KB261892

교육조직 연구

교육조직 연구

충남대학교 교수
주 삼 환 저

한국학술정보㈜

머리말

　학교조직은 군대조직이나, 정부조직, 회사조직과 다른 특성을 갖고 있다. 그 두드러진 특성의 하나가 학교조직의 관료성과 전문직성을 동시에 포함하고 있다는 점이다. 그런데 관료제의 역기능을 욕하면서도 학교조직은 점점 더 관료화하고 동시에 그 조직 속에서 하는 일(예: 수업)과 일하는 사람(예: 교사)은 점점 더 관료화의 반대인 전문직의 특성으로 가고 있다는 점이다. 교육행정가와 지도자는 이런 학교조직의 특성을 이해하고 교육행정을 해야 하는 것이다. 이에 착안하여 연구한 것이 저자의 박사학위 논문이다. 이 책의 제1부에서는 이와 관련한 연구물을 묶어 놓았다.

　인간은 조직 속에서 일을 하면서 인생의 대부분의 시간을 보낸다. 그런데 어떤 사람은 일을 하면서도 행복을 느끼고 어떤 사람은 일하기를 싫어하고 불행해 하며 때로는 지겨워한다. 일에 대한 태도에 따라 인간은 행복하게 일할 수도 있고 불행하게 살 수도 있다. 일에 대한 동기에 대하여 통속적인 생각을 넘은 이론을 제기한 사람이 Herzberg이고 그 이론이 동기-위생이론이다. 이 허즈버그 이론을 검증하는 것이 저자의 석사학위 논문이었다. 이 책의 제2부는 허즈버그 이론과 관련된 연구물을 묶어 놓았다.

　연구에 관심이 있는 사람들은 이들 이론과 연구물과 관련하여 더 연구할 소재와 아이디어를 발견할 것으로 본다. 그리고 교장, 교감, 장학사 등 교육 지도자들은 학교조직의 특성에 맞게 행정을 하고 직원의 동기유발을 이해하여 교육행정 실천에 도움이 될 것으로 본다. 이 연구물들이 교육행정 이론가와, 교육 연구자, 교육행정 실천가의 직무수행에 도움에 되었으면 한다.

2006. 3.

저자 주삼환 識

차 례

제1부
관료제(官僚制)와 전문주의(專門主義)

1. School Bureaucratization and Professionalization

(RELATIONSHIPS OF SCHOOL BUREAUCRATIZATION, ELEMENTARY SCHOOL TEACHERS' PROFESSIONAL AND BUREAUCRATIC ORIENTATION, CONFLICT, AND JOB SATISFACTION IN A SELECTED SCHOOL DISTRICT)

A THESIS

SUBMITTED TO THE FACULTY OF THE GRADUATE SCHOOL OF THE UNIVERSITY OF MINNESOTA

By

Sam Hwan Joo

IN PARTIAL FULFILLMENT OF THE REQUIREMENTS

FOR THE DEGREE OF

DOCTOR OF PHILOSOPHY

August 1981

ACKNOWLEDGMENT

This volume made possible by the cooperation, assistance, support, advice, encouragement, and patience of many people. The writer wishes to acknowledge his sincere appreciation to those individuals who helped make a dream come true.

A special word of appreciation must be given to Dr. Ronald T. Lambert, advisor and committee chairman, who made "impossible" a "possible," "weakness" a "strength," and "stranger" a "friend." The writer enjoyed his teaching assistantship, and could learn much through personal contact with him throughout Ph. D. program. Thousands of words cannot express completely this writer's lifelong debt of gratitude to him.

The writer expresses the deepest appreciation to committee members, Dr. Harlan S. Hansen, for his suggestions, teaching assistantship and personal kindness; Dr. Gary N. McLean, for his time in correction of writing, his suggestions, his scholarship and friendship; Drs. Donald G. MacEachern, William M. Ammentorp and Tim L. Mazzoni for their critical reading and suggestions.

The writer will always remember the strong cooperation and support of the superintendent, elementary school principals and teachers who were involved in this study, and the kindness of many other American friends.

The writer is especially grateful to Drs. Young-Shik Kim, Jongchol Kim and Kilsoo Kang, Seoul National University in Korea, M Ed. advisor and professors, for their encouragement, guidance, and psychological and spiritual support, and to many other elementary school colleagues and friends in Seoul, Korea, for their endless prayers and wishes for the writer's success.

Finally, the writer weeps thanks to his late father, his mother, brothers and sisters who wanted to have a doctoral son and brother, for their patience and support. The writer thanks his wife, Mija, and children, Eun-Sun, Eun-Jee and Eun-Joong, for their love and support and their willingness to sacrifice holidays and vacations for this writer's study.

Sam Hwan Joo
August, 1981

CONTENTS

Ⅰ. INTRODUCTION

A. Nature and Research Framework of the Study

"Our society is an organizational society. We are born in organizations, educated by organizations, and most of us spend much of our lives working for organizations"(Etzioni, 1964, p.1). For us to live without organizations is similar to a fish living out of water. An organization is formulated because of our social and personal needs. Individuals devote their time and energy for the organization and in turn the organization rewards individuals in payment for their service.

School teachers who have their own "personalities" and "need-dispositions" which represent the "idiographic" dimension are working in a school organization which has certain "roles" and "expectations": these represent the "nomothetic" dimension in the Getzels-Guba Model(Getzels and Guba, 1957; Getzels, 1958). When individual personalities and need-dispositions are incongruous with organizational roles and expectations, conflicts are inevitable. This kind of conflict is natural in some aspects because almost all organizations have this kind of problem. Much pervious research has examined this kind of conflict.

However, a more serious problem is that, on the one hand, modern school organization is becoming increasingly more bureaucratized and is demanding more strict bureaucratic (1) roles and (2) expectations from teachers who are thinking of themselves as professional, and, on the other hand, teaching is becoming increasingly more professionalized. In other words, even though "the man, the job, and the social setting must be combined into sufficient harmony so that goals of institution can be achieved"(Otto and Sanders, 1964. p.393), school structure, a major part of 'the social setting' in the school system, is moving to more strict bureaucratization, while 'the man' dimension(the teacher) and 'the job' dimension(teaching) are moving in the opposite direction, professionalization.

When the history of educational administration is reviewed briefly, the principle of the Hegelian dialectic can be applied. The Hegelian "thesis" is the Classical Theory of Taylorism which emphasized the organizational dimension. With the passage of time, its "antithesis" came into vogue as Mayo's Human Relations which placed greater emphasis on the individual dimension. A "synthesis" of these two theses incorporates and harmonizes both dimensions. The present study deals with both dimensions, the organization and the individual, and, at the same time, organizational behavior. School bureaucratization is the organizational variable, while the teachers' professional and bureaucratic orientations are the individual variables. Teachers' conflict and job satisfaction, as outcome variables between the organization and the individual, are the organizational behavior variables.

One cannot deny the fact that the history of the development of the public school has been characterized by the process of bureaucratization. Schools have traditionally adopted a bureaucratic system as a means to achieve their goal. Particularly in the last decade, bureaucratic symptoms have been increasing in school organization.

As administering the financial, building, and maintenance functions of school organization have become more complex, responsibility and decision-making have become increasingly centralized and specialized. Central office staffs have increased markedly, as have office personnel and paper work. Computers are being used more frequently as a means to standardize, regulate, and program decision-making. All of these developments are symptoms of an expanding bureaucracy(Sergiovanni and Carver, 1973, p.24).

At the same time, another tendency is also clear in the school system.

Parallel changes in complexity and sophistication have also occurred in the nature, scope, and breadth of programs and in instructional learning systems. This expansion of knowledge in teaching, content, and instructional technology is combined with a renewed and vigorous sense of responsibility for student welfare. A drive for status for teachers and an interest in upgrading teaching are related phenomena. All of these are symptoms of professionalism(Sergiovanni and Carver 1973, p.25).

"The growth of teacher professionalization thus challenges the traditional ideology of lay control and the hierarchical control of administrators"(Robinson. 1966, p.9). Because bureaucratic principles and professional principles in organizational theory are too different to be represented by the same line, this study adds one more line at the bottom to the Getzels-Guba Model(See Figure 1), that is, professional roles and expectations as a professional teacher. Because the differences between bureaucratic

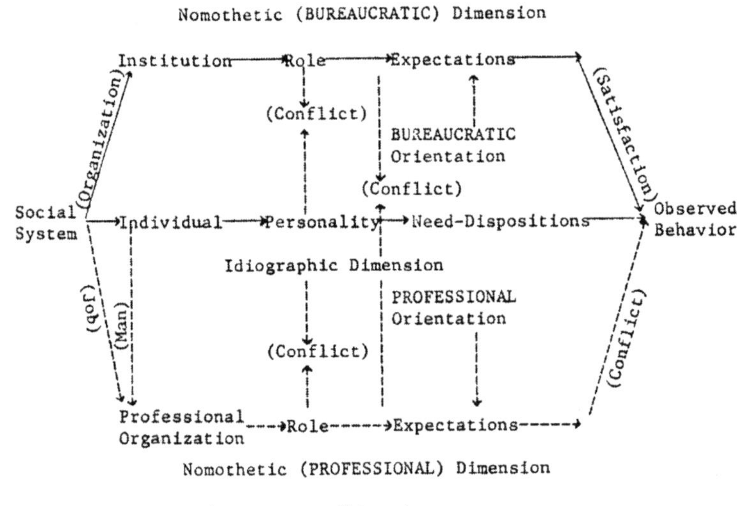

Figure 1

Adapted Getzels-Guba Model

role-expectations and professional role-expectations are greater than those between role-expectations and personality-needs in many organizations, the resulting conflicts are assumed to be greater. In Figure 1 the distance from the upper line to the middle, or from the bottom to the middle is shorter than that from the upper to the bottom. Following this logic, highly professionally-oriented teachers(approaching the bottom line) are predicted to conflict with the bureaucratic hierarchy, rule, procedure, and the impersonality of the upper line. However, bureaucratically-oriented teachers(those approaching the upper line) in a bureaucratic school(the upper line), will be more satisfied with school life and with their jobs than will professionally-oriented teachers, because the organizational environment reinforces and rewards more for bureaucratically-oriented teachers.

It should be noted that the added bottom line does not reflect another institution, but reflects different organizational principles in the same institution. This line for the professional dimension, which has been hidden under the shade of school bureaucracy, is separated and is treated at the same level of bureaucratic dimension for three reasons. First, the two tendencies of school bureaucratization and teaching professionalization are emergent; second, the public school is classified as a semi-professional organization of bureaucracy and profession(Etzioni, 1964); third, bureaucratic characteristics and professional characteristics are almost inversely related.

Figure 2 depicts the research framework and relationships of five major variables identified. Dependent variables, teachers' Conflict and Job Satisfaction of the central part, are produced by the interaction among three independent variables, School Bureaucratization of upper side and teachers' Professional Orientation and Bureaucratic Orientation of the bottom side. Teachers' Conflict are viewed here as the discrepancies between the pattern of expectations attached to a given role and pattern of need-disposition characteristics of the incumbent in the role, or between Bureaucratic role-expectations and Professional role-expectations(according to the Getzels-Guba Model). Job Satisfaction is explained as an internal indicator of correspondence between environmental and individual(according to the Theory of Work Adjustment(Dawiset. al., 1986)).

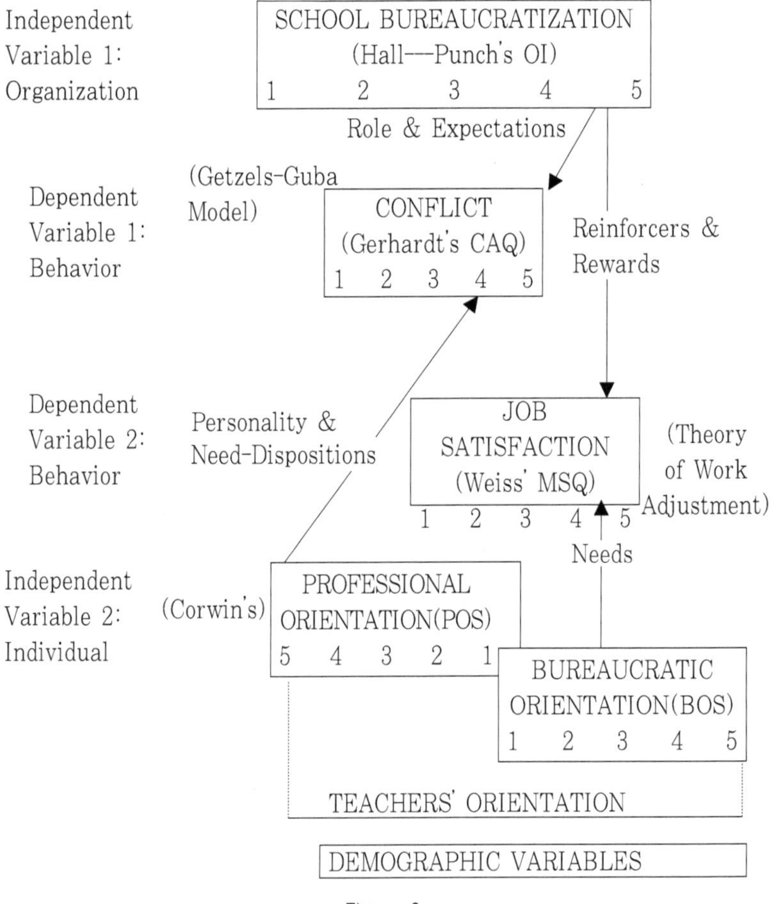

Figure 2

Research Framework

> Correspondence between an individual and his environment implies conditions that can be described as: a harmonious relationship between individual and environment, suitability of the individual to the environment and of the environment for the individual, consonance or agreement between individual and environment, and a reciprocal and complementary relationship between the individual and his environment(Dawis et al., 1968. p.3).

Thus, job satisfaction is decided by the degree that individual needs correspond to the reinforcers or rewards of the work environment. Numbers from 1 to 5 in each variable of Figure 2, except the demographic variable, mean the degree, level of intensity of each variable as measured by each instrument, such as the Organizational Inventory(OI), the Professional Orientation Scale(POS), the Bureaucratic Orientation Scale(BOS), the Conflict Assessment Questionnaire(CAQ), and the Minnesota Satisfaction Questionnaire(MSQ). Demographic variables are located with the other independent variables. School bureaucratization is conceptualized according to Punch's argument, originally Hall's concept; teachers' professional orientation and bureaucratic orientation according to Corwin's work; teacher's conflict, according to Getzels-Guba Model and Gerhardt's instrument; job satisfaction, according to the Theory of Work Adjustment. A discussion of these theories or arguments and instruments will follow in the next chapters.

In this research framework it is assumed that all schools have bureaucratic characteristics, although there are differences in the degree of bureaucratization, and that schools differ significantly on the bureaucratic dimensions. This difference can be classified by the Organizational Inventory(OI). The school is the unit of analysis in school bureaucratization variable, but in using teachers' perception of school bureaucratization the unit of analysis is the teacher. Teacher also is a unit in teachers' orientation, conflict, and job satisfaction. It is also assumed that teachers differ in professional and bureaucratic orientation scores, conflict scores, and job satisfaction scores.

In summary, this study focuses on two dependent variables, (1) teachers' conflict, as measured by the CAQ, and (2) job satisfaction, as measured by the MSQ. They are conceptualized as the outcome of interaction of three independent variables, (1) school bureaucratization, as measured by the OI, (2) teachers' professional orientation, as measured by the POS, and (3) teachers' bureaucratic orientation, as measured by the BOS.

B. Purpose of the Study

This study seeks to describe and analayze for a school district school organizational characteristics or patterns, teachers' perceptions of school bureaucratization, teachers' orientation toward professionalization and bureaucratization, conflict, job satisfaction, and the interrelationships of these variables.

One of the major purposes of the proposed study, as a pilot

study, is to explore the possibility of more comprehensive and larger-scale investigation of these variables. Applicability of the research framework, usage of the composite instrument, possible other research questions, adaptability of statistical treatment for follow-up studies, and other problems are expected to be suggested from this pilot study.

To accomplish its purpose this study will describe current conditions concerning school bureaucratization, teachers' professional and bureaucratic orientation, teachers' conflict and job satisfaction, in a suburban school district in Minnesota which has been selected for access and willingness to cooperate. It then will analyze the relationships of school bureaucratization, teachers' professional orientation, bureaucratic orientation, teachers' conflict, job satisfaction, and selected demographic variables.

Specifically, the purposes of the study are

(1) to determine and describe the degrees of school bureaucratization, teachers' professional orientation, bureaucratic orientation, teachers' conflict, and job satisfaction.

(2) to analyze the relationships of school bureaucratization, teachers' professional orientation, bureaucratic orientation, teachers' conflict, job satisfaction, and selected demographic variables.

With respect to these stated purposes of the study the following questions will be answered:

(1) What are the degrees of school bureaucratization, the level of teachers' professional orientation, bureaucratic orientation, the inte-

nsity of teachers' conflict, and the level of job satisfaction in one
selected school district?

(2) What are the relationships among major variables of school bureaucratization, teachers' professional orientation, bureaucractic orientation, teachers' conflict, job satisfaction, and some demographic
variables?

The combinations of variables to identify the relationships
are as follows:

(1) School bureaucratization: Professional orientation
(2) School bureaucratization: Bureaucratic orientation
(3) Professional orientation: Bureaucratic orientation

(4) School bureaucratization: Conflict
(5) Professional orientation: Conflict
(6) Bureaucratic orientation: Conflict
(7) Job Satisfaction: Conflict

(8) School bureaucratization: Job Satisfaction
(9) Professional orientation: Job Satisfaction
(10) Bureaucratic orientation: Job Satisfaction

(11) Demographic variables: School bureaucratization
     (Sex, Age, Teaching Experience,
     Academic degree,……)
(12) Demographic variables: Professional orientation
(13) Demographic variables: Bureaucratic orientation
(14) Demographic variables: Conflict
(15) Demographic variables: Job Satisfaction

C. Significance of the Study

This is a descriptive and exploratory study of school organization, individual teachers, and their behavior. It deals with many related variables and instruments at the same time. Therefore, this study is expected to suggest some comprehensive implications for a study on a broader scale which may have importance for theory and practice. School organizational patterns have changed and will continue to change. Organizational factors are very important for the achievement. of institutional goals and individual feelings of happiness in work. A larger study might be expected to give some suggestions concerning organizational change in elementary schools. Are educators satisfied with the present elementary school organization? If not, in what direction should clementary school organization be changed?

How do the interaction of organizational characteristics and individual members' orientation affect their job satisfaction and conflict? It is believed that it will be more revealing to accomplish an interaction study which examines organizational and individual variables concurrently than to do separate studies of each variable. Whether individual teachers have conflict or satisfaction in work is also very important, not only for the goals of the school, but also for the teachers themselves. The research results will suggest the impact on conflict and job satisfaction of school bureaucratization and teachers' orientation. Some teachers conflict with organization, however, other teachers are satisfied in the same school or in the same conditions. Why do these phenomena happen?

Many past empirical studies have tested only a small portion of a theory or a single variable, such as the student, the teacher, or administrator attitudes, thus the focus has been too narrow (Miskel, Fevurly and Stewart, 1979, p.97). The present study is significant in dealing comprehensively with organizational structure, teachers' value orientation, conflict, and job satisfaction or motivation.

The limited generalizability of many previous studies stemmed from the use of inappropriate units of analysis. Much published research has used the individual as the unit of analysis in the investigation of bureaucracy. Bureaucratic structure is clearly related to characteristics that would be more appropriately examined in terms of the school building or district(Miskel, Fevurly and Stewart 1979, p.98). In order to overcome this weakness, school building is used as the unit of analysis for the organizational variable, but teacher is a unit for other variables, such as highly bureaucratically-oriented teachers or highly professionally-oriented teachers. However, teachers' perception of school bureaucratization uses teacher as the unit.

When feelings of job isolation and alienation are high, the study of conflict and job satisfaction has an important meaning. The effective goal achievement of schools without teachers' job satisfaction is unlikely. When the teachers' definition of themseleves as professionals and their desire for professional autonomy are strong, is the traditional supervision style acceptable? This study will give some insight into appropriate style of supervision, personnel administration. and relationships of professional administrators and professional teachers.

D. Limitation of the Study

The conclusions drawn from this study are necessarily limited by the nature of the population, the instruments used, and the statistical treatment applied. The following limitations, in particular, should be noted:

(1) The study is limited to elementary school teachers in a selected school district in the Twin Cities Metropolitan Area. No attempt will be made to determine the representativeness of the population studied to the entire teacher population in Minnesota or the United States of America, nor to generalize the research results and conclusions. This is only an exploratory pilot study.

(2) Instruments measure limited concepts with limited subscales. The Organizational Inventory, especially, should be viewed with caution as it is used as four reduced subscales which focus only on the major bureaucratic characteristics among six dimensions, and it measures indirectly the degree of school bureaucratization by teachers' perception.

(3) The Organizational Inventory and the teachers' Bureaucratic Orientation Scale should be based on the same bureaucratic characteristics, but there are minor differences.

Subscales of the Hall's Organizational Inventory are Hierarchy of authority, Rules for incumbents, Procedural specifications, and Impersonality, while subscales of Corwin's Bureaucratic Orientation Scale are Administrative orientation, Loyalty to the organization, Experience orientation, Standardization orientation, Rules and procedures orientation, and Orientation to the public. This incompatibility will be examined through a correlation of the OI scores and the BOS scores. A lack of significant positive relationship between the OI and the BOS would be problem of instrumentation in this study. Yet, it is generally accepted that both instruments are best for each purpose.

(4) It is assumed that schools are differentiated in degree of bureaucratization and that teachers differ in their degree of professional and bureaucratic orientation, conflict, and job satisfaction. Although evidence exists for each of these assumptions(MacKay, 1964; Robinson, 1966; Corwin, 1964), if these assumptions are not supported in the present study, the significance of the study will be reduced.

E. Definition of Terms

Major terms are defined briefly here, with more detailed discussion provided in Chapter 2

1. Bureaucracy

A form of organization which exists along a number of dimensions: Hierarchy of authority, Rules for incumbents, Procedural specifications, and Impersonality. The OI score operationally defines the degree of school bureaucratization, the BOS measures the degree of teachers' bureaucratic orientation with six subscales: Administrative orientation, Loyalty to the organization, Experience orientation, Standardization orientation, Rules and procedures orientation, and Orientation to the public.

2. Profession

An occupation which has the following characteristics; a general and systematic body of knowledge, a degree of autonomy, responsibility, service to clients, self-governing, and specialized training. Teachers' professional orientation is measured by the POS based on Clients orientation, Colleague orientation, Monopoly of knowledge, and Decision-making.

3. Orientation

Orientation refers to a person's conception of the total environment. Orientations are a part of a value system(Corwin, 1966, p.116). Teachers' orientation is classified into two types; professional orientation and bureaucratic orientation.

4. Professionally-Oriented Teachers

Teachers who have a higher Professional Orientation Scale scores than the mean score and at the same time have a lower Bureaucratic Orientation Scale scores than the mean.

5. Bureaucratically-Oriented Teachers

Teachers who have a higher Bureaucratic Orientation Scale scores than the mean score and at the same time have a lower Professional Orientation Scale scores than the mean.

6. Conflict

Discrepancies between the pattern of expectations attaching to a given role and the pattern of need-dispositions characteristic of the incumbent of the role or the pattern of value orientation. Conflict is operationally defined as scores of the CAQ in this study.

7. Job Satisfaction

The individual assessment of the degree of fulfillment of the requirement by work environment. The MSQ scores substitute for the degree of individual job satisfaction.

8. Teachers

For purposes of this study. the term will include classroom teachers in grades k-6, teachers in special areas such as music and art and special education teachers.

F. Summary and Overview

The introductory chapter has covered: (1) nature and research framework of the study, (2) purpose of the study, (3) significance of the study, (4) limitation of the study, and (5) definition of terms. The remaining part of this chapter will overview the next chapters.

Chapter 2 will review the literature related to: (1) bureaucratization, (2) professionalization, (3) conflict, (4) job satisfaction, (5) relationships among variables, and (6) a summary of the reviewed literature.

Chapter 3 will present a description of the design of the study: (1) the population, (2) the instruments, and (3) the treatment of the data.

Chapter 4 will present an analysis of the data. This chapter will be divided into three parts: (1) general profile of major variables, (2) relationships among variables, and (3) a summary of the data analysis.

Chapter 5 will contain (1) a summary of the study, (2) conclusions, and (3) implications for theory, practice and research.

Ⅱ. REVIEW OF RELATED LITERATURE AND RESEARCH

In this chapter major concepts, related literature and empirical research are reviewed. The last sections of the chapter include a discussion of the relationships of variables and the chapter summary.

A. Bureaucratization

1. Definition

A vast literature exists on the general topic of bureaucracy. There are different approaches and controversies in defining bureaucracy. Following a broad review of the literature, Punch (1969) summarized these definitional issues by identifying three disctinct approaches:

> Firstly, bureaucracy, used globally in macroscopic, often historical and cross-cultural analysis, denotes the characteristically modern form of social organization: ours is 'the bureaucratic society.' In this view, bureaucracy is organizational form '--- designed to accomplish large scale administrative tasks by systematically coordinating the work of many individuals.' It is here that bureaucracy becomes synonymous with large organization or formal organization. Secondly, bureaucracy refers in detail to the internal structure of organizations. The emphasis here is on differentiating between contemporary organizations. They differ in

bureaucratization according to their stress in operation on typically bureaucratic characteristics. Thirdly, bureaucracy is used pejoratively to symbolize arbitrary power, inefficiency, red tape, and so on. Though value-loaded, this use points to the dysfunctions of bureaucracy, an area of considerable research interest(Punch, 1969, p.44).

Dimock(1965) defined bureaucracy as a way of life in which institutions overshadow the individual, and Blau and Scott(1962, p.8) defined it as "the amount of effort that an organization expends in maintaining itself rather than in pursuing its objectives." These two definitions are examples of the foregoing third approach used by Punch. Owens'(1970, p.56) definition— "an administrative system that is adapted to the needs of large and complex organizations that deal with large members of clients"— is an example of the first approach.

The preference of this study is the use of Punch's second approach, the internal characteristics or dimensions of bureaucracy as they allude to school organizations. In the second dimensional approach, bureaucracy is separated into component parts or dimensions, such as hierarchy of authority, division of labor, rules for incumbents, procedural specifications, impersonality, and technical competence. Because, according to Hall(1966), this dimensional approach could be particularly useful in research when organizational structure is treated as an independent variable, and factors such as conflict between professionals and non-professionals or interdepartmental relations are handled as dependent variables, the present research follows this dimensional approach.

Discussion of whether or not an organization is a bureaucracy is meaningless. The dimensions are "not all present nor all absent in any one organization"(Hall, 1963, p.33), but all organizations have some bureaucratic characteristics. The only existing differences are those differences in the degree of bureaucracy. This "degree of bureaucracy" makes the word, "bureaucratization" possible. Complex administrative problems confront most large organizations. Therefore, "bureaucracy is not confined to the military and civilian branches of government but is also found in business, unions, churches, universities, and even in baseball clubs"(Blau and Meyer, 1971, p.4). Gouldner(1948) and Udy(1959) suggested that bureaucracy is a condition that exists along a continuum, rather than being a condition that is either present or absent. "This point may be expanded to state that bureaucracy is a form of organization which exists along a number of continua or dimensions"(Hall, 1966, p.33). As a result, the term, "bureaucratization," is more possible than "bureaucracy" and is appropriate in this study to be used as a contrasting concept to professionalization.

Bureaucratization refers to the degree of emphasis on characteristics—since they vary together—in the school organization (Punch, 1969, p.53). In other words, bureaucratization is the level of bureaucraticness in an organization. The concept of bureaucracy is used for both school organizational structure and teachers' orientation in this study.

To summarize, bureaucracy is defined as a form of organization which exists along a number of continua or dimensions. These bureaucratic dimensions or characteristics are discussed in the following section of this chapter. The terms, "bureaucratic" or "bureaucratization," implying a dynamic meaning, are used in this study rather than the term "bureaucracy." Whether one organization can be classified as a bureaucracy or not is meaningless, but to classify an organization as high bureaucratic or low bureaucratic is possible and useful.

2. Characteristics of Bureaucracy

Many scholars have based their discussions of bureaucratic characteristics on Weber's theory. Although their expressions often differ, they have generally agreed on the commonalities of Weber's formulation(Weber, 1947). Merton, Friedrich, Udy, Heady, Parsons, Berger, and Litwak have generally agreed on the bureaucratic characteristics as shown on the following table(Hall, 1961, p.7; 1963, p.34).

Table 1

Characteristics of Bureaucracy as Listed by Major Authors

Dimensions of Bureaucracy	Weber	Litwak	Fried-rich	Merton	Udy	Heady	Parsons	Berger
Hierarchy of Authority	*	*	*	*	*	*	*	*
Division of Labor	*	*	*	*	*	*	*	
Technically Competent Participants	*	*	*	*	*		*	*
Procedural Devices for Work Situations	*	*	*	*		*		*
Rules Governing Behavior of Members	*	*	*	*				*

Dimensions of Bureaucracy	Weber	Litwak	Fried-rich	Merton	Udy	Heady	Parsons	Berger
Limited Authority of Office	*			*		*	*	
Differential Rewards by Office	*				*			
Impersonality of Personal Contact		*		*				
Administration Separate from Ownership	*	*						
Emphasis on Written Communication	*							
Rational Discipline	*							

Hall used six dimensions on his Organizational Inventory(OI) subscales to measure the degree of bureaucratization of an organization. They were:

1. The hierarchy of authority—the extent to which the locus decision making is prestructured by the organization.
2. Division of labor—the extent to which work tasks are subdivided by functional specialization decided by the organization.
3. Rules for incumbents—the degree to which the behavior of organizational member is subject to organizational control.
4. Procedural specifications—the extent to which organizational members must follow organizationally defined techniques in dealing with situations which they encounter.
5. Impersonality—the extent to which both organizational members and outsiders are treated without regard to individual qualities.
6. Technical competence—the extent to which organizationally difined "universalistic" standards are utilized in the personal selection and advancement process(Hall, 1961, p.20; 1968, p.95).

As mentioned earlier, all characteristics are not either all present nor all absent in any one organization, but there will be only a difference in degree in which they are present. In highly bureaucratic organizations all characteristics are present to a high degree, while in non-bureaucratized or professional organizations, they are low.

In Weber's view, bureaucracy is the most efficient form of organization because trained experts are best qualified to make correct decisions and because impersonal relationships guided by abstract rules and coordinated by the authority hierarchy promote a rational and consistent accomplishment of organizational goals(Faber and Shearron, 1970, p.81).

When functioning properly, a bureaucracy is characterized by four distinct advantages that become increasingly important with the passage of time: (1) efficient, (2) predictable, (3) impersonal and (4) fast(Presthus, 1962, p.5), but when dysfunctions of bureaucracy emerge, criticisms of these qualifications quickly follow. It is unquestionably true that all bureaucracies are not equally effective, and a given bureaucracy varies in its state of health from time to time. A typical catalogue of the more serious faults of bureaucracy would include tendencies toward the following:

(1) Bureaucracy encourages overconformity, inducing "group think."
(2) In time, bureaucracy modifies the very personality of bureaucrats such that they become the drab, colorless, routinized "organization man."
(3) Innovative ideas wilt from the distortion and long delays which result from communication overloading as attempts are made to transmit ideas through the hierarchical layers of organization.

(4) Bureaucracy does not take into account the presence of informal organizations, including the primary groups to which role-incumbents belong(Owens, 1970, p.59).

In many cases school bureaucracy also is dysfunctional, as is evident by encoded phrases such as "trained incapacity," "displacement of goals," and "bureaupathology." Because school organizations have special goals different from other organizations, bureaucracy in schools has to adapt to the school's own nature. Anderson(1966, p.31) used the term "Janus-like character" after discussing functional and dysfunctional consequences of bureaucratic rules. Gouldner(1964) also discussed organizational rules with respect to "function" and "dysfunction," and Hoy and Miskel (1978) devised the following table to summarize their concepts and those of the Weberian model, conceived as existing in continua. It is evident that function and dysfunction both exist on the continuum.

Table 2

Functions and Dysfunctions of the Weberian Model(Hoy and Miskel, 1987, p.5)

Dysfunction	Bureaucratic Characteristics	Function
Boredom————————	Division of Labor————	Expertise
Lack of Morale———————	Impersonal ——————— Orientation	Rationality
Communication ——————— Blocks	Hierarchy of ——————— Authority	Disciplined Compliance and Coordination
Rigidity and Goal —— Displacement	Rules and ————————— Regulations	Continuity and Uniformity
Conflict between ——————— Achievement and Seniority	Career Orientation———	Incentive

In brief summary of the several scholarly discussions of the characteristics of a bureaucracy which were reviewed, the researcher has selected Hall's six characteristics as having the greatest utility for his research: (1) Hierarchy of Authority, (2) Division of Labor, (3) Rules for Incumbents, (4) Procedural Specifications, (5) Impersonality, and (6) Technical Competence. However, dimensions (2) and (6) are tentatively excluded in measuring major bureaucratic characteristics as contrasted with professional orientation, according to Punch's suggestion. These characteristics sometimes function well but sometimes are dysfunctional and can be expressed along continua.

3. Bureaucratization in Schools

Individuals living in modern society find that an increasingly large proportion of their activities take place in bureaucratic settings. "Most sociologists agree that schools have become increasingly bureaucratized"(Parelius and Parelius, 1978, p.106).

In the Pre-Industrial Period, educational form was the least bureaucratized of all, with small and relatively undifferentiated internal form, but during the Early Industrial Period numerous far-reaching bureaucratic characteristics began to occur in the structure of education. "This bureaucratization was essentially complete, in its modern form, by as early as 1880" (Parelius and Parelius, 1978, p.106). With the coming of the Mature Industrial Period, bureaucratization was more enforced in the school system, side by side with organizational size and complexity.

Many factors have contributed to the dramatic growth in size: increases in school-age populations; radical urbanization; increased rates of enrollment, attendance, and graduation; and consolidation of school districts. In 1932, the first year for which reasonably accurate data are available, there were over 127,000 public school districts in the United States, but in 1960, there were 40,520; in 1967, fewer than 22,000; and in 1973, the numbers decreased to 16,960(Boyan, 1969, p.200; Campbell et al., 1975, p.85; McNally, 1974, p.9; Faber and Shearron, 1970, p.338; Parelius and Parelius, 1978, p.120). Together, growth and consolidation have resulted in almost 80 per cent of all school districts enrolling 3,000 or more students and more than 40 per cent enrolling 12,000 or more during the 1971-1972 school year(Golladay, 1976, p.20). These phenomena mean that the larger the urban or suburban school and school district, the more centralized and consequently the more bureaucratized the school system. Centralized authority is a symptom of bureaucratization and is an indication that the superintendent's power has been increasing. The superintendent influences the building principal who, in turn, influences the teachers. Even though recently there is the declining enrollment phenomenon in the United States of America, the degree of bureaucratization is thought not to be reduced in school systems since this phenomenon.

Many factors, such as team teaching, differentiated staffing, open school system, and various grouping of pupils, have contributed to complexity. One important factor of complexity is increased public expectation of the roles of the elementary school. "No longer is the school concerned only with teaching children basic skills. It is now expected to promote the development of the whole child. This means having individuals who are concerned with physical, psychological, social and emotional, as well as intellectual, growth"(Parelius and Parelius, 1978, p.120). School roles were expanded to include food, transportation, and even social work. The more complex the organization, the greater the need for internal coordination, which enhances the power of administrators whose primary internal function is coordination.

School administrative work continuously increases. Principals who want to spend much of their time on instructional supervision cannot do so because too much time is necessarily spent in administrative work chores, clerical work, and management (Krajewski, 1978, p.65; Faber and Shearron, 1970, p.214; Lipham and Hoeh 1974, p.127). This explosion of administrative work is one outcome of bureaucratic dysfunction.

Federal, state and local pressures exert influence on individual schools which then tend to develop more school uniformity(Campbell et al., 1975, pp.22-27, and p.74). Uniformity is also a product of bureaucratization.

"In recent years, many parents and community groups have grown increasingly dissatisfied with the effectiveness of school programs, achievements and personnel—and in turn desire more meaningful involvement in the establishment and modification of school policies and in the evaluation of the extent to which the school and its personnel are meeting their responsibilities"(Gorton, 1972. pp.24-25). These groups have sometimes complained that "Teacher Can't Teach!"(Time, 16 June, 1980). These are major challenges to professional teachers. In severe cases, some parents do not want to send their children to school and the parents teach them in their homes themselves. This fundamentally comes from the tradition of strong local and lay control over education. The employee status and image of teachers are that of "public servant" of the community. These deep roots have hindered teachers from professionalizing.

In conclusion, schools traditionally adopted bureaucracy, and the bureaucratic symptom has been reinforced and expanded in school organization in recent years.

4. Empirical Studies on Bureaucratization

Much empirical research into the bureaucratic structure has been the case study style in the past, but after the development of objective measurement instruments, empirical research has multiplied. This subsection covers empirical studies related to school bureaucratization and teachers' bureaucratic orientation.

Before beginning a review of the empirical studies, it may be meaningful to describe some of the objective instruments which have been developed for the measurement of bureaucracy.

The first attempt to measure the degree of bureaucracy was made by Berger(1956) who used a scale of three dimensions of bureaucratic behavior; Rationality and Universalism, Hierarchy, and Discretion for Egyptian civil servants.

Udy(1958, 1959) developed a measurement instrument from the Weberian ideal type of bureaucracy. When characteristics of bureaucracy appeared, he classified that organization as having bureaucratic structure. He used the "present versus absent" variable concept. When different types of organization are differentiated, this method is appropriate, but when differentiating between organizations of the same type, it is less appropriate.

Stinchcombe(1959) compared mass production and construction industries with respect to (1) the social location of work planning, (2) administrative status structure, and (3) content of administrative communication.

In education, Moeller(1962, 1969) attempted to measure the degree of school bureaucratization by using a rating scale to judge school structure. This rating scale also used "present versus absent" attributes rather than continuous variables, as in Udy's study. Moeller's eight-item forced-choice instrument was based on Blau's characterization of bureaucracy and used the Guttman scale analysis.

Hartley(1964) developed a 30-item Likert scale based on more than 20 bureaucratic characteristics derived from the literature. This instrument was based on two assumptions: that bureaucratization was unidimensional, and that all dimensions were intended to be of equal importance.

A more systematic and comprehensive study was done by Hall(1961) with an Organizational Inventory. This instrument was developed originally to be used in measuring the bureaucratization of business and governmental organizations. This was the most rational instrument reviewed and the dimensions which he isolated from the literature occurred on continua, but not in a "present versus absent" form. Mackay(1964, 1969), Robinson (1966), and Punch(1967, 1969) revised and used Hall's Organizational Inventory in education. Detailed discussion of the OI will follow in Chapter 3.

Sorensen(1965) pointed out that less experienced persons in lower positions feel that there is too much bureaucracy, while the more experienced people in higher positions feel that there is too little. This phenomenon is explained by Corwin's(1961) and Kuhlman and Hoy's(1974) socialization studies. Beginning teachers tended to perceive the same school structure more bureaucratically than experienced teachers. As they gained experience, they began to adapt to bureaucracy.

Some confusion exists in research results concerning bureaucratic orientation. Berger(1956) indicated that the older, western-exposed civil servants are highly predisposed to emphasize rationality, efficiency, and universality, and less predisposed to emphasize the power of position, the authority of the superior official, and the propriety of obedience by the subordinate, and that age, civil-service grade, social mobility, and job satisfaction are related to the bureaucratic scale.

Wermuth(1977) also indicated that age, sex, marital status, level of education and tenure status are related to loyalty and acceptance of rules.

Corwin's(1970) study pointed out that men and younger teachers have a statistically lower bureaucratic orientation than their opposites. Kuhlman and Hoy's(1974) study resulted in no significant difference between the bureaucratic orientations of men and women, but experience for beginning teachers is related to increased bureaucratic orientation.

The present study assumes that the difference in the degree of bureaucratization between schools comes mainly from organizational characteristics plus some from individual characteristics. Mackay(1964) and Robinson(1966) certainly found that schools differed in degree of bureaucratization, but they did not clarify the causes of this condition. Generally, size, complexity and goal statement were believed to be predictors of bureaucratization, but Hall(1966) said that they were not necessarily so. Hall's (1966, p.272) findings suggested that bureaucracy was too complex to be explained in terms of such simple factors as size, number of divisions, or type of goals. One of the goals of the present study is to determine whether differences in bureaucratization come from different organizational characteristics, individual characteristics or an interaction of both.

B. Professionalization

1. Definition

The concept of "professionalization" is a dynamic process that may affect any occupation to a greater or lesser degree. After reviewing numerous attempts to define a profession, Cogan(1953) categorized five types of definitions: (1) dictionary and legal definitions, (2) arbitrary and applied definitions, (3) definitions expressed in terms of power and prestige, (4) profession as formal association, and (5) definitions in terms of techniques of internal regulations. He also attempted to provide a comprehensive definition:

> A profession is a vocation whose practice is founded upon an understanding of the theoretical structure of some department of learning or science, and upon the abilities accompanying such understanding. This understanding and these abilities are applied to the vital practical affairs of man. The practices of the profession are modified by knowledge of a generalized nature and by the accumulated wisdom and experience of mankind, which serve to correct the errors of specialism. The profession, serving the vital needs of man, considers its first ethical imperative to be altruistic service to the client(Cogan, 1953, p.49).

Contrary to Cogan, Bell(1969, p.73) used professionalization to mean that workers have received technical training to achieve a recognized occupational competence. Becker(1962, p.33) accepted the position that profession is an honorific title, and Parsons(1970, p.17) emphasized the importance of higher education, stating that a profession is an integral part of a complex, of which the system of higher education is also a part.

A typical approach to defining 'profession' has been to list several characteristics of a profession and to use these as criteria in testing any given occupational group for professionalism (MacKay, 1969, p.228). This approach has, of course, limitations in that it is premised on an ideal typology of professionalism and that kind of empirical measurement of the characteristics of a profession is usually difficult, if not impossible.

Except for the references which have been cited, the many other attempts were usually lists of characteristics, standards, or criteria. There were some operational definitions. However, "generally speaking, a mature profession is an organized work group that has a legal monopoly to establish procedures for recruiting and policing members and for maximizing control over a body of theoretical knowledge and applying it to the solution of social problems"(Corwin, 1970, p.43).

This section concludes that professionalization is a drive for status as a process, and it must be viewed as a dimension on a continuum(Goode, 1970, p.46), just as bureaucratization was defined. To clarify the concept of professionalization, one must reflect upon the characteristics of a profession, as presented in the next section.

2. Characteristics of a Profession

Many scholars have pointed out the characteristics of a profession. Such efforts have had similar results even though expressed in different terms. After quoting some lists of characteristics of a profession, this section will determine the common elements expressed in the literature.

Lieberman regarded a profession as an occupation which exhibited the following characteristics:

(1) A unique, definite, and essential social service.

(2) An emphasis upon intellectual techniques in performing its service.

(3) A long period of specialized training.

(4) A broad range of autonomy for both the individual practitioners and for the occupational group as a whole.

(5) An acceptance by the practitioners of broad personal responsibility for judgments made and acts performed within the scope of professional autonomy.

(6) An emphasis upon the practitioners, as the basis for the organization and performance of the social service delegated to the occupational group.

(7) A comprehensive self-governing organization of practitioners.

(8) A code of ethics which has been clarified and interpreted at ambiguous and doubtful points by concrete cases(1956, pp.1-5).

Greenwood maintained that professions are distinguishable by profession of (1) a systematic body of theory, (2) professional authority, (3) sanction of the community, (4) a regulative code of ethics, and (5) the professional culture(1966, pp.9-19). In 1976 the

American Association of Colleges for Teacher Education(AACTE),
through its Commission on Education for the Profession of Teaching,
categorized teaching as a "semi-profession" and provided a set of
characteristics of professions and of semi-professions. This AACTE
description was very detailed and comprehensive(Howsam, et al.,
1976). The central meanings of their 12 characteristics of professions were summarized as follows;

(1) Essential services
(2) Identified areas of need or function
(3) Body of knowledge and a repertoire of behavior and skills
(4) Involving in decision making
(5) One or more undergirding disciplines
(6) Professional associations
(7) Performance standards
(8) Preparation in professional school
(9) Public trust and confidence
(10) Service motivation and lifetime commitment
(11) Authority to practice and accountability
(12) Freedom from direct on supervision and evaluation(pp.6-7).

The following table summarizes the review of literature
dealing with characteristics of a profession in a manner to
that used by Hall in showing the characteristics of bureauc-
racy(Table 1).

Table 3

Characteristics of Profession as Listed by Major Authors

	Lieberman	NEA	Hoy	MacKay	Corwin	Flexner	Kornhauser	Goode	Hall
Unique social service	*				*				
Intellectual techniques	*	*	*		*	*	*		
Specialized training	*	*		*		*		*	
Autonomy of Professional	*		*		*		*		*
Responsibility	*					*	*		
Service to clients	*	*		*	*	*		*	*
Self-governance	*	*	*	*	*				*
Code of ethics	*		*	*					
Colleague, Association		*	*	*	*	*		*	*
Career, Research	*				*	*	*		

(Lieberman, 1956; NEA 1948; Hoy & Miskel, 1978; MacKay, 1964; Flexner, 1955; Kornhauser, 1962; Goode, 1961; Hall, 1968; Corwin, 1965a)

From these characteristics can be construed some common elements, such as a theoretical body of knowledge, autonomy, responsibility, a service spirit, self-governance, specialized training, and code of ethics.

Teachers who consider themselves as professionals are now challenging the traditional bureaucratic structure of school organizations with claims of their special competence and desire for more control over their own work. This professional image propels teaching in quite another direction away from the bureaucracy. Professional characteristics tend to differ greatly from the characteristics of a bureaucracy as discussed

earlier. When both professional and bureaucratic characteristics exist in the same school system, conflict is predicted.

As mentioned earlier, professionalization was expressed along a
continuum from the established professions, the new professions,
the emerging professions, the semi-professions, and other occupa-
tions(Howsam, 1980, p.93). Etzioni(1964) and Howsam et al.(1976)
classified public school teachers as semi-professional and many
others agree that public school teachers are not at the same professional level as medical doctors or lawyers. However, according
to one survey, over ninety per cent of the public believed that
teaching is a profession(Corwin, 1965b, p.312).

In brief summary, teaching is classified as semi-professional, some teachers are striving to be recognized as
full-professionals, and a profession has a number of unique
characteristics expressed along continua. In some aspects
these characteristics become sources of conflict within a bureaucratic structure.

3. Professionalization in Schools

Many occupations are emerging as new professions. At the
same time each occupation has been emphasizing its degree of
professionalization. Public school teaching is one of these occupations. "During most of the Pre-Industrial Period there
was little that might be identified as a teaching profession"
(Parelius and Parelius, 1978, p.187), but the end of the nineteenth century, through the Early Industrial Period, teaching
had emerged as an occupation widely recognized as a pro-

fession, with specialized, body of expertise, formal training programs, and national organizations. The Early Industrial Period saw teaching make enormous strides in the direction of professionalization. Over the last several decades, during the Mature Industrial Period, teaching has developed as a profession in aspects of recruitment and selection, expertise, training and socialization, and professional organizations and unions; however, as some sociologists have suggested, teaching is not yet fully professionalized as is medicine and law. Unfortunately, "teachers currently work in settings that are highly bureaucratized, where they are often treated as employees rather than as professional workers"(Parelius and Parelius, 1978, p.233).

Nevertheless, various conditions are flowing in the direction of professionalization in schools. First, teacher education and training standards have become higher, preparation periods longer and are projected to be continuously higher in the future. "A long period of specialized education" is an important characteristic of professionalization. "In 1925, few teachers possessed bachelor's degrees, but by 1970, almost 95% held bachelor's degrees, and more than 28% held masters degrees; some states reported more than half of their elementary teachers as holding master's degrees"(Hencley, et al., 1970, p.6). Ten years later, 1980, their educational level might be expected to be higher than in 1970.

Modern teaching technologies—such as computer-assisted instruction, competency-based education, etc.—necessarily demand more specialized preparation for teaching. The current explosion of knowledge encourages the professionalization of teaching.

The reference group for teachers is changing. In the past, teachers would look to their superior, the school principal, to receive help, but now most of the help they obtain comes from other teachers, and some comes from university professors. For special assistance, the teachers turn to colleagues whom they view as experts with the authority of competence. This trend will be continuously strengthened in the future(Faber and Shearron, 1970, p.378).

The fact teachers and administrators began to have different professional organizations, such as AFT, AASA, NAESP, NASSP, etc. is a trend toward professionalization in which groups are functionally differentiating themselves from other groups. This indicates that teaching and administration are functionally different from each other with unique professionality.

The increase of professional positions in elementary schools, such as guidance counselors, curriculum materials specialists, and partial departmentalization, is an indication of a process of professionalization.

In conclusion, many teachers strongly argue that they are professional and therefore should have academic autonomy and total authority over matters concerning instruction, curriculum, teaching materials, and classroom environment. This kind of argument is assumed to conflict with the bureaucratic structure of schools.

4. Empirical Studies on Professionalization

This subsection mainly reviews the empirical research related to professional orientation. However, prior to beginning such a review, it may be useful to describe instruments which have been developed to measure professional orientation. Colombotos(1962) used a four-item index of teacher professionalism; it pertained to technical competence, the autonomy of teachers, and the service ideal. Respondents expressed the importance of each of these elements.

Webb(1964) developed multiple-item and Likert-type professional and employee scales. The professional scale was based on the four professional principles of functional specialization, horizontal differentiation, competence-based integration, and uniformity based on general principles.

Using a Likert technique, Hall(1968) also developed a professionalism scale. From a review of structural and attitudinal attributes, he developed subscales which were: (1) professional organization as reference, (2) belief in service to public, (3) sense of calling to the field, and (4) feeling of autonomy.

This researcher has chosen to use Corwin's "Professional Orientation Scale." Discussion of this instrument appears in Chapter 3.

According to Colombotos'(1962) study males teaching in academic subject matter areas were more professional than nonacademic subject matter teachers; teachers with advanced training were found to be more professional than those less well-educated; liberal arts graduates were more professional than graduates of teachers' colleges; and generally, women tended to be more professionally oriented than men.

Kuhlman and Hoy's(1974) study added some new and conflicting results. Experience in the school organization for beginning teachers was related to decreased professional orientation, but there was no significant difference in the professional orientations of men and women, and between elementary and secondary teachers.

Kornacher's(1966) study showed that relatively more males than females were classified as professional, but Corwin(1970) found that professional orientation did not differ between the sexes or different age groups. Fris(1978) concluded his study by saying that differences in professional aspiration were found for sex and teaching experience.

Robinson's(1966) research results indicated that teachers with a university degree collectively exhibited more professionalism than those without degrees. From a study of police officers, social workers and teachers, Peabody(1962) pointed out that younger, career-oriented police officers with college training, and small-town police attached importance to authority of professional competence which was related to level of graduate education.

The foregoing empirical research results are seen by researchers to be inconsistent. Wells(1977) recommended that further study was needed in order to know more about the effect of such variables as age, sex, race, educational training, and teaching experience upon militancy and professional orientation. A part of the study also seeks to identify the more professionally-oriented teacher.

C. Conflict

1. Definition

From the literature, it would appear that it has been diffi-cult for scholars to develop a clear definition of conflict. This difficulty may be due to the many types, sources, and classi-fications of conflict. Therefore, in many cases researchers have used operational definitions which have limited value beyond their immediate purposes.

According to Boulding, conflict referred to a "situation of com-petition in which the parties are aware of the incompatibility of potential future positions and in which each party wishes to oc-cupy a position that is incompatible with the wishes of the other" (1962, p.5; 1964, p.46). Coser's definition was "a struggle over values and claims to scarce status, power and resources in which the aims of the opponents are to neutralize, injure, or eliminate the rivals"(1967, p.8). Frost and Wilmot defined conflict in terms of communication perspective as "an expressed struggle between at least two interdependent parties, who perceive incompatible goals, scarce rewards, and interference from the other party in achieving their goals"(1978, p.9).

Common elements of these definitions are actor and system. Actors are expressed here as parties and system is position, power, status, rewards, or goals. A party may be a person or a group. These definitions usually require at least

two parties, but such is not necessarily so because an individual can conflict internally. These definitions exclude the
"internal conflict" area which occurs within the individual, in
addition to those conflicts which occur outside. Keltner(1970,
pp.225-28) listed three conflict areas: "Internal Conflict,"
"Interpersonal Conflict," and "Intergroup Conflict." However,
when two people, two groups, or two alternatives cannot oc-
cupy the same space at the same time, a conflict situation
occurs. Therefore, the following assumptions are premised for
conflict:

1. Conflict involves interaction between two or more individuals or
   alternatives in which actions and counteractions are mutually opposed.
2. A conflict situation is one in which gains in one alternative are
   made at the other's expense.
3. Conflict arises as either a result of position scarcity or of resource
   scarcity(Mack and Snyder, 1957, pp.218-19).

In their model which was mentioned earlier, Getzels and
Guba defined conflict simply as the "mutual interference of
adjustive and integrative reactions." They pointed to three
primary sources of conflict between individual and institution:
Role-personality Conflicts, Role Conflicts, and Personality Conflicts.
Because the present study is interested in conflict between
bureaucratic structure and individual professional orientation,
and between bureaucratic characteristics and professional
characteristics, the present study follows Getzels and Guba's
definition of Role-personality Conflict; "discrepancies between

the pattern of expectations attaching to a given role and pattern of need-dispositions characteristics of the incumbent of the role"(1957, p.431). However, because there is no developed instrument to measure only these specific areas, the Conflict Assessment Questionnaire(CAQ), which attempted to measure general and comprehensive conflicts in school situations, will be used in this study. Therefore, conflict is operationally defined as the score on the CAQ.

Katz and Kahn's model(1966) was similar to the Getzels-Guba model. An organization provides offices to an individual which defines the individual's role set, which, in turn, defines role behavior. The individual responds according to perceptions of the information and to perception of roles. This response affects the behavior. An individual experiences conflict when he/she perceives contradictory information and role demands.

Katz and Kahn identified five types of conflict from their model; (1) Intrasender Conflict in which a role incumbent must choose one at the other's expense among incompatible alternatives; (2) Intersender Conflict which occurs when contradictory expectations are demanded by other rolesenders; (3) Interrole Conflict which occurs when various roles for the same office are incompatible; (4) Person-Role Conflict occurs when the demanded role violates the role incumbent's personality, needs, values, and capacities; and (5) Role Overload occurs when a role incumbent must perform too many expectations at the same time.

Types of conflict also are explained according to Role Theory. When two persons cannot establish a satisfactory complementary or reciprocal role relationship, conflict appears. There are many possible conflicts; conflict from differences between role expectation and role perception, conflict from role expectation clashing with the individual personality needs, conflict from role ambiguity, conflict from concurrent roles, conflict between manifest role and latent role, etc.

Bailey(1971, p.233), from the viewpoint of hierarchy, identified three types of conflict: (1) Subordinate Conflict, (2) Superordinate Conflict, and (3) Lateral Conflict. Evan(1965, pp.57-58) listed three: (1) Technical Conflict, (2) Administrative Conflict, and (3) Interpersonal Conflict. These kinds of conflict types are all related to previously mentioned definitions, to sources of conflict, and to functions of conflict.

Nebgen(1977-78, p.2) categorized four sources of conflict: (1) Communication Problems, (2) Structural Factors, (3) Human Factors, and (4) Conflict-Promoting Interactions. Unclear messages from semantic differences, insufficient exchange of information, and noise often become causes of conflict. Communication channels are also very important in communication problems. Structural Factors correspond to the nomothetic dimension of the Getzels-Guba model. Therefore, these factors are major interest areas to the present study, in addition to the Human Factors which correspond to the idiographic dimension. Nebgen indicated that size of organization, bureaucratic characteristics, reward structure, power structure and overloading information are related to conflict. Her point was compatible with the assumptions underlying the present study. She pointed out that the Human Factors of personality, role satisfaction, role status, and differing goals will contribute to conflict. These factors partially support the assumptions of the present study that personal value orientation will contribute to conflict with bureaucratic structure. Conflict-promoting Interactions are those that involve competition, domination, and/or provocation according to her explanation, but these seem to describe conflict situations. Her comments were, however, congruous with the bases for this study.

Before turning to conflict management, it is useful to refer briefly to the function of conflict. In 1950, Bernard(1950) indicated that the study of sociological theory of conflict in the United States had been comparatively neglected, while Communists, on the other hand, had assiduously cultivated this field. He pointed out the following six reasons:

(1) Cultural explanations of sociological phenomena are easier on our own personalities than interactional ones;
(2) Sociologists have wished to avoid identification with Marxism or socialism;
(3) There is a widespread fear that, if studies conflict, he is aggravating, advocating, or approving it;
(4) Powerful fighting organizations do not want to see a science of conflict developed;
(5) We do not wish to face the existence of certain conflicts; and finally,
(6) The difficulty in securing adequate data is very great(1950, p.11)

One of the most important, but comparatively little studied, areas is, still, conflict and conflict management. As Pois(1969) indicated, conflict has been frequently viewed as a negative function for an organization; however, recently, its positive viewpoints have been recognized. In other words, conflict has begun to be seen as a sign of health in an organization(LaCrosse, 1979).

"We all have often assumed that competition, controversy, and combat are undesirable processes and that the prime efforts of social scientists and practitioners should be directed toward eliminating struggle from our living systems or at least reducing their frequency and significance"(Keltner, 1970, p.229). From this viewpoint, efforts of many sociologists were directed at reducing conflict because they saw it as a disruptive element in society. Thus, their central emphasis became "roads to agreement" and mutual adjustment by reducing conflict. However, another sociologist(i.e., Lewis A. Coser, 1967) argued that conflict had socially desirable qualities as well as negative values. In his view, conflict created associations and coalitions by bringing together people who might otherwise have nothing to do with each other. Darendorf(1958) also adopted the "conflict model of society" as the ideal model of society.

Whether conflict is harmful or helpful depends on how it is used—on how constructively one copes with it. Spence's(1978, pp.17-18) position was that when properly managed, conflict could even enhance organizational effectiveness.

Follet(Metcalf and Urwick, 1940, pp.31-49) viewed conflict

as negative and suggested three approaches to reducing or resolving conflict within and among groups: (1) Domination is where one side wins and others lose. It is often the easiest and quickest way in the immediate sense, but in the long run is not usually successful. (2) Compromise involves each party giving up something. Compromise is a lose-lose situation. Because the parties give up something in this situation, at some point the conflict will rise in another form. (3) Integration, is the only truly effective method of dealing with conflict. This is a process by which the involved parties seek a new solution rather than staying within the confines of existing mutually exclusive alternatives. In integration all parties "win."

Nebgen(1978) summarized her review of the literature on conflict management techniques as (1) Avoidance Techniques, (2) Use of Force, (3) Use of a Third Party, and (4) Rational Approaches. Avoidance techniques include non-response or withdrawal, isolation, procrastination, smoothing, and the bringing about of a deadlock situation. Non-response or withdrawal is based on the belief that "silence is golden." Isolation involves removing or reducing contact with the source of conflict. In procrastination, the conflict manager adopts a "let's wait and see" stance. The smoothing technique is to play down the differences but to emphasize the common interests of the group. In deadlock technique, the conflict manager has an attitude that nobody wins, but then no one loses either.

Use of force techniques include coercion, suppression, domination, and forcing or imposition. These techniques assume that one party is in a superordinate position to the other. The coercion technique uses implied or explicit threats to the other. Suppression is the conscious attempt to avoid unpleasantness through denial by one party of the existence of conflict. In domination one party dominates the other to settle the conflict. Forcing or imposition is a win-lose situation in which the stronger party settles the conflict by forcing a solution.

In the use of third party, arbitration and mediation are common. In arbitration the contending parties may agree in advance that the recommendations of the arbitrator will be binding. A mediator is not empowered to settle the conflict as an arbitrator is, but serves to clarify the positions of both parties and to suggest compromises.

Rational approaches are persuasion, compromise or bargaining, and confrontation or problem-solving. In persuasion, one or both parties try to persuade the other side. In compromise, the idea is that half-a-loaf is better than none, as mentioned earlier. In problem-solving, there is an open exchange of information regarding the problem as each side sees it and a working through of their differences to arrive at a solution that is mutually beneficial to both. The emphasis is on solving the problem, not accommodating different points of view.

There are many other conflict management techniques, but, there is no absolute or single, best technique. The best management technique depends on the situation of the conflict.

To sum up, the present study follows Getzels-Guba's definition and recognizes communication problems, structural factors, human factors, and conflict-promoting interaction as
major sources of conflict. Whether conflict is helpful or harmful depends on how it is managed, and how it is managed depends on the situation of the conflict.

2. Conflict in Schools

In this subsection, examples or symptoms of conflict in
schools will be presented. These are based on a comprehensive review of the literature and on field observations, not
on specific citations.

While professional teachers are obliged to serve the best
interests of their clients—students or parents—and to provide
them with needed services, tension may exist between professionals and clients. On the other hand, when a problem
student is found, a rigid bureaucratic structure may demand
punishment of the student by school rule or due process, but
a professionally-oriented teacher may stand on the student's
side, arguing that this student is in a special situation; therefore, punishment should be suited to the individual case.

When a bureaucratic school dysfunctions in a routinized and
uniform way, but professional teachers dislike this kind of routinization, the administration is challenged on its insistence that,
what is perceived as extra or worthless paperwork, be completed anyway.

Much organizational tension can be attributed to the fact that administrators frequently supervise and evaluate professional subo-rdinates who are more competent in their work than super-ordinates(Gouldner, 1959). The problem of evaluation is compounded by the fact that the reputations of professionals are based on the opinions of their colleagues outside of the organization.

Bureaucratic standardization probably discourages a pro-fessional's creativity and original thought. Bureaucrats are too busy following the standardized rules and procedures to create new ideas, but endlessly persuing new ideas is one of the professional's characteristics. So conflict follows.

In a bureaucratic organization, one derives authority pri-marily from the position that is held, but professionals attach their authority to competence. Therefore, professional author-ity will conflict with hierarchical authority. Becker(1953) pointed out that conflict arises when the principal ignores teachers' need for professional independence and defense against attacks on authority. If a school principal wants to supervise the instruction of a teacher who believes himself or herself better than the principal, at least in teaching the spe-cific subject matter and the specific grade, conflict cannot be avoided.

Professional teachers argue for autonomy in classroom con-trol and curriculum management, but still many parts are controlled by the building principal or district superintendent.

Now, professional teachers are not satisfied with just partic-ipating in decision-making but may demand the right to actually make the decisions in matters concerning their professional area.

The terms participatory decision-making and shared decision-making may not motivate all professionally-oriented teachers today.

In conclusion, because of increased teachers' work preparation, teacher expertise and advancing technology, a series of conflicts have grown in schools. As Corwin(1965) summarized, conflict areas in school are authority, distribution of scarce rewards, and value conflicts.

3. Empirical Studies on Conflict

There were few objective instruments to measure conflict. Corwin's 'critical incident' method through interviews has been used, but a more systematic and objective instrument was Gerhardt's(1971) Conflict Assessment Questionnaire(CAQ). Gerhardt(1971) found that secondary teachers and female teachers reported a significantly higher intensity of conflict than did elementary teachers or male teachers, and that older respondents and those with more experience reported a significantly lower intensity of conflict than did those who were younger or who had less teaching experience. Miskel and Gerhardt(1974) confirmed previous results from 642 teachers studied in Kansas school districts. Age, sex, and teaching level were significant predictors of conflict; namely, younger teachers and secondary teachers experienced higher conflict, but contrary to the previous study, male teachers had higher conflict. In their research the relationships were consistent with conflict increasing as the bureaucracy dimensions increased.

McEwen(1956) was interested in professional positions in

the military services. Between professional skill and military rank, he found that most of the enlisted male M. D. s and Ph. D. s refused officer ranks and concluded that the professional roles of physicians in the military had been found incompatibile with the bureaucracy in which they operate.

Dalton(1950) studied conflicts between staff and line managerial officers. It was concluded that the struggle between line and staff organizations were attributable mainly to (1) functional differences between the two groups; (2) differentials in the ages, formal education, potential occupational ceilings, and status group affiliations of the members of the two groups; (3) need of the staff groups to justify their experience; (4) fear in the line that staff members, by their expansion and well-financed research activities, would undermine line authority; and (5) the fact that aspirations to higher staff offices could gain promotion only through approval of influence line executives.

Evan's study of superior-subordinate conflict(1965) related conflict types to position. The incidence of superior-subordinate conflicts was positively associated with organizational position in both government and individual laboratories. There was a tendency for technical conflicts to decrease and administrative conflicts to increase with organizational position.

The relationship between individual orientation and conflict, generally speaking, revealed that professionally-oriented teachers experience more conflict than others in school(Scott, 1965; Lusthaus, 1975; and Corwin, 1965a). However, the configuration of professional and bureaucratic role conceptions seemed to be more important than either role considered separately(Corwin, 1965b). Corwin(1965b) found that high professional-low bureaucratic orientation teachers conflict more than those with low professional-high bureaucratic orientations.

Lusthaus(1975) suggested that organizational structure was related to role conflict, and Miskel and Gerhardt(1974) concluded in their study that the relationships were consistent with conflict increasing as the bureaucratic dimensions increased. However, Stahl's(1975) study reported that bureaucratism might not influence attrition.

In sum, demographic variables, such as age, sex, teaching experience, teaching level, academic degree; are related to intensity of conflict. However, it is assumed that more important variables are structural variables and individual values or attitudinal variables, i.e. school bureaucracy and teachers' professional and bureaucratic orientation.

D. Job Satisfaction

1. Definition

Hoppock(1935) defined job satisfaction as any combination of psychological, physiological, and environmental circumstances. This is a very broad definition, but the elements of job satisfaction are clear. Lock's(1969) definition was "the pleasurable emotional state resulting from appraisal of one's job as achieving or facilitating one's value." Ivancevich and Donnelly(1968) defined job satisfaction as "the favorable viewpoint of the worker toward the work role he presently occupies." This implies that the "unfavorable" viewpoint means "dissatisfaction." Vroom's(1964) statement was almost the same. 'Job satisfaction' and 'job attitudes' were used interchangeably since both refer to the affective orientation of the individual toward the work role being occupied. Positive attitudes are equated with satisfaction and negative attitudes with dissatisfaction. Another definition which was similar to the previous definitions, but which included both the organization and the individual, is that of Salinas'(1964): "the evaluation of one's job and the employing company as contributing suitably to the attainment of one's personal objectives"(p.7). Miskel and Gerhardt(1974) defined job satisfaction in an education setting, as "a willingness to continue as a teacher because the personal needs of expectations are being fulfilled in the job"(p.86).

Smith, Kendall and Hulin(1969) defined job satisfaction as feelings of affective responses which are best explained by a discrepancy between the work motivation attitudes and the incentives offered by the organization to the work situation. Similarly March and Simon's(1958) inducement-contributions theory, Festinger's(1957) cognitive dissonance theory, Adam's(1963) inequity theory, and Dawis et al. 's(1968) theory of work adjustment indicated that "job satisfaction levels are related to the perceived difference between what is expected or desired as a fair and reasonable return(individual motivation) and what is actually experienced in the job situation(organizational incentives)", (Miskel, Glasnapp & Hartley, 1975). In school organizations, Abbott(1965) anticipated a relationship between the expected performance and the rewards offered by the school. If the anticipated rewards are not forthcoming, following performance, or if the rewards are perceived as negative, a condition of dissonance or inequity will exist.

A concept closely related to job satisfaction is that of morale. Beer(1964) distinguished between these two concepts. Job satisfaction was seen as the attitude of workers toward the company, their job, their fellow workers and other psychological objects in the work environment, while morale was defined as a group phenomenon similar to "esprit de corps" or a "group enthusiasm in the pursuit of a common goal." While job satisfaction is related to the individual and morale is related to the group, Gordon(1963) included both the individual and the group in his concept of morale. "Perhaps it may be said that job satisfaction is commonly used to refer to the reactions of individuals to specific elements in their working environment, whereas morale often is applied to the general level of satisfaction and enthusiasm of individuals and groups"(p.387).

As reviewed, job satisfaction has been defined from the viewpoint of the relationship between the organization and the individual. This viewpoint is consistent with the Getzels-Guba Model and Dawis et al. 's Theory of Work Adjustment which are the bases of the present study. Getzels and Guba defined satisfaction as "a function of the congruence of institutional expectations with individual need-dispositions"(1957, p.435). In their Theory of Work Adjustment, Dawis et al. defined satisfaction as "a function of the correspondence between the reinforcer system of the work environment and the individual's needs provided that the individual's abilities correspond with the ability requirements of the work environment"(1968, p.11). Even though most of the definitions are similar, because the Minnesota Satisfaction Questionnaire(MSQ) will be used to measure the teachers' degree of job satisfaction, this study uses the definition developed for the Theory of Work Adjustment and the MSQ: "Job satisfaction is the individual assessment of the degree of fulfillment of the requirments by the work environment"(Lofquist and Dawis, 1969).

Job satisfaction is a dependent variable in this investigation. Holdaway(1978) supported the position that job satisfaction is generally viewed as an organizational outcome, not as a determinant. Because improving job satisfaction is a humanitarian value and is a legitimate goal in itself(Smith, Kendall and Hulin, 1969), it has been used as a dependent or output variable(Carlson, 1965; Miskel, Fevurly and Stewart, 1979).

2. Theories of Job Satisfaction

In this subsection several theories concerning job satisfaction are reviewed briefly only insofar as such theories have a direct bearing on this study.

a. Traditional theory. Traditionally, researchers in job satisfaction assumed that "if the presence of a variable in the work situation leads to satisfaction, then its absence will lead to job dissatisfaction, and vice versa."(Ewen et al., 1966). In other words, factors which account for job dissatisfaction are the same and are only arranged on a conceptual continuum as shown in Figure 3.

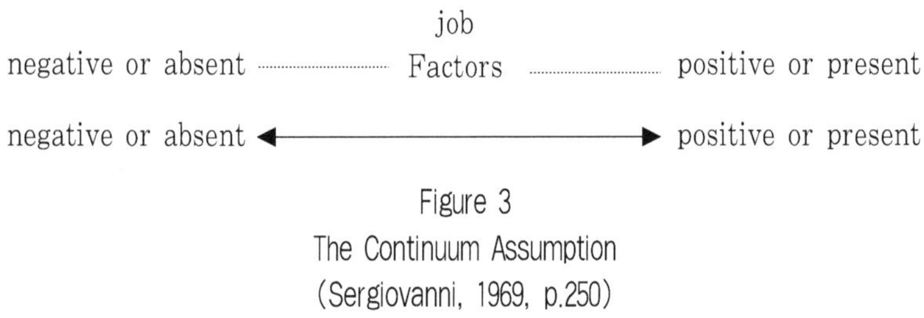

Figure 3
The Continuum Assumption
(Sergiovanni, 1969, p.250)

If a factor on the continuum is absent or negative, then it will lead to job dissatisfaction, but if this factor is altered to be present or positive, then the same factors will lead to job satisfaction. For example, if salary increases, the worker will be satisfied; if it decreases, then worker will be dissatisfied. Managers, believing this theory, set out to develop a pleasant work environment, pay incentives and pension plans, job security, etc., especially since the Hawthorn Study, in order to change dissatisfaction to satisfaction.

b. Need hierarchy theory. Maslow(1954) noted that people at work are motivated by a desire to satisfy their needs which appear in a hierarchical order. When the lowest order of needs in the hierarchy is satisfied, a higher-order need appears, and, since it has the greater potency at the time, this higher-order need causes the individual to attempt to satisfy it. Owens simplified Maslow's need hierarchy as shown in Figure 4, but the terms were somewhat changed and others added.

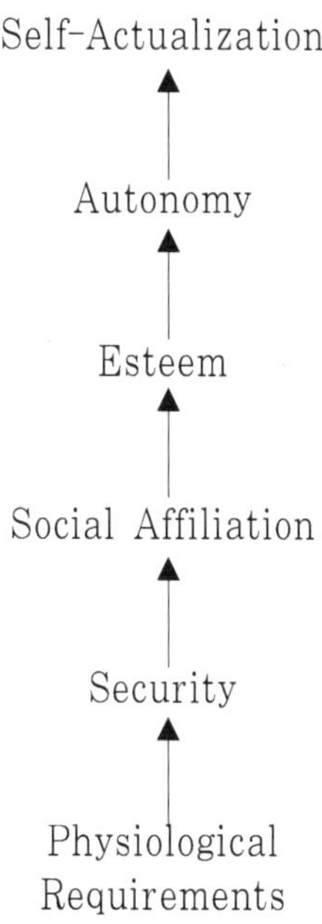

Figure 4
Typical Hierarchy of Human Needs Related to Motivation
(Owens, 1970, p.32)

Maslow's propositions are widely supported in business schools through theories developed by McGregor(1969), Herzberg(1959), and others, and at the same time has been criticized because of vagueness in concept, looseness in laguage, and lack of adequate empirical evidence(Wahba and Bridwell, 1976). It is clear, however, that this theory provides many implications for the study of job satisfaction.

c. Motivation-hygiene theory. Herzberg, Mausner and Snyderman(1959) developed the Motivation-Hygiene Theory or Two-Factor Theory, in contrast to the Traditional Theory, from the results of interviewing about 200 engineers and accountants in the Pittsburgh area. Herzberg hypothesized, and at last confirmed, "that some factors were satisfiers when present but not dissatisfiers when absent; other factors were dissatisfiers, but when eliminated as dissatisfiers did not result in positive motivation" (Sergiovanni, 1969, p.249) as like Figure 5.

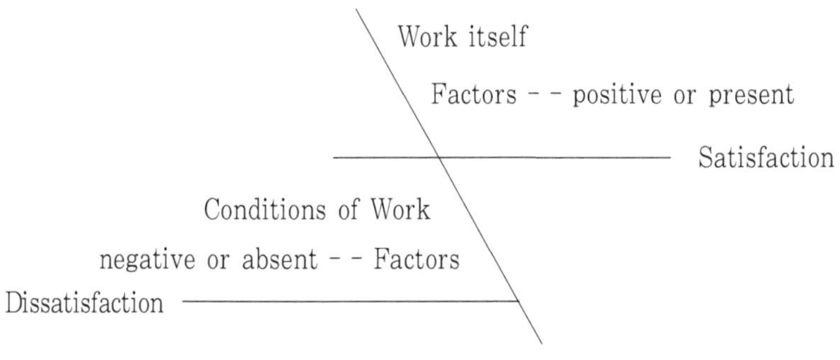

Figure 5

Herzberg Hypothesis: Satisfaction Factors and Dissatisfaction Factors are Mutually Exclusive(Sergiovanni, 1969, p.250)

Herzberg identified two sets of needs: satisfaction needs(satisfiers or motivators) which are related to "work itself" and "intrinsic factors," and hygienic needs(dissatisfiers) which are related to "conditions of work" and "extrinsic factors." Satisfiers are achievement, recognition, work itself, responsibility and advancement, and dissatisfiers are salary, possibility of growth, interpersonal relations(subordinates), status, interpersonal relations (superiors), interpersonal relations(peers), supervision-technical, company policy and administration, working conditions, personal life, and job security.

Herzberg's "ideas are not in contradiction to Maslow's, but are an enlargement, refinement, and extension of the kind of theorizing that Maslow and McGregor have engaged in"(Owens, 1970, p.32). Joo(1974) summarized the relationships of Maslow's, Herzberg's, McGregor's, and Argyris' theory as shown in Figure 6.

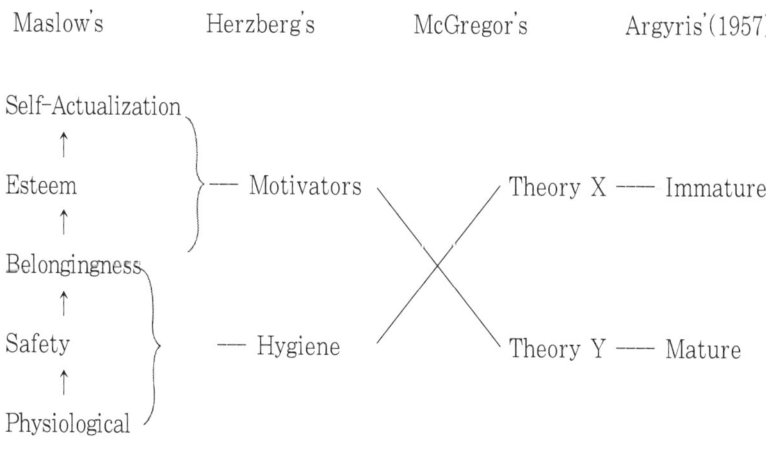

Figure 6
The Relationship of Herzberg Theory and Others
(Joo, 1974, p.33)

Sergiovanni(1969) and Schmidt(1976) replicated Herzberg's research in school and concluded that, generally, the results tended to support Herzberg's findings. While Herzberg's theory has been widely accepted by empirical researchers and especially by practitioners, it also has been heavily criticized, especially in methodology, by academicians.

This theory called the manager's attention to the importance of job content factors which had been neglected since the Hawthorn study. Herzberg's findings opened a new chapter in the literature on job satisfaction.

d. Cognitive dissonance theory Festinger(1957) emphasized and added the idea of cognitive balance. Festinger's Cognitive Dissonance Theory is based on the assumption that people strive to avoid inconsistencies in their beliefs. "Dissonance between two cognitive elements will motivate an individual to do whatever is easiest to achieve a consistency between the disparate beliefs"(Carroll, 1969, p.9). The individual who comes to a job with needs, but who meets dissonance between input and output, will attempt to alleviate the dissonance, strive toward assonance and readjust his inner attitudes. Carroll(1969, p.10) pointed out three ways of solving dissonance: (1) changing individual needs or expectations, (2) leaving the job, and (3) lowering of the input.

Similar theories to Cognitive Dissonance are the Inequity Theory and the Theory of Work Adjustment.

e. Theory of work adjustment. A Theory of Work Adjustment, a conceptual framework, was developed to organize the accumulated research results and to give direction to future research activity by the research team of the Work Adjustment

Project in the Industrial Relations Center at the University of Minnesota.

This theory is based on the concept of correspondence between individual and environment which is described as: "a harmonious relationship between individual and environment, suitability of the individual to the environment and of the environment for the individual, consonance or agreement between individual and environment, and a reciprocal and complementary relationship between the individual and his environment" (Dawis et al., 1968, p.3). The basic assumption of this theory is that each individual seeks to achieve and maintain correspondence with his environment. In other words, if individuals find a correspondent relationship between themselves and the work environment, they seek to maintain it, but if they do not, they seek to establish correspondence, or failing in this, to leave the work environment.

Satisfactoriness and satisfaction are used as indicators of the degree of correspondence between individuals and their work environment, or the degree of success an individual has achieved in maintaining correspondence. Satisfactoriness is an external indicator of correspondence between job requirement and an individual's abilities, and satisfaction is an internal indicator of correspondence between reinforcers or rewards fulfilled by the work environment and an individual needs as displayed in Figure 7.

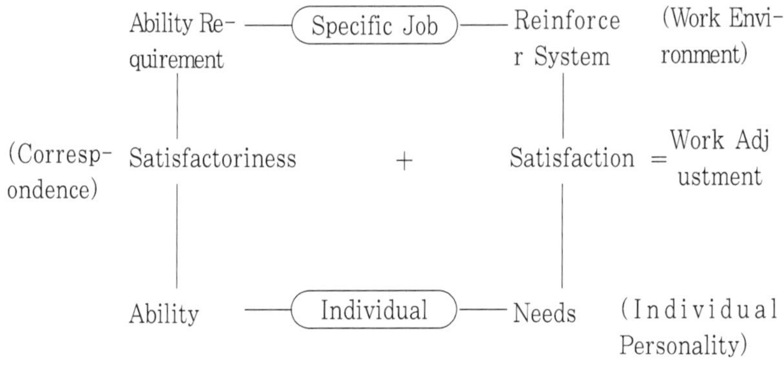

Figure 7
Theory of Work Adjustment
(adapted form Dawis et al., 1968, p.6)

Because the present study is interested in teachers' job satisfaction as a product of interaction between school bureaucracy and teachers' orientation, satisfactoriness is not treated separately but is included in the concept of satisfaction. Because the Minnesota Satisfaction Questionnaire(MSQ), an instrument to measure the degree of job satisfaction, was developed by the same team which developed the Theory of Work Adjustment, and because this theory was developed on almost the same basis as the Getzels-Guba Model for conflict, another dependent variable of the present study, this Theory of Work Adjustment provides the best background for the framework of the present study.

Major theories concerning job satisfaction have been reviewed briefly. Most theories deal with job satisfaction as an outcome of the organization and the individual. Therefore,

job satisfaction is not inconsistent with the basic framework
of the study and with another dependent variable, conflict,
as a product of interaction between organizational structure
and individual orientation. Here one important question is
suggested: Is job satisfaction the opposite of conflict or vice
versa? If there is no conflict or there is little conflict, will
teachers necessarily be satisfied with their work or vice versa?

3. Empirical Studies on Job Satisfaction

Before embarking on a review of empirical studies of job
satisfaction. it may be more meaningful to first discuss instruments which have been to measure job satisfaction.
Among the oldest and best known instrument is the "Hoppock
Job Satisfaction Blank"(1935). This short form consists of four
items, each of which requires the responding individual to
choose from among seven statements the one which best represents that person's opinion or perception of job satisfaction.
Responses were weighted from 1(the most unfavorable or dissatisfied response) to 7 (the most favorable or satisfied response). Each person's total score consists of a summation of
responses to each of the four items.

Another well-known approach is Herzberg's "Two-Factor
Theory" and "Critical Incident Technique"(1959). This technique consists of asking each individual during an interview to
relate any incidents indicative of an extremely good or bad
experience on the job. Two distinct sets of factors emerge

from the results: (1) those which lead to satisfaction, including the work itself, responsibilities, achievement, and advancement, are labeled "intrinsic factors" or "motivators"; and (2) those which caused dissatisfaction, including company policy and administration, interpersonal relations, working conditions, and technical supervision, are called "extrinsic factors" or "hygienes." This is an appropriate method for finding the factors leading to satisfaction or dissatisfaction rather than the degree of satisfaction or dissatisfaction.

Smith and others'(1965) Job Description Index has been used by many researchers. This index has two major advantages: simplicity in terms of response demands, and brevity in terms of completion time—both significant considerations in collecting data by questionnaire. This instrument approaches job satisfaction somewhat indirectly asking the respondent to describe the job by checking a list of words or phrases divided into five subscales. These five subscales measure satisfaction in the areas of pay, promotion, supervision, the work itself, and the work group. Scores on the work and work group subscales can be summed to obtain a measure of intrinsic satisfaction, and the sum of the remaining subscales provides a measure of extrinsic satisfaction. The sum of all five subscales is a measure of overall job satisfaction.

The instrument chosen for this study is the Minnesota Satisfaction Questionnaire(MSQ) Short Form developed by Weiss and other members of a research team of the Work

Adjustment Project in the Industrial Research Center at the University of Minnesota. Detailed discussion of the MSQ will appear in Chapter 3.

Schultz(1973) pointed out that employees between the ages of 30 to 35 had a high level of job satisfaction, while employees in their middle and late twenties were relatively dissatisfied. However, Herzberg et al.(1957) found a U-shaped relationship between morale and age as a result of reviewing 33 studies, but Hulin and Smith's study(1965) failed to confirm Herzberg's conclusion. Chen (1977) summarized his review that 9 among 17 studies showed a positive relationship, 1 a moderate relationship, 1 a few differences between ages, and 6 with no relationship.

Closely related to age is experience or length of service variable. Siegel(1969) indicated that, following the first year, job satisfaction tended to decrease; after six or seven years, to increase to a moderate high; and at about 20 years to reach a maximum high. Tenure status also seemed to correlate with higher job satisfaction(Carroll, 1969). As a result, it was inferred that "the longer the worker has been on a job, the more he knows what to expect, the better his equilibrium adjustment can be made"(Carroll, 1969, p.13).

Concerning position and education level of worker, Loke(1973) reported that white-collar employees ranked task events significantly more often and reward and context events significantly less often than blue-collar worker as sources of satisfaction or dissatisfaction. McDonald and Gunderson(1974) reported that job satisfaction was negatively correlated with level of education.

In studying the relationship of sex of employee and job satisfaction, Siegel(1969) and Novak(1975) found that overall job satisfaction of women was higher than that of men, but Broadwell(1969) reported that males were slightly more satisfied. Another group reported that the relationship between sex of employees and job satisfaction was inconsistent(Herzberg et al., 1957; Centers and Bugetal, 1966; Schultz, 1973).

In general, job satisfaction in school appeared to be related to such demographic variables as age, sex, education and teaching experience(Hamlin, 1966; Evans and Mass, 1969; Becvar, 1969; Novak, 1975).

A number of researchers have shown that organizational size was inversely related to job satisfaction(Porter, 1963; Beer, 1964; Davis, 1972; Talacci, 1960; Longenecker, 1973). In education, research results were divided into two groups; one, no relationship between organizational size and job satisfaction(Lacy, 1969; Morris, 1973; Talbot, 1975), and two, an inverse relationship(Mifflin, 1976; Harshberger, 1976; Anton, 1974).

In relation to organizational structure, Jennings(1978) indicated that school bureaucratization was predictable for job satisfaction. Danese(1977) suggested a negative relationship between bureaucracy and satisfaction, and Blazovsky(1977) indirectly supported Danese's suggestion; highly centralized and formalized schools were characterized by alienation from work. However, Moeller and Charters(1969) unexpectedly found the opposite result that teachers in highly bureaucratic systems had a significantly higher, not lower, sense of power than those in less bureaucratic systems. Enerio's study(1977) supported Moeller and Charters' result. Jain(1978) reported that intrinsic motivation was affected by bureaucratic level; however, Stewart(1977) obtained a different result which indicated that structural change did not affect job satisfaction.

In general, it has been believed that a high bureaucratic structure produces low job satisfaction, and that organizational size is inversely related to job satisfaction.

E. Relationships among Variables

As reviewed earlier, bureaucratization and professionalization differ from each other in basic principles. However, diverse concepts tend to be emphasized commonly in schools. School organization is increasingly becoming bureaucratized, while at the same time teachers want to be recognized as professional and are tending toward professionalization. This tendency is expressed as teachers' professional orientation in this study.

This study will attempt to compare the different professional and bureaucratic expectations, and to review the relationships between independent variables and dependent variables, and the relationships among three independent variables and between two dependent variables.

1. Relationships between Independent and Dependent Variables

In the present study, (1) school bureaucratization, (2) teachers' professional orientation, and (3) bureaucratic orientation are treated as independent variables, and (1) teachers' conflict and job satisfaction are dependent variables. It is premised that school organization is structured with bureaucracy, even though there are some differences in the degree of bureaucratization among schools. As bureaucratic characteristics this study has chosen four dimensions from among Hall's six dimensions(1961, 1963): (1) Hierarchy of authority, (2) Rules for incumbents, (3) Procedural specifications, and (4) Impersonality, because, according to many scholars' arguments, bureaucratic structure is a two-factor and not a unitary concept(Gouldner, 1964; Udy, 1959; Hage, 1965; Robinson, 1966; Punch, 1969; Isherwood and Hoy, 1973). Corwin(1965a) extracted bureaucratic expectations and professional expectations from bureaucratic characteristics and professional characteristics, and contrasted them as shown in Table 4.

Table 4.
Contrasts in the Bureaucratic- and Professional-Employee Principles of
Organization(Corwin, 1965a, p.7)

Organizational Characteristics	Bureaucratic-Employee Expectations	Professional-Employee Expectations
1. Standardization:		
a. Routine of work	Stress on Uniformity of clients' problems	Stress on uniqueness of clients' problems
b. Continuity of procedure	Stress on records and files	Stress on research and change
c. Specificity of rules	Rules stated as universal; and specific	Rules stated as alternatives; and diffuse
2. Specialization:		
a. Basis of division of labor	Stress on efficiency of techniques; task orientation	Stress on achievement of goals; client orientation
b. Basis of skill	Skill based primarily on practice	Skill based primarily on monopoly of knowledge
3. Authority:		
a. Responsibility for decision-making	Decisions concerning application of rules to routine problems	Decisions concerning policy in professional matters and unique problems
b. Basis of authority (continued)	Rules sanctioned by the public	Rules sanctioned by legally sanctioned professions
	Loyalty to the organization and to superiors	Loyalty to professional associations and clients
	Authority from office(position)	Authority from personal competence

Teachers who are trying to adapt to these bureaucratic expectations are called "bureaucratically-oriented teachers" and

teachers who are trying to fulfill other professional expectations are called "professionally-oriented teachers." The degree of orientation is measured by Corwin's Bureaucratic(Employee) Orientation Scale and Professional Orientation Scale(1964, 1966, 1970). Their subscales also are contrasted as follows:

Table 5
Teachers' Orientation Scale Subscales

Bureaucratic Orientation Scale	Professional Orientation Scale
1. Administrative orientation	1. Client orientation
2. Loyalty to the organization	2. Colleague orientation
3. Experience orientation	3. Monopoly of knowledge
4. Standardization orientation	4. Decision making
5. Rules and procedures orientation	
6. Orientation to the public	

It is inferred that, if teachers are professionally oriented in a bureaucratic school organization, they will experience conflict. The higher the professional orientation teachers have, the higher conflict they will have, and the higher school bureaucratization is, the higher conflict such teachers will have. However, if teachers are bureaucratically oriented in a bureaucratic school organization, then there is little conflict or little problem, but rather job satisfaction. This is an inference about the relationship between the independent variables and the dependent variables.

On the one hand, Corwin(1965a) indicated only differences or contrasts between bureaucratic expectations and professional expectations. On the other hand, Hoy and Miskel(1978) and

Blau and Scott(1962) pointed out both similarity and conflict sources between professional orientation and bureaucratic orientation as shown in the following table. Unfortunately, this study cannot include these similarities because there is no developed instrument to measure teachers' professional and bureaucratic orientation including similarities between bureaucratic orientation and professional orientation.

Several empirical studies have confirmed that professionally-oriented teachers experience more conflict in school, as reviewed earlier in the section on conflict(Scott, 1965; Lusthaus, 1975; Corwin, 1965a). Freed's study(1979) also suggested a significant correlation between teachers' grievance and the degree of professional latitude. However, Corwin(1965b) argued that the configuration of professional and bureaucratic role conceptions seemed to be more important than either role considered separately. Lusthaus'(1974)

Table 6

Basic Characteristics of Professional and Bureaucratic
Orientations: Similarities and Contrasts
(Hoy and Miskel, 1978, p.71)

Professional Orientation		Bureaucratic Orientation
Technical Expertise		Technical Expertise
Objective Perspective		Objective Perspective
	SIMILARITIES	
Impersonal and Impartial Approach		Impersonal and Impartial Approach
Service to Clients		Service to Organization
Colleague-Oriented Reference Group	MAJOR	Hierarchical Orientation
Autonomy in Decision Making	SOURCE OF	Disciplined Compliance
Self-Imposed Standards of Control	CONFLICT	Subordinated to the Organization

and Miskel and Gerhardt's(1974) empirical studies suggested that the relationships were consistent with conflict increasing as the bureaucratic dimensions increased in school, but Spence(1978) and Stahl(1975) reported no relationship between conflict and school bureaucratization.

Concerning the relationship between professionalism and job satisfaction, Mawter(1975) reported an inverse relationship. However, results of empirical studies have not supported the claim that bureaucratically-oriented teachers in low bureaucratic schools are more satisfied in their jobs.

In summary, from the foregoing logic and empirical evidence it may be tentatively predicted that school bureaucratization and teachers' professional orientation are positively related to teachers' conflict, but teachers' bureaucratic orientation is negatively related to teachers' conflict, and that professional orientation and school bureaucratization are inversely related to job satisfaction, and teachers' bureaucratic orientation is positively related to job satisfaction.

The tentative prediction about the relationships between three independent variables and two dependent variables of the present study is represented in Figure 8. This tentative prediction will be re-examined and clarified as part of the analysis of the data from this study.

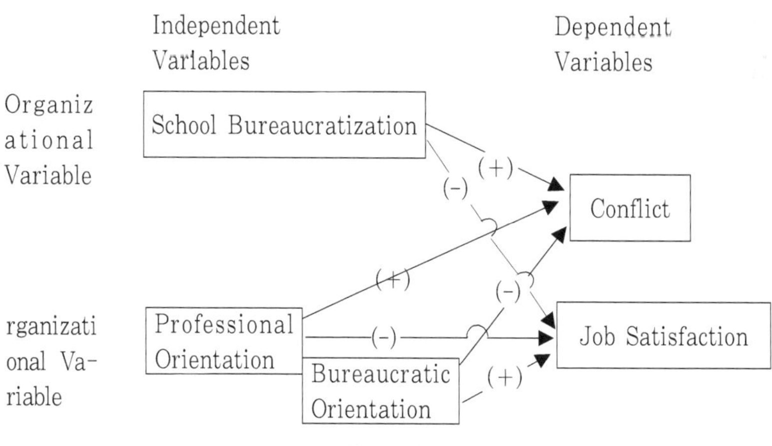

Figure 8

Tentative Prediction of Relationships between Independent and Dependent Variables

2. Relationships among Independent Variables and
between Dependent Variables

First, the relationship between teachers' professional and bureaucratic orientation is of interest. Because professional and bureaucratic concepts are not only different from each other, but also complementary, a negative relationship is theoretically expected. However, empirical studies have indicated that there was no
significant relationship between teachers' bureaucratic orientation
and professional orientation(Corwin, 1965b; Berger, 1956; Punch,
1967; Kuhlman and Hoy, 1974). This phenomenon was explained
in terms of teachers' socialization to bureaucracy by means of
their increasing experience. In other words, some teachers showed
high professional orientation and at the same time high bureaucratic orientation. This is evidence that some teachers adjust,
adapt or socialize well to even bureaucratic situations.

Second, the relationship between perception of bureaucratization and teachers' professional and bureaucratic orientation is another possible interest area. This study is designed to measure the degree of bureaucratization in school
by teachers' perceptions about school bureaucracy. The individual school will be used as a unit for the school bureaucratization by using the Organizational Inventory(OI) total
score in a school, but the teacher will be a unit when this
study deals with difference in teachers' perceptions of
bureaucratization. How teachers perceive their school bureaucratization is more important than the actual degree to
which the school organization is bureaucratized. If teachers

perceive the same school differently and in turn behave differently toward school organization, teachers' perceptions of bureaucracy give rise to another problem in educational administration. Because professionalization and bureaucratization generally have a negative relationship, and because the more professionalized groups are found in less bureaucratic settings, according to Hall's study(1968), there is a possibility that professionally-oriented teachers will perceive their school bureaucratization differently from bureaucratically oriented teachers in the same schools. Thus far, these have been evidence of this possible phenomenon.

Third, a generally negative relationship has been believed to exist between conflict and job satisfaction(Miskel and Gerhardt, 1974). Gerhardt reported that "teachers who are satisfied experience less conflict than those who are less satisfied"(Gerhardt, 1971, p.81). Getzels, Lipham and Campbell(1968) maintained that satisfaction resulted from the absence of conflict in job. However, this relationship was not always the same. Koopman-Boyden and Adams(1974) found that the relationship between job satisfaction and consensus which is thought to be the opposite of conflict, was shown to be far from strong. Therefore, although common belief holds conflict and job satisfaction to be negatively related, lack of agreement in the research which has examined such relationships makes re-examination of that belief a necessary part of this study.

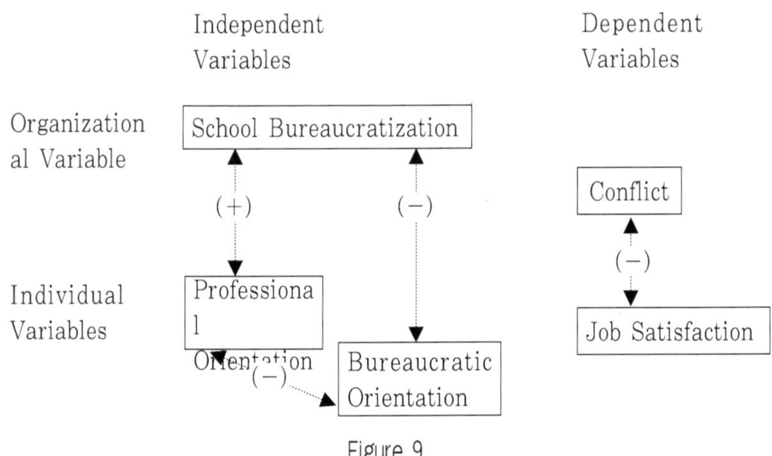

Figure 9

Tentative Prediction of Relationships among Independent
Variables and between Dependent Variables

In summary three relationships are of interest in this area: (1) the relationship between teachers' professional orientation and bureaucratic orientation, (2) the relationship between perception of school bureaucratization and teachers' professional and bureaucratic orientation, and (3) the relationship between teachers' conflict and job satisfaction. Tentatively predicted relationships are represented in Figure 9.

3. Relationships between Major and Demographic Variables

To identify the relationships between the five major variables and demographic variables is another interest area of this study. As indicated in the foregoing sections of this chapter which deal with each of the variables, the results of research do not provide a clear picture of the relationships of the major variables and demographic variables.

This research framework has assumed that teachers' conflict score and job satisfaction score may be explained by organizational effects, plus individual value orientation and demographic effects, plus interactional effects of organizational, individual and demographic effects, plus error effects.

At present, this study presumes that there is some relationship between the major five variables and demographic variables without speculating as to the direction, (+) or (−), of the relationship as shown in Figure 10.

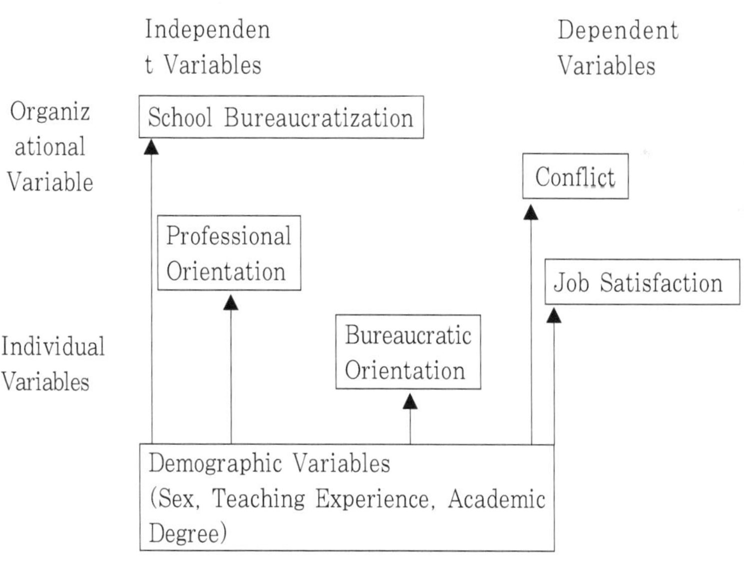

Figure 10
Relationships between Major and Demographic Variables

F. Summary

School teachers perform their job in a school organization. Teachers' behavior is observed as an interaction of an organizational, nomothetic dimension and an individual, idiographic dimension. The organization and individual have been discussed as the most important concepts in educational administration, and the person, the job, and the social setting also have been seen as important tridimensions in the school. Recently, as a major part of the social setting, school structure has become more bureaucratized and, on the other hand, the person—teacher—and the job—teaching—are becoming increasingly professionalized. Conflict is assumed between these two tendencies, bureaucratization and professionalization. When individual teachers with a professionally-oriented work value are working in a bureaucratic school structure, they may experience conflict which may, in turn, their observed behavior. However, if individual teachers in the same setting have a bureaucratically-oriented work value toward bureaucratic school structure, they may experience satisfaction which may, in turn, effect their observed behavior.

A summary of this chapter and of the proposed research framework is shown in Figure 11. In this figure, the bottom line, professional dimension was added to the Getzels-Guba Model with the same weight as bureaucratic dimension. This line had been hidden as an informal organization under the shade of strong bureaucratic or formal organization line, but it is separated and emphasized in this framework. Hanson(1975) indirectly supported this logic, indicating that "the specter of two very different sources of organizational authority in the school comes into the picture—one rooted in the classical bureaucratic tradition of formal centralized authority and the other footed in the informal professionalism of the teacher"(p.22). Therefore, conflict in this figure includes conflicts between the bureaucratic and professional sub-systems as well as conflicts between the organization and the individual. Bureaucratic characteristics and professional characteristics are examples of each structure, and bureaucratic expectations and professional expectations are individuals' work value if they show orientation to one side or the other. According to Hall(1968) and Wilensky(1964), the former are "structural attributes," and the latter, "attitudinal attributes." The combination of both, structural and attitudinal attributes, serves as the basis for each model and produces individual behavior, in this study, conflict or job satisfaction. OI, POS, BOS, CAQ, and MSQ in the rectangles are the abbreviations of the instruments to be used in this study.

Empirical studies are generally divided into two groups; one, supporting assumptions underlying this study, and the other, confusing results. These latter results make the present study possible and necessary. Figure 12 shows the summarized and tentatively predicted relationships of variables to be used in this study. Whether or not these tentatively predicted relationships are confirmed is hoped to be clarified by this study.

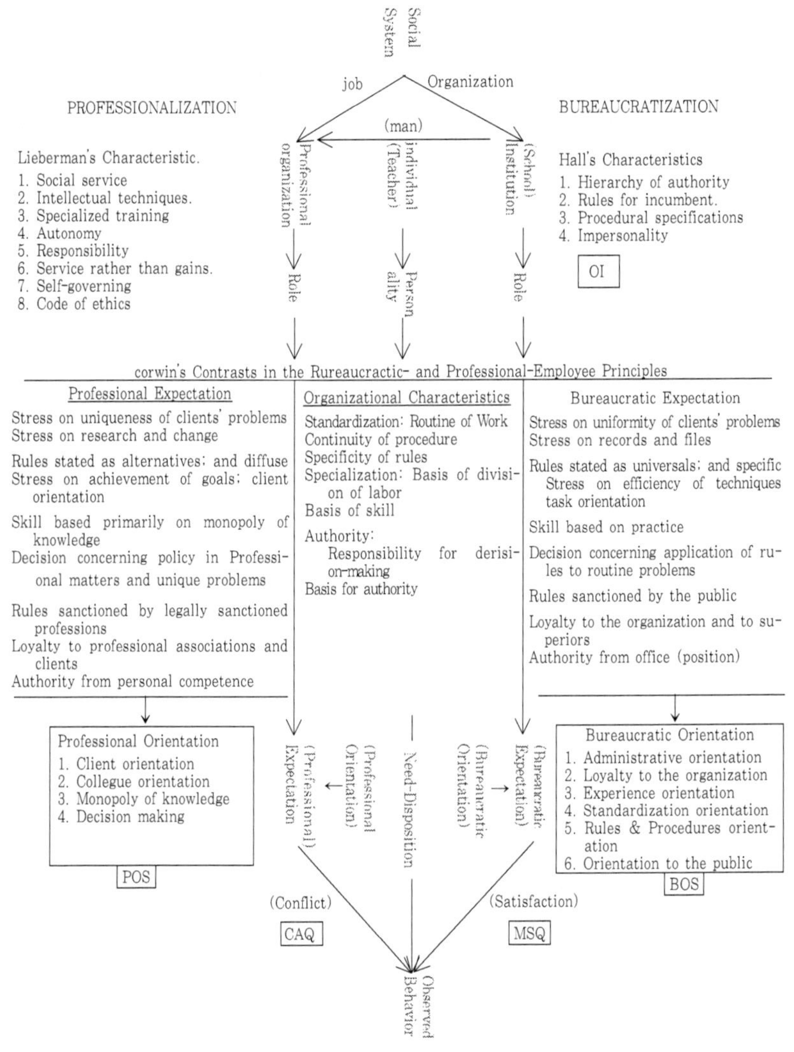

Figure 11

Summary of Review of Literature and Research Framework

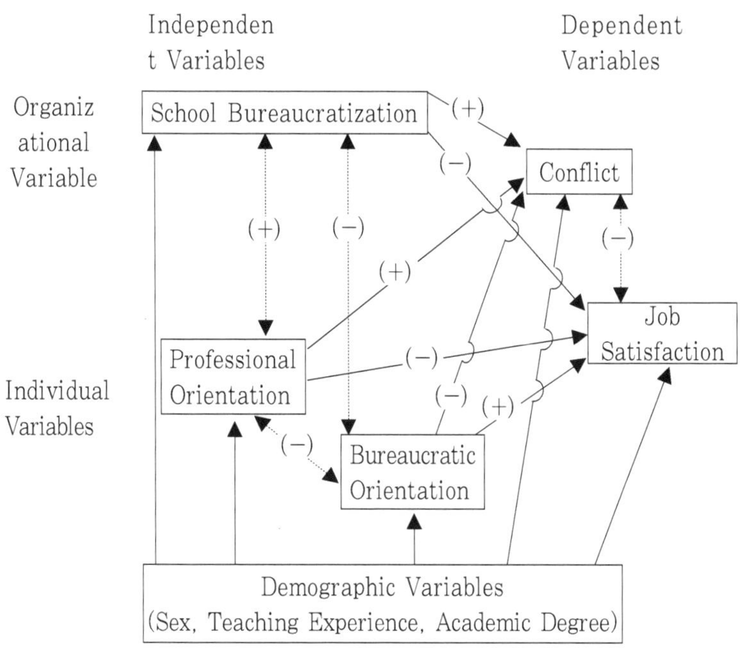

Figure 12
Summary of Tentatively Predicted Relationships of Variables

III. DESIGN OF THE STUDY

The purpose of this chapter is to describe the design of the study. Chapter sections of the population, the instrument, and the treatment of the data.

A. The Population

As a pilot study, this study was consisted in one suburban school district in Minnesota which consisted of 6 elementary schools, 2 junior high schools and 1 senior high school. The school district which was utilized was selected for the following reasons:

(1) Strong support and cooperation of the superintendent of schools and elementary school principals and teachers was essential.

(2) Of particular importance was the willingness of the elementary school classroom and special area teachers to complete the lengthy instrument used to gather data.

(3) One of the major purposes of the pilot study was to (1) determine the possibility of a more comprehensive, larger-scale study, and (2) confirm the rationale of the research framework, use of the composite instrument and adaptability of the statistical treatment.

Although the school district shall be anonymous In this report, a brief description of some of the characteristics of the district may be helpful to the reader. The district is located about 12 miles from the Twin Cities. It contains all or parts of 12 counties, cities or towns. A school population of about 6,200 students, of which about 3,000 are K-6, are drawn from the 28,000 residents of the district. About 600 people in full and part-time are employed by the district. Two-thirds are professionally licensed teachers and administrators. Others serve as aids, nurses, clerical workers, custodians, maintenance personnel and food service employees.

The superintendent of the school district was contacted to explain the purposes and procedures of the proposed study and to solicit possible interest in participation in the study. The superintendent discussed the proposal with the elementary school principals and other members of administrative cabinet and the principals, in turn, discussed the proposal with the teachers in the six elementary schools. After the principals reported the willingness on the part of the majority of teachers to participate in the study, the superintendent made the decision to approve the accomplishment of the study. Only those teachers who voluntarily chose to complete the questionnaire which was used to gather data were involved in the study. Therefore, the population became 158 elementary school classroom and special area teachers of six elementary schools in one suburban school district in Minnesota.

This researcher visited each school to administer the composite questionnaires. Regular faculty meeting time was used for this purpose in four schools. In the other two schools, principals distributed questionnaires and teachers completed and returned the questionnaires at their earliest convenience. One hundred forty-two questionnaires were returned from among 158 teachers(return rate=89.8%), of those returned, 139 questionnaires were usable. The sample consisted of 111 female(79.9%) and 28 male(20.1%) teachers, and of 98 classroom teachers(70.5%) and 41 special area teachers(29.5%). Age, teaching experience, experience in district were high: average age=40.6 years, average teaching experience=16.3 years, and average experience in district=13.6 years. With the respect to degree, 89 BA/S degree holders(64.0%) 49 MA/S(35.3%), and 1 doctorate(.7%) were included in this sample. The number of usable questionnaires from each school and the demographics of sample are shown in Tables 7 and 8.

It may be important to remind the reader that, as stated in Chapter 1, since the population was drawn from only a single school district, generalizations may not be applicable to other districts.

Table 7

The Population Surveyed

(Return Rate=89.9%, N=139)

School*	Total Teachers	Teachers Absent	Incomplete Questionnaires	Usable Questionnaires
A	19	0	1	18
B	24	0	0	24
C	26	13	1	12
D	27	0	1	26
E	31	0	0	31
F	31	3	0	28
Totals	158	16(10.1%)	3(1.9%)	139(88.0%)

* Schools are listed by size from smallest to largest.

Table 8

Demographics of Sample

Demographic Data		School						Total	Percent	Mean
		A	B	C	D	E	F			
Sex	Female	14	18	8	21	26	24	111	79.9	
	Male	4	6	4	5	5	4	28	20.1	
Age	20's	1	2	2	2	6	1	14	10.1	40.6
	30's	7	14	7	11	8	11	58	41.7	

Demographic Data		School						Total	Percent	Mean
		A	B	C	D	E	F			
	40's	6	4	2	7	12	10	41	29.5	
	50's	4	4	1	6	3	5	23	16.5	
	60's	0	0	0	0	2	1	3	2.2	
Years of Teaching Experience	1-9	1	3	2	3	6	3	18	13.0	16.3
	10-19	9	16	7	11	13	16	72	51.8	
	20-29	7	5	3	9	11	7	42	30.2	
	30-39	1	0	0	3	1	2	7	5.0	
Years of Teaching Experience in District	1-9	5	3	3	4	10	5	30	21.6	13.6
	10-19	8	19	7	15	15	20	84	60.4	
	20-29	5	2	2	7	6	3	25	18.0	
Teaching Area	Special	6	7	4	7	11	6	41	29.5	
	Classroom	12	17	8	19	20	22	98	70.5	
Degree	BA/S	13	14	7	12	23	20	89	64.0	
	MA/S	5	10	5	13	8	8	49	35.3	
	Doctorate	0	0	0	1	0	0	1	.7	
Total		18	24	12	26	31	28	139		
Percent		13.0	17.3	8.6	18.7	22.3	20.1		100.0	

B. The Instruments

This section describes the instruments used; the Organizational Inventory(OI) to measure the degree of school bureaucratization or teachers' perception of school bureaucratization, the Professional Orientation Scale(POS) to measure the degree of teachers' professional orientation, the Bureaucratic Orientation Scale(BOS) to measure the degree of teachers' bureaucratic orientation, the Conflict Assessment Questionnarie(CAQ) to measure the intensity of teachers' conflict, and the Minnesota

Satisfaction Questionnaire(MSQ) to measure the level of teachers' job satisfaction. The foregoing instruments were combined into one composite instrument which was completed by the respondents.

1. The Organizational Inventory

The Organizational Inventory was developed by Hall(1966) originally to be used in measuring the bureaucratization of business and governmental organization. Hall isolated six differing from the literature which occurred along a continuum, differing in degree, but not in the sense of "present versus absent" as discussed previously in Chapter 2. Hall's six dimensions were: Hierarchy of Authority, Division of Labor, Rules for Incumbents, Procedural Specifications, Impersonality, and Technical Competency. The split-half reliabilities reported by Hall for the scales were .83, .34, .59, .64, .56, and .71.

In education, MacKay(1964) used a revision of Hall's Organizational Inventory. The dimension, Technical Competency was changed to focus on technical competency 'within' the school because this dimension was identified at the system level. Wording changes followed to adapt the instrument to the school situation before using it. The instrument was revised again, and renamed "School Organizational Inventory" by Robinson(1966) who retested it for internal consistency. As a result the number of items were reduced from 62 to 48. Because Technical Competency did not differentiate between schools more wording changes were necessary to assess de facto instead of expected school operations. Punch(1967) developed new items and administered this inventory to 913 teachers. Analysis of variance was used to determine the power of each item response to differentiate between schools while clustering within schools; and correlation was applied to test the internal consistency of the scale. Punch concluded that bureaucratic structure is a two-factor and not a unitary construct: Factor A being Hierarchy of Authority, Rules for Incumbents, Procedural Specifications, and Impersonality; and Factor B being Division of Labor and Technical Competency. Punch considered Factor A as the central notion of bureaucracy and Factor B as a partial index of "professionalization." He did not name the "School Organizational Inventory" but used the original name, "Organizational Inventory." Hoy and Miskel also followed Punch's point of view and summarized school organization as shown in Table 9. For purposes of this study, a measure of the degree of central bureaucratization in the school, especially as in contrast to professionalization, is desired. Therefore, Hall's four dimensions(excluding Technical Competency and Division of Labor) and the original name are used in the present study, following Punch's argument.

Table 9

Two Types of Rational Organization in the School Setting(1978, p.64)

Organizational Characteristics	Organizational Patterns
Hierarchy of Authority Rules for Incumbents Procedural Specifications Impersonality	Bureaucratic
Technical Competence Specialization	Professional

The following items are sample items from the "Organizational Inventory"(The complete instrument used is reproduced in the Appendix A.).

(1) I get approval for decisions I make.

(2) Rules stating when teachers arrive at and depart from the building are strictly followed.

(3) The time for informal get-together during the school days is strictly regulated.

(4) Red tape is a problem in getting a job done in this school.

(5) The organization sponsors staff get-togethers.

The Organizational Inventory is a systematic instrument for the measurement of school bureaucratization; it has been analyzed at various stages and its usefulness has been shown by a number of users. Its dimensional approach and continuum logic are consistent with the rationale of this study.

The most fundamental difficulty with the Organizational Inventory is that it is a perceptual measurement of the bureaucratic structure. The instrument only indirectly measures the degree of bureaucratization through teachers' perceptions about schools. It, thus, does not avoid the criticism that it is possible for the same school to be perceived differently by individual teachers.

Measuring the school structure directly, for example, through observation of the degree of hierarchy, rigidity of rules, complexity of procedures, and degree of impersonality would be the best and most accurate method. However, such an observation measure is not available at this time, and the degree of measurement error by a single researcher due to subjectivity should also be recognized. Therefore, the Organizational Inventory was chosen for this study.

2. The Professional and Bureaucratic Orientation Scale

"The term 'orientation' refers to a person's understanding of his relationship to a selected part of his total environment" (Corwin, 1970, p.75) and is a part of a value system. English and English(1958) defined orientation as "a set or predisposition toward certain behavior patterns." By analogy from this definition, "a teacher's understanding of his relationship to professionalism" is interpreted as professional orientation and "a teacher's understanding of his relationship to bureaucracy" is teacher's bureaucratic orientation. There were a few instruments to measure professional and bureaucratic orientation.

Corwin(1964) developed a 16-item Likert-type "Professional Orientation Scale(POS)" by contrasting it with a 29-item "Bureaucratic Orientation Scale." These instruments, especially the Professional Orientation Scale, have been used by many researchers. The Professional Orientation Scale, items 1-16, consists of four subscales: (1) Client Orientation, (2) Colleague Orientation, (3) Monopoly of Knowledge, and (4) Decision Making. Responses were weighted from 1 to 5 and summed to indicate the four subscales. The split-half reliability of the POS was reported as .48, or .65 when corrected by the Spearman-Brown formula (The complete instrument is reproduced in Appendix A.). Following are sample items from the POS:

(1) It should be permissible for the teacher to violate a rule if he / she is sure that the best interests of the students will be served in doing so.
(2) Unless she is satisfied that it is best for the student, a teacher should not do what she is told to do.
(3) Good teachers should not do anything that they believe may jeopardize the interests of students regardless of who tells them to or what the rules state.
(4) Teachers should try to live up to what they think are the standards of their profession even if the administration or the community does not seem to respect them.
(5) One primary criterion of a good school should be the degree of respect it commands from other teachers around the state.

The Bureaucratic Orientation Scale(BOS), items 17-45, consisted of six subscales; (1) Administrative Orientation, (2) Loyalty to the Organization, (3) Experience Orientation, (4) Standardization Orientation, (5) Rules and Procedures Orientation, and (6) Orientation to the Public. Linear correlations among the subscale scores of individuals ranged from .37 to .79, and correlation between the subscales and total scores of the Bureaucratic Orientation Scale from .85 up as reported by Corwin.

Sample items from the BOS are illustrated as follows:

(17) Teachers should adjust their teaching to the administration's view of good educational practice.

(18) The school administration should be better qualified than the teacher to judge what is best for education.

(19) Teachers should be obedient, respectful and loyal to the principal.

(20) In case of a dispute in the community over whether a controversial textbook or controversial speaker should be permitted in the school, the teacher should look primarily to the judgment of the administration for guidance.

(21) Personnel who openly criticize the administration should be encouraged to go elsewhere.

3. The Conflict Assessment Questionnaire

There are few objective instruments to measure conflict. Corwin used the "critical incident" method through interviews, but this method is not appropriate to use in this study because of the difficulty of interviewing, its lack of objectivity, and inconsistency of instruments with others.

The most systematic and objective instrument was Gerhardt's(1971) "Conflict Assessment Questionnaire"(CAQ).

CAQ was designed to measure the intensity of conflict represents a synthesis of the empirical developments of Corwin and the theoretical assertions of Barnard. The first step in the synthesis was to classify Corwin's 125 content analysis categories for conflict into the two primary groups of Barnard's method of incentives. Using the definitions of the two groups a panel of two professors and three graduate students classified the conflict categories as either a specific inducement or general incentive. The panel further classified the items in each group into the four subgroups proposed by Barnard. First, the items in the specific inducement group were classified as Material inducements, Personal non-material opportunities, Desirable physical conditions, or Ideal benefactions; second, the items in the general incentive group were classified as associational attractives, adaptation of conditions to habitual methods and attitudes, opportunity of enlarged participation, or condition of communion(Miskel and Gerhardt, 1974, pp.87-89).

This instrument consisted of 47 items with 8 subscales: (1) Desirable Physical Work Conditions, (2) Material Inducements, (3) Personal, Non-material Opportunities, (4) School Priorities and Standards, (5) Decision-sharing, (6) Student Relationships, (7) Administrative Relationships, and (8) Staff Relationships.

The validity of the item content and the relatively clear and stable factor structure of the CAQ were supported by empirical findings. Moreover, the alpha coefficients as estimates of reliability add further support to the assertion that the CAQ is a potentially useful measure of conflict in the educational setting. The reliability estimates of the foregoing 8 subscales were reported by Gerhardt to be .89, .75, .73, .79,

.78, .78, .83, and .64, respectively. The total instrument reliability estimate is .94. Following are sample items of the
CAQ(The complete instrument is reproduced in Appendix A.).
I have experienced disagreements or misunderstandings
over:

(1) salary paid for sponsoring extra-curricular activities.
(2) a personality clash with a student.
(3) adequacy of teaching supplies.
(4) the appropriate number of assemblies.
(5) the administration's idea of proper teaching techniques and methods.

Because the CAQ was developed in the school setting, it
can be used directly in schools without rewording or adapting.
Since this instrument has the same Likert-type scale as the
previous two instruments, and the Minnesota Satisfaction
Questionnaire to be described later, consistency is afforded respondents in the manner of indicating their responses. Another
strength is that instrument is based on a valid theoretical,
and at the same time empirical background.

However, the CAQ does not focus on professional-bureau-
cratic conflict, but deals with general conflict. Therefore, one
notes that the CAQ score measures the intensity of teachers'
general conflict. The overall mean of 1.78 on the original
study was lower than the panel expected, but this is the
best instrument found to date for systematically, objectively
and easily measuring the degree of conflict in schools.

4. The Minnesota Satisfaction Questionnaire

The instrument chosen for this study is the Minnesota Satisfaction Questionnaire(MSQ) Short-Form which consists of 20 items, each reflecting one of 20 dimensions, and two subscales. Weiss et al.(1967) developed this Likert-type scale to measure job satisfaction. The MSQ is consistent with the "Theory of Work Adjustment" formulated by Dawis et al.(1968), the same research team of the Work Adjustment Project in the Industrial Research Center at the University of Minnesota.

The MSQ Long-Form consists of 100 items scored on 20 dimensions. A Short-Form of the MSQ was developed by choosing 20 representative items, one from each dimension. The items chosen were those which correlated the highest with their respective scale. The MSQ 20 dimensions are: (1) Ability utilization, (2) Achievement, (3) Activity, (4) Advancement, (5) Authority, (6) Company Policies and practice, (7) Compensation, (8) Coworkers, (9) Creativity, (10) Independence, (11) Moral values, (12) Recognition, (13) Responsibility, (14) Security, (15) Social service, (17) Supervision-human relations, (18) Supervision-technical, (19) Variety, and (20) Working conditions. The resulting data were factor-analyzed. Two factors resulted, intrinsic and extrinsic satisfaction, while the 20 items indicate general satisfaction.

For the Intrinsic Satisfaction subscale of the Short-Form, the reliability coefficients ranged from .84(for the two assembler groups of the original study) to .91(for engineers). For the Extrinsic Satisfaction subscale, the coefficients varied from .77 to .82. On the General Satisfaction, the coefficients varied from .87 to .92. Median reliability coefficients were .86 for Intrinsic Satisfaction, .80 for Extrinsic Satisfaction, and .90 for General Satisfaction.

Sample items of the MSQ Short-Form are illustrated and the complete instrument is reproduced in Appendix A.

On my present job, this is how I feel about……

(1) being able to keep busy all the time.

(2) the chance to work alone on the job.

(3) the chance to do different things from time to time.

(4) the chance to be "somebody" in the community.

(5) the way my boss handles his/her workers.

The MSQ was developed at the University of Minnesota and has been identified as an instrument that measures satisfaction with several different aspects of the work environment. Therefore, there was no difficulty in administering it to Minnesota teachers. An additional advantage was that it took little time, only 5 minutes to respond, according to the Manual for the MSQ. Furthermore, it was easy to read and met the accepted standards for reliability and validity.

The reliability of the five instruments used for the present study was calculated to examine the internal consistency for the study group. A split-half reliability coefficient was calculated for the Organizational Inventory instrument. The reliability of the total score was .75 and the reliabilities of each of the subscales were .64, .66, .50 and .37. A correlation matrix which indicates the intercorrelations among the subscales is shown in Table 10.

Table 10

Internal Correlations of the OI Subscales

Subscale	(2)	(3)	(4)
(1) Hierarchy of Authority	.51**	.54**	.19*
(2) Rules for Incumbents		.60**	.19*
(3) Procedural Specifications			.31**
(4) Impersonality			

* Significant at .05 level.
** Significant at .01 level.

The split-half reliability of the POS total score was .57 and the reliabilities of each of the subscales were .62, .55, .16, and .59 in this study. A correlation matrix for the POS subscales is shown in Table 11.

Table 11

Internal Correlations of the POS Subscales

Subscale	(2)	(3)	(4)
(1) Client Orientation	.20*	.14*	.19*
(2) Colleague Orientation		.23**	.13
(3) Monopoly of Knowledge			.05
(4) Decision Making			

* Significant at .05 level.
** Significant at .01 level.

A split-half reliability of the total BOS score was .76 and the reliabilities of each of the subscales were .64, .74, .18, .67, .64, and .66 in this study. Table 12 shows the intercorrelations among the subscales.

Table 12

Internal Correlations of the BOS Subscales

Subscale	(2)	(3)	(4)	(5)	(6)
(1) Administrative Orientation	.33**	.27**	.35**	.51**	.41**
(2) Loyalty to the Organization		.24**	.30**	.22**	.53**
(3) Experience Orientation			.15*	.11	.11
(4) Standardization Orientation				.45**	.20**
(5) Rules & Procedures Orientation					.46**
(6) Orientation to the Public					

* Significant at .05 level.
** Significant at .01 level.

The alpha reliability of the total CAQ score was .94 and the reliabilities of each of the subscales were .84, .69, .69, .61, .78, .73, .80, and .67. Table 13 shows the intercorrelations among the subscales.

Table 13

Internal Correlations of the CAQ Subscales

Subscale	(2)	(3)	(4)	(5)	(6)	(7)	(8)
(1) Work Conditions	.55**	.44**	.49**	.56**	.56**	.57**	.37**
(2) Material Inducements		.14**	.48**	.50**	.51**	.59**	.31**
(3) Non-material Opportunities			.30**	.49**	.36**	.47**	.47**
(4) School Priority & Standards				.51**	.58**	.46**	.48**
(5) Decision-sharing					.62**	.71**	.54**
(6) Student Relationships						.56**	.48**
(7) Administrative Relationships							.60**
(8) Staff Relationships							

** Significant at .01 level.

A split-half reliability of the MSQ total score was .80 and the reliabilities of each of the subscales were .80 and .71. A correlation matrix which indicates the intercorrelations among the subscales is shown in Table 14.

Table 14
Internal Correlations of the MSQ Subscales

Subscale	(2)	(3)
(1) Intrinsic Satisfaction	.61**	.90**
(2) Extrinsic Satisfaction		.87**
(3) General Satisfaction		

** Significant at .01 level.

Generally reliabilities for this study were somewhat lower than those reported by the instrument developers. Correlations among the subscales were all positive and ranged from low on the POS, to fairly high on the MSQ. The comparisons of reliabilities of this study with developers' are shown in Table 15.

In summary, the five instruments used in this research have been identified and described. These were all simplified questionnaires. Because they are all Likert-type with five-response-choices, consistency could be maintained by respondents and in treating the data. These instruments were combined into a single composite questionnaire. A demographic data sheet was also a part of the total questionnaire.

It took an average of 20-30 minutes, ranged 15-45 minutes for teachers to respond to all 146 items and 8 personal data items. Table 15 is the summary of the instruments used.

Table 15

The Instruments Used

(All 5 scale Likert-type)

Instrument	Developer (Year)	Subscale	Reliability		No.of Items
			Developers'	This Group	
OI	Hall (1961)			.75	34
		1. Hierarchy of Authority	.83	.64	10
		2. Rules, for Incumbents	.59	.66	8
		3. Procedural Specifications	.64	.50	8
		4. Impersonality	.56	.37	8
POS	Corwin (1964)		.65	.57	16
		1. Client Orientation	.54	.62	3
POS		2. Colleague Orient.	.66	.55	6
		3. Monopoly of Knowledge	.18	.16	4
		4. Decision Making	.90	.59	3
BOS	Corwin (1964)		.84	.76	29
		1. Administrative Orientation	.81	.64	7
		2. Loyalty to the Organization	.80	.74	4
		3. Experience Orientation	.21	.18	2
		4. Standardization Orientation	.70	.67	4
		5. Rules & Procedures Orientation	.84	.64	6
		6. Orientation to the Public	.84	.66	6

Instru-ment	Developer (Year)	Subscale	Reliability		No.of Items
			Develo-pers'	This Group	
CAQ	Gerhardt		.94	.94	47
	(1971)	1. Work Conditions	.89	.84	7
		2. Material Inducements	.75	.69	7
		3. Non-material Opportunities	.73	.69	6
		4. School Priorities	.79	.61	6
		5. Decision-sharing	.78	.78	7
		6. Student Relationships	.78	.73	5
		7. Administrative Relationships	.83	.80	6
		8. Staff Relationships	.64	.67	3
MSQ	Weiss				20
	(1967)	1. Intrinsic Satisraction	.86	.80	12
		2. Extrinsic Satisraction	.80	.71	6
		3. General Satisfaction	.90	.80	20

C. The Treatment of the Data

All returned questionnaires were examined and questionnaires that contain six or more unanswered items were discarded from the treatment. Three questionnaires were discarded in this study. The usable data were transferred from questionnaires to computer cards and verified. The data were then programed and computer analyzed by using Statistical Package for the Social Science(SPSS) at the University of Minnesota Computer Center during April 2-27, 1981.

Responses to the instruments were scored by summing the

scores of the statements in each dimension according to the scoring key which appeared on the Appendix C. All instruments were categorized for subscales as Appendix B.

Summary data are presented for major variables of the study. These data are produced from the Condescriptive subprogram of SPSS to determine the current reality of each variable in accord with the first stated purpose of this study(Chapter 1).

The basic statistical method used in analysis of the data was correlation analysis. Because this analysis provides the researcher with a technique for measuring the linear relationship between two variables and produces a single summary statistic describing the strength of the association(Nie, Hull, Jenkins, Steinbrenner and Bent, 1975), it is appropriate for this study of the relationships of variables. According to the SPSS manual, "a correlation coefficient not only summarizes the strength of association between a pair of variables, but also provides an easy means for comparing the strength of relationship between one pair of variables and a different pair"(p.276). Pearson product-moment correlation procedures used for this study are appropriate for normally distributed data with an interval scale.

The next statistical treatment was a stepwise regression procedure which is appropriate to enter independent variables one by one on the basis of some pre-established statistical criteria. This procedure was used to isolate a subset of available predictor variables for dependent variables, conflict and job satisfaction. Forward(stepwise) inclusion was used. At first seven demographic variables and 14 subscales from three independent variables were entered only if they met certain statistical criteria(minimum F value=3.84, and other parameters set=default), and non-forced variables were automatically removed when their F values become too low. In the next stepwise regression, only three independent variables were entered as predictors of conflict or job satisfaction, and conflict and job satisfaction were entered as an additional predictor of the other.

In a further examination of the data, a two-way and a three-way analysis of variance were used to determine the interaction effect of independent variables to dependent variables.

Further comparisons among means were made when warranted. Data on several other demographic variables: sex, teaching area, degree earned and school were coded and used in several analyses.

The SPSS package was used for most calculations. This package is shown in detail in the SPSS Manual(Nie, Hull, Jenkins, Steinbrenner and Bent. 1975); therefore, statistical methods are not presented in detail here.

Ⅳ. ANALYSIS OF THE DATA

In a sense this study was exploratory in nature and was an attempt to refine the conceptual framework and the instruments and procedures for an investigation of the possibility of a similar but more comprehensive study on a larger scale. More specifically, the purpose was twofold: first, to describe the degree of School Bureaucratization, teachers' Professional and Bureaucratic Orientation, and teachers' Conflict and Job Satisfaction in a selected school district, and second, to analyze the relationships among the above major variables and selected demographic variables.

In this chapter the description of each variable will be presented and relationships among variables will be studied. The Condescriptive, Pearson Correlation, and Stepwise Regression programs of the SPSS package were utilized. In addition the ANOVA program was used in supplementary analyses.

A. General Profile of Major Variables

This section presents for each variable and subscale with the mean scores and standard deviations, and presents a general profile of the selected school district. Table 16 summarizes the results for all variables. Almost all distributions of variables were not badly skewed except Conflict and conflict subscale distributions which were skewed to the right(positive skew).

Table 16

Means and Standard Deviations for Each Variable

(n=139)

Variable	Mean	Standard Deviation
1. SCHOOL BUREAUCRATIZATION	2.81	.37
(1) Hierarchy of Authority	2.44	.50
(2) Rules for Incumbents	2.92	.61
(3) Procedural Specifications	3.14	.46
(4) Impersonality	2.61	.41
2. PROFESSIONAL ORIENTATION	3.61	.38
(1) Client Orientation	3.29	.71
(2) Colleague Orientation	3.43	.54
(3) Monopoly of Knowledge	3.58	.63
(4) Decision Making	4.00	.51
3. BUREAUCRATIC ORIENTATION	2.75	.47
(1) Administrative Orientation	2.63	.62
(2) Loyalty to the Organization	2.36	.68
(3) Experience Orientation	3.12	.72
(4) Standardization Orientation	2.65	.70
(5) Rules & Procedures Orientation	2.82	.57
(6) Orientation to the Public	3.09	.57
4. CONFLICT	1.78	.53
(1) Physical Work Conditions	1.85	.76
(2) Material Inducements	1.76	.68
(3) Non-material Opportunities	1.25	.42
(4) School Priorities and Standards	1.50	.54
(5) Decision-sharing	1.87	.70
(6) Student Relationships	2.03	.72

Variable	Mean	Standard Deviation
(7) Administrative Relationships	2.02	.87
(8) Staff Relationships	2.10	.92
5. JOB SATISFACTION	3.71	.56
(1) Intrinsic Satisfaction	4.06	.50
(2) Extrinsic Satisfaction	2.97	.90
6. DEMOGRAPHICS		
(1) School size (1=small, …6=large)	3.81	1.72
(2) Sex (1=F, 2=M)	1.20	.40
(3) Age	40.62	8.82
(4) Teaching Experience	16.26	7.18
(5) Experience in the District	13.62	6.15
(6) Teaching Area (1=special, 2=classroom)	1.71	.46
(7) Academic Degree (1=BA/S, 2−MA/S, 3=Doctorate)	1.37	.50

1. School Bureaucratization

School Bureaucratization was the organizational independent variable in this study. The overall mean score on School Bureaucratization treatment, as measured by the Organizational Inventory of teachers' perceptions about their schools, was 2.81 on a 5-point Likert-type scale. This mean score was slightly lower than that(3.39) found by Gerhardt(1971). The subscale scores ranged from 2.44(Hierarchy of Authority) to 3.14(Procedural Specifications). School C had the lowest mean and B had the highest mean. Schools B, D and F were above the overall mean for the six schools, and schools A, C and E were below this overall mean for the district. Table 17 shows the mean scores of each school.

Table 17
Degree of School Bureaucratization of Each School

School	Mean of the OI
A	2.74
B	2.98
C	2.57
D	2.81
E	2.75
F	2.90
District	2.81

2. Teachers' Professional and Bureaucratic Orientation

Other independent variables related to individual teacher value orientations were Professional Orientation and Bureaucratic Orientation. The overall mean score for Professional Orientation as determined by the 5-point Likert-type scale was 3.61, and the subscale, Decision Making, had the highest mean(4.00). The Bureaucratic Orientation overall mean score was 2.75 and the subscales, Experience Orientation(3.12) and Orientation to the Public(3.09), had the highest. Data on these variables are included in Table 16.

The mean score for Professional Orientation is higher than that for Bureaucratic Orientation, which perhaps is explained as a reflection of teacher Professionalization. The ratio of the

Professional Orientation to Bureaucratic Orientation was 1.31:1.

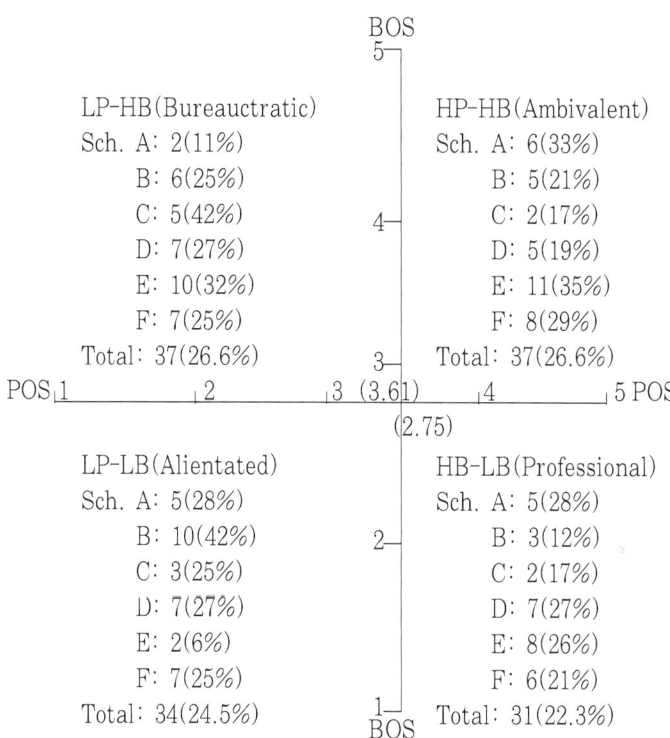

Figure 13

The Distribution of Teaches on the POS and BOS

Sixty-seven teachers scored above the mean on the POS, and seventy-two fell below the mean of 3.61. Seventy-five teachers obtained scores above 2.75, the mean on the BOS, and sixty-five were below the mean. Distributing of subjects above and below the means on the two treatments yielded

37(26.6%) in the High Professional-High Bureaucratic(named Ambivalent) category, 31(21.6%) in the HP-LB(Professional), 37(26.6%) in the LP-HB(Bureaucratic) and 34(24.5%) in LP-LB(Alienated) as shown in Figure 13. Figure 13 also shows that the subject teachers were distributed almost evenly into the four subgroups. One notes that only 6% of School E teachers had contributions of scores that placed them in the Alienated group. This seemed to be a much smaller percentage than for any of the other schools.

3. Conflict

Conflict was designated as a dependent variable for teacher behavior in the school system. When measured by the Conflict Assessment Questionnaire, the mean was 1.78 on a 5-point Likert scale. This mean Conflict score appears to be low and equals the score found by Gerhardt(1.78), the CAQ developer with his subject pool. The data also show that teachers in this school district obtained higher conflict scores on several of the subscales: Student Relationships(2.03), Administrative Relationships(2.02) and Staff Relationships(2.10). According to Gerhardt's study, the Work Conditions subscale with a mean of 2.17 gave the highest subscale mean, however, this subscale in the present study was not high(1.85). Personal, Non-material Opportunities(1.25) in the present study was the subscale with the lowest mean. This is congruent with Gerhardt's mean of 1.39(1971). Table 18 compares this study's results with Gerhardt's(1971).

Table 18

Comparison of Teachers' Conflict with Gerhardt's Study

Subscale	Present Study	Gerhardt's Study
(1) Physical Work Conditions	1.85	2.17
(2) Material Inducements	1.76	1.88
(3) Non-material Opportunities	1.25	1.34
(4) School Priorities and Standards	1.50	1.85
(5) Decision-sharing	1.87	1.70
(6) Student Relationships	2.03	1.99
(7) Administrative Relationships	2.02	1.80
(8) Staff Relationships	2.10	1.92
OVERALL MEAN	1.78	1.78

In summary, the teachers' overall Conflict level was low(1.78). Personal, Non-material Opportunities gave the lowest sub-scale, and Student Relationships, Administrative Relationships and Staff Relationships yielded the highest subscales means. These results are similar to Gerhardt's results.

4. Job Satisfaction

Job Satisfaction was also considered to be a dependent variable in this study and was measured by the 20-item Minnesota Satisfaction Questionnaire. Teachers' satisfaction level was found to be high with a mean score of 3.71 on the 5-point scale. The Intrinsic Satisfaction mean(4.05) appeared to be higher than the Extrinsic Satisfaction mean(2.97).

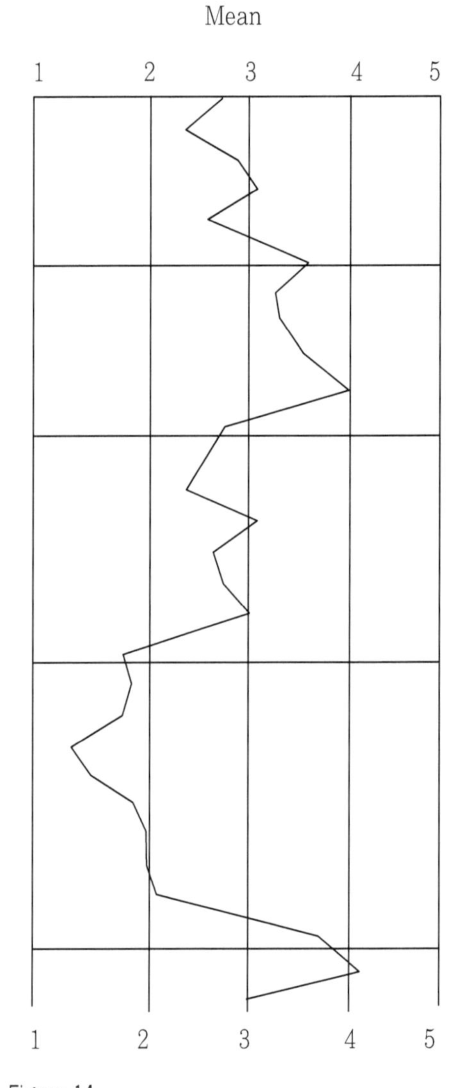

Figure 14

Summary Profile of Major Variables

5. The Profile of the District

Figure 14 shows the general profile of major variables in the district. The degree of School Bureaucratization is low. Teachers' Professional Orientation is somewhat high, while their Bureaucratic Orientation is low. Teachers' Conflict in this district appears to be low, while Job Satisfaction is high.

B. Relationships among Variables

This section presents the results of the data analyses on the relationships among variables. Various combinations of possible relationships were suggested on page 9, and tentative predictions of relationships among variables from the review of the literature were presented on pages 72, 75, 76, and 80. The researcher has attempted in several ways to study the relationships of the independent variables(School Bureaucratization as the organizational variable, and teachers' Professional and Bureaucratic Orientation as individual variables) to the dependent variables(teachers' Conflict and Job Satisfaction as organizational behavioral variables) based on the Getzels-Guba model.

This section will present the results of the data analyses. First, a summary of the relationships between the independent variables and the dependent variables will be examined. Second, the relationships among the independent variables and between the dependent variables will be examined. Finally, the relationships among the major variables and the demographic variables will be studied. Several statistical techniques will be used in the analysis.

1. Relationships between Independent and Dependent Variables

a. Correlation analysis. As a result of the Pearson correlation analysis, only two correlations, Bureaucratic Orientation and Job Satisfaction($r=.23$), and Professional Orientation and Job Satisfaction($r=.14$) among the six predicted relationships, were significant at the .05 level(See Figure 15). Four other relationships were in the predicted direction but were not significant. Figure 15 summarizes the relationships of independent and dependent variables. The direction of the observed relationships can be compared with the predicted relationship given on p.72.

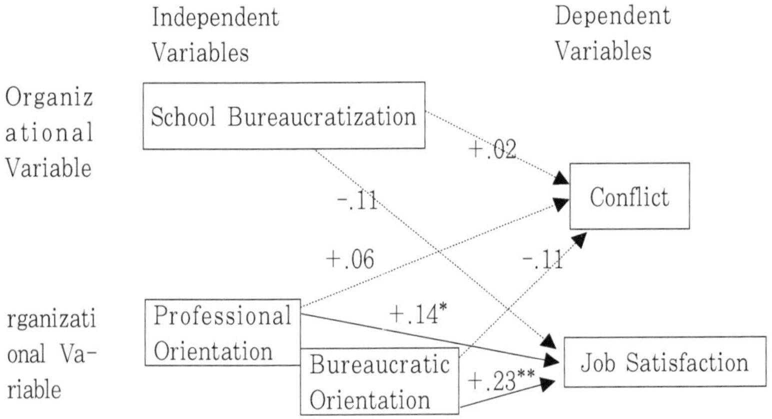

* Significant at .05 level.
** Significant at .01 level.

Figure 15

Relationships between Independent and Dependent Variables

All observed relationships were in the predicted directions. In other words, School Bureaucratization tended to be related positively to Conflict but negatively to Job Satisfaction(non-significant). Professional Orientation tended to be related positively to both Conflict(non-significant) and Job Satisfaction. Bureaucratic Orientation tended to be negatively related to Conflict(non-significant) but positively related to Job Satisfaction.

b. Stepwise regression. A stepwise regression analysis procedure was applied to the data to determine significant predictors for Conflict and Job Satisfaction. The minimum F value for a variable to be entered into the equation was chosen to be 3.84(Other parameters set were a maximum step=42, tolerance=.001, and F to remove=.005.).

Seven demographic variables and 14 subscales from the OI, POS and BOS were used in a stepwise regression procedure for predictors of Conflict and Job Satisfaction; the significant predictors are shown in Table 19.

Significant predictors of Conflict were: (1) Loyalty to the Organization from the BOS, (2) Hierarchy of Authority from the OI, and (3) Rules for Incumbents from the OI. However, these three subscales explained only 9% of the variance of Conflict. Significant predictors of Job Satisfaction were (1) Teaching Experience from the demographic variables, (2) Rules & Procedures Orientation from the BOS, (3) Sex from the demographic variables, (4) Hierarchy of Authority from the OI, and (5) Rules for Incumbents from the OI. These five subscales explained 30% of the variance of Job Satisfaction. The OI subscales, Hierarchy of Authority and Rules for Incumbents, were significant predictors of both Conflict and Job Satisfaction.

Table 19
Significant Predictors of Conflict and Job Satisfaction Using Demographic
Variables and All Independent Subscales

Dependent Variable	Predictor	Multiple R	R Square	R Square Change	F
1. Conflict	(1) Loyalty to the Organization	.17	.03	.03	4.19*
	(2) Hierarchy of Authority	.24	.06	.04	4.10*
	(3) Rules for Incumbents	.31	.09	.04	4.68**
2. Job Satisfaction	(1) Teaching Experience	.28	.08	.08	11.78**
	(2) Rules & Procedures Orientation	.39	.16	.08	12.53**
	(3) Sex	.46	.21	.06	12.12**
	(4) Hierarchy of Authority	.51	.26	.05	11.75**
	(5) Rules for Incumbents	.55	.30	.04	11.57**

Variables Entered: School Size, Sex, Age, Teaching Experience, Experience in District, Teaching Area, Degree, Hierarchy of Authority, Rules for Incumbents, Prodecural Specifications, Impersonality, Client Orientation, Colleague Orientation, Monopoly of Knowledge, Decision Making, Administrative Orientation, Loyalty ot the Organization, Experience Orientation, Standardization Orientation, Rules & Procedures Orientation, Orientation to the Public

* Significant at .05 level.

** Significant at .01 level.

In the next stepwise regression analysis, only the major variables were entered as predictors of Conflict or Job Satisfaction and Conflict and Job Satisfaction were also entered as an additional predictor of the other. Table 20 shows the results of these stepwise regressions.

Table 20

Significant Predictors of Conflict and Job Satisfaction Using Major Variables

Dependent Variable	Predictors	Multiple R	R Square	R Square Change	F
1. Conflict	(1) Job Satisfaction	.42	.18	.18	29.31**
Variables Entered: School Bureaucratization, Professional Orientation, Bureaucratic Orientation, Job Satisfaction					
2. Job Satisfaction	(1) Conflict	.42	.18	.18	29.31**
	(2) Bureaucratic Orientation	.46	.21	.03	18.19**
	(3) Professional Orientation	.49	.24	.03	13.90**
Variables Entered: School Bureaucratization, Professional Orientation, Bureaucratic Orientation, Conflict					

** Significant at .01 level.

When only the major variables were entered as predictors, the results of the stepwise regression were similar to the results of the correlation analysis. Conflict has no significant predictors among the independent variables, and Professional Orientation and Bureaucratic Orientation were significant predictors of Job Satisfaction. However, Bureaucratic Orientation and Professional Orientation each changed only 3% of the variance of Job Satisfaction. Conflict and Job Satisfaction were significant predictors of each other. They explained 18% of the variance of the other.

c. Analysis of variance. In a further examination of the data, a two-way analysis of variance was also run for the two dependent variables, Conflict and Job Satisfaction. The independent variables, Professional Orientation and Bureaucratic Orientation, were obtained by categorizing the scores of subjects(as shown earlier in Figure 13) into high and low groups on each treatment by the mean scores of 3.61 for the POS and 2.75 for the BOS. Tables 21 and 22 show the results. There was no significant effect of PO, BO or interaction on Conflict. However, for Job Satisfaction a significant main effect was found for BO, but not for PO. In the stepwise regressions, both variables were significant predictors of Job Satisfaction.

Table 21

Summary of Analysis of Variance for Conflict, with Two Levels of
Professional Orientation and Two Levels of Bureaucratic Orientation

SV	SS	df	MS	F
PO	294.83	1	294.83	.42(ns)
BO	164.55	1	164.55	.61(ns)
PO×BO	1440.05	1	1440.05	2.35(ns)
Explained	82879.71	135	613.92	
Total	84168.60	138	614.27	

Table 22

Summary of Analysis of Variance for Job Satisfaction, with Two Levels of
Professional Orientation and Two Levels of Bureaucratic Orientation

SV	SS	df	MS	F
PO	258.77	1	258.77	2.19
BO	1062.14	1	1062.14	9.00**
PO×BO	124.04	1	124.04	1.05
Residual	15938.89	135	118.07	
Total	17410.36	138	126.16	

** Significant at .01 level.

Table 23

Subgroup Means for Conflict and Job Satisfaction

Group	N	Conflict		Job Satisfaction	
		Mean	Order	Mean	Order
Low PO	72	82.15	2	72.82	2
High PO	67	85.01	1	75.69	1
Low BO	64	84.67	1	71.17	2
High BO	75	82.56	2	76.79	1
LP-LB	34	80.02	4	70.85	4
HP-HB	37	81.02	3	79.05	1
LP-HB	38	84.05	2	74.58	2
HP-LB	30	89.93	1	71.53	3

L=Low, H=High, P=Professional, B=Bureaucratic, O=Orientation

The means for each of the subgroups are presented in Table
23. Examining the subgroup means in Table 23. one sees that
the groups with the lowest and highest Conflict means, LP-LB

(Alienated) and HP-LB(Professional), have the lowest Job Satisfaction means. Apparently levels of Professional Orientation are not as important as levels of Bureaucratic Orientation. The groups with a high Bureaucratic Orientation(LP-HB and HP-HB, namely Bureaucratic and Ambivalent), both exhibited higher Job Satisfaction means.

When a three-way analysis of variance was run, there was no significant effect of School Bureaucratization(SB), Professional Orientation(PO), Bureaucratic Orientation(BO) nor any significant interactions on the Conflict variable.

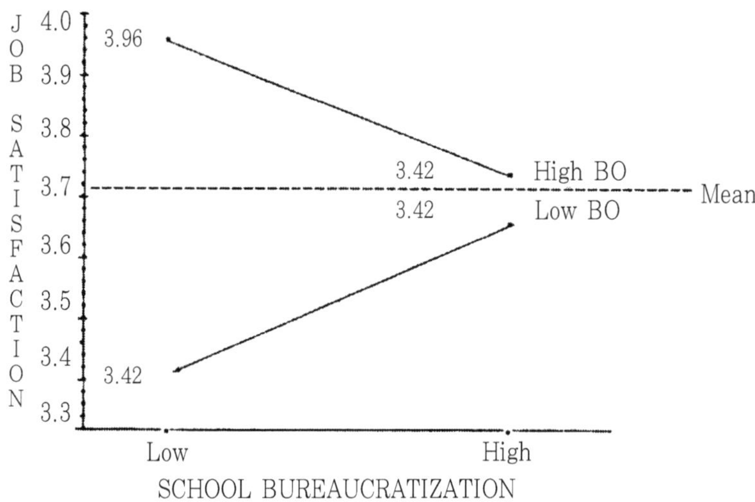

Figure 16

The Mean Scores of Job Satisfaction for Bureaucratic Orientation and School Bureaucratization

However, for Job Satisfaction a significant main effect was found for BO, and a significant interaction effect, SB×BO was also found(See Appendix D-1 and D-2). At both high and low levels of School Bureaucratization, high BO teachers had higher Job Satisfaction than low BO teachers as shown in Figure 16. High BO teachers in low Bureaucratic Schools showed much the highest Job Satisfaction.

2. Relationships among Independent Variables and between Dependent Variables

Figure 17 shows the Pearson correlations and significance levels. Among the variables only one relationship was significant—that between Conflict and Job Satisfaction(−.42). The results may be compared with the predicted relationship given in Figure 9 on page 75.

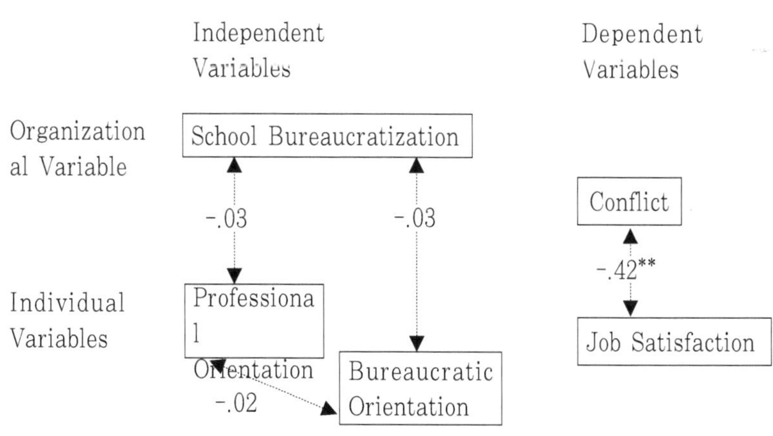

** Significant at .01 level.

Figure 17
Relationships among Independent Variables and
between Dependent Variables

One direction of the relationship differed from the prediction on page 75. The positive relationship between perceptions of School Bureaucratization and Professional Orientation
was predicted but non-significant negative relationship
appeared. Others were the same directions as predicted.

3. Relationships between Major and Demographic Variables

The relationships between the five variables and the seven
demographic variables were examined under the assumption
that demographic variables will impact on both independent
and dependent variables.

Pearson product-moment correlation coefficients are shown
in Table 24.

Table 24

Correlations between Major and Demographic Variables

Demographic Variables	Major Variables				
	SB	PO	BO	C	JS
1. School Size (1=small, —, 6=large)	.02	.01	.03	.01	.05
2. Sex(1=F, 2=M)	−.09	−.10	−.13	.12	−.27**
3. Age(actual age)	−.19*	.19*	−.04	−.12	.25**
4. Teaching Experience (years)	−.18*	.16*	−.07	.02	.28**
5. Experience in District (years)	−.12	.12	−.10	.08	.15*
6. Teaching Area (1=special area, 2=classroom)	−.01	−.08	.04	.07	.02

Demographic Variables	Major Variables				
	SB	PO	BO	C	JS
7. Academic Degree (1=BA/S, 2=MA/S, 3=Doctorate)	−.06	.06	−.20*	.15*	−.16*

SB=School Bureaucratization, PO=Professional Orientation
BO=Bureaucratic Orientation, C=Conflict, and JS=Job Satisfaction.
 * Significant at .05 level.
** Significant at .01 level

From this table of correlations the following observations can be made.

(1) The negative correlation of −.27 indicates that female teachers reported a significantly higher level of job satisfaction than did male teachers.

(2) Older teachers reported significantly lower perceptions of School Bureaucratization, and a higher Professional Orientation, and a higher Job Satisfaction than did younger teachers.

(3) Teachers with more teaching experience overall reported significantly lower perceptions of School Bureaucratization, but a higher Professional Orientation, and a higher Job Satisfaction than did teachers with less experience.

(4) Teachers with more experience in the district, reported significantly higher Job Satisfaction than did teachers with less experience in the district.

(5) Teachers who had earned higher degrees reported a significantly lower Bureaucratic Orientation, a higher Conflict, and a lower Job Satisfaction than did lower degree holders.

(6) Neither school size nor area of teaching were related to major variables.

It should be noted that age, teaching experience overall and experience in the district are closely related variables(Age: Teaching Experience=.81, Age: Experience in District=.70, and Experience in District: Teaching Experience=.85). Therefore, it may be summarized that teachers who are older, more experienced overall and more experienced teaching in the district tended to express lower perceptions of School Bureaucratization, and higher Professional Orientation, and a higher Job Satisfaction than did their counterparts.

C. Summary of the Data Analysis

This section summarizes the results of the data analyses presented in the previous sections.

(1) The degree of School Bureaucratization was low; level of teachers' Professional Orientation was higher than their Bureaucratic Orientation level; teachers' Conflict was low while Job Satisfaction was high.

(2) Teachers' Professional Orientation and Bureaucratic Orientation showed significantly positive relationships to Job Satisfaction. School Bureaucratization tended to be related positively to Conflict but negatively to Job Satisfaction(non-significant). Professional Orientation tended to be related negatively to Conflict, but Bureaucratic Orientation tended to be related positively to Conflict(non-significant).

(3) The significant predictors of Conflict were ① Loyalty to the Organization from the BOS, ② Hierarchy of Authority from the OI and ③ Rules for Incumbents from the OI(These three subscales explained only 9% of the variance of Conflict.), and those of Job Satisfaction were ① Teaching Experience from the demographic variables, ② Rules & Procedures Orientation from the BOS, ③ Sex from the demographic variables, ④ Hierarchy of Authority from the OI and ⑤ Rules for Incumbents from the OI(These five subscales explained 30% of the variance of Job Satisfaction.), when seven demographic variables and 14 subscales from the OI, POS and BOS were used in a stepwise regression procedure for predictors of conflict and Job Satisfaction. The OI subscales, Hierarchy of Authority and Rules for Incumbents were significant predictors of both Conflict and Job Satisfaction.

(4) When only major independent variables were entered into the stepwise regression as predictors, Conflict had no significant predictors, and Professional Orientation and Bureaucratic Orientation were significant predictors of Job Satisfaction. However, these two variables changed only 6% of the variance of Job Satisfaction.

(5) As the result of two-way ANOVA, both Professional Orientation and Bureaucratic Orientation failed(not significant) to explain the variance of Conflict, but Bureaucratic Orientation explained(significant) the variance of Job Satisfaction. High Bureaucratic Orientation teachers had significantly higher Job Satisfaction than did low Bureaucratic Orientation teachers. A

three-way ANOVA added one more significant effect of "interaction between School Bureaucratization and teachers' Bureaucratic Orientation(SB×BO) for Job Satisfaction" to the result of two-way ANOVA. At both high and low levels of School Bureaucratization, high Bureaucratic Orientation teachers had higher Job Satisfaction than low Bureaucratic Orientation teachers.

(6) In the comparison of subgroup means for Conflict and Job Satisfaction, the groups with the lowest and highest Conflict means, LP-LB(Alienated) and HP-LB(Professional), had the lowest Job Satisfaction means. The groups with a high Bureaucratic Orientation level(LP-HB(Bureaucratic) and HP-HB(Ambivalent)), both exhibited higher Job Satisfaction means. The "Ambivalent" group had a low Conflict mean and the highest Job Satisfaction mean, the "Alienated" group had the lowest Conflict mean and the lowest Job Satisfaction mean, and "Professional" group had the highest Conflict mean and a low Job Satisfaction mean.

(7) Conflict and Job Satisfaction had a strong negative correlation.

(8) Female teachers reported higher Job Satisfaction than did male teachers.

(9) Older and more experienced teachers reported lower perceptions of School Bureaucratization, higher Professional Orientation, and higher Job Satisfaction than did younger and less experienced teachers.

(10) Teachers with more experience in the district reported higher Job Satisfaction than did teachers with less experi-

ence in the district.

(11) Higher degree holders reported lower Bureaucratic Orientation, higher Conflict, and lower Job Satisfaction than did lower degree holders.

V. SUMMARY, CONCLUSIONS AND IMPLICATIONS

This final chapter briefly summarizes the previous chapters, presents conclusions from the analysis of the data, and provides implications for theory, practice and research.

A. Summary

This section contains brief summaries of each of the preceding chapters and presents those findings of the study judged to be most important.

1. The Nature and Purpose of the Study

Humans live and work in organizations and their behaviors in such settings are expressed as an interaction between organizational and individual characteristics. Teachers are no exception. Teachers work in school organizations and their behaviors are assumed to be impacted by organizational structure, their own value orientation, and/or interaction of both. The organization, the individual and individual behavior were the variables of interest in this study. The organizational variable, school organization, has traditionally been bureaucratic and is becoming increasingly more bureaucratized due to the growth in size and complexity of modern schools. At the same time, the individual variable, teachers, are becoming increasingly more professionalized due to the increase in (1) systematic knowledge of teaching, (2) teachers' sense of responsibility for student welfare and (3) length of preparation programs for teachers. The behavioral variable, teachers' conflict, was expected to exist between these two tendencies of increased school bureaucratization and increased teacher professionalization, but bureaucratically-oriented teachers in bureaucratic school organizations might be presumed to have greater job satisfaction than professionally-oriented teachers. Therefore, this research studied five variables: (1) School Bureaucratization as an organizational variables, teachers' (2) Professional Orientation and (3) Bureaucratic Orientation as individual variables, and teachers' (4) Conflict and (5) Job Satisfaction as behavioral variables.

The general purpose of this pilot, exploratory study was to refine the conceptual base of the study as well as the instruments and the procedures used and to determine the possibility of a more comprehensive larger-scale study. To accomplish this overall purpose, the specific purposes of this research were to secure the cooperation of a selected school district in order to (1) determine and describe the degrees of school bureaucratization, teachers' professional and bureaucratic orientation, teachers' conflict, and job satisfaction; (2) analyze the relationship of these major variables, including relationships with demographic variables. Generalization based on the specific results of the study would, by the nature of the research, be limited to the selected school district.

2. Review of Related Literature and Research

This study reviewed the concepts of the major variables from the literature and empirical research. For the variable, bureaucratization, this study followed Hall's dimensional approach and used four dimensions from among Hall's six dimensions. This selection of dimensions was in accord with Punch's research results and argument that bureaucratic structure has two-factors, the major bureaucratization factor and the professionalization factor. The four dimensions were: (1) Hierarchy of Authority, (2) Rules for Incumbents, (3) Procedural Specifications, and (4) Impersonality. Chapter 2 covered the tendency toward increased bureaucratization of the schools and empirical research related to school bureaucracy which was believed to impact teacher conflict and job satisfaction.

Teachers' Professional and Bureaucratic Orientation were based on Corwin's studies and his instrument, the Professional and Bureaucratic(Employee) Orientation Scale. Generally, the literature and research supported the observation that teachers' professionalization in bureaucratic schools resulted in conflict.

The variable, conflict was based on the Getzels-Guba Model, Katz and Kahn's Model, and Gerhardt's Conflict Assessment Questionnaire. Conflict was the dependent variable produced by competition between organizational structure or goals and in-dividual value orientation or goals.

Job Satisfaction, chosen as one of the behavioral variables, was also based upon the Getzels-Guba Model as well as Dawis et al.'s Theory of Work Adjustment. This variable, too, was defined from the viewpoint of the relationship between the organization and the individual.

From the review of the literature and research, this study predicted some tentative relationships among the five major variables and demographic variables in Chapter 2 rather than adopting exact hypotheses to test.

3. Design of the Study

This study was designed as an exploratory and descriptive pilot study. In order to refine the instrument and procedures used for possible use in further study, the data were sub-jected to several treatments which were deemed appropriate. Because the population was selected from a single school dis-trict generalizations based on the analysis of the data were limited to that district.

a. The population. The population consisted of 158 elementary school teachers from six schools in one selected suburban school district in Minnesota. This researcher visited each school to ad-minister the composite questionnaires. Regular faculty meeting time was used for this purpose in four schools. In the other two schools, the principals distributed the questionnaires and the teachers completed and returned the questionnaires at their earliest convenience. One hundred forty-two questionnaires were returned(89.9%); of those returned 139 were usable(88.0%). Demographically, the respondents were 79.9 per cent female and 20.1 per cent male; 70.5 per cent classroom teachers and 29.5 per cent special area teachers; 64.0 per cent BA/S degree holders and 36.0 per cent MA/S(including one doctorate) degree holders. Average age(40.6 years), teaching experience(16.3 years) and experience in the district(13.6 years) were high.

b. The instruments. The instruments which were combined to make-up the composite questionnaire used in this study were: the Organizational Inventory(OI) to measure the degree of school bureaucratization, the Professional Orientation Scale(POS) to measure teachers' professional orientation, the Bureaucratic Orientation Scale(BOS) to measure teachers' bureaucratic orientation, the Conflict Assessment Questionnaire(CAQ) to measure the intensity of conflict, and the Minnesota Satisfaction Questionnaire(MSQ) to measure the level of job satisfaction. The composite questionnaire consisted of 24 subscales and 146 items, 8 entries for demographic data and took an average of 20-30 minutes to complete. The reliability indeces for most of the subscales were somewhat lower than those cited by the original developers of the instruments.

c. The treatment of the data. All returned questionnaires were examined; those containing six or more unanswered items were discarded from treatment. Three such questionnaires were discarded leaving an N of 139. Each instrument was scored as shown in Appendices B and C. Pearson product-moment correlation, multiple regression and analysis of variance were used to examine relationships among variables.

4. The Findings

From the data analysis the following findings were cited in Chapter 4:

(1) The degree of School Bureaucratization in this school district was low(2.81). Procedural Specification was the highest(3.14), and Hierarchy of Authority was the lowest(2.44) subscale.

(2) Teachers' Professional Orientation(3.61) was higher than Bureaucratic Orientation(2.75). Teachers were highly professionally oriented on Decision Making(4.00), highly bureaucratically oriented on Experience(3.12), and Public(3.09), and low bureaucratically oriented on Loyalty to the Organization(2.36).

(3) Teachers were distributed almost evenly into four groups by the combinations of the POS and BOS; High Professional-High Bureaucratic(HP-HB, 26.6%), High Professional-Low Bureaucratic(HP-LB, 21.6%), Low Professional-High Bureaucratic(LP-HB, 27.3%), and Low Professional-Low Bureaucratic(LP-LB, 24.5%).

(4) Teachers' Conflict intensity was low(1.78), especially on the Personal, Non-material Opportunities subscale(1.25). High conflict areas were Student Relationships(2.03), Administrative Relationships(2.02) and Staff Relationships(2.10).

(5) Teachers' Job Satisfaction level was high(3.71), especially on the Intrinsic Satisfaction subscale(4.06).

(6) Both Bureaucratic Orientation and Professional Orientation were significantly(BO:JS=.14, PO:JS=.23) and positively related to Job Satisfaction and were also significant predictors(Each changed only 3% of the variance.), of Job Satisfaction. This means that highly bureaucratically-oriented teachers and highly professionally-oriented teachers tended to have high Job Satisfaction.

(7) As the result of correlation analysis, Conflict was not significantly related to any of the major independent variables, but as the result of stepwise regression, Conflict had significant predictors among subscales of independent variables such as Loyalty to the Organization from the BOS, Hierarchy of Authority from the OI, and Rules for Incumbents from the OI(These three subscales explained only 9% of the variance of Job Satisfaction.).

(8) As the result of stepwise regression, Teaching Experience and Sex from the demographic variables, Hierarchy of Authority, and Rules for Incumbents from the OI subscales, and Rules & Procedures Orientation from the BOS subscales were significant predictors of Job Satisfaction(They explained 30% of the variance of Job Satisfaction.).

(9) When only the major variables were entered in stepwise regression, Conflict had no significant predictor from the independent variables.

(10) When only the major variables were entered in stepwise

regression, Conflict, Bureaucratic Orientation and Professional Orientation were significant predictors of Job Satisfaction. These three variables explained 24% of the variance of Job Satisfaction.

(11) School Bureaucratization was not related to either of the dependent variables, Conflict and Job Satisfaction, and was not a predictor of either dependent variable in this study.

(12) As the result of two-way ANOVA, Professional Orientation, Bureaucratic Orientation, and interaction of Professional Orientation and Bureaucratic Orientation failed to explain significantly the variance of Conflict. Professional Orientation, Bureaucratic Orientation and interaction of both could not impact to the intensity of Conflict.

(13) As the result of two-way ANOVA, the main effect for Bureaucratic Orientation was significant at the .01 level to explain the variance of Job Satisfaction. Bureaucratic Orientation only independently impacted to Job Satisfaction and highly bureaucratically-oriented teachers had higher Job Satisfaction than low bureaucratically-oriented teachers.

(14) No significant relationships were found among School Bureaucratization, Professional Orientation and Bureaucratic Orientation, but the relationship between Conflict and Job Satisfaction was a significant and negative correlation.

(15) In the comparison of subgroup means for Conflict and Job Satisfaction, the group with the lowest and highest Conflict means, LP-LB(Alienated) and HP-LB(Professional),

had the lowest Job Satisfaction and the groups with a high Bureaucratic Orientation, LP-HB(Bureaucratic) and HP-HB (Ambivalent), both exhibited higher Job Satisfaction.

(16) To the result of the two-way ANOVA, a three-way ANOVA added one more significant effect of interaction between School Bureaucratization and teachers' Bureaucratic Orientation for Job Satisfaction. At both high and low levels of School Bureaucratization, high Bureaucratic Orientation teachers had higher Job Satisfaction than low Bureaucratic Orientation teachers.

(17) Female teachers reported a significantly higher level of Job Satisfaction than did male teachers.

(18) Older teachers reported significantly lower perceptions of School Bureaucratization, higher Professional Orientation and higher Job Satisfaction than did younger teachers.

(19) Teachers with more teaching experience reported significantly lower perceptions of School Bureaucratization, higher Professional Orientation and higher Job Satisfaction than did teachers with less experience.

(20) Teachers with more experience in the district reported significantly higher levels of Job Satisfaction than did teachers with less experience in the district.

(21) Teachers who had earned higher degrees reported significantly lower Bureaucratic Orientation, higher intensity of Conflict and lower levels of Job Satisfaction than did lower degree holders.

(22) School Size and Teaching Area(special area or class-

room) were not related significantly to any major variables.

B. Conclusions

Based on the findings from the data analysis, the following conclusions are made. Conclusions 1-4 are directly related to specific purpose one of this study(p.9): to describe the degree of School Bureaucratization, teachers' Professional and Bureaucratic Orientation, and teachers' Conflict and Job Satisfaction in a selected school district.

(1) This research began with a detection of two emergent tendencies of school bureaucratization and teacher professionalization. In other words, the organization and the individual were viewed as going to opposite poles; therefore, conflict or job satisfaction would be affected. However, the research results were somewhat different from what had been anticipated. The degree of school bureaucratization in this district was low, and teachers' professional orientation was somewhat higher than bureaucratic orientation. Measurements of the conditions in this district do not confirm the fact that schools are increasingly becoming bureaucratized and that teachers are increasingly becoming professionalized. Teachers' conflict level was low while the level of job satisfaction was high.

This school organization is doing well; structure does not appear over-bureaucratized, organizational members are professionally oriented with a low level of bureaucratic orientation which matched with the degree of organizational bureaucratization, and member teachers' behavior is expressed as low conflict−a symptom of a healthy organization−and high job satisfaction.

(2) Teachers expressed high professional orientation on Decision Making of the POS subscale compared with other subscales. This may be explained as an expression of teachers that they want to participate in decision making regarding their own work. Indeed, some highly professionally-oriented teachers may not be satisfied with only participating in decision making, but may want to actually make decisions by themselves concerning their professional work.

In the Bureaucratic Orientation, teachers expressed high orientation on the subscales, Experience Orientation and Orientation to the Public. High orientation on the Experience subscale may be explained as teachers perceiving teaching experience not as simple labor experience, but as an important part of professional experience. High Orientation to the Public may be a reflection of sensitivity to community expectations.

(3) Teachers reported high Intrinsic Satisfaction(4.06) than Extrinsic Satisfaction(2.97), and they showed the lowest conflict with Non-material Opportunities(1.25). This may indicate that teachers are more motivated by intrinsic factors than by external factors.

(4) Conflict scores on Student Relationships, Administrative Relationships, and Staff Relationships, while higher than those on the other factors, were still low. This would appear to indicate that where conflict is perceived by teachers it is in

people relationships. There is insufficient data available to attempt to explain this condition.

Conclusions 5-11 are directly related to the specific purpose two of this study(p.9): to analyze the relationships among the major variables and selected demographic variables.

(5) Teachers' behavior was assumed to be a function of inter-action or organizational and individual varibles. This study adopted School Bureaucratization as an organizational variable and teacher's value orientations as individual variables. However, in the results of this study, School Bureaucratization was not significantly related either to Conflict or to Job Satisfaction. Even so, it cannot be concluded that organizational variables are not related to organizational behavior, because "School Bureaucratization" is only a part of a complex of organizational variables, and because in this specific district the degree of bureaucratization was low. Therefore, despite the findings of this study of a single school district, it is still possible to maintain that the variable, School Bureaucratization is conditional; if the organization is highly bureaucratized, then the variable will be significantly and positively related to conflict and negatively to job satisfaction, but if it is not highly bureaucratized, it is not significantly related to them. In support of this belief it should be noted that in this study School Bureaucratization was significantly related to Conflict and Job Satisfaction only through the subscales, Hierarchy of Authority and Rules for Incumbents; those subscales were significant predictors of both Conflict and Job Satisfaction. School

Bureaucratization tended to be related positively to Conflict, but negatively to Job Satisfaction(non-significant), and the interaction effect of School Bureaucratization and teachers' Bureaucratic Orientation impacted Job Satisfaction as the result of the three-way ANOVA. These results suggest that although the relationships were not significant, they were in the predicted direction and that School Bureaucratization has the potential related.

(6) Conflict was not significantly related to any independent variables. Conflict was expected between high school bureaucratization and high teacher professionalization, but neither of these variables was very high. Therefore, it is still possible to maintain that when school bureaucratization and teachers' professional orientation are high, conflict also appears high, and is related significantly to other variables; positively to School Bureaucratization and Professional Orientation, but negatively to Bureaucratic Orientation.

(7) The results showed significant relationships only between teachers' Professional Orientation and Job Satisfaction, and between Bureaucratic Orientation and Job Satisfaction as relationships between independent and dependent variables. Both teachers' Professional Orientation and Bureaucratic Orientation were positively related to Job Satisfaction somewhat differently from what had been expected. This study anticipated that highly professionally-oriented teachers would have low Job Satisfaction under the assumption that all schools were highly bureaucratized. In the comparison of subgroup means for Job Satisfaction, HP-HB(Ambivalent) had the highest Job Satisfaction, and there

was no relationship between Professional Orientation and Bureaucratic Orientation. This may mean that teachers can be both highly professionally and bureaucratically oriented. In fact, teachers were distributed quite evenly into four groups; HP-HB (26.6%), HP-LB(21.6%), LP-HB(27.3%) and LP-LB(24.5%). In this school district, teachers who reflected ambivalence or high professional or high bureaucratic orientation were highly satisfied in teaching.

(8) Since there was found to be a strong negative correlation between Conflict and Job Satisfaction, this study confirms previous research results that "teachers who are satisfied experience less conflict than those who are less satisfied"(Gerhardt, 1971, p.82), and that satisfaction results from the absence of conflict in job.

(9) Demographic variables tended to be more closely related to behavioral variables than to organizational or individual orientation variables. This suggests that teacher behavior is impacted by demographic variables as well as by organizational and individual value orientations. School Size and Teaching Area were not significantly related to any major variables.

(10) Older teachers expressed significantly higher professional orientation, higher job satisfaction and lower perception of school bureaucratization than did younger teachers. More experienced teachers also reported higher professional orientation and lower perception of school bureaucratization, and teachers with more experience in the district reported

higher job satisfaction than did their counterparts. These results are explained by the close relationships of age, teaching experience, and experience in the district. However, the high Professional Orientation of older teachers was unusual when compared with previous research results. Previous research had shown that younger teachers reflected higher professional orientation than older teachers. The conclusion from the results of this study would be that older teachers in this district appear to be moving in the ideal direction; higher professional orientation and higher job satisfaction.

(11) The variable, Academic Degree earned, was an important variable in this study. Higher degree holders tended to report signigicantly lower Bureaucratic Orientation, lower Job Satisfaction and higher intensity of Conflict. This phenomenon is very unfortunate not only for the educational system but also for the higher degree holders, themselves. It may be that such teachers believe that the educational system does not fully reward higher degrees earned.

Conclusions 12-16 are related to the overall purpose of this study(pp.8-9): to refine the conceptual base of the study as well as the instruments and procedures used: and to determine the possibility of a more comprehensive larger-scale study.

(12) The correlation analyses which were computed were checked with several statistical treatments, but different approaches did not add many new findings. Therefore, this study concludes that the several statistical treatments which were utilized produced almost the same results.

(13) From the results of tests of reliability the instruments which were used proved to be appropriate and the composite questionnarie presented no difficulty for use in this and future studies.

(14) The results of this exploratory study suggest that, for future use, the research framework should be revised somewhat; the variable, Conflict, and the School Bureaucratization variable are conditional. It would appear that ① only when a school is highly bureaucratized is School Bureaucratization related to Conflict and Job Satisfaction, and ② only when the degrees of School Bureaucratization and teachers' Professional Orientation are high will teachers' Conflict appear as high. The relationships between Professional Orientation and Job Satisfaction, Bureaucratic Orientation and Job Satisfaction, and Conflict and Job Satisfaction, were clearly significant as shown in Figure 18, but the relationships between School Bureaucratization and Conflict, and between School Bureaucratization and Job Satisfaction, were indirectly related through the subscales of Hierarchy of Authority and Rules for Incumbents, and through interaction between School Bureaucratization and Bureaucratic Orientation(SB×BO). Demographic variables are more closely related to Job Satisfaction than to others.

Based on the findings of this study, this researcher has concluded that teachers' Conflict(conditional) and Job Satisfaction may be viewed as a product of interaction of School Bureaucratization(conditional), teachers' Professional Orientation and Bureaucratic Orientation, plus Demographic variables such as Sex, Age, Teaching Experience and Academic Degree earned. It may be denoted as:

C & JS=f(SB×PO×BO)+D;

where C=Conflict, JS=Job Satisfaction, SB=School Bureaucratization, PO=Professional Orientation, BO=Bureaucratic Orientation, and D=Demographic variables.

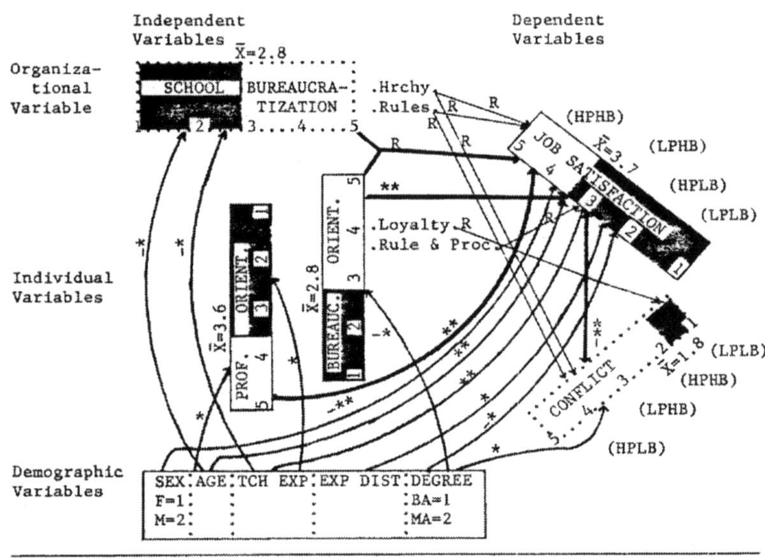

= Conditional Variable

* r is significant at .05 level.
** r is significant at .01 level.
R=Multiple R, Significant predictor.
Hrchy.=Subscale, Hierarchy of Authority
Rules.=Subscale, Rules for Incumbents.
Loyalty.=Subscale, Loyalty to the Organization.
Rule & Proc.=Subscale, Rules & Procedures Orientation.
HPHB=Ambivalent.
LPHB=Bureaucratic.
HPLB=Professional.
LPLB=Alienated.

Figure 18

The Revised Framework and Summary of Findings

Figure 18 shows this revised conceptual framework and reflects the summary of findings. The reader may wish to compare Figure 18 with Figures 2 and 12 in Chapters 1 and 2, respectively. Individual orientations, PO and BO, are more closely related to teachers' behavior than is organizational structure, SB, both high professionally and bureaucratically oriented teachers have high Job Satisfaction(significant), and highly bureaucratically-oriented teachers tend to have low conflict(non-significant), and highly professionally-oriented teachers tend to have high conflict(non-significant). Demographic variables also are closely related to Job Satisfaction.

(15) Based on the several analyses of the composite questionnaire used in this study, it may be concluded that this instrument is appropriate for future, larger-scale investigations which focus on the revised research framework as discussed in the preceding conclusion.

(16) From this researcher's experience in this exploratory study, it may be concluded that, with the exception of the sampling recommendation which is suggested in the implications section, the procedures used would lend themselves to replication in a larger-scale investigation.

C. Implications

Provided the conclusions based on the findings of this study have validity for the population of a selected school district in Minnesota, the following implications for theory, practice and research seem warranted. The theory-practice-research subsections are, of course, closely interconnected.

1. For Theory

(1) This school distr was not over-bureaucratized and teachers were not over-professionally oriented, consequently, teachers were highly satisfied in their jobs with low conflict. However, previous studies reviewed in Chapter 2 had detected conflict between bureaucratization and professionalization(i.e. Corwin, 1965a; Gerhardt, 1971). This may suggest that when the degree of organizational bureaucratization is well harmonized with the appropriate degree of members' professional orientation, the school organization maintains members' high job satisfaction with low conflict and is stable and developmental.

Many people argue that school organization "ought to be" professional but "is" bureaucratic or semiprofessional. When "ought to be" and "is" balance well, the school system will be stable. The implication may be that the public school system should accept the bureaucratic-professional model at this stage and work towards the development of the "professional model" as suggested by Litwak's term(1969). How to harmonize bureaucratic characteristics with professional orientation may be turned over to the organizational theorists. Continuous longitudinal studies are needed.

(2) This study concluded that "teachers' job satisfaction and conflict(conditional) are viewed as a product of the interaction of school bureaucratization(conditional) and teachers' professional

and bureaucratic orientation, plus demographic variables such as sex, age, teaching experience and degree earned." This conclusion suggests that organizational behavior is more closely related to individual variables or characteristics than to organizational variables. It may even be speculated that individual variables such as professional and bureaucratic orientation and demographic variables impact behavior to a greater degree than to organizational structure or characteristics of task. Furthermore, organizational structure and climate are influenced by such individual variables. Regardless of this sepeculation, it appears that the individual may be the most important variable in studies of organizational behavior.

2. For Practice

(1) Teacher professionalization has long been a desire of many educators and of educational consumers. To increase professionalization, much money and time have been devoted to teachers' pre-and in-service education. Many administrators have recommended that teachers take post-baccalaureate course work and teachers have been busy completing course credits during summer and professional leaves. Lengthened preparation programs for teachers and improved continuing teacher education programs have been implemented to produce teachers with increasingly higher qualifications and, hopefully, the improved education of children. However, one of the results of this study has raised a question about this common belief; higher degree holders tended to have lower job satisfaction and higher conflict. Higher earned de-

grees have been an important component of professionalization. It is assumed that neither administrators nor teachers would see the conditions of low job satisfaction and high conflict as desirable. If these results from a selected school district appear in other studies so that generalizations may be drawn, it may mean that the public school system has failed to sufficiently reward teachers who earn higher degrees. It is not the purpose of this study to discuss reward systems, however, at least in this selected school district, administrators may wish to attempt to develop additional intrinsic and external recognitions of teachers with higher earned degrees and may wish to examine motivational theories for approaches to improving job satisfaction for such teachers.

(2) Individual characteristics such as sex, age, teaching experience, experience in the district, and academic degree earned, were identified as important variables which impact to teacher behavior. Teachers have different perceptions of school bureaucratization, professional orientation and bureaucratic orientation, and conflict and job satisfaction. In other words, each teacher has her/his own individuality and this different individuality will produce different attitudes and behaviors. If administrators and other supervisors apply the same style of administration and supervision to each unique teacher, administration and supervision will be ineffective. Therefore, it is recommended that supervisors develop an "individualized supervision"[1] approach to working with individual teachers just as teachers are encouraged to individualize the in-

struction of children. If individualized supervision is difficult because of limitations of ratio of teachers to supervisors, time and fi-
nance, at least the demographic variables such as sex, age, experience, district experience and earned degree as used in this study,
should be given speical consideration in supervision and
administration.

(3) The majority of teachers who participated in this study
expressed low conflict and high job satisfaction. It is suggested that principals and other administrators in this district examine current practices in an attempt to identify
those which contribute to this favorable condition. The intent
of such an exercise would, of course, be the continuation and
reinforcement of such practices and procedures in order to
maintain and even improve these desirably low conflict and
high job satisfaction levels.

(4) The majority of teachers who participated in this study reported higher conflict with Student Relationships, Administrative
Relationships and Staff Relationships compared with other
five subscales. It is suggested that district administrators attempt to identify factors which contribute to such conflict and
plan an approach to helping teachers and administrators improve people relationships.

(5) School principals and other administrators need to be
aware of the relatively low job satisfaction of younger and
less experienced teachers: when beginning teachers first

---

1) This term appears in some of the recent literature which describes the
   clinical supervision process.

come to the field with hope and a sense of mission, school principals can provide special motivational support which can help teachers to deal with the frustrations of a demanding job. Beginning teachers should be given special consideration in appropriate personnel policies and reinforcement systems.

(6) Increasing professionalization of teachers is clearly a worldwide tendency. This study showed that teachers reflected a high professional orientation, especially on the Decision Making factor. Highly professionally-oriented teachers tended to express high conflict(non-significant), in fact higher degree holders, an important criterion of professionalization, reported high conflict, low job satisfaction and low bureaucratic orientation. Appropriate administrative and supervisory techniques and more suitable reward systems for teachers should be examined as potential alleviators of this conflict. Professional teachers continue to work toward increased ① participation in decision making, ② autonomy, ③ academic freedom and ④ accountability.

What is the leader's role among professional members who are striving toward increased professionalization? One suggestion that appears to merit consideration is that school principals, as leaders of professionals, begin to share some of their leadership functions with age / grade-level coordinators and other teachers whose abilities and interests warrant such sharing. In this manner the school principal, as a leader of professionals, may adopt an increasingly "delegating style" of leadership as suggested by Gates, Blanchard and Hersey(1976) in their situational leadership theory for working with highly mature groups.

3. For Research

(1) This study was, to a large extent, exploratory and descriptive in nature and one of the few to utilize standardized questionnaires to investigate this specific realm of educational administration in one district of Minnesota. It is recommended that additional investigations be made in this specific area of school administration in Minnesota and nationwide. The conceptual framework was partially proved as sound, it has been revised, and the instruments used presented no major difficulty.

(2) This study was confined to public elementary schools in one selected school district in Minnesota. The number of sample teachers, schools and district were too small to be broken down into some of the subgroups which might be desirable for purposes of comparison. Schools used also were homogeneous in size, geographic region and socio-economic status. Thus, for further study, a sufficient sample size of heterogeneous schools from different school districts which represent a variety of geographic regions and socio-economic levels is recommended as is a random sampling procedure. Future studies may also be extended to include secondary schools, non-public schools, and principals and other school administrators.

(3) This study tentatively concluded that school bureaucratization(conditional), and teachers' professional orientation

and bureaucratic orientation are related to conflict(conditional) and job satisfaction. To clarify the positions of conditional variables, another comprehensive study is recommended. This conclusion is important because it implies an assumption that conflict and job satisfaction will be related to job performance, student achievement, school goal achievement, organizational development and the happiness of the individual teachers. Extended further study of the relationship between conflict or job satisfaction, and school goal achievement or student achievement, is recommended. For instance, "do highly satisfied teachers effectively achieve school goals or facilitate student achievement?" is a worthwhile question for extended study. "The relationship between teachers' professional /bureaucratic orientation and student achievement" also is a challenging research topic as the next step of this study. Figure 19 shows possible further study areas; the solid line represents the present study area and the dotted line represents further study areas which have been suggested.

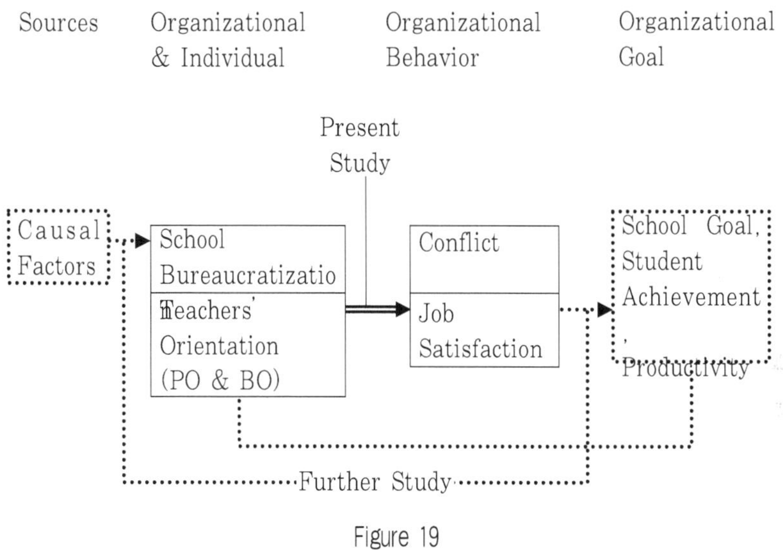

Figure 19
Further Study Areas Suggested

(4) This study did not differentiate between "general life satisfaction" and "job satisfaction in teaching." Further study is suggested to isolate "the job satisfaction in teaching" from "general life satisfaction." For example, whether or not there are teachers who have high job satisfaction in teaching among teachers who have low general life satisfaction will be one of the questions of interest.

(5) This study examined the relationships among School Bureaucratization, Professional Orientation, Bureaucratic Orientation, Conflict and Job Satisfaction, but, by intent, did not investigate the causal realtionships among these variables. Further study is suggested to attempt to utilize "path analysis" to determine possible causal relationships among these variables.

BIBLIOGRAPHY

Abbott, M. G. "Hierarchical Impediments to Innovation in Educational Organizations." In Fred D. Carver and Thomas J. Sergiovanni(eds.), *Organizations and Human Behavior: Focus on Schools.* N. Y.: McGraw-Hill Book Co., 1969, 42-52.

Abbott, M. G. "Intervening Variables in Organizational Behavior." *Educational Administration* Quarterly, 2: 1-13. 1965.

Adams, J. S. "Toward an Understanding of Inequity." *Journal of Abnormal Psychology,* LXVII: 422-36. 1963.

Anderson, J. G. *Bureaucracy in Education.* Baltimore: The John Hopkins Press, 1968.

Anderson, J. G. "The Teacher: Bureaucrat or Professional?" *Educational Administration Quarterly,* 3: 291-300. Autumn, 1967.

Anderson, J. G. "Bureaucratic Rules: Bearers of Organizational Authority." *Educational Administration Quarterly,* 2: 7-34. Winter, 1966.

Anton, K. O. "Identification and Analysis of Pressures on the Secondary School Principal Relative to Job Satisfaction." *Dissertation Abstracts International,* 35: 116A-117A. 1974.

Argyris, C. and D. A. Schön. *Theory in Practice: Increasing Professional, Effectiveness.* San Francisco: Jossey-Bass Publishers, 1974.

Argyris, C. and D. A. Schön. *The Applicability of Organizational Sociology.* London: The Cambridge University Press, 1974.

Argyris, C. and D. A. Schön. *Personality and Organization: The Conflict between System and the Individual.* N. Y.: Harper & Row Publishers, 1957.

Bailey, S. K. "Preparing Administrators for Conflict Resolution." *Educat-*

ional Record, 52: 233, Summer, 1971.

Barnard, C. I. *The Functions of the Executive.* Cambridge: Harvard University Press, 1968.

Barnard, C. I. "Functions and Pathology of Status Systems in Formal Organizations." In Fred D. Carver and Thomas J. Sergiovanni(eds.), *Organizations and Human Behavior: Focus on Schools.* N. Y.: McGraw-Hill Book Co., 1969. 51-62.

Becker, H. S. "The Nature of a Profession." In *Education for the Professions.* Sixty-first yearbook, Part Ⅱ, The National Society for the Study of Education, Chicago: University of Chicago Press, 1962. 27-46.

Becker, H. S. "The Teacher in the Authority System of the Public School." *Journal of Educational Sociology,* 27: 128-41. Nov., 1953.

Becvar, R. J. "Job Satisfaction of First-Year Teachers: A Study of Discrepancies between Expectations and Experiences." Unpublished doctoral dissertation, The University of Minnesota, 1969.

Beer, M. "Organizational Size and Job Satisfaction." Academy of Management Journal, *7: 34-44. March, 1964.*

Bell, G. D. "Formality Versus Flexibility in Complex Organizations." In Fred D. Carver and Thomas J. Sergiovanni(eds.), *Organizations and Human Behavior: Focus on Schools.* N. Y.: McGraw-Hill Book Co., 1969. 71-81.

Berger, M. "Bureaucracy East and West." *Administative Science Quarterly,* 1: 518-29. Sep., 1956.

Bernard, J. "Where is the Modern Sociology of Conflict?" *American Journal of Scoiology,* 56: 11-16. 1950.

Bidwell, C. E. "The School as a Formal Organization." In James G. March(ed.), *Handbook of Organizations.* Chicago: Rand McNally & Co., 1965.

Blau, P. M. The Dynamics of Bureaucracy: *A Study of Interpersonal Relations in Two Government Agencies*(Rev. ed.). Chicago: The University of Chicago Press, 1955.

Blau, P. M. and M. W. Meyer. *Bureaucracy in Modern Society*(2nd ed.). N. Y.: Random House, 1971.

Blau, P. M. and W. R. Scott. "The Nature and Types of Formal Organizations." In Fred D. Carver and Thomas J. Sergiovanni(eds.), *Organizations and Human Behavior: Focus on Schools.* N. Y.: McGraw-Hill Book Co., 1969. 5-18.

Blau, P. M. *Formal Organizations.* San Francisco: Chandler Publishing Co., 1962.

Blazovsky, R. A. "School Bureaucracy and Teacher Alienation." *Dissertation Abstracts International,* 38: 3820A. 1977.(Rutgers University, The State University of New Jersey).

Boulding, E. *Conflict Management in Organizations.* Ann Arbor, Michigan: Foundation for Research on Human Behavior, 1968.

Boulding, K. "A Pure Theory of Conflict Applied to Organizations." In Robert L. Kahn and Elise Boulding(eds.), *Power and Conflict in Organizations.* N. Y.: Basic Books, Inc., 1964.

Boulding, K. *Conflict and Defense.* N. Y.: Harper and Row, 1962.

Boyan, N. J. "The Emergent Role of the Teacher in the Authority Structure of the School." In Fred D. Carver and Thomas J. Sergiovanni(eds.), *Organizations and Human Behavior: Focus on Schools.* N. Y.: McGraw-Hill Book Co., 1969. 200-11.

Bratton, S. E. Jr. "A Study of Role Conflict Among Elementary Principals and Its Relationship to Organizational Climate and Central Office Evaluation Procedures." Unpublished doctoral dissertation, University of Tennessee, 1973.

Bridges, E. M. "A Model for Shared Decision Making in the School Principalship." *Educational Administration Quarterly,* 3: 49-61. Winter, 1967.

Bridges, E. M. "Bureaucratic Role and Socialization: The Influence on the Elementary Principal." *Educational Administration Quarterly,* 1: 19-28. Spring, 1965.

Broadwell, G. J. "Job Satisfactions of Professionals: A Study of the Job Satisfactions of Cooperative Extension Agents in New York State." *Dissertation Abstracts International,* 30: 843A. 1969.

Bunch, R. and J. G. Stelling. *Becoming Professional.* Beverly Hill: SAGE, 1977.

Campbell, R. E. and others. *The Organization and Control of American Schools*(3rd ed.). Columbus, Ohio: A Bell & Howell Co., 1975.

Carlson, R. E. "An Empirical Evaluation of Selected Hypotheses from A Theory of Works Adjustment." Unpublished doctoral dissertation, The University of Minnesota, 1965.

Carroll, B. "Job Satisfaction-A Review of the Literature." *Industrial Relations Library, Key Issues Series-No.3.* N. Y.: New York State School of Industrial and Labor Relations, Cornell University, Feb., 1969.

Carver, F. D. and T. J. Sergiovanni. *Organizations and Human Behavior: Focus on Schools.* N. Y.: McGraw-Hill Book Co., 1969.

Centers, R. and D. E. Bugental. "Intrinsic and Extensic Job Motivations Among Different Segments of the Working Population." *Journal of Applied Psychology,* 50: 193-97. 1966.

Chen, W. S. "The Job Satisfaction of School Teachers in the Republic of China as Related to Personal and Organizational Characteristics." Unpublished doctoral dissertation, The University of Minnesota, 1977.

Coble, L. D. "The Effect of the Implementation of Comprehensive Planning and Management by Objectives on the Bureaucratization of A School Organization." *Dissertation Abstracts International,* 39: 1940A. 1978(University of North Carolina at Greensbaro).

Cogan, M. L. "Toward a Definition of Profession." *Harvard Educational*

Review, 23: 33-50. Winter, 1953.

Colombotos, J. L. "Sources of Professionalism: A Study of High School Teachers." Cooperative Research Project No.330, U. S. Office of Education. Ann Arbor: Department of Sociology, University of Michigan, 1962.

Coogle, F. E. "Instructional Freedom and the Influence of Organizational Characteristics as Perceived by Teachers in Kentucky Secondary Schools." *Dissertation Abstracts International,* 36: 1199-100A. 1975(University of Kentucky).

Corwin, R. G. *Education in Crisis: A Sociological Analysis of Schools and University in Transition.* N. Y.: John Wiley & Sons. 1974.

Corwin, R. G. *Reform and Organizational Survivial.* N. Y.: John Wiley & Sons, 1973.

Corwin, R. G. *Militant Professionalism: A Study of Organizational Conflict in High Schools.* N. Y.: Meredith Corporation, 1970.

Corwin, R. G. *Staff Conflicts in the Public Schools.* Washington, D. C.: U. S. Office of Education, Cooperative Research Project No.2637, 1966.

Corwin, R. G. "Professional Persons in Public Organizations." *Educational Administration Quarterly,* 1: 1-22. Autumn, 1965(a).

Corwin, R. G. "Militant Professionalism, Initiative and Compliance in Public Education." *Sociology of Education,* 38: 310-31. 1965(b).

Corwin, R. G. "The Development of An Instrument for Examining Staff Conflicts in the Public Schools." U. S. Office of Education, Cooperative Research Project No.1934, Department of Sociology and Anthropology, Ohio State University, 1964.

Corwin, R. G. "The Professional Employee: A Study of Conflict in Nursing Roles." *American Journal of Sociology,* 66: 604-15. May, 1961.

Corwin, R. G. and R. A. Edelfelt. *Perspectives on Organizations Viewpoints for Teachers.* Washington, D. C.: Association of Teacher Educators. 1976.

Coser, L. A. *Continuities in the Study of Social Conflict.* N. Y.: The Free Press, 1967.

Dahrendorf, R. "Out of Utopia: Toward a Reorientation of Sociological Analysis." *The American Journal of Sociology,* 64: 115-27. Sep., 1958.

Dalton, M. "Conflicts Between Staff and Line Managerial Officers." *American Sociological, Review,* 15: 342-51. June, 1950.

Danese, G. "Perceptions of Bureaucracy and Faculty Satisfaction with Participations in Decision Making at Unionized and Non-Unionized Institutions of Higher Education." *Dissertation Abstracts International,* 38: 1143-44A. 1977 (State University of New York at Albany).

Davis, K. *Human Behavior at Work: Human Relations and Organizational Behavior*(4th ed.). N. Y.: McGraw-Hill, 1972.

Dawis, R. V. and others. "A Theory of Work Adjustment." *Minnesota Studies Vocational Rehabilitation:* 23. Industrial Relation Center, University of Minnesota, Bulletin 47, Apr., 1968.

Dempsey, V. F. "An Assessment of Conflict Between Bureaucracy and Professionalism in a School System." Unpublished doctoral dissertation, New York University, 1969.

Dimock, M. E. "Expanding Jurisdictions: A Case Study in Bureaucratic Conflict." In Robert Merton, A. P. Gray, B. Hockey and H. C. Selvin(eds.), *Reader in Bureaucracy.* N. Y.: Free Press, 1965.

Dubin, R. *Human Relations in Administration*(3rd ed.). Englewood Cliffs, N. J.: Prentice Hall, Inc., 1968.

Eisenstadt, S. N. "Bureaucracy, Bureaucratization, and Debureaucratization." *Administrative Science Quarterly,* 4: 302-20. Sep., 1959.

Elliott. P. *The Sociology of Professions.* N. Y.: Hender. 1972.

Enerio. J. M. "Perceived Bureaucratic Structure in the Universities and Four-Year Colleges of the State University of New York and Its Relation to the Academic Deans' Perceived Sense of Power." *Dissertation Abstracts International.* 37: 5480A. 1977(University of New York at Albany).

English. H. B. and A. C. English. *A Comprehensive Dictionary of Psychological and Psychoanalytical Terms.* N. Y.: Longmans Green, 1958.

Erickson, D. A. *Educational Organization and Administration.* Berkeley, California: McCutchan Publishing Co., 1977.

Etzioni, A. *Modern Organizations.* Englewood Cliffs, New Jersey: Prentice-Hall, Inc., 1964.

Evan, W. M. "Superio-Subordinate Conflict in Research Organizations." *Administrative Science Quarterly,* 10: 52-81. Jun., 1965.

Evans, G. A. and J. M. Mass. *Job Satisfaction and Teacher Militancy: Some Teacher Attitudes.* Danville, Ill: Interstate Printers and Publishers, 1969.

Ewen, R. B. et al. "An Empirical Test of the Herzberg Two-Factor Theory." *Journal of Applied Psychology,* 50: 544-50. 1966.

Faber, C. F. and G. F. Shearron. *Elementary School Administration,* N. Y.: Holt, Rinehart and Winston, Inc. 1970.

Festinger, L. *A Theory of Cognitive Dissonance.* Evanston, Ill.: Row Peterson, 1957.

Flexner, A. "Is Social Work A Profession?" In Proceedings of the National Conference of Charities and Correction. Chicago: Hildmann Printing Co., 1955. 576-90.

Foshay, A. W. (ed.) *The Professional As Educator.* N. Y.: Teachers College Press of Columbia University, 1970.

Freed, A. S. "A Descriptive Study of the Relationship of Organizational

Structure and Teacher Professional Orientation to Teachers' Grievances." *Dissertation. Abstracts International,* 40: 1175-76A. Sep., 1979(New York University).

Freidson, E. and B. Rhea. "Knowledge and Judgment in Professional Evaluations." *Administrative Science Quarterly,* 10: 107-124. Jun., 1965.

Fris, J. "Professionalization and Militancy among Ontario Secondary School Teachers." *Dissertation Abstracts International,* 38: 5154-55A. 1978(University of Toronto, Canada).

Frost, J. H. and W. W. Wilmot. *Interpersonal Conflict.* Dubuque, Iowa: WM. C. Brown Co. Publishers, 1978.

Gates, P. E., K. H. Blanchard, and P. Hersey. "Diagnosing Educational Leadership Problems: A Situational Approach." *Educational Leadership,* 33: 348-354, Feb., 1976.

Gerhardt, E. "Staff Conflict, Organizational Bureaucracy and Individual Satisfaction in Selected Kansas School Districts. "Unpublished doctoral dissertation, The University of Kansas, 1971.

Getzels, J. W. "Administration as a Social Process." In Andrew W. Halpin(ed.), *Administrative Theory in Education.* Midwest Administration Center, University of Chicago, 1958. 150-65.

Getzels, J. W. and E. G. Guba. "Social Behavior and the Administrative Process." *School Review,* 65: 423-41. Winter, 1957.

Getzels, J. W. J. M. Lipham and R. E. Campbell. *Educational Administration as a Social Process.* New York: Harper and Row, 1968.

Goldstein, B. "Some Aspects of the Nature of Unionism among Salaried Professionals in Industry." *American Sociological Review,* 20: 199-205. Apr., 1955.

Golladay, M. A. *The Condition of Education.* 1976 ed. Washington, D. C.: Government Printing Office, 1976.

Goode, W. J. "The Theoretical Limits of Professionalization." In Arthur W. Foshay(ed.), *The Professional As Educator.* N. Y.: Teachers College Press, Columbia University, 1970.

Goode, W. J. "The Librarian: From Occupation to Profession?" *Library Quarterly,* 31: 306-320. Oct., 1961.

Gordon, G. G. "Conditions of Employment and Service in Elementary and Secondary Schools" *Review of Educational Research,* 33: 387. Oct., 1963.

Gorton, R. A. *Conflict, Controversy and Crisis in School Administration and Supervision: Cases and Concepts for the '70s.* Dubuque, Iowa: WM. C. Brown Co. Publishers, 1972.

Gouldner, A. *Patterns of Industrial Bureaucracy.* N. Y.: Free Press, 1954.

Gouldner, A. "Organizational Tensions." In Robert Merton *et al.* (ed.), *Sociology Today.* N. Y.: Basic Books, 1959. 400-28.

Gouldner, A. "Discussion." *American Sociological Review,* 8(4): 396. Aug., 1948.

Greenwood, E. "The Elements of Professionalization." In Howard M. Vollmer and Donald L. Mills(eds.), *Professionalization.* Englewood Cliffs, N. J.: Prentice-Hall, Inc., 1966. 9-19.

Hage, J. "An Axiomatic Theory of Organizations." *Administrative Science Quarterly,* 10: 289-320. Dec., 1965.

Hall, R. H. *Organizations: Structure and Process*(2nd ed.). Englewood Cliffs, N. J.: Prentice-Hall, Inc., 1972.

Hall, R. H. "Professionalization and Bureaucratization." *American Sociological Review,* 33: 92-104. Feb., 1968.

Hall, R. H. and C. R. Tittle. "A Note on Bureaucracy and Its Correlates." *American Journal of Sociology,* 72: 267-72 Nov., 1966.

Hall, R. H. "The Concept of Bureaucracy: An Empirical Assessment." *American Journal of Sociology,* 64: 32-40. Jul., 1963.

Hall, R. H. "An Empirical Study of Bureaucratic Dimensions and Their Relations to Other Organizational Characteristics." Unpublished doctoral dissertation, The Ohio State University, 1961.

Hall, R. H. "Intraorganizational Structural Variation: Application of the Bureaucratic Model." *Administrative Science Quarterly,* 7: 295-308. Dec., 1962.

Hamlin, M. M. "Relationships Between Organizational Climate of Elementary Schools and the Degree of Job Satisfaction of Teachers in the Schools." Unpublished doctoral dissertation, The University of Minnesota. 1966.

Hanson, E. M. "The Modern Educational Bureaucracy and the Process of Change." *Educational Administration Quarterly,* 11: 21-36. Autumn, 1975.

Harshberger, R. F. "Job Satisfaction / Dissatisfaction and the Motivation to Work of Full-Time University Teaching Faculty: An Analysis." *Dissertation Abstracts International,* 36: 5738A-39A. 1976.

Hartley, H. J. "Bureaucracy and Local-Cosmopolitan Orientation Examined with Selected Criterion Variables." Unpublished doctoral dissertation, The Pennsylvania State University, 1964.

Havighust, R. and D. U. Levine. *Society and Education*(5th ed.). Boston: Allyn and Bacon, Inc., 1976.

Heady, F. "Bureaucratic Theory and Comparative Administration." *Administrative Science Quarterly,* 4: 509-25. 1959.

Hencley, S. P., L. E. McClearly and J. H. McGrath. *Elementary School Principalship.* N. Y.: Dodd, Mead & Co., 1970.

Herzberg, F., B. Mausner, and B. B. Snyderman. *The Motivation to Work.* N. Y.: John Wiley & Sons, Inc., 1959.

Herzberg, F., B. Mausner, and B. B. Snyderman. *et al. Job Attitudes: Review of Research and Opinion.* Pittsburgh: Psychological Services of Pittsburgh, 1957.

Hills, J. "Obstacles to Professional Self-Governance in Education." *Administrator's Notebook,* 24(4): 1-4. 1975-76.

Holdaway, E. A. *Teacher Satisfaction: An Alberta Report.* Edminton: The University of Alberta, 1978.

Hoppock, R. *Job Satisfaction.* N. Y.: Harper, 1935.

Howsam, R. B. "The Workplace: Does It Hamper Professionalization of Pedagogy?" *Phi Delta Kappan,* 93-96. Oct., 1980.

Howsam, R. B. *et al. Educating a Profession.* Washington D. C.: American Association of Colleges for Teacher Education, 1976.

Hoy, W. K. and C. G. Miskel. *Educational Administration: Theory, Research and Practice.* N. Y.: Random House, 1978.

Hulin, C. L. and P. CP. Smith. "A Linear Model of Job Satisfaction." *Journal of Applied Psychology,* 49: 209-16. 1965.

Inkson, J. H., D. S. Pugh and D. J. Hickson. "Organization Context and Structure: An Abbreviated Replication." *Administrative Science Quarterly,* 15: 318-29. 1970.

Isherwood, G. and W. K. Hoy. "Bureaucracy, Powerlessness and Teacher Work Values." *Journal of Educational Administration,* 11: 124-38. 1973.

Ivancevich, J. M. and J. H. Donnelly. "Job Satisfaction Research: A Management Guide for Practitioners." *Personnel Journal,* 47: 172-77. March, 1968.

Jackson, J. A. (ed.) *Professions and Professionalization.* London: Cambridge University Press, 1970.

Jain, T. K. "Bureaucracy and Motivation: An Empirical Assessment of Weber's and Bennis' Theoretical Positions." *Dissertation Abstracts International,* 38: 3845A. 1978 (University of Kansas).

Jennings, P. D. "A Study of the Relationship between the Organizational Structure of Schools, the Role Orientation of Teachers, and Teacher

Morale." *Dissertation Abstracts International,* 39: 3270-71A. 1978 (Columbia University Teachers College).

Joo, S. H. "A Study on Professionally Oriented Teachers' Conflicts in Bureaucratic School Organization." *The Journal of Educational Research,* 14(3): 155-68. Oct., 1976 (Published by The Korean Society for the Study of Education).

Joo, S. H. "A Test of Herzberg's Motivation-Hygiene Theory." Unpublished M. Ed. thesis, The Seoul National University. 1974.

Katz, D. and R. L. Kahn. *The Social Psychology of Organizations.* N. Y.: John Wiley and Sons, Inc., 1966.

Keltner, J. W. *Interpersonal Speech-Communication: Elements and Structures.* Belmont, Calif.: Wadsworth Publishing Co., Inc., 1970.

Kimbrough, R. B. and M. Y. Nunnery. *Educational Administration.* N. Y.: Macmillan Publishing Co., Inc., 1976.

Koopman-Boyden, P. G. and R. S. Adams. "Role Consensus and Teacher Job Satisfaction." *The Journal of Educational Administration,* 7: 98-113. May, 1974.

Kornacher, M. "How Urban High School Teachers View Their Job." U. S. Office of Education Cooperative Research Project No.5-8144. 1966.

Kornhauser, W. "Scientists in Industry: Conflict and Accommodation." with the assistance of Warren O. Hagstrom. Berkeley: University of California Press, 1962.

Krajewski, R. J. "Secondary Principals Want to Be Instructional's Leader." *Phi Delta Kappan,* 60(1): 65. Sep., 1978.

Kramer, L. J. "Kansas Professioanl Teaching Standards Advisory Board: A Five-Year Review." *Dissertation Abstracts International,* 37: 4751A. 1977(University of Kansas).

Kuhlman, E. L. and W. K. Hoy. "The Socialization of Professionals into

Bureaucracies: The Beginning Teacher in the School." *The Journal of Educational Administration,* 7(2): 18-27. Oct., 1974.

LaCrosse, E. R. "Thoughts for New Administrators." In Dorothy W. Hewes(ed.), *Administration: Making Programs Work for Children and Families.* Washington D. C.: National Association for the Education of Young Children, 1979. 3-12.

Lacy, A. "An Analysis of Factors That Affect Job Satisfaction of Public High School Business Teachers in Ohio." *Dissertation Abstracts International,* 30: 67A-68A. 1969.

Lane, W. R., R. G. Corwin and W. G. Monahan. *Educational Administration.* N. Y.: The Macmillan Co., 1967.

Lieberman, M. *Education As A Profession.* Englewood Cliffs, N. J.: Prentice-Hall, Inc., 1956.

Lipham, J. M. and J. A. Hoeh, Jr. *The Principalship: Foundations and Functions.* N. Y.: Harper & Row, Publishers, 1974.

Litwak, E. "Models of Bureaucracy Which Permit Conflict." In Fred D. Carver and Thomas J. Sergiovanni(eds.), *Organizations and Human Behvaior: Focus on Schools.* N. Y.: McGraw-Hill Book Co., 1969. 82-90.

Locke, E. A. "Satisfiers and Dissatisfiers among White-Collar and Blue-Collar Employees." *Journal of Applied Psychology,* 58: 67-76. 1973.

Locke, E. A. "What is Job Satisfaction?" *Organizational Behavior and Human Performance,* 4: 309-36. 1969.

Lofquist, L. H. and R. V. Dawis. *Adjustment to Work: A Psychological View of Man's Problems in a Work-Oriented Society.* N. Y.: Appelton-Century-Crofts, 1969.

Longenecker, J. G. *Principles of Management and Organizational Behavior*(3rd ed.). Columbus, Ohio: Charles E. Merrill, 1973.

Lusthaus, E. W. "Role Conflict and Special Education Teachers: Effects of

Organizational Structure of Schools." *Dissertation Abstracts International,* 36: 1218A. 1975(State University of New York at Buffalo).

McEwen, W. J. "Position Conflict and Professional Orientation in A Research Organization." *Administrative Science Quarterly,* 1: 208-24. Sep., 1956.

McDonald, B. W. and E. K. E. Gunderson. "Correlates of Job Satisfaction in Naval Environment." *Journal of Applied Psychology,* 59: 371-73. 1974.

McGregor, D. "The Human Side of Enterprise." In Fred D. Carver and Thomas J. Sergiovanni(eds.), *Organizations and Human Behavior: Focus on Schools.* N. Y.: McGraw-Hill Book Co., 1969.

Mack, R. W. and R. C. Snyder. "The Analysis of Social Conflict-Toward an Overview and Synthesis." *Journal of Conflict Resolution,* 1: 212-48. June, 1957.

MacKay, D. A. "An Empirical Study of Bureaucratic Dimensions and Their Relations to Other Characteristics of School Organizations." Unpublished doctoral dissertation, The University of Alberta, Edmonton, 1964.

MacKay, D. A. "Using Professional Talent in A School Organization." In Fred D. Carver and Thomas J. Sergiovanni(eds.), *Organizations and Human Behavior: Focus on Schools.* N. Y.: McGraw-Hill Book., 1969. 228-34.

McNally, J. "Summing Up." *National Elementary Principal,* 54(1): 6-15. Sep. / Oct., 1974.

March, J. G. and H. A. Simon. "Dysfunctions in Organizations." In Fred D. Carver and Thomas J. Sergiovanni(eds.), *Organizations and Human Behavior: Focus on Schools.* N. Y.: McGraw-Hill Book Co., 1969. 63-70.

March, J. G. and H. A. Simon. *Organizations.* N. Y.: John Wiley and Sons, 1958.

Maslow, A. H. *Motivation and Personality.* N. Y.: Harper & Row, Publishers, 1954.

Mattingly, P. H. *The Classless Profession: American Schoolmen In The Nineteenth Century.* N. Y.: New York University Press, 1965.

Mawter, P. T. "Teacher Professionalism and Decision-Making Modes In Selected Elementary Schools As Determinants of Job Satisfaction." Unpublished doctoral dissertation, University of Oregon, 1975.

Mayhew, J. R. "The Development of A Conceptual Framework to Describe and Analyze Nonformal Education Systems: A Case Study of Action Cultural Popular." Unpublished doctoral dissertation, Florida State University, 1978.

Metcalf, H. C. and L. Urwick(eds.) *Dynamic Administration: The Collected Paper of Mary Parker Follett.* N. Y.: Harper, 1940.

Mifflin, J. W. "A Study of the Work Adjustment and Job Satisfaction of Elementary and Secondary Principals." *Dissertation Abstracts International,* 36: 5702A-5703A. 1976.

Miller, G. A. "Professionals in Bureaucracy, Alienation Among Industrial Scientists and Engineers." *American Sociological Review,* 32: 755-68. Oct., 1967.

Miskel, C. G., R. Fevurly and J. Stewart. "Organizational Structures and Processes, Perceived School Effectiveness, Loyalty, and Job Satisfaction." *Educational Administration Quarterly,* 15(3): 97-118. Fall, 1979.

Miskel, C. G., and E. Gerhardt. "Perceived Bureaucracy, Teacher Conflict, Central Life Interests, Voluntarism, and Job Satisfaction." *The Journal of Educational Administration,* 12: 84-97. May, 1974.

Miskel, C. G., G. Glasnapp and R. Hartley. "A Test of the Inequity Theory for Job Satisfaction Using Educators' Attitudes Toward Work Motivation and Work Incentives." *Educational Administration Quarterly,* 11(1): 38-54. Winter, 1975.

Moeller, G. H. "The Relationship Between Bureaucracy in School System Organization and Teachers' Sense of Power." Unpublished doctoral dissertation, Washington University, 1962.

Moeller, G. H. and W. W. Charters. "Relation of Bureaucratization to Sense of Power Among Teachers." In Fred D. Carver and Thomas J. Sergiovanni(eds.), *Organizations and Human Behavior: Focus on Schools.* N. Y.: McGraw-Hill Book Co., 1969. 235-48.

Morris, J. V. "Factors Influencing Job Satisfaction / Dissatisfaction Among Faculty in Selected Private Liberal Arts Colleges." *Dissertation Abstracts International,* 33: 3211A. 1973.

National Education Association. *Elementary School Organization.* Washington, D. C.: National Education Assocation, 1961.

National, Education Association. Division of Field Service. "The Yardstick of A Profession." *Institutes on Professional and Public Relations. Washington,* D. C.: The National Education Association, 1948. p.8. Cited by T. M. Stinnett, *Professional Problems of Teachers.* N. Y.: The Macmillan Co., 1968. 54-55.

Nebgen, M. K. "Conflict Management in Schools." *Administrator's Notebook.* 26(6): 1-4. 1977-78.

Nie, N. H., C. H. Hull, J. G. Jenkins, K. Steinbrenner, and D. H. Bent. SPSS(2nd ed.). N. Y.: McGraw-Hill Book Co., 1975.

Novak, K. D. "Preferred Job Reinforcers and the Job Satisfaction of Faculty in Minnesota's Area Vocational Technical Institutes." Unpublished doctoral dissertation, The University of Minnesota, 1975.

Otto, H. J. and D. C. Sanders. *Elementary School Organization and Administration(4th ed.).* N. Y.: Appleton-Century-Crofts, 1964.

Owens, R. G. *Organizational Behavior in Schools.* Englewood Cliffs, N. J.: Prentice-Hall, Inc., 1970.

Parelius, A. P. and R. J. Parelius. *The Sociology of Education.* Englewood Cliffs, N. J.: Prentice-Hall, 1978.

Parsons, T. "The Professional As Educator." In Arthur W. Foshay(ed.),

The Professional As Educator. N. Y.: Teachers College Press, Columbia University, 1970.

Parsons, T. "The Professions and Social Structure." *Social Forces,* 17(4): 457-67. May, 1939.

Peabody, R. "Perceptions of Organizational Authority: A Comparative Analysis." *Administrative Science Quarterly,* 6: 463-82. March, 1962.

Pois, J. "The. Board and the General Superintendent." In Alan Rosenthal(eds.), *Governing Education.* N. Y.: Doubleday and Company, Inc., 1969.

Porter, L. W. "Job Attitudes in Management: III. Perceived Deficiencies in Need Fulfillment As A Function of Line Versus Staff Type of Job." *Journal of Applied Psychology,* 47: 267-75. 1963.

Presthus, R. *The Organizational Society.* N. Y.: Alfred A. Knoph, Inc., 1962.

Pugh, D. S. and Others. "A Conceptual Scheme for Organizational Analysis." *Administrative Science Quarterly,* 8: 289-315. Dec., 1963.

Punch, K. F. "Bureaucratic Structure in Schools: Toward Redefinition and Measurement." *Educational Administration Quarterly,* 5(2): 43-57. Spring, 1969.

Punch, K. F. "Bureaucratic Structure in Schools and Its Relationship to Leader Behavior: An Empirical Study." Unpublished doctoral dissertation, The University of Toronto, 1967.

Quaid, C. A. "Professional Bureaucratic Orientations, Perceptions of Bureaucratic Structure and Climate in Irish Secondary Schools." *Dissertation Abstracts International,* 38: 1801A. 1977(Fordham University).

Robinson, N. "A Study of the Professional Role Orientations of Teachers and Principals and Their Relationship to Bureaucratic Characteristics of School Organizations." Unpublished doctoral dissertation, The University of Alberta, 1966.

Sajecki, A. D. "The Relationship of Teacher Orientation and Perceived Structural Characteristics of Schools to Decisional States of Teachers." *Dissertation Abstracts International,* 28: 59-60A. 1977. (Columbia University, Teachers College).

Salinas, R. C. "An Exploratory Study of Job Satisfaction Attitudes Among Non-academic University Personnel." Unpublished MA. thesis, New York State School of Industrial and Labor Relations, Cornell University, 1964.

Sarber, M. L. "Teacher Perception of Professional Autonomy Under Varying Conditions of Negotiations in Arizona, California, and Nevada." *Dissertation Abstracts International,* 38: 1805A. 1977(The University of Arizona).

Schackmuth, T. G. "Creating Job Satisfaction in A Static Teacher Market." *Clearing House,* 52(5): 229-32. Jan., 1979. ERIC Document EJ 199128.

Schmidt, G. L. "Job Satisfaction Among Secondary School Administrators." *Educational Administration Quarterly,* 12: 68-86. 1976.

Schultz, D. *Psychology and Industry Today.* N. Y.: Macmillan, 1973.

Scott, W. R. "Reactions to Supervision in A Heteronomous Professional Organization." *Administrative Science Quarterly,* 10(1): 65-81. Jun., 1965.

Sergiovanni, T. J. and F. D. Carver. *The New School Executive: A Theory of Administration.* N. Y.: Harper & Row, 1973.

Sergiovanni, T. J. and F. D. Carver. "Factors Which Affect Satisfaction and Dissatisfaction of Teachers." In Fred D. Carver and Thomas J. Sergiovanni(eds.), *Organizations and Human Behavior: Focus on Schools.* N. Y.: McGraw-Hill Book Co., 1969. 249-260.

Sheppard, F. D. "Differences in Professional and Bureaucratic Self-Perceptions of Public School Teachers." Unpublished doctoral dissertation, State University of New York at Buffalo, 1965.

Siegel, L. *Industrial Psychology*(Rev. ed.). Homewood, Ill.: Richard D. Irwin, 1969.

Smith, P. C., L. M. Kendall, and C. L. Hulin. *The Measurement of Satisfaction in Work and Retirement: A Strategy for the Study of Attitudes. Chicago:* Rand McNally and Co., 1969.

Smith, P. C., L. M. Kendall, and others. *Cornell Studies of Job Satisfaction: I - VI.* Mimeo, Cornell University, 1965.

Sobong, L. C. "A Study of the Relationship Between Teachers' Beliefs Regarding Dimensions of Academic Freedom and Their Professional and Employee Role Orientations." *Dissertation Abstracts International,* 36: 83A. 1975(University of Missouri-Columbia).

Sorensen, J. E. "Professional and Bureaucratic Organizations in Large Public Accounting Firms." Unpublished doctoral dissertation, The Ohio State University, 1965.

Spence, J. A. "Perceived Bureaucracy, Teacher Work Value, Conflict and Organizational Effectiveness." Unpublished doctoral dissertation, University of Kansas, 1978.

Stahl, B. G. "Community College Bureaucraticism as Related to Student and Faculty Attrition." *Dissertation Abstracts International,* 36: 83A. 1975.(University of Missouri-Columbia).

Stewart, D. A. "Changing Organizational Structure to Affect Perceived Bureaucracy, Organizational Climate, Loyalty, Job Satisfaction." *Dissertation Abstracts International,* 38: 587A. 1977(University of Kansas).

Stinchcombe, A. L. "Bureaucratic and Craft Administration of Production: A Comparative Study." *Administrative Science Quarterly,* 4: 168-187. Sep., 1959.

Stinnett, T. M. *Professional Problems of Teachers.* N. Y.: The Macmillan Co., 1968.

Tagiuri, R. "Value Orientations, and the Relationship of Managers and Scientists." *Administrative Science Quarterly,* 10(1): 39-51. Jun., 1965.

Talacchi, S. "Organizational Size, Individual Attitudes, and Behavior." *Administrative Science Quarterly,* 5: 398-420. 1960.

Talbot, R. J. "An Investigation of Expressed Factors Related to the Job Satisfaction and Dissatisfaction of Industrial Arts Teachers in Suffolk County, New York." *Dissertation Abstracts International,* 36: 755A-56A. 1975.

Thom, C. G. "The Relationship Between Principals' Power Behavior and Their Evaluations of Teacher Performance." *Dissertation Abstracts International,* 39: 5841-42A. 1978(Maruette University).

Thompson, V. A. "Hierarchy Specialization, and Organizational Conflict." In Fred D. Carver and Thomas J. Sergiovanni(eds.), *Organizations and Human Behavior: Focus on Schools.* N. Y.: McGraw-Hill Book Co., 1969. 19-41.

Time, 16 June, 1980. 54-63.

Tofte, T. G. "The Role of the Elementary School Principal: A Review and Analysis of the Literature." Unpublished MA. thesis, The University of Minnesota, 1977.

Udy, H. Jr. "'Bureaucracy' and 'Rationality' in Weber's Organization Theory: An Empirical Study." *American Sociological Review,* 24: 791-95. Dec., 1959.

Udy, H. Jr. "'Bureaucratic Elements in Organizations: Some Research Findings." *American Sociological Review.* 23: 415-18. Aug., 1958.

Vollmer, H. M. and D. L. Mills(eds.) *Professionalization.* Englewood Cliffs, N. J.: Prentice-Hall, Inc., 1966.

Vroom, V. H. *Work and Motivation.* N. Y.: John Wiley and Sons, Inc., 1964.

Wahba, M. A., and L. G. Bridwell. "Maslow Reconsidered: A Review of Research on the Need Hierarchy Theory." *Organizational Behavior and Human Performance,* 15: 212-40. 1976.

Wardwell, W. "Social Integration, Bureaucratization," *Social Forces,* 33: 356-59. 1955.

Warren, D. I. "Power, Visibility and Conformity in Formal Organizations." *American Sociological Review,* 33(6): 951-70. Dec., 1968.

Washburne, C. "The Teacher in the Authority System." *Journal of Educational Sociology,* 30: 390-94. May, 1957.

Webb, T. W. "Classification of Teachers by Bureaucratic and Professional Normative Orientations to Educational Issues." Unpublished doctoral dissertation, The Ohio State University, 1964.

Weber, M. *The Theory of Social and Economic Organization.* Translated by A. M. Henderson and Talcott Parsons and edited by Talcott Parsons. N. Y.: Free Press, 1947.

Weiss, D. J. and others. "Manual for the Minnesota Satisfaction Questionnaire." *Minnesota Studies in Vocational Rehabilitation:* 22. Bulletin 46. Industrial Relations Center, University of Minnesota. Oct., 1967.

Wells, J. C. "Teacher Militancy and Professional Orientation Among Black Teachers in New York State." *Dissertation Abstracts International,* 37: 5524A. 1977(New York University).

Wermuth, M. A. "Relationship of Professional Orientation and Organizational Involvement to Organizational Commitment." *Dissertation Abstracts International,* 38: 67A. 1977(Columbia University, Teachers College).

Wilensky, H. L. "The Professionalization of Everyone?" *American Journal of Sociology,* 70: 137-58. Sep., 1964.

Whyte, W. H. Jr. *The Organization Man.* N. Y: Simon and Schuster, 1956.

Williams, J. O. "Professionalism and Bureaucracy: Natural Conflict." *NASSP Bulletin,* 61-68. Dec., 1971.

Wolf, E. P.(ed.) *Conflicts and Tensions in the Public Schools.* SAGE Contemporary School Science Issues-38. Beverly Hills: SAGE, 1977.

APPENDICES

APPENDIX A: QUESTIONNAIRE

YOUR WILLINGNESS TO PARTICIPATE IN THIS STUDY IS GREATLY APPRECIATED

....

***** BACKGROUND INFORMATION ABOUT TEACHER *****

Sex: Female_____, Male_____

Age:_____

Total Number of Years of Teaching Experience:

Number of Years of Teaching Experience in This School

Mstrict:_____

Total Years of Teaching Experience by Grades Tau□:

    Kindergarten_____

    Grade 1_____   Grade 2_____

    Grade 3_____   Grade 4_____

    Grade 5_____   Grade 6_____

     Other(Special: Area Teacher, Please Specify)___________

                          ____

Current Teaching Assignment: Grade_____

    Number of Years in Current Teaching Assignment:_____

Highest Academic Degree:

    Bachelor______

    Bachelor+__________Credits
            (Enter No.)

    Masser______

    Master+_________Credits
            (Enter No.)

    Doctorate______

    Hold Tenure______ or Nontenure______

    ....

PLEASE PROCEED TO THE QUESTIONNAIRE

READ THE QUESTIONS CAREFULLY AND ANSWER ALL QUESTIONS.
SOME OF THE QUESTIONS MAY BE DIFFICULT TO ANSWER WITH
THE LJNIYDD INFORMATION GIVER, BUT PLEASE RESPOND TO
EACH STATEMENT AS BEST YOU CAN.

***** ORGANIZATIONAL INVENTORY *****

DIRECTION: In the following statements you are asked to indvcate how well each one describes the organizational characteristics of YOUR SCHOOL. CIRCLE the number in the appropriate column that best reflects your opinion according to the key:

AT: Always True, OFT: Often True, OCT: Occasionally True, ST: Seldom True, NT: Never True

<u>AT OFT OCT ST NT</u>

5   4   3   2   1   1. I get approval for decisions I make.

5   4   3   2   1   2. Rules stating when teachers arrive at and depart from the building are strictly followed.

5   4   3   2   1   3. The time for informal get-togethers during the school days is. strictly regulated.

5   4   3   2   1   4. Red tape is a problem in getting a job done in this school.

5   4   3   2   1   5. The organization sponsors staff get-togethers.

5   4   3   2   1   6. Staff members here do almost as they please in classroom work.

5   4   3   2   1   7. Students are treated within the rules of the school, no matter how serlous a problem they have.

5   4   3   2   1   8. We follow strict operating procedures at all times.

5   4   3   2   1   9. A person who wants to make his own decisions would quickly become discouraged in this school.

5   4   3   2   1   10. Teachers in this school follow a set of rules and regulations.

5   4   3   2   1   11. Going through the proper channels is important in this school.

5   4   3   2   1   12. Staff meetings proceed in a friendly and informal manner.

5   4   3   2   1   13. Even small matters are referred to someone higher up for a final answer.

5   4   3   2   1   14. Standardized classroom methods and procedures are used by all teachers.

5   4   3   2   1   15. For student behavior problems, the school has standard punishments for standard offenses, regardless of the individual involved.

5   4   3   2   1   16. There can be little action until decisions are approved.

5   4   3   2   1   17. Teachers do not leave their classrooms unless they have permission.

5   4   3   2   1   18. Whenever we have a problem, we go to the same person for an answer.

5   4   3   2   1   19. No matter how special a pupil's or parent's problem appears to be, he is treated the same way as anyone else.

AT OFT OCT ST NT

5　4　3　2　1　20. Nothing is said if you got to school just before soli call or leave right after dismissal occasionally.

5　4　3　2　1　21. Relationships among staff members are formal and impersonal.

5　4　3　2　1　22. No one can get necessary supplies without permission from the principal or vice-principal.

5　4　3　2　1　23. Written orders from higher up are followed unquestioningly.

5　4　3　2　1　24. We follow standard procedures in dealing with most situations which arise.

5　4　3　2　1　25. People make their own decisions here without checking with anyone else.

5　4　3　2　1　26. Teachers are careful not to violate rules in this school.

5　4　3　2　1　27. Teachers follow clearly specified procedures for doing the job here.

5　4　3　2　1　28. I ask someone higher up before I do almost anything.

5　4　3　2　1　29. Teachers are aware of rules regarding their behavior in and around the school.

5　4　3　2　1　30. I feel that I am my own boss in most matters.

5　4　3　2　1　31. Teachers have fun socializing together during school time.

5　4　3　2　1　32. Teachers experiment with procedures for classroom teaching and other school work.

5　4　3　2　1　33. Teachers' closest friends are other staff members at this school.

5　4　3　2　1　34. How things are done in the classroom is pretty much up to the individual teacher.

***** PROFESSIONAL AND BUREAUCRATIC ORIENTATION SCALE *****

DIRECTION: The following statements concern YOUR ATTITUDES. Please CIRCLE the number of the appropriate response according to the key:

SA: Strongly Agree, A: Agree, ?: Undecided, D: Disagree, SD: Strongly Disagree

SA　A　?　D　SD

5　4　3　2　1　　1. It should be permissible for the teacher to violate a rule if he/she is sure that the best interests of the students will be served in doing so.

5　4　3　2　1　　2. Unless she is satisfied that it is best for the student, a teacher should not do what she is told to do.

5　4　3　2　1　　3. Good teachers should not do anything that they believe may jeopardize the interests of students regardless of who tells them to or what the rules state.

5　4　3　2　1　　4. Teachers should try to live up to what they think are the standards of their profession even if the administration or the community does not seem to respect them.

```
SA  A  ?  D  SD
```

5 4 3 2 1   5. One primary criterion of a good school should be the degree of respect it commands from other teachers around the state.

5 4 3 2 1   6. Teachers should try to put their standards into practice even if the rules or procedures of the school prohibit it.

5 4 3 2 1   7. Teachers should subscribe to and diligently read the standard professional journals.

5 4 3 2 1   8. Teachers should be active members of at least one professional teaching association, and attend most conferences and meetings of the association.

5 4 3 2 1   9. Teachers should consistently practice their ideas of the best educational practices even though the administration prefers other views.

5 4 3 2 1   10. A teacher's skill should be primarily based on acquaintance with subject matter.

5 4 3 2 1   11. Teachers should be evaluated primarily on the basis of their knowledge of the subject to be taught, and their ability to communicate it.

5 4 3 2 1   12. Schools should hire no one to teach unless they hold at least a 4-year bachelor's degree.

5 4 3 2 1   13. If there were a teacher shortage, it should be permissible to hire teachers trained at non-accre○ted colleges.

5 4 3 2 1   14. A teacher should be able to make his own decisions about problems that come up in the classroom.

5 4 3 2 1   15. Small matters should not have to be referred to someone higher up for a final answer.

5 4 3 2 1   16. The ultimate authority over the major educational decisions should be exercised by professional teachers.

5 4 3 2 1   17. Teachers should adjust their teaching to the administration's views of good educational practice.

5 4 3 2 1   18. The school administration should be better qualified than the teacher to judge what is best for education.

5 4 3 2 1   19. Teachers should be obedient, respectful and loyal to the principal.

5 4 3 2 1   20. In case of a dispute in the community over whether a controversial textbook or controversial speaker should be permitted in the school, the teacher should look primarily to the judgment of the administration for guidance.

5 4 3 2 1   21. Personnel who openly criticize the administration should be encouraged to go elsewhere.

5 4 3 2 1   22. Teachers should not be influenced by the opinions of those teachers whose thinking does not reflect the thinking of the administration.

5 4 3 2 1   23. The only way a teacher can keep out of "hot water" is to follow the wishes of the top adminstration.

5 4 3 2 1   24. What is best for the school is best for education.

5 4 3 2 1   25. A good teacher should put the interests of his school above everything else.

SA A ? D SD

5 4 3 2 1   26. In case of doubt whether a particular practice is better than another, the primary test should be what seems best for the overall reputation of the school.

5 4 3 2 1   27. A good teacher Should put the interests of his department above everything else.

5 4 3 2 1   28. Pay should be in relation to teacher experience.

5 4 3 2 1   29. Often, classroom experience simply gives a teacher the opportunity to practice his mistakes.

5 4 3 2 1   30. Teachers of the same subject throughout the system should follow the same kind of lesson plan.

5 4 3 2 1   31. Teachers should teach their course in such a way that a substitute can take over at a moment's notice without serious interruption.

5 4 3 2 1   32. The work of a course should be so planned that every child taking the same kind of course throughout the state eventually will cover the same material.

5 4 3 2 1   33. A good teacher should be able to efficiently teach the children what they need to know in the limited time available.

5 4 3 2 1   34. Teachers should be completely familiar with the written descriptions of the rules, procedures, manuals and other standard operating procedures for running the classroom.

5 4 3 2 1   35. The school should have a manual of rules and regulations which are actually followed.

5 4 3 2 1   36. Rules stating when the teachers should arrive and depart from the building should be strictly enforced.

5 4 3 2 1   37. To prevent confusion and friction among the staff, there should be a rule covering almost every problem that might come up at the school.

5 4 3 2 1   38. There should be definite rules specifying the topics that are not appropriate for discussion in a classroom.

5 4 3 2 1   39. When a controversy arises about the interpretation of school rules, a teacher should not "stick his neck out" by taking a definite position.

5 4 3 2 1   40. Teachers should take into account the opinions of their community in guiding what they say in class and in their choice of teaching materials.

5 4 3 2 1   41. Teachers should not publicly advocate a position on the place of religion in the school which differs greatly from the majority opinion of the community.

5 4 3 2 1   42. A good teacher is one who conforms, in general, to accepted standards in the community.

5 4 3 2 1   43. The criterion of a good school should be one that serves the needs of the local community.

5 4 3 2 1   44. Teachers should not attempt to discuss any controversial issues(such as abolishing the House Un-American Activities Committee) which may jeopardize the school's public relations.

5　4　3　2　1　　　45. Local control over schools by school boards represents the most fundamental form of democracy in public education.

***** CONFLICT ASSESSMENT QUESTIONNAIRE *****

DIFECTION: Most teachers have experienced misunderstandings, disagreements, conflict, or tense situations at some time in their teaching career. Some evidence indicates that the items below are sources of misunderstandings for many teachers. The teaches. The items are arranged on a scale from 5(Serious Conflict) to 1(No Conflict). A serious misunderstanding or disagreement resulted in major tensions or disconfort for you. A minor conflict(misunderstanding or disagreement) resulted in little or no change in attitude. Please CIRCLE the number in the appropriate column for each item reflecting the intensity of misunderstanding or disagreement YOU have experienced in the past five years.

Serious-Minor-None

I have experienced disagreements or misunderstandings over:

5　4　3　2　1　　　1. salary paid for sponsoring extra-curricular activities.

5　4　3　2　1　　　2. a personality clash with a student.

5　4　3　2　1　　　3. adequacy of teaching supplies.

5　4　3　2　1　　　4. the appropriate number of assemblies.

5　4　3　2　1　　　5. the administration's idea of proper teaching techniques and methods.

5　4　3　2　1　　　6. the opportunity to communicate my ideas to the central office.

5　4　3　2　1　　　7. requirements for student achievement.

5　4　3　2　1　　　8. the determination of teacher load for extra-curricular activities.

5　4　3　2　1　　　9. the amount of sick leave.

5　4　3　2　1　　　10. my behavior and actions after school hours.

5　4　3　2　1　　　11. appropriate disciplinary treatment or suspension of pupils.

5　4　3　2　1　　　12. scheduling or frequency of field trips.

5　4　3　2　1　　　13. the right to have a voice in determining curriculum.

5　4　3　2　1　　　14. what the "best policy" for the school is.

5　4　3　2　1　　　15. enforcing rules on student behavior.

5　4　3　2　1　　　16. my overall control in the classroom.

5　4　3　2　1　　　17. determining the frequency of achievement or mental measurement testing.

5　4　3　2　1　　　18. availability of proper facilities.

5　4　3　2　1　　　19. the retirement program.

5　4　3　2　1　　　20. moral standards for teacher.

5　4　3　2　1　　　21. my promotion to a better teaching position.

5　4　3　2　1　　　22. ethical standards related to the school.

5　4　3　2　1　　　23. policies for getting students out at class.

5　4　3　2　1　　　24. recognition of teacher prestige by the administration.

Serious-Minor-None

I have experienced disagreements or misunderstandings over:

5	4	3	2	1	25. a personality clash with a teacher.
5	4	3	2	1	26. fringe benefits such as health insurance and workmen's compensation.
5	4	3	2	1	27. cleanliness of the classroom or building.
5	4	3	2	1	28. emphasis on academic work versus activities.
5	4	3	2	1	29. availability of instructional material or equipment.
5	4	3	2	1	30. the salary being too low.
5	4	3	2	1	31. socializing with students.
5	4	3	2	1	32. cooperation on the teaching staff.
5	4	3	2	1	33. personal teacher responsibilities in selection of textbooks.
5	4	3	2	1	34. emphasis placed on the importance of the child.
5	4	3	2	1	35. joint teacher-administrator determination of job description.
5	4	3	2	1	36. the amount of emphasis on extra-curricular activities.
5	4	3	2	1	37. inequity among teachers in salaries paid.
5	4	3	2	1	38. inequities in distribution of equipment or supplies.
5	4	3	2	1	39. having audio-visual equipment available.
5	4	3	2	1	40. having a personality clash with an administrator.
5	4	3	2	1	41. participation of students in extra-curricular activities.
5	4	3	2	1	42. pleasantness of the physical work conditions.
5	4	3	2	1	43. administrative recognition for my teaching abilities.
5	4	3	2	1	44. allocation of student grades—failure or low grades.
5	4	3	2	1	45. who is to teach prestige or advanced courses.
5	4	3	2	1	46. the backing of the administrator or department head.
5	4	3	2	1	47. privileges taken by certain faculty members.

***** MINNESOTA SATISFACTION QUESTIONNAIRE *****

The purpose of this questionnaire is to give you a chance to tell HOW YOU FEEL ABOUT YOUR PRESENT JOB, which things you are SATISFIED with and what things you are NOT SATISFIED with. Please CIRCLE the number in the appropriate column for each item according to the key:

Ask yourself: HOW SATISFIED am I with this aspect of my job?

VS (Very Satisfied): means I am very satisfied with this aspect of my job.

S (Satisfied): means I am satisfied with this aspect of my job.

N (Neither Satisfied not Dissatisfied): means I can't decide whether I am satisfied or not with this aspect of my job.

D (Dissatisfied): means I am dissatisfied with this aspect of my job.

VD (Very Dissatisfied): means I am very dissatisfied with this aspect of my job.

VS S N D VD

On my present Job, this is how I feel about……

1 2 3 4 5   1. being able to keep busy all the time.

1 2 3 4 5   2. the chance to work alone on the job.

1 2 3 4 5   3. the chance to do different things from time to time.

1 2 3 4 5   4. the chance to be "somebody" in the community.

1 2 3 4 5   5. the way my boss handles his / her workers.

1 2 3 4 5   6. the competence of my supervisor in making decisions.

1 2 3 4 5   7. being able to do things that don't go against my conscience.

1 2 3 4 5   8. the way my job provides for steady employment.

1 2 3 4 5   9. the chance to do things for other people.

1 2 3 4 5   10. the chance to tell people what to do.

1 2 3 4 5   11. the chance to do something that makes use of my abilities.

1 2 3 4 5   12. the way school district policies are put into practice.

1 2 3 4 5   13. my pay and the amount of work I do.

1 2 3 4 5   14. the chance for advancement on this job.

1 2 3 4 5   15. the freedom to use my own judgment.

1 2 3 4 5   16. the chance to try my own methods of dong the job.

1 2 3 4 5   17. the working conditions.

1 2 3 4 5   18. the way my co-worker get along with each other.

1 2 3 4 5   19. the praise I get for doing a good job.

1 2 3 4 5   20. the feeling of accomplishment I got from the job.

THANK YOU VERY MUCH!

APPENDIX B: KEY TO THE CATEGORICAL
BREAKDWN OF EACH INSTRUMENT

Instruments and Subscales	Items
The Organizational Inventory	
(1) Hierarchy of Authority	1,6,9,13,16,22,25,28,30,34.
(2) Rules for Incumbents	2,3,10,17,20,23,26,29.
(3) Procedural Specifications	4,8,11,14,18,24,27,32.
(4) Impersonality	5,7,12,15,19,21,31,33.
The Professional Orientation Scale	
(1) Client Orientation	1-3
(2) Colleague Orientation	4-9
(3) Monopoly of Knowledge	10-13
(4) Decision Making	14-16
The Bureaucratic Orientation Scale	
(1) Administrative Orientation Scale	17-23
(2) Loyalty to the Organization	24-27
(3) Experience Orientation	28-29
(4) Standardization Orientation	30-33
(5) Rules and Procedures Orientation	34-39
(6) Orientation to the Public	40-45
The Conflict Assessment Questionnaire	
(1) Desirable Physical Work Conditions	3,18,27,29,38,39,42.
(2) Material Inducements	1,9,19,26,30,37.
(3) Personal, Non-Material Opportunities	10,20,21,22,31,45.
(4) School Priorities and Standards	4,8,28,36,41.
(5) Decision-Sharing	7,12,13,14,17,33,34.
(6) Student Relationships	2,11,15,16,23,44.
(7) Administrative Relationships	5,6,24,35,40,43,46.
(8) Staff Relationships	25,32,47.

Instruments and Subscales	Items
The Minnesota Satisfaction Questionniare	
(1) Intrinsic Satisfaction	1,2,3,4,7,8,9,10,11,15,16,20.
(2) Extrinsic Satisfaction	5,6,12,13,14,19.
(3) General Satisfaction	1-20.

APPENDIX C: KEY TO SCORING EACH INSTRUMENT

The Organizational Inventory

For the item 5, 6, 12, 20, 25, 30, 31, and 34

AT (Always True)   =1
OFT (Often True)   =2
OCT (Occasionally True) =3
ST (Seldom True)   =4
NT (Never True)   =5

For other all items

AT (Always True)   =5
OFT (Often True)   =4
OCT (Occasionally True) =3
ST (Seldom True)   =2
NT (Never True)   =1

The Professional and Bureaucratic Orientation Scale

For all items except item 13

SA (Strongly Agree)   =5
A (Agree)   =4
? (Undecided)   =3
D (Disagree)   =2
SD (Strongly Disagree) =1

For item 13; SA=1, A=2, ?=3, D=2, SD=1.

The Conflict Assessment Questionnaire

For all items; Serious (5) - Minor - None (1)

The Minnesota Satisfaction Questionnaire

For all items

VS (Very Satisfied) =5
S (Satisfied) =4
N (Neither Satisfied nor Dissatisfied) =3
D (Dissatisfied) =2
VD (Very Dissatisfied) =1

Items left blank were scored with a three but items left blank on the CAQ were with a one as developers.

APPENDIX D: SUPPLEMENTAL TABLES; TABLES; THREE-WAY ANOVA

APPENDIX D-1

Summary of Analysis of Variance for Conflict, with School Bureaucratization, Professional Orientation and Bureaucratic Orientation

SV	SS	df	MS	F
SB	537.05	1	537.05	.86(ns)
PO	195.10	1	195.10	.31(ns)
BO	219.10	1	219.10	.35(ns)
SB×PO	708.70	1	708.70	1.14(ns)
SB×BO	90.99	1	90.99	.15(ns)
PO×BO	1039.02	1	1039.02	1.67(ns)
SB×PO×BO	249.64	1	249.64	.40(ns)
Residual	81418.22	131	621.52	
Total	84768.60	138	614.27	

APPENDIX D-2

Summary of Analysis of Variance for Job Satisfaction, with School Bureaucratization, Professional Orientation and Bureaucratic Orientation

SV	SS	df	MS	F
SB	1.93	1	1.93	.08
PO	248.47	1	148.47	2.14
BO	1046.18	1	1046.18	9.01*
SB×PO	1.14	1	1.14	.01
SB×BO	708.51	1	708.51	6.10*
PO×BO	50.79	1	50.79	.44
SB×PO×BO	17.72	1	17.72	.15
Residual	15207.56	131	116.09	
Total	17410.36	138	126.16	

** Significant at .05 level.

APPENDIX E: PERMISSION ON THE USE OF
HUMAN SUBJECTS IN RESEARCH

RE: Methodological Protocol #   1   .

Dear Mr. Joo:

Your Methodological Protocol Request for Approval was received in the Committee office on   9/18/80   , and has
been administratively approved on   4/14/81   as within
the guidelines of the referenced Methodological Protocol.

I would like to remind you that it is the responsibility of the
investigator to bring to the attention of the Committee any
proposed change in the project or any emergent problems
that will affect human subjects.

On behalf of the Committee, I wish you luck with your
research.

Sincerely,

Anne Munro

Executive Secretary to the

Committee on the Use of

Human Subjects in Research

2. 학교조직의 관료화, 교사의 전문지향성과 관료지향성, 갈등, 직무만족 간의 관계연구[*2]

I. 조직과 개인

"우리 사회는 조직사회이다. 인간은 조직 속에 태어나고, 조직에 의하여 교육을 받고, 또 대부분의 인간은 조직을 위해서 일하면서 생의 대부분을 보내게 된다"(Etzioni 1964. p.1). 물고기가 물을 떠나서 살 수 없듯이 인간도 조직을 떠나서는 잠시도 생활할 수 없다.

조직이란 우리의 사회적인 욕구와 개인적인 욕구 때문에 형성된 것이다. 개인이 조직을 위해서 시간과 정력을 바치는 대가로 조직은 개인의 봉사에 대하여 금전으로써 보상한다.

교육행정의 발전 역사를 잠깐 살펴볼 때도 이와 같은 조직과 개인에 대한 헤겔의 법칙이 적용될 수 있다.

헤겔 법칙의 "정"은 조직적 측면을 강조한 "과학적 관리시대"이다. 시간의 흐름에 따라 개인적 측면을 보다 더 강조했던 "인간관계시대"가 헤겔의 "반"

---

* 이 논문은 <u>새교육</u> 34권 8호(1982. 8) 대한교육연합회에 박사학위논문 서론 부분을 요약하여 우리말로 쓴 것임.

으로 전성시대를 이루기도 했다. "합"은 조직과 개인의 양 측면을 동시에 강조하고 조화를 이루고자 하는 것이다. 어쨌든 교육행정에 있어서 조직과 개인과의 관계는 중요한 한 연구의 영역이다.

자기 자신의 독특한 "성격"과 "욕구성향"–개인적 측면–을 가지고 있는 교사들은 어떤 역할과 "기대"–조직규범적 측면–를 요구하는 학교조직 속에서 일하고 있다(Getzels and Guba, 1957; Getzels, 1958).

개인의 성격과 욕구성향이 조직의 역할과 기대와 부합되지 않을 때 갈등상태는 피할 길이 없다. 거의 모든 조직이 이런 문제를 안고 있기 때문에 어떤 의미에서 이 종류의 갈등은 당연한 것인지도 모른다. 그리고 많은 연구들이 이런 갈등의 문제를 다루어 온 것이다.

그러나 보다 더 심각한 문제는 다른 데 있다. 즉, 현대 학교조직은 점점 더 관료화되어 가고, 자기 스스로 전문가라고 생각되는 교사에게 보다 더 엄격한 관료적 역할과 기대를 요구하는 반면, 교사들의 주업인 가르치는 일은 점점 더 전문화되어 가고 있다는 사실에 있다.

바꾸어 말하면, "사람과 일, 사회적 환경"의 삼자는 조직의 목적이 달성될 수 있도록 충분히 조화를 이루어야 힘에도 불구하고(Otto and Sanders, p.393) 학교체제에서의 "사회환경"의 주요 부분인 학교조직은 보다 더 엄격한 관료화의 방향으로 나아가고 있는 반면, "사람"차원(교사)과 "일"차원(교수)은 그 반대 방향인 전문화의 방향으로 나아가고 있다는 데 문제가 있는 것이다.

공립학교 발전의 역사가 바로 관료화의 과정이었다는 사실은 아무도 부인할 수 없을 것이다. 학교는 전통적으로 자신의 목적을 달성하기 위한 수단으로써 관료제를 채택해 온 것이다. 특히 지난 수세기 동안 학교조직에서 관료화의 증세가 점점 증가해 온 것이다.

학교조직의 재정·시설·유지기능 등이 점점 복잡해짐에 따라 책임성과 의사결정이 보다 더 중앙집권화하고 특수화되고 있다. 인원과 사무가 증가함에 따라 중앙, 교육위원회, 행정가의 수가 현저히 증가해 왔다. 의사 결정을 표준화하고 규제하고, 프로그램화하기 위한 수단으로 컴퓨터가 보다 자주 사용되고 있다. 이런 모든 현상은 관료제가 확대되고 있다는 증거이다 (Sergiovanni and Carver, p.24).

동시에 다른 경향이 또한 학교체제 내에서 분명히 일어나고 있는 것이다.

> 교육프로그램의 성격, 범위, 다양성과 교수학습 체제에 있어서 똑같은 복잡화와 정교화의 변화가 일어나고 있다. 교수 방법·내용, 교수공학에 있어서의 이러한 폭발적인 지식은 학생의 복지에 대한 새롭고도 강한 책임감과 결합하여 나타나게 되었다. 교사의 지위 향상과 교수 방법을 향상시키기 위한 운동이 이와 관련된 현상이다. 이러한 모든 증세가 전문화의 증거이다(Sergiovanni and Carver, 1973, p.25).

이리하여 "교사의 전문화의 성장은 교육에 대한 비전문가의 관리와 행정가의 계층에 의한 통제란 전통에 도전하게 되는 것이다"(Robinson, 1966, p.9).

요약하면 교사라는 개인은 학교라는 조직 속에서 생활하게 되며, 그들의 행동은 "조직"의 "역할", "기대"와 "개인"의 "성격", "욕구성향"의 상호작용에 의하여 나타나게 되는데, 학교조직은 점점 더 관료화되어 가고, 교사와 교수하는 일은 점점 더 전문화되어 가고 있다는 데 문제가 있을 것으로 예상된다. 좀더 학교조직의 관료화 경향과 교사의 전문화 경향을 살펴보고자 한다.

Ⅱ. 학교조직의 관료화와 교사의 전문화

학교조직의 관료화 경향과 교사의 전문화 경향을 나누어서 고찰하고자 한다.

A. 학교조직의 관료화 경향

먼저 관료제의 개념부터 정의하고 학교에 있어서의 관료화 경향 몇 가지

증거를 열거한다.

관료제를 정의하기 위하여 많은 접근이 시도되었다. Punch(1969)는 많은 문헌을 광범하게 연구한 다음 관료제 정의의 종류를 세 가지로 압축·요약하였다.

그 하나는, 거시적, 때로는 역사적·문화적 분석에서 흔히 사용되는 것으로 관료제를 특징적으로 사회조직의 현대적 형태라는 것이다. 즉, 우리 조직은 "관료사회이다"라는 접근이다.

이러한 관점에서는 관료제는 많은 개개인의 일을 체계적으로 조정함으로써 대형화된 행정과업을 성취할 수 있도록 고안된 조직형태라 정의된다. 이런 의미에서 관료제는 대형조직 또는 공식조직과 동의어로 쓰인다.

두 번째 접근은 보다 상세히 조직의 내적 구조에 관심을 갖는다. 여기서는 현존 조직들을 하나하나 구별하는 데 강조점이 주어진다. 전형적으로 관료제의 특성에 의하여 조직들을 구별하고자 하는 접근이다.

마지막으로 관료제는 독재적 권력, 비능률, 형식적 서류로 상징되는 좀 나쁜 의미로 쓰이는 것이다. 이것은 가치가 부여된 것으로 많은 연구의 관심영역이며, 관료세의 역기능이란 점을 이용한나(Punch, 1969, p.44.).

Owens(1970, p.56)는 위의 첫 번째 접근으로 "많은 고객을 다루는 대형이며, 또 복잡한 조직의 필요성에 알맞은 하나의 행정조직"이라고 정의하였다. 그런가 하면 Dimock(1965)는 기관리 개인을 압도하는 생활 방도로서 관료제를 정의하였다.

Blau와 Scott(1962, p.8)도 "하나의 조직이 그 목적 달성을 위해서라기보다 그 조직 자체를 유지하기 위하여 바치는 노력의 양"이라고 정의하였는데, 이 둘은 Punch의 분류에서 볼 때 세 번째 접근에 속한다.

이 논문은 Punch의 분류에서 두 번째 접근으로 정의하고자 한다. 두 번째 내적 특성에 의한 차원적 접근은 관료제의 특성을 (1) 권위의 위계(hierarchy of authority), (2) 일의 분화(divisison of labor), (3) 규정(rules for incumbents), (4) 절차의 명세화(procedural specifications), (5) 비정

(impersonality), (6) 기술적 능력(technical competence)(Hall, 1963)
과 같은 구성요소 또는 차원으로 나누어 조직을 관찰하는 것이다.

이러한 접근에서 볼 때는 하나의 조직이 관료조직이냐 아니냐를 따지는
것은 무의미하고 그 조직의 위의 6가지 특성 또는 차원을 어느 정도 나타내
고 있느냐, 즉 "관료화"가 어느 정도 되어 있느냐를 따지는 것이 오히려 유
용하다는 것이다.

그렇다면 학교조직이 점점 더 관료화되어 가고 있다는 증거는 무엇인가?

첫째: 학교의 크기가 점점 대형화되어 감에 따라 더욱 관료화되고 있다.
취학 연령층과 인구의 증가, 급격한 도시화, 증가 일로에 있는 진학률, 졸
업률, 교육구의 통합(미국에 있어서)으로 학교체제가 대형화하고 있다.

이렇게 학교체제가 대형화하면 교육구가 점점 더 커지고, 그에 따라 점점
더 중앙집권화되면 교육감의 권한이 확대되어 교장의 영향력이 커지고, 이
어서 교장의 교사에 대한 압력이 강해지게 마련이다.

우리나라에서도 교장의 "재량권 확대"니 "학교장 중심행정"이니 "교사왕국"
을 만드느니 하는 말이 자주 쓰이게 되는데, 이런 말들이 자주 쓰이면 쓰일
수록 그것이 이루어지지 않고 있다는 증거이다.

교육행정가들이 의도한 것도 아닌데 어느새 학교체제가 대형화되고, 또
그에 따라 모르는 사이에 행정은 중앙집권화되어 있다는 것을 뒤늦게 느껴
권한을 학교장이나 교사의 재량권이나 자율성에 맡겨야 되겠다는 생각에 미
치는 것이다.

둘째로, 학교조직과 기능의 복잡화에 따라 학교의 관료화가 촉진되고 있다.

Team Teaching, 과목전담제, 개방학교체제, 학생들을 다양한 집단으
로 구성하는 방법 등은 학교체제의 "복잡화"에 기여해 온 것이다.

복잡화에 기여한 또 하나의 중요한 요인은 학교의 역할에 대한 기대가 증
가하고 있다는 사실이다. 더 이상 학교는 학생들의 기본 기능만을 가르치는
역할에만 머물러 있을 수가 없다. 학교는 읽고, 쓰고, 셈하는 또는 단지 지
식만 가르치는 역할만 담당하던 시대는 지나간 것을 우리는 잘 알고 있다.

학교는 전인적 아동발달을 돕도록 기대되고 있다. 즉, 학교는 지적인 것은 물론이고 신체적·심리적·사회적·정서적인 발달도 도와주도록 기대되고 있다(Parelius and Parelius, 1978, p.120).

학교의 역할은 학생의 영양, 급식, 교통, 사회사업의 역할까지 확대되게 되었다. 조직이 더욱 복잡해지고 학교의 역할이 더욱 다양화되면 될수록 내적 조정의 필요성은 증대되어 행정가의 주요 내적 기능은 "조정"이란 것이기 때문에 행정가의 권한은 확대되는 것이다.

셋째로, 행정업무가 계속적으로 증가 일로에 있다. 교장들도 수업장학(Supervision of Instruction)에 그들의 대부분의 시간을 바치고 싶어 하고, 또 그것이 이상적이라고 생각하지만 실제로는 그렇지 못하고 어쩔 수 없이 행정적 잡무와 사무적인 일, 관리에 너무나 많은 시간을 바치지 않을 수 없다는 것이다(Krajewski, 1978, p.50: Faber and Shearron, 1970, p.214: Lipham and Hoeh, 1974, p.127).

우리나라에서도 공문 처리건수가 너무 많다고 줄이려는 노력을 하고 있다. 하지만 원래 행정가들이 공문건수를 늘리려고 했던 것이 아니고, 그만큼 할일이 많나 보니까 그렇게 된 경우가 낳을 것이며, 공문건수가 너무 낳아서 학교의 본업인 가르치는 일에까지 영향을 준다고 하여 문제가 됨으로써 억지로 줄이려 하다 보니 공문과 다름없는 전화에 의한 업무 연락이 많아진다는 것이다. 어쨌든 이러한 행정사무의 폭발은 하나의 관료적 역기능의 산물인 것이다.

넷째로, 미국에서는 연방 정부, 주정부, 지방교육구의 개개 학교에 대한 압력이 증가되고, 학교가 점점 더 획일화하고 있는 경향이다(Campbell 외 1975, pp.22~27, p.74).

원래 미국은 학교, 지방교육구 수준에서 학교가 운영되어 왔던 것인데, 점점 연방정부, 주정부의 교육에 대한 관여가 심해지고 있으며, 우리나라에서는 이미 중앙의 관여가 너무 심하다는 것을 스스로 느끼고 지방에 권한을 이양하려고 노력하고 있다. 중앙의 간섭에 의한 획일성도 또한 관료제의 산물인 것이다.

다섯째로, "최근 많은 학부모와 지역 사회집단은 학교 프로그램과 학업 성취도, 교직원의 효과성에 점점 더 실망하게 되고 따라서 학교 정책의 수립과 수정에, 그리고 학교가 달성해야 할 책임성에 대한 평가에 깊이 참여하기를 원하고 있다.(Gorton, 1972, pp.24~25). 심한 경우 "교사는 가르칠 수 없다(Time, 1980. 6. 16)"고까지 불평하고 있다.

이 모든 현상은 전문가라 자부하는 교사에 대한 심각한 도전이다. 더욱 심한 경우는 자기 집 아이들을 자기 집에서 학부모가 직접 가르치고 학교에 보내지 않으려고까지 한다는 것이다.

이러한 것들은 모두 전통적으로 관료제를 채택해 왔으며, 이 관료제의 증세가 최근 점점 더 학교 조직에서 강화되고 또 확대되고 있다는 증거이다.

B. 교사의 전문화경향

전문화란 개념도 관료화를 정의할 때와 비슷한 방법으로 정의된다. Cogan(1953)은 전문직을 정의하기 위한 많은 시도들을 고찰한 후 다섯 종류의 정의의 형태를 발견하였다. 즉, (1) 사전식 정의, (2) 응용적인 면을 강조한 정의, (3) 권한과 특권이란 관점에서 본 정의 (4) 공식(전문가) 집단에 의한 정의, (5) 내적 규제에 의한 방법에 의한 정의이다 이들 전문직 또는 전문화의 정의의 예를 일일이 다 들지 않고 관료제를 정의할 때와 같이 정의한다.

"전문직"을 정의하는 전형적인 접근은 전문직에 해당되는 특성들을 열거하고 주어진 직업이 전문주의에 해당되는지 검토하기 위한 기준으로 이들 특성을 사용하는 것이다.(MacKay, 1969, p.228). "일반적으로 말하면 성숙된 전문직도 구성원 채용과 정책에 대하여 절차를 마련하고 이론적 지식을 최대한 구사하며, 또 사회문제 해결에 이를 최대로 적용하는데 합법적으로 독점적이다(Corwin, 1970, p.43). 이들 기준의 특성에는 여러 사람들의 것이 있으나 Liebeberman(1956)의 8개의 기준을 예로 들고자 한다.

(1) 특수하고, 명확하고, 중요한 일에의 사회적 봉사

(2) 봉사하는 데 있어서의 지적 기능의 강조

(3) 장기간에 걸친 전문교육

(4) 집단이나 개인에 대한 광범한 자율성

(5) 전문적 자율성의 범위 내에서 행한 판단과 행동에 대한 책임성의 수락

(6) 직업집단에 주어진 사회봉사와 조직에 바탕을 둔 개인의 강조

(7) 완전한 자치조직

(8) 불분명하고 의심스러운 점에 대하여 구체적인 사례로 명확하게 해석된 윤리강령

이러한 특성을 가진 전문직의 증세가 점점 학교에서 나타나고 있다. 다시 말하면 교직의 전문화 경향이 점점 확실히 나타나고 있는데, 그 실례를 몇 가지 지적하고자 한다.

전산업시대에 교직을 전문직으로 생각한 사람은 거의 없었다.(Parelius and Parelius, 1978, p.187). 그러나 19세기 말 초기산업시대에 교직의 전문화, 숙연, 전국 교직 단체의 구성과 함께 전문직으로 인정받게 되었다. 초기산업시대 교직은 전문화의 방향으로 장족의 발전을 하였다.

지난 수십 년 동안 성숙산업시대에 교직은 유인과 선발 체제, 숙련, 교육기간과 특수화, 전문 조직과 조합의 측면에서 전문직으로 발전해 왔으나 많은 사회학자들이 지적하는 것처럼 교직은 아직 의사나 변호사처럼 완전전문화되지 못한 것으로 보이고 있다.

그러나 여러 조건은 교직의 전문화의 방향으로 진행되어 가고 있다.

첫째, 교사교육과 교육의 기준이 점점 더 향상되어 가고, 그 준비 기간이 길어지며, 또 앞으로도 계속 질이 향상되고 기간이 길어질 전망이다. "장기간에 걸친 전문교육"은 전문화의 중요한 특성의 하나인 것이다. "1925년에 미국에서 학사학위를 가진 교사는 거의 없었다. 그러나 1970년에는 거의 95%가 학사학위를 가졌으며, 28% 이상이 석사학위를 가졌으며, 어떤 주에서는 초등학교 교사의 80% 이상이 석사학위 소지자로 되어 있다(Hencley 외,

1970, p.6).

1980년대에는 교사들이 더 높은 학위를 소지할 것이며, 우리나라에서도 교육대학의 4년제 승격과 많은 교사의 교육대학원 수료로 교사교육 기간과 질은 높아지고 있는 것이다.

둘째, 컴퓨터 보조학습(Computer-assisted Instruction), 능력기준 교육(Competency-based Education) 같은 현대 교수공학에 의해서 교수 준비과정에 보다 깊은 전문화가 요구되고 또 실제로 전문화되고 있다.

셋째, 교사의 참조집단이 변하고 있다. 과거에 교사가 가르치는 데 어떤 문제점이 있을 때는 상사인 교장을 찾아가서 도움을 청했었다. 그러나 지금은 다른 동료 교사나 대학교수를 찾아가서 문제를 해결하려 한다. 교사들은 능력에 있어서 권위를 가졌다고 생각하는 동료에게 특별한 도움을 청하려고 하는데, 이러한 경향은 앞으로 계속 더욱 강화될 될 것이다(Faber and Shearron, 1970, p.378).

넷째, 교사와 행정가들이 서로 각각 다른 전문가 조직을 갖기 시작했다. 예를 들면,

American Federation of Teachers(AFT), American Association of School Administrators(AASA), National Association of Elementary School Principals(NAESP), National Association of Secondary School Principals(NASSP)들은 교사조직과 행정가조직으로 구별되고 있다. 이러한 사실은 교사의 전문조직이 행정가 전문조직과 기능적으로 서로 분화·전문화되고 있다는 증거이다.

다섯째, 전문성이 약하다고 하는 초등학교에서까지도 생활지도 카운슬러, 교육자료 전문가, 과목 담임제 같은 전문적 자리가 증가하고 있는데, 이것도 전문화과정을 알려 주는 지표의 하나가 된다.

결국 많은 교사들은 자기들 스스로가 전문가라고 강력히 주장하고 있으며, 전문가이기 때문에 교수, 교육과정, 교수자료, 학급 환경 문제에 관한 한은 학문적 자유와 절대적 권위가 인정되어야 한다고 목청 높여 주장하는 것이다.

Weber의 이상적인 관료제는 전문주의의 요소도 포함하고 있다. 그래서 조직의 관료화 정도를 재기 위한 Hall(1961, p.20:1968, p.95)의 Organizational Inventory에는 이미 언급한 6개의 특성 속에 있는 "일의 분화"와 "기술적 능력" 같은 전문주의의 요소를 포함하고 있는 것이다.

그러나 Punch(1969) 등의 연구에 의하면, 이들 두 특성은 다른 네 특성과 서로 관련이 없는 집단으로 나타났으며, 서로 반대되는 특성들인 것이다. 그래서 학교조직은 관료화의 경향으로 나아가고 그 조직 속에서 일하는 교사와 가르치는 일 자체가 점점 더 전문화되어 가는 경향이라면 필연적으로 갈등의 문제가 따르게 되면, 교육행정에 있어서 앞으로 맞이해야 될, 그리고 해결해야 될 중요한 과제가 될 것이다.

그러나 교사가 관료주의와 전문주의 중 어느 쪽으로 지향하느냐, 또는 양쪽으로 다 지향할 수 있느냐에 따라 문제는 달라질 것이므로 교사의 관료지향성과 전문지향성을 잠깐 논하고자 한다.

Ⅲ. 교사의 관료지향성과 선문지향성

조직 속에서 생활하는 개인이 조직에 대하여 어떠한 태도를 갖고 있으며, 조직의 요구에 대하여 어떻게 반응하느냐는 조직의 발전과 개인의 행복을 위해서도 매우 중요하다.

전술한 관료적 특성에 적응하려 하고, 관료적 기대에 맞추려는 경향이 강한 사람을 관료지향적(bureaucratic orientation)이라고 하고 전문주의 특성을 갖고 전문성을 살리려는 경향을 전문지향성(professional orientation)이라 한다. 관료제와 전문주의 중 어느 쪽으로 얼마나 강하게 지향하는지를 알기 위하여 Corwin(1964)은 관료지향척도, 전문지향척도(Bureaucratic (Employee)-Professional Orientation Scale)를 개발하였다. 그 하위 척도는 다음 표와 같다.

교사의 지향성척도 하위척도

관료지향척도	전문지향척도
1. 행정 지향적	1. 고객지향적
2. 조직에의 충성	2. 동료지향적
3. 경험 지향적	3. 전문지식 지향적
4. 표준화 지향	4. 의사결정권
5. 규정과 절차 지향적	
6. 공중지향적	

관료지향 전문지향척도에 의하여 관료지향성이 높고 전문지향성이 낮은 집단을 "관료집단"이라 하고, 전문지향성이 높고 관료지향성이 낮은 집단을 "전문가 집단"이라 하고, 양쪽 다 높은 집단을 "능력자 집단", 양쪽 다 낮은 점수를 가질 때 "소외자"라 한다.

만일 학교조직의 관료화 정도가 높은데 교사가 강한 전문지향을 갖는다면 그들의 갈등이 높을 것으로 예상되고, 학교가 관료화되었더라도 교사가 높은 관료지향성을 가져서 "관료집단"에 분류된다면 그들은 갈등이 낮고 대신 직무 만족이 높을 것으로 기대된다.

이론적으로만 생각한다면 능력자집단은 갈등과 만족이 동시에 높아야 할 것이고, "소외집단"은 조직에 대하여 무관심하고 개인의 행복을 조직의 밖에서 찾는 집단이기 때문에 갈등도 직무만족도 낮을 것으로 가정되는 것이다.

Ⅳ. 연구방법

이 연구는 조직과 개인, 개인의 조직행위를 다루었다. 독립변인으로서 조직 측면에서 (1) 학교 조직의 관료화를 Punch(Hall의 것을 학교 조직에 맞게 고친)의 Organizational Inventory로 교사의 지각에 의하여 재고, 역시 다른 독립변인으로서 개인 측면의 (2) 교사의 관료지향성과 (3) 전문지향성을 재어 이들 세 변인이 종속변인인 조직행위로 나타날 (4) 갈등(Conflict Assessment Questionnaire로 잼)과 (5) 직무만족(Minnesota Satisfaction Questionnaire로 잼)에 어떻게 영향을 미치며, 이들 다섯 변인들 사이에 어떤 관계가 있는가를 상관관계, 중다회귀분석 등에 의하여 탐색적 방법(pilot study의 성격)으로 연구하였다.

위의 질문지들을 하나로 통합하여 미국 미네소타 주에 있는 한 교육구의 6개 초등학교 교사 139명에게 적용하여 자료 수집하여 분석했다.

V. 연구결과

연구결과를 간단히 요약하면 다음과 같다.

(1) 교사의 지각에 의한 학교의 관료화 정도는 5점 척도에서 평균 2.81로 비교적 예상 외로 낮았다. 교사의 전문지향성은 3.61로 높았고, 관료지향성은 2.75로 낮았다. 이들 독립변인이 이상적인 방향임에 따라 역시 종속변인인 교사의 갈등의 정도도 1.78로 낮은 반면, 직무 만족의 정도는 3.71로 높았다. 그리고 관료지향성·전문지향성척도에 의하여 나누어진 교사의 하위집단은 관료집단에는 26.6%, 전문가 집단에는 22.3%, 능력자 집단에는 26.6%, 소외집단에는 24.5%의 교사가 속하여 4집단에 거의 골고루 분포되었다.

(2) 교사의 전문지향성과 관료지향성 둘 다 교사의 직무 만족과 정적 상관관계가 있었다. 다시 말하면, 전문지향성이 높은 교사도 관료지향성이 높은 교사도 모두 직무만족이 높은 것이다. 그러나 관료지향성이 높은 사람이 전문지향성이 높은 교사보다 더 직무만족이 높았다.

(3) 교사의 갈등을 예언할 수 있는 변인은 학교의 관료화를 측정하는 하위변인 중 권위의 "위계와 규정", 그리고 교사의 관료지향성 하위변인인 "조직에의 충성"이었다. 직무 만족을 의의 있게 예언할 수 있는 변인은 인구변

인 중 "교사경역(경력 많은 사람이 직무 만족도 높았음)과 "성별"(여자의 직무 만족이 높았음), 학교관료화 측정 하위변인 중 "권위의 위계", "규정", 그리고 관료지향성 하위변인인 규정과 절차였다.

(4) 주요 독립변인만(학교의 관료화, 교사의 전문 지향성, 관료 지향성) 종속변인의 예언변인으로 컴퓨터에 넣었을 때 교사의 전문지향성과 관료지향성 둘 다 직무만족의 의의 있는 예언변인이었다. 결과 (2)의 단순상관관계와 회귀분석의 결과와 일치하였다.

(5) 교사의 전문지향성과 관료지향성의 조합에 의한 4개의 교사 집단 중에서 소외집단(전문 지향, 관료 지향 둘 다 낮은)은 갈등도 직무 만족도 모두 낮았다. 그 다음 전문가 집단은 두 번째로 직무 만족이 낮은 반면 갈등은 제일 높았고, 관료집단은 직무만족도 갈등도 두 번째로 높았고, 능력자 집단은 직무 만족은 제일 높은 반면 갈등은 두 번째로 낮았다.

(6) 갈등과 직무 만족은 서로 강한 부적 상관관계에 있었다.

(7) 여교사가 남교사보다 더 직무만족이 높고, 나이 많은 교사, 경력이 많은 교사들은 같은 학교를 그 상대 교사들보다 학교의 관료화 정도를 낮게 지각하고, 전문지향성도 높고 동시에 관료지향성도 높은 것으로 나타났다.

(8) 한 교육구에 오래 근무한 교사들은 다른 교사들 보다 직무만족이 더 높았다.

(9) 높은 학위를 가진 교사일수록 관료지향성은 낮고 갈등은 높았으며, 직무만족은 낮았다.

VI. 결 론

연구결과로써 추출된 결론의 요약은 다음과 같다.

(1) 이 연구는 학교조직의 관료화 경향과 교사의 전문화 경향의 탐지로부터 출발되었었다. 즉, 조직과 그 조직 속에서 일하는 개인이 잘 조화를

이루어야 할 텐데 서로 반대 극으로 가는 경향이 교사의 갈등감과 직무만족감에 영향을 줄 것이라는 가정에서부터 연구가 출발되었던 것이다.

그러나 연구 결과 이 연구의 대상이 되었던 교육구는 학교조직의 관료화 정도가 낮은 것으로 교사들에 의하여 지각되고, 교사의 전문지향성은 높고, 관료지향성은 낮아서 갈등은 적은 반면 직무 만족은 아주 높은 것으로 나타났다. 이런 연구 결과로부터 이 교육구는 아주 이상적인 방향으로 나아가고 있으며, 건전한 조직이라고 할 수 있으며, 보다 확실한 연구 결과를 얻기 위해서는 보다 광범한 표집에 의한 연구가 요구된다.

(2) 교사들은 높은 "내적 만족"과 "비물질적 기회"에 낮은 갈등을 보고하였다. 이것은 교사들이 외적 요인보다 내적 요인에 의하여 더 동기부여가 될 수 있다는 것을 의미한다.

(3) 갈등에 있어서는 "학생과의 관계" "행정과의 관계" "직원과의 관계"에 보다 높은 갈등을 표시하였었다. 이것은 다른 요인들 보다 인간관계가 더 갈등의 요인이 된다는 것을 말해 준다.

(4) 이 교육구에서는 학교의 관료화 정도가 낮았다. 그리고 학교의 관료화가 직접석으로 갈능과 직부 만속에 영향을 수지는 못하는 것으로 나타났다. 그러나 간접적으로 하위척도를 통해서 영향을 주었었기 때문에 학교의 관료화는 조건적 변인이라고 결론을 내릴 수 있다. 즉, 만일 학교의 관료화 정도가 높으면 갈등과 직무 만족에 의의 있게 영향을 줄 것이라는 조건적 변인이라고 잠정적으로 결론짓는다.

(5) 갈등변인 역시 직접적으로 의의 있게 관련이 없었다. 이도 역시 학교의 관료화 정도가 높고 교사의 전문지향성이 높을 때(조건) 의의 있게 독립변인에 의하여 영향을 받는 조건변인이라고 잠정적으로 결론을 맺는다.

(6) 교사의 전문지향성과 관료지향성 둘 다 교사의 직무만족과 의의 있게 정적 상관관계에 있었고, 또 직무 만족의 예언변인이었다. 이것은 학교의 관료화 정도가 낮은 조건일 때 교사가 전문지향성이든 관료지향성이든, 어느 쪽으로든 강한 지향성을 갖고 적극적일 때 직무 만족이 높다는 것을

말한다. 둘 다 높을 때는 더 직무만족이 높다.

(7) 직무만족과 갈등은 부적 상관관계로 갈등이 없는 곳에서 만족이 생긴다.(Gerhardt, 1971, p.82)"는 종래의 연구결과를 재인식하였다.

(8) 인구변인들과 개인변인이 조직변인보다 더 밀접하게 갈등이나 직무만족에 영향을 주는 경향이었다(단 학교의 관료화가 낮을 때).

즉, 개인 변인이 조직행위에 영향을 더 주는 것이라 할 수 있다.

(9) 나이가 많고, 경험이 많고, 한 교육구에서 오래 근무한 교사들이 그 반대의 교사들보다 더 전문지향성이 높고, 직무 만족도 높고, 조직의 관료화를 낮게 지각하는 경향이어서 바람직한 방향이었다. 특히 나이 많고 경험 많은 교사가 더 전문지향이라는 것은 종래의 많은 연구들의 결과(Corwin, 1961)를 뒤엎은 것으로 이 교육구의 나이 먹은 교사들은 이상적인 방향으로 나아가고 있다고 할 수 있다.

(10) 높은 학위를 가진 교사들이 직무만족이 낮고, 반대로 높은 갈등을 갖는다는 것은 불행한 일이다. 학교체제가 높은 학위소지자에 대하여 충분한 보상을 해주지 못한다고 할 수 있다.

(11) 탐색 연구의 특질로 여러 통계적 방법으로 자료를 분석하였으나 결과는 거의 일치하였다.

(12) 네 개의 질문지를 하나로 합쳐서 사용하였으나 큰 문제가 없었으며, 신뢰도도 높아 후속연구에 문제가 없을 것이다.

(13) 갈등과 직무만족은 학교의 관료화 정도, 교사의 전문지향성과 관료지향성의 함수에 인구적 변인의 영향을 더한 산물이다. 즉, 갈등과 직무 만족=f(학교 관료화×교사의 전문지향성×관료지향성)+인구적 변인

(14) 이 탐색 연구의 경험에 바탕을 두어 광범하게 무선표집한다면 보다 완전한 본 연구가 가능하다고 본다.

이 연구는 이론·실제·연구에 많은 시사점을 주고 있으나 지면 관계로 여기서 생략한다.

참고문헌

Blua, P. M. and W. R. Scott. "The Nature and Types of Formal Organizations." In Fred D. Carver and Thomas J. Sergiovanni(eds.), *Organizations and Human Behavior: Focus on Schools,* N. Y.: McGraw-Hill Book Co., 1969, 5-18.

Compbell, R. E. and others. *The Organization and Control of American Schools*(3rd ed.). Columbus, Ohio: A Bell & Howell Co., 1975.

Cogan, M. L. "Toward a Definition of Profession." *Harvard Educational Review,* 23: 33-50. Winter, 1953.

Corwin, R. G. *Militant Professionalism: A Study of Organizational Conflict in High Schools.* N. Y.: Meredith Corporation, 1970.

Corwin, R. G. *Staff Conflict in the Public Schools. Washington,* D. C.: U. S. Office of Education, Cooperative Research Project No.2637, 1966.

Corwin, R. G. "The Professional Employee: A Study of Conflict in Nursing Roles." *American Journal of Sociology,* 66: 604-15, May, 1961.

Dimock, M. E. "Expanding Jurisdictions: A Case Study in Bureaucratic Conflict." In Robert Merton A. P. Gray, B. Hockey and H. C. Selvin(eds.), *Reader in Bureaucracy.* N. Y.: Free Press, 1965.

Etzioni A. *Modern Organizations.* Englewood Cliffs, New Jersey: Prentice-Hall, Inc., 1964.

Faber, C. F. and G. F. Shearron. *Elementary School Administration.* N. Y.: Halt, Rinehart and Winston, Inc., 1970.

Gerhardt, E. "Staff Conflict, Organizational Bureaucracy and Individual Satisfaction in Selected Kansas Districts." Unpublished doctoral disertation, The University of Kansas, 1971.

Getzels, J. W. "Administration as a Social Process." In Andrew W. Halpin(ed.), *Administrative Theory in Education.* Midwest Administration Center, University of Chicago, 1958. 150-65.

Getzels, J. W. and E. G. Guba. "Social Behavior and the Administrative Process." *School Review,* 65: 423-41. Winter, 1957.

Gorton, R. A. *Conflict, Controversy and Crisis in School Administration and Supervision: Cases and Concepts for the '70s.* Bubuque, Iowa: WM. C. Brown Co. Publishers, 1972.

Hall, R. H. "Professionalization and Bureaucratization." *American Sociological Review,* 33: 2-104. Feb., 1968.

Hall, R. H. "The Concept of Bureaucracy: An Empirical Assessment." American Journal of Sociology, 64: 32-40. Jul., 1963.

Hall, R. H. "An Empirical Study of Bureaucratic Dimensions and Their Relations to Other Organizational Characteristics." Unpublished doctoral dissertation, The Ohio State University, 1961.

Hencley, S. P., L. E. McClearly and J. H. McGrath. *Elementary School Principalship.* N. Y.: Dodd, Mead & Co., 1970.

Krajewski, R. J. "Secondary Principals Want to be Instructional's Leader." *Phi Deltat Kappan,* 60(1): 65, Sep., 1978.

Lieberman, M. *Education As A Profession.* Englewood Cliffs, N. J.: Prentice-Hall, Inc., 1956.

Lipham, J. M. and J. A. Hoth, Jr. *The Principalship: Foundations and Functions,* N. Y.: Harper & Row, Publishers, 1974.

MacKay, D. A. "Using Professional Talent in A School Organization," In Fred D. Carver and Thomas J. Sergiovanni(eds.), *Organizations and Human Behavior: Focus on Schools.* N. Y.: McGraw-Hill Book, 1969.

Otto, H. J. and D. C. Sanders, *Elementary School Organization and Adm-*

inistration(4th ed.), N. Y.: Appleton-Century-Crofts, 1964.

Owens, R. G. *Organizational Behavior in Schools,* Englewood Cliffs, N. J.: Prentice-Hall, Inc., 1970.

Parelius, A. P. and R. J. Parelius, *The Sociology of Education. Englewood Cliffs,* N. J.: Prentice-Hall, 1978.

Punch, K. F. "Bureaucratic Structure in Schools: Toward Redefinition and Measurement," *Educational Administration Quarterly,* 5(2): 43-57, Spring, 1969.

Robinson, N. "A Study of the Professional Role Orientations of Teachers and Principals and Their Relationship to Bureaucratic Character-istics of School Organizations." Unpublished doctoral dissertation, The University of Alberta, 1966.

Sergiovanni, T. J. and F. D. Carver. *The New School Executive: A Theory of Administration,* N. Y.: Harper & Row, 1973.

Time, 16 June, 1980. 54-63.

3. Bureaucratization and Professionalization Tendencies in Public Schools

I. INTRODUCTION

"Our society is an organization society. We are born in organizations, educated by organizations, and most of us spend much of our lives working for organizations."[2] For us to live without organizations is similar to a fish living without water. An organization is formulated because of our social and personal needs. Individuals devote their time and energy for the organization and in turn the organization rewards to individuals in payment for their service.

---

* 이 논문은 교육학연구 18권 2호(1980. 10) 한국교육학회에 김영식과 공동으로 발표한 것임. 박사학위논문의 골격이 되고 있어 많은 부분이 박사학위 논문의 내용과 중복되고 있으나 여기서도 앞으로 더 많은 논문이 나올 수 있음.

2) Amitai Etzioni, *Modern Organizations*(Englewood Cliffs, New Jersey: Prentice-Hall, Inc., 1964), p.1.

Weber defines the organization as "a system of continuous purposive activity of a specified kind."[3] Barnard emphasizes that organizational activities are "a system of consciously co-ordinated activities or forces of two or more persons."[4] The concept of organization as collectivities is introduced by Scott: "collectivities that have for the pursuit of relatively specific objectives on a more or less continuous basis."[5] An organization is "a social unit which pursues specific goals; its very raison d'etre is the service of these goals."[6]

The primary purpose of studying school organization, educational administration and of discussing professional and bureaucratic problems is to find the means to achieve effectively the ends of school. The writer interest in the definition of organization, and its purposes is in relation to the concept of school which is considered organization pursuing special goals. Needless to say, a common goal of the school is the growth and development of the students it serves. All too often, the goals of the school are forgotten and means become the master. In other words, we haveseen many ex-

---

3) Richard H. Hall, Organizations: Structure and Process, 2nd ed. (Englewood Cliffs, New Jersey: Prentice-Hall, Inc., 1972), p.18, citing Max Weber, The Theory of Social and Economic Organization, A. M. Henderson and Talcott Parsons, trans.(New York: The Free Press, 1947), p.151.
4) Chester I. Barnard, The Functions of the Executive(Cambridge: Harvard University Press. 1968), p.73.
5) W. Richard Scott, Theory of Organizations, in Robert E. L. Fris(ed.), Handbook of Modern Sociology(Chicago: Paul McNally and Co., 1964), p.488.
6) Amitai Etzioni, Op. Cit., p.5.

amples of "displacement of goal"[7] phenomenon. Clarification of the importance of goals is necessary at this point. Adding one more remark, school organization is the framework facilitating the achievement of the school's educational aims. School organization is "a means to end, not an end in itself."[8] In order words, organization is the servant of function.

We cannot negate the fact that school has traditionally adopted bureaucratic system as a means to achieve its goals. Particularly in the last decade bureaucratic culture has been increasing in school organization.

> As administering the financial, building, and maintenance functions of school operation have become more complex, responsibility and decision-making have become increasingly centralized and specialized. Central office staff have increased markedly, as have office personnel and paper work. Computers are being used more frequently as a means to standardize, regulate, and program decision-making[9]

As school size increases so does its complexity and the bureaucratic phenomenon is exacerated by other social and economic trends.

At the same time,

---

7) Robert G. Owens, Organizational Behavior in Schools(Englewood Cliffs, N. J.: Prentica-Hall, Inc., 1970), p.91.
8) Henry J. Otto and David C. Sanders, Elementary School Organization and Administration, 4th ed. (N. Y.: Appleton-Century-Crofts, 1964), p.22.
9) Thoms J. Sergiovanni and Fred D. Carver. The New School Executive: A Theory of Administration(N. Y.: Harper & Row, 1973), p.24.

Parallel change in complexity and sophistication have also occurred in the nature, scope, and breadth of educational programs and in instructional learning systems. This expansion of knowledge in teaching, content, and instructional technology is combined with a renewed and vigorous sense of responsibility for student welfare. A drive for status for teachers and an interest in upgrading teaching are related phenomena. All of these are symptoms of professionalism. Often they are expressed militantly as teachers seek to increase power in co-opting more responsibility and more authority.[10]

If professionalization of teachers and school bureaucratization tendencies are movement in parallel fashion in the same direction, they will not likely conflict with each other, but instead their complementarity will be helpful for the effective achievement of school goals. However, problems arise when they assume different organizational principles, and conflict is the outcome. For example, highly professionally oriented teachers will conflict severely with a highly bureaucratic administrator and organization, whereas highly bureaucratic oriented teachers will be more satisfied in their jobs. Conflict will be inversely proportional to teachers' job satisfaction and ultimately be reflected in classroom teaching and directed toward the goals of the school. These are the basic assumtions underlying in this paper. These assumtions will be dealt with further in research question section. Attention will now be given to the discussion of the definition of bureaucratization and its characteristics and tendencies in schools.

---

10) Ibid., p.25

II.
BUREAUCRATIZATION

A. Definition

A vast literature exists on the general topic of bureaucracy. There are some different approaches and controversies regarding the definition of bureaucracy. Following a broad review of the literature, Punch summarized these definitional issues by identifying three distinct approaches to such definition.

Firstly, bureaucracy, used globally in macroscopic, often historical and cross-cultural analysis, denotes the characteristically modern form of social organization: ours is "the bureaucratic society." In this view, bureaucracy is organizational form "designed to accomplish large scale administrative tasks by systematically coordinating the work of many individuals." It is here that bureaucracy becomes synonymous with large organization or formal organization. Secondly, bureaucracy refers in detail to the internal structure of organizations. The emphasis here is on differentiating between contemporary organizations. They differ in bureaucratization according to their stress in operation on typically bureaucratic characteristics. Thirdly, bureaucracy is used pejoratively to symbolize arbitrary power, inefficiency, red tape, and so on. Though value-loaded. this use points to the dysfunctions of bureaucracy, an area of considerable research interest.[11]

Dimock defines bureaucracy as "a way of life in which in-

---

11) Keith F. Punch, Bureaucratic Structure in Schools: Towards Redefinition and Measurement, Educational Administration Quarterly, 5: 2(Spring, 1968), p.44.

stitutions overshadow the individual."[12] Blau and Scott define it as "the amount of effort that an organization expands in maintaining itself rather than in pursuing its objectives."[13] Above both definitions are examples of the third approach of previous Punch's distinction. Owens' definition as "an administrative system that is adapted to the needs of large and complex organizations that deal with large members of clients,"[14] is the first approach.

The preference of the writers is the use of Punch's second approach, i. e. the internal characteristics or dimensions of bureaucracy as they allude to school organizations. In the second approach, dimensional approach, bureaucracy is separated into component parts or dimensions such as hierarchy of authority, division of labor, rules for incumbents, procedural specifications, impersonality and technical competence. Because according to Hall, "……this dimensional approach can be particularly useful in research when organizational structure is treated as an independent variable and factors such as conflict between professionals and non-professionals or interdepartmental relations are handled as dependent variables,"[15] this paper follows this dimensional approach.

---

12) March E. Dimock, Expanding Jurisdictions: A Case Study in Bureaucratic Conflict, in Robert K. Merton, A. P. Gary, B. Hockey and H. V. Selvin(eds.), Reader in Bureaucracy(N. Y.: Free Press, 1965).
13) P. M. Blau and W. R. Scott, Formal Organizations(San-Francisco: Chandler Publishing Co., 1962), p.8.
14) Owens, Op. Cit., p.56.
15) Richard H. Hall and Charles R. Tittle, A Note on Bureaucracy and Its Correlates, American Journal of Sociology, 72: 267(Nov., 1966).

Discussion of whether or not an organization is a bureaucracy is meaningless. The dimensions are "not all present not all absent in any one organization,"[16] but all organizations have some bureaucratic characteristics. Only existing differences are those differences in the degree of bureaucracy. This "degree of bureaucracy" makes the word "bureaucratization" possible. Complex administrative problems confront most large organization. Therefore "bureaucracy is not confined to the military and civilian branches of the government but is also found in business, unions, churches, universities, and even in baseball clubs."[17] Gouldner,[18] and Udy[19] suggest that bureaucracy is a condition that exists along a continuum, rather than being a condition that is either present or absent. "This point may be expanded to state that bureaucracy is a form of organization which exists along a number of continua or dimensions."[20] As a result, the term "bureaucratization" is more possible and appropriate in this paper to be used as a contrasting concept to professionalization.

Bureaucratization refers to the degree of emphasis on character-

16) Richard H. Hall, The Concept of Bureaucracy: An Empirical Assessment, American Journal of Sociology, 64: 33(July, 1963).
17) Peter M. Blau and Marshall W. Meyer, Bureaucracy in Modrn *Society, 2nd ed.(N. Y.: Random Houe, 1971), p.4.*
18) Alvin Gouldner, Disenssion, American Sociological Review, 8: 4 (August, 1948), p.396.
19) Stanley H. Udy, Jr., 'Bureaucracy' and 'Rationality' in Weber's Organizational Theory: An Empirical Study, American Sociological Review, 24(Dec., 1959). pp.781~95.
20) Richard H. Hall, The Concept of Bureaucracy: An Empirical Assessment, Op. Cit., p.33.

istics-since they very together-in the school organization.[21] In other words, bureaucratization is the level of bureaucraticness in an organization.

To summarize, bureaucracy is defined as a form of organization which exists along a number of continua or dimensions. These bureaucratic characteristics or dimensions are dealt with in just next section. The terms of "bureaucratic" or "bureaucratization" which have the meaning of changeable concept in the degree of bureaucracy, are preferably used present paper rather than the term "bureaucracy." One organization cannot be classified as bureaucracy or as not bureaucracy but can be classified as high bureaucratic or high bureaucratized organization, or as its opposite.

B. Characteristics of Bureaucracy

Many scholars have based their discussions of bureaucratic characteristics on Weber's theory. Although their expressions often differ, generally, have agreed on the commonalities of Weber's formulation.[22] Merton, Friedrick, Udy, Heady, Parsons, Berger, and Litwak have generally agreed on the bureaucratic characteristics as shown on the following table.[23]

---

21) Keith F. Punch, Op. Cit., p.53.
22) Max Weber, The Theory of Economic and Social Organization, trans. A. M. Henderson and Talcott Parsons(N. Y.: Free Press, 1947), pp.330~34, cited by Richard H. Hall, Intraorganzational Structural Variation: Application of the Bureaucratic Model, Administrative Science Quarterly 7(Dec., 1962). p.296.
23) Richard H. Hall, An Empirical Study of Bureaucratic Dimensions and Their Relations to Other Organizational Characteristic, (Ph. D. Dissertation, The

<Table 1> Characteristics of Bureaucracy as Listed by Major Authors

Dimensions of bureaucracy	Weber	Litwak	Friedrich	Merton	Udy	Hcady	Parsons	Berger
Hierarchy of authority	*	*	*	*	*	*	*	*
Division of labor	*	*	*	*	*	*	*	
Technically competent participants	*	*	*	*	*		*	*
Procedural devices for work situations	*	*	*	*		*		*
Rules governing behavior of members	*	*	*	*				*
Limited authorithy of office	*			*		*	*	
Dimensions of bureaucracy	Weber	Litwak	Friedrich	Merton	Udy	Hcady	Parsons	Berger
Differential rewards by office	*				*			
Impersonality of personal contact		*		*				
Administration separate from ownership	*	*						
Emphasis on written communication	*							
Rational discipline	*							

Hall used six dimensions as his Organizational Inventory

Ohio State University, 1961), p.7., Intraorganizational Structural Variation: Applications of the Bureaucratic Model and The Concept of Bureaucracy: An Empirical Assessment. Op. Cit., p.34.

subscale to measure the degree of bureaucratization of an organization. They are:

(1) The hierarchy of authority; the extent to which the locus of decision making is prestructured by the organization.

(2) Division of labor; the extent to which work tasks are subdivided by functional specialization decided by the organization.

(3) Rule for incumbents; the degree to which the behavior of organizational member is subject to organizational control.

(4) Procedural specifications; the extent to which organizational members must follow organizationally defined techniques in dealing with situations which they encounter.

(5) Impersonality; the extent to which both organizational members and outsiders are treated without regard to individual qualities.

(6) Technical competence; the extent to which organizationally defined "universalistic" standards are untilized in the personal selection and advancement process.[24]

As described in previous definitions, all characteristics are not either all present or all absent in any one organization and there will be difference in degrees to which they are present. In highly bureaucratic organizations all characteristics are present to a high degree, while the degrees differ in non-bureaucratized or professional organizations.

In Weber's view, bureaucracy is the most efficient form of organization because trained experts are best qualified to make correct decisions and because impersonal relationships guided by abs-

---

24) Ibid Dissertation., p.20., and Professionalization and Bureaucratization, American Sociological Review, 33: 1(Fed., 1968).

tract rules and coordinated by the authority hierarchy promote a rational and consistent accomplishment of organizational goals.[25]

When functioning properly, a bureaucracy is characterized by four distinct advantages that become increasingly important with the passage of time: (1) efficient, (2) predictable, (3) impersonal and

(4) fast.[26]

On the one hand bureaucracy has such strengths as above, on the other hand it is also a proven fact that went when dysfunctions of bureaucracy are emergent, criticisms of these qualifications quickly follow. It is unquestionably true that all bureaucracies are not equally effective, and a given bureaucracy varies in its state of health from time to time over the year. A typical catalogue of the more serious faults of bureaucracy would include tendencies toward the following:

(1) Bureaucracy encourages overconformity, inducing "group think."

(2) In time, bureaucracy modifies the very personality of bureaucrats such that they become the drab, colorless, routinized "organization men."

(3) Innovation ideas wilt from the distortion and long delays which result from communication overloading as attempts are made to transmit ideas through the hierachical layers of organization.

(4) Bureaucracy does not take into account the presence of informal organizations, including the primary groups to which role-incumbents belong.[27]

---

25) Charles F. Faber and Gilbert F. Shearron, Elementary School Administration(N. Y.: Holt, Rinehart and Winton, Inc., 1970), p.81.

26) Robert Presthus, The Organizational Society(N. Y.: Alfred A Knoph, Inc., 1962), p.5.

In many cases school bureaucracy also is disfunctional, as is evident encoded phrases such as "trained incapacity," "displacement of goals" and "bureaupathology." Because school organizations have different special goals from other organizations, bureaucracy in schools should be adapted well to the schools own nature. Anderson[28] uses the term "Janus like character" after discussing functional and dysfunctional consequences of bureaucratic rules. Gouldner[29] also discussed organizational rules with to "function" and "dysfunction," and Hay and Miskel devised the following tables to summarize his concepts and those concepts of Weberian model as conceived of existing on continua.

⟨Table 2⟩ Functions and Dysfunctions of the Weberian Model[30]

Dysfunction	Bureaucratic Characteristic	Function
Boredom ⟵	Division of Labor ⟶	Expertise
Lack of Morale ⟵	Impersonal Orientation ⟶	Rationality
Communication Blocks ⟵	Hierachy of Authority ⟶	Discplined Compliance and Coordination
Rigidity and Goal Displacement ⟵	Rules and Regulations ⟶	Continuity and Uniformity
Conflict between Achievement and Seniority ⟵	Career Orientation ⟶	Incentive

27) Robert G. Owens, Op. Cit., p.59.
28) James G. Anderson, Bureaucratic Rules: Bearers of Organizational Authority. Educational Administration Quarterly, 2 : 2(Winter, 1966), p.31.
29) Alvin Gouldner, Patterns of Industrial Bureaucracy(N. Y.: Free Press, 1964), pp.162~180.
30) Wayna K. Hoy and Cecil M. Miskel, Educational Administration:

We can know that the degree of function and dysfunction also exists on the continuum from following table as in the case of degree of bureaucratization. In brief summary of the several scholarly discussions of the characteristics of a bureaucracy which were reviewed, the writers have selected Hall's six characteristics as having the greatest unlity for his research: (1) Hierarchiy of Authority, (2) Division of Labor, (3) Rules for Incumbents, (4) Procedural Specification, (5) Impersonality, and (6) Technical Competence. These characteristics sometimes function well but sometimes are dysfunctional and these also can be expressed along a continuum.

C. Bureaucratization Tendencies in Schools

Bureaucratic characteristics tend to more visible and to be more emphasized. A survey of the literature indicated a number of symptoms of bureaucratization in schools. At the same time field observation supports these bureaucratization tendencies.

(1) The school system viewed as a bureaucratic organization exhibits a strong tradition of local, lay control over educators.[31] Employee status and the image of teachers are that of "public servant" of the community. Because this tradition is deeply rooted, this element has become a hinderance to the concept of professionalization of teaching.

(2) The explosion of pupil population and enlargement of school size tend to

---

Theory, Research and Practice(N. Y.: Random House, 1978), p.55.

31) Ronald G. Corwin, Militant Professionalism: A Study of Organizational Conflict in High Schools(N. Y.: Meredith, Corporation, 1970), p.7.

generate bureaucratization tendencies.[32] The 1932 enrollment to-
tal(elementary and secondary) was about 26,000,000 pupils;
thirty-five years later, 1967, 43,000,000 pupils were enrolled
in public schools.[33] Schools have developed from one-teach-
er, one-group, one-room types of schools[34] to present type
of schools which have large number of students. Despite the
recent declining enrollment phenomenon, large sizes continue
by way of consolidation. Organizational size is an important viable
of the degree of bureaucratization. Increased size is indication of
increased bureaucratization.[35]

(3) Modern urbanization and eduction in the number of local
school districts leads to school bureaucratization.[36] In 1932, the
first year for which reasonably accurate data a vailable, there
were over 127,000 public school districts in the United States.
Thirty-five years later, in 1967, there were fewer than 22,000 such
districts.[37] Thus the average number of pubils per district

---

32) Norman J. Bayan, The Emergent Role of the Teacher in the
    Authority Structure of the School, in Fred D. Carver and Thomas
    J. Sergiovanni(eda.), Organizations and Human Behavior: Focus
    on Schools(N. Y.: McGraw-Hill Book Co., 1969), p.200.
33) Charles F. Faber and Gilbert F. Shearron, Op. Cit., p.338.
34) National Education Association, Elementary School Organization
    (Washington, D. C.: National Education Association, 1961), p.50.
35) Richard H. Hall and Charles R. Tittle, A Note on Bureaucracy and
    Its Correlates, Op. Cit., p.269 and Terry George Tofte, The Role of
    the Elementary School Principal: A Review and Analysis of the
    Literature(M. A. Thesis, University of Minnesota, 1977), p.25.
36) Norman J. Boyan, Op. Cit., p.200, Roald F. Canpbell and others, The
    Organization and Control of American School, 3rd ed. (Columbus, Ohio: A
    Bell & Howell Co., 1975), p.85, and Harold J. McNally, Summing Up National
    Elementary Principal, 54: 1: 9 (Sep./Oct., 1974).
37) Charles F. Faber and Gilbert F. Shearron, Op. Cit., p.338.

was fewer than 200 in 1967, it was over 1,600, or eight times as great as before. These are some old statistical number, but it is fact that school district has been larger and larger. "The tremendous growth of cities during twentieth century and the dramatic increase in population of metropolitan areas within the last thirty years means that most pupils now live in cities and attend urban schools."[38] These phenomena mean that the bigger the district and urban school, the more centralized and consequently, the more bureaucratized the school system. Centralized authority is a symptom of bureaucratization. This is an indication of fact that the superintendent's power has been increasing. The superintendent presses the building principal who in turn, presses the teachers.

(4) School organization is becoming increasingly complex. Team teaching, differentiated staffing, open schools, various grouping of pupils, or other strategies necessarily increase school complexity. The more complex the organization, the greater the need for internal coordination, which enhances the power of administrators whose primary internal function is coordination.[39]

(5) Increased public expectation of the roles of the elementary school is accerlerating the school bureaucratization. The school is now expected to assume responsibility for the child's physical and mental health, his social and emotional adjustment,[40] food, transportation and even for

---

38) Ibid.

39) Ronald G. Corwin, Professional Persons in Public Organizations, Educational Administration Quarterly, 1: 3: 9(Autumn, 1965).

social work, as well as for his intellectual growth. These roles require more administrative functions, thus exacerbating school bureaucratization.

(6) School administration continuously increases principals who want to spend much of their time for instructional supervision, can not to do so because too much time of necessity is spent in administrative chores, clerical work, and management.[41] This increased administrative work is one of evidences of school bureaucratization tendencies.

(7) Federal, state and local pressures exert influence on individual schools which then tend to become more school uniformity.[42]

(8) The community and parents increasingly challenge the teaching profession.

> In recent years, many parent and community groups have grown increasingly dissatisfied with the effectiveness of school programs, achievements and personnel,... and in turn desire more meaningful involvement in the establishment and modification of school policies and in the evaluation of the extent to which the school and its personnel are meeting their responsibilities. These expectations represent a direct challenge to the professional norms of many educators.[43]

---

40) Charles F. Faber and Gilbert F. Shearron, Op. Cit., p.340.

41) Robert J. Krajewski, Secondary Principals Want to be Instructional Leader, Phi Delta Kappan, 60: 1: 65(Sep., 1978), Chales F. Faber and Gilbert F. Shearron, Op. Cit., p.214, and James M. Lipham and James A Hoeh, Jr., The Principalship: Foundations and Functions(N. Y.: Harper & Row, 1974), p.127.

42) Roald F. Campbell and others, Op. Cit., pp.22~27, pp.50~54 and p.74.

43) Richard A. Gorton, Conflict, Controversy and Crisis in School Administration

This lay interuption and challenge to the school lays more bureaucratic regulations and procedures, and at last enforces school bureaucratization and weaken teaching professionalization.

Ⅲ. PROFESSIONALIZATION

A. Definition

Bell[44] uses professionalization to mean that workers have received a technical training to achieve a recognized occupational competence. Becker[45] accepts the position that profession is an honorific title but Parsons[46] indicates that profession is an integral part of a complex, of which the system of higher education is also a part.

A typical approach to defining profession has been to list several characteristics of a profession and to use these as criteria in testing any given occupational group for professionalism.[47] This approach has, of course, limitations in that it is prem-

---

and Supervision: Issues, Cases and Concepts for the '70s(Dubuque, Iowa: W. M. C. Brown Co. Publishers, 1972), pp.24~25.

44) Gerald D. Bell, Formaliy Verus Flexibility in Complex Organizations, in Fred D. Carver and Thomas J. Sergiovanni(eds.), Op. Cit., p.73.

45) Howard S. Becker, The Nature of A Profession, in The National Society for The Study of Education, Education For the Professions, The Sixty-First Yearbook, Part Ⅱ. (1962), p.33.

46) Talcott Parsons, The Professional As Educator, in Arthur W. Foshay(ed.), The Professional As Educator(N. Y.: Teachers College Press, Columbia University, 1970), p.17.

47) D. A. Mackay, Using Professional Talent in a School Organization, in Fred D. Carver and Thomas J. Sergiovanni(eds.), Op. Cit., p.228.

ised on an ideal typology of professionalism and in that empirical measurement of the characteristics of the profession is usually difficult, if not impossible.

Except for the above cited references these have been many attempts, but they are usually lists of characteristics, standards, or criteria. There are also some operational definitions. However, "generally speaking, a mature profession is an organized work group that has a legal monopoly to establish procedures for recruiting and policing members and for maximizing control over a body of theoretical knowledge and applying it the solution of social problems."[48]

A clear definition at this time is difficult, and the writer can only conclude that professionalization is a drive for status as process and it must be viewed as a dimension on continuum[49] in the same manner that bureaucratization was defined. In order to clarify the concept of professionalization one must reflect upon the next section, characterisrics of profession.

B. Characteristics of Profession

Many scholars have pointed out the characteristics of profession, but content seems to be similar and only expressional terms differ. After quoting one of classic but famous characteristics of profession, the writer will determine common elements

---

48) Ronald G. Corwin, Militant Professionalism: A Study of Organizational Conflict in High School, Op. Cit., p.43.
49) William J. Goode, The Theoretical Limits of Professionalization, in Arthur W. Foshay(ed.), The Professional As Educator(N. Y.: Teachers College Press, Columbia University, 1970), p.46.

expressed in the literature.

Myron Lieberman regards a profession as an occupation which exhibits the following characteristics:

(1) A unique, definite, and essential social service.

(2) An emphasis upon intellectual techniques in performing its service.

(3) A long period of specialized training.

(4) A broad range of autonomy for both the individual practitioners and for the occupational group as a whole.

(5) An acceptance by the practitioners of broad personal responsibility for judgments made and acts performed within the scope of professional autonomy.

(6) An emphasis upon the service to be rendered, rather than the economic gain to the practitioners, as the basis for the organization and performance of the social service delegated to the occupational group.

(7) A comprehensive self-governing organization of practitioners.

(8) A code of ethics which has been clarified and interpreted at ambiguous and doubtful points by concrete cases.[50]

The following table summarizes the reveiew of literature as the case of characteristics of bureaucracy.

---

50) Myron Lieberman, Education As A Profession(Englewood Cliffs, N. J.: Prentice-Hall, Inc., 1956), pp.1~5.

〈Table 3〉 Characteristics of Profession as Listed by Major Authors

Characteristics of profession	Lieberman	NEA[51]	Hoy	Mackay	Corwin	Flexner[52]	Kornhauser[53]	Goode[54]	Hall[55]
Unique social	*				*				
Intellectual techniques	*	*	*		*	*	*		
Specialized training	*	*		*		*		*	
Autonomy of Professional	*		*		*		*		*
Responsibility	*					*	*		
Service to clients	*	*		*	*	*		*	*
Self-governing	*	*	*	*	*				*
Code of ethics	*		*	*					
Colleague, Association		*	*	*	*	*		*	*
Career, Research		*			*	*	*		

From these characteristics can be construed some common elements, such as social service, intellectualism, autonomy,

51) National Education Association, Division of Field Service, The Yardstick of A Profession, Institutes on Professional and Public Realions(Washington, D. C.: The National Education Association, 1948), p.8., cited by T. M. Stinnett, Professional Problems of Teachers(N. Y.: The Macmillan Co., 1968), pp.54~55.

52) Abraham Flexner, Is Social Work A Profession? in Proceedings of the National Conference of Charities and Correction(Chicago: Hildmann Printing Co., 1915), pp.576~90, cited by Howard S. Becker, The Nature of A Profession, Op, Cit., pp.27~28.

53) William Kornhauser, Scientists in Industry: Conflict and Accomo*dation, with the assistance of Harren O. Hagstrom(Berkeley: Univer*sity of California Press, 1962), p.8.

54) William Goode, The Librarian: From Occupation to Profession? Library Quarterly, 31(Oct., 1961), pp.306~320.

55) Richard H. Hall. Professionalization and Bureaucratization. Ameri*can Sociological Review 33: 1(Feb, 1968). pp.93~104.

responsibility, service, continuous growth, life long career, specialized knowledge, long professional preparation, professional organization, and code of ethics.

Teachers who consider themselves as professionals are now challenging the traditional bureaucratic structure of school organizations with claims of their special competence and desire for more control over their own work. This professional image propels teaching in quite another direction. The professional characteristics tend to differ from the characteristics of bureaucracy discussed earlier. When different both professional and bureaucratic characteristics exist commonly in same school, conflicts are predicted.

As previously explained in this paper, professionalization is expressed along continuum from nonprofessional through semiprofessional to a ful-fledged professional. Etzioni[56] classifies public school as semiprofessional and many other do not think of public school teachers as having the same professional level of doctors or lawyers.

However, according to one survey, over ninety percent of the public said that teaching was a profession.[57] For the purposes of present paper it is helpful to accept Etzioni's classification and the fact that teachers are more militant to recognize teaching as ful-fledged profession.

As a brief summary, professionalization has a number of different characteristics which will become sources of conflict.

---

56) Amitai Etzioni, Op. Cit., p.87.
57) Ronald G. Corwin, Militant Professionalism, Sociology of Education, 38(1965), p.312.

C. Professionalization Tendencies in Schools

The traditional bureaucratic viewpoint is now being challenged by the progressively vocal claims of teachers that they have special competence and hence deserve more control over their own work. Detailed discussion of these kind of tendencies follows.

(1) Teacher education and training standards have become higher and longer and are projected to be continuously higher in the future. A long period of specialized education is an important characteristic of professionalization. In 1925, few teachers possessed bachelor's degrees, but 1970, almost 95% held bachelor's degrees, and more than 28% held master's degrees; some states reported more than half of their elementary teachers as holding master's degrees.[58] Ten years later 1980, their educational level might be produced to be far higher than in 1970.

(2) Modern teaching technologies-such as computer-assisted instruction, teaching machines, team teaching etc-necessarily demand more specialized training which is one characteristics of increased professionalization. Complexity and sophistication have also occured in the nature, scope, and breadth of educational programs and instructional learning systems. This expansion of knowledge in teaching, content, and instructional technology is combined with a renewed and vigorous sense of responsibility for student welfare. A drive for status for teachers and an interest in upgrading teaching are related phenomena. All of these are symptoms

---

58) Stephen P. Hencley, Lloyed, E. McCleary and J. H. McGrath, *Elementary School Principalship(N. Y.: Dodd, Mead & Co., 1970), p.6.*

of professionalism.[59]

(3) Teacher militancy has increased and the power of professional organizations is becoming stronger. These are symptoms of the process of professionalization. The stronger the professional organization is, the more professionalization teachers' status become.

(4) The reference group of teachers is changing. In the past, teachers would look to their superior, the school principal to receive help, but now most of the help they obtain comes from fellow teachers, and some comes from university professors. For special assistance, the teachers turn to colleagues whom they view as fellow experts with the authority of competence. This trend will be continuously strengthened in the future.[60]

(5) The fact that teachers and administrators began to have different professional organization such as AFT, AASA, NAESP, NASSP, etc, is a tendency toward professionalization functionally differentiating each other. This indicates a feeling that teaching and administration are different from each other in unque professionality.

(6) The increase of new professional positions in elementary schools such as guidance counselors, curriculum materials specialists,[61] and partial departmentalization are indicators of a process of professionalization.

In conclusion many teachers strongly argue that they are

59) Thomas J. Sergiovanni and Fred D. Carver(ed.). Op. Cit., p.25.
60) Charles F. Faber and Gilbert F. Shearron, Op. Cit., p.378.
61) Ibid., p.352.

professional and therefore should have academic autonomy and total authority over matters concerning instruction, curriculum, teaching materials and classroom environment.

IV. BUREAUCRATIZATION, PROFESSIONALIZATION AND CONFLICT

A. The Relationship of Bureaucratization and Professionalization

As one looks about, bureaucratization and professionalization differ from each other in many ways. However, these diverse concepts tend to be emphasized commonly in schools. Namely, school organization is increasingly becoming bureaucratized, while at the same time teachers want to be recognized as professionals and are tending toward professionalization.

The purpose of this section is to compare directly the two different principles. Because these differences tend to become the sources of conflicts when, for example, different behaviors are expected from a teacher, and begin to conflict.

Corwin[62] contrasts these two principles on the following table. He subsequently devised the teacher's Employee(Bureaucratic) and Professional Orientation Scale.

---

62) Ronald G. Corwin, Professional Persons in Public Organization, Op. Cit., p.7.

<Table 4> Contrasts in Bureaucratic-and Professional-Employee Principles

organizational Characteristics	Bureaucratic-Employee Expectations	Professional-Employee Expectations
1. Standardization		
(1) Routine of work	Stress on uniformity of Clients' problem	Stress of on uniqueness of clients' problem
(2) Continuity of Procedure	Stress on records and files	Stress on research and change
(3) Specificity of rules	Rules stated as universal; and specific	Rules stated as alterna tives; and diffuse
2. Specialization		
(1) Basic of division of labor	Stresss on efficieny of techniques; task orientation	Stress on achievement of goals; client orientation
(2) Basis of skill	Skills based primarily on practice	Skills based primarily on monopoly of knowledge
3. Authority		
(1) Responsibility for decision-making	Decisions concerning application of rules to routine problems	Decisions concerning policy in professional matters and unique problems
(2) Basis of autononomy	Rules sanctioned by public	Rules sanctioned by legally sanctioned professions.
	Loyalty to the organization and to superiors.	Loyalty to professional association and clients.
	Authority from office (position)	Authority from professional competence

⟨Table 5⟩ Teachers' Orientation Scale

Bureaucration Orientation Scale	Professional Orientation Scale
1. Administrative orientation	1. Client orientation
2. Loyalty to the organization	2. Colleague orientation
3. Experience orientation	3. Monopoly of knowledge
4. Standardization orientation	4. Decision making
5. Rules and procedures orientation	
6. Orientation to the public	

The term, 'orientation' refers to a person's conception of his total environment;……. Orientations are a part of a value system. As such they are normative, representing a person's beiefs about what ought to occur, although they are less diffuse than attitudes which(in addition to beliefs) include feelings and emotions.[63]

Although there are some similarities between the concepts of professionalization and bureaucratization, Corwin indicated only differences and contrasts, but did not mention common elements. Avoiding detailed explanation, Hoy and Miskel's table[64] summarizes major similarities and contrasts between professional orientation and bureaucratic orientation.

---

63) Ronald G. Corwin, Staff Conflicts in the Public Schools Cooperative Research Proiect(Department of Sociology and Anthropology, The Ohio State University, 1996), p.116.
64) Wayne K. Hoy and Cecil M. Miskel, Op. Cit., p.71.

<Table 6> Basic Characteristics of Professional and Bureaucratic Orientations:
Similarities and Contrasts

Professional Orientation		Bureaucratic Orientation
Technical Expertise	SIMILARITIES	Technical Expertise
Objective Perspective		Objective Perpective
Impersonal and Impartial Approach		Impersonal and Impartial Approach
Service to Clients		Service to Organization
Colleague-Oriented Reference Group	MAJOR SOURCES OF CONFLICT	Hierarchical Orientation
Autonomy in Decision Making		Disciplined Compliance
Self-Imposed Standards of Control		Subordinated to the Organization

B. Conflict

We can find basic sources of conflicts from the above tables of contrasting different principles. These conflicts are not alway individual-organizational conflict from individual personality, but parts of system conflict.

The writer is going to find some examples of potential sources of conflict in schools.

(1) While professionals are obliged to serve the best interests of their clients and to provide them with needed services regardless of their considerations, tension exists between the professionals and clients. For example, when a problem student is found, static bureaucratic rules will demand punishment of the student by school rule and due process, but the professional orientation teacher will argue this student is in

a special situation and punishment should be suited to the individual case.

(2) When a bureaucratic school functions in a routinized and uniform way but professional teachers dislike this kind of routinization, administration is challenged for insistence upon extra of worthless paperwork.

(3) Much organizational tension can be attributed to the fact that administrators frequently supervise and evaluate professional subordinates who are more competent in their work than superordinates.[65] The problem of evaluation is compounded by the fact that the reputations of professionals are based on the opinions of their professional colleagues outside the organization.

(4) Bureaucratic standardization probably discourages a professionals creativity and original thought. Bureaucrats are too busy to follow the standardized rules and procedures to create new idea. But professionals persue new one and conflict is natural.

(5) In bureaucratic organization, one derives his authority primarily from the position that he holds, but professionals attach their competency as the base of their authority. Therefore professional authority will conflict with hierarchical authority.

(6) Professional teachers argue their autonomy in classroom control and curriculum management.

(7) Professional teachers are not satisfied only by participating in decision-making but demand actual decision-mak-

---

65) Alvin W. Gouldner, Organizational Tensions, in Robert Merton et al(ed.), Sociology Today,(N. Y.: Basic Books 1959), pp.400~28.

ing in matters their professional area.

We can assume that professionally oriented teachers will be in more conflict than bureaucratically oriented teachers in bureaucratic organization. Thus, it is predicted that patterns of conflict, such as open discussion, heated discussion, major incident, and group conflict will predominate.

A little conflict is helpful for organizational health and development and is a sign of health,[66] but over conflict is harmful to an individual teacher's mental, physical health as well as to the school organization. Serious conflict having serious repercurssions on the well-being of the professionals and the organization are said to: (1) affect job performance, (2) cause high teacher turnover, (3) tension, psychiatric problem and neurosis, (4) affect human relations, (5) increase absenteeism, sabotage and frustration, and (6) foster militancy.[67]

In summary professionalization and bureaucratization both can be indicated on the continuum, as having different characteristics from each other but with some similarities. Both tend to be emphasized at the same time in school organizations. The professional model originally is changed form from bureaucratic model and is adapted model to organizational conditions. That

---

66) E. Robert Lacrosse, Thouht for New Administrators, in Dorothy W. Hewes(ed.), Administration: Making Programs Work for Children and Families(Washington, D. C.: National Association for the Education of Young Children, 1979).

67) Sam Hwan Joo, A Study on Professionally Oriented Teachers' Coflicts in Bureaucratic School Organization, The Journal of Educational Research, 14: 3: 168(Published by The Korean Society for The Study of Education, Oct., 1976).

is, the concepts of professionalization and bureaucratization were formerly considered to be not antagonistic but complementary. However, in order to compare or to contrast major concept of bureaucratization to major concept of professionalization, the writer needs to reduce the concept of bureaucratization, four dimensions among Hall's six dimensions except two professional characteristics, the division of labor and technical competence which were included in ideal bureaucracy.

V. POSSIBLE RESEARCH QUESTIONS AND EMPIRICAL LITERATURE

This section is organized so as to summarize the research frame-work. first, and then to extract the major research questions and the empirical literature related to these questions.

A. Research Framework

Teachers perform in school organization which have certain role structures and expectations; these represent the nomothetic dimensions, and at the same time have their own personality structures and need-dispositions which represent the idiographic dimensions. In the past, many researches focused on the conflict between individual personalty and needs, and institutional roles and expectations, but the writers add one more line to the Getzels-Guba model; that is, professional roles and expectations. Modern school organization is increasingly becoming bureaucratized, while on the other hand the teaching job is increasingly requiring greater professionalization. As discussed earlier, bureaucratic and professional concepts have different characteristics and expectations, and thus require different roles and expectations from the same individual teacher. The next figure explains research framework and summarizes previous whole discussion.

Figure. 7. Research Framework

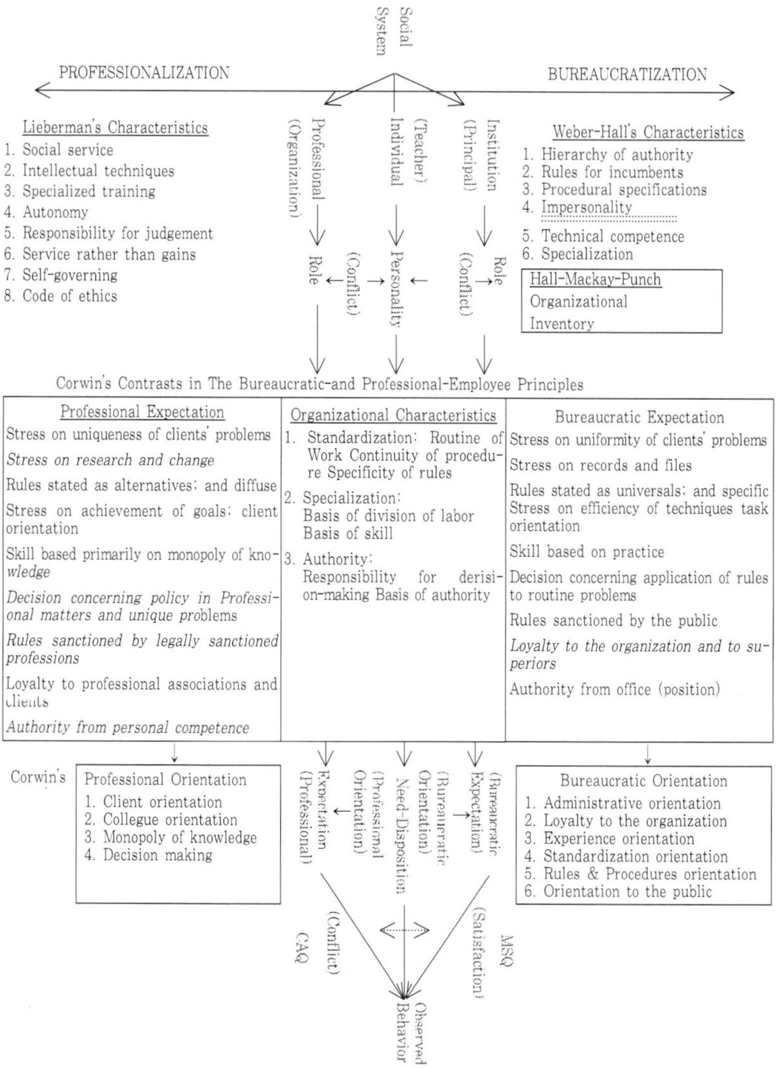

At the left side, Lieberman's professional characteristics produce Corwin's professional expectations which produce his

Professional Orientation Scale and in turn produces "Conflict." Right side also produces different results, "Job Satisfaction." Middle line, individual will conflict or will be satisfied between different.

The tendency for teachers to act properly toward bureaucratic expectations is defined as "Bureaucratic Orientation" measured by Corwin's "Bureaucratic Orientation Scale (BOS)," in opposition, the tendency for teachers to act professional expectations is termed as "Professional Orientation," measured by Corwin's "Professional Orientation Scale(POS)." In Getzels-Guba Model, organizational behavior can be viewed as the product of interaction; $B=f(R \cdot P)$, where B=organizational behavior, R=role, and P=personality. Professionally oriented teacher's behavior is expected to be significantly different from bureaucratically oriented techer's, in high bureaucratic school. That is, their behavior will be high "Conflict," and bureaucratically oriented teach's behavior will be "Satisfaction."

Basic assumptions underlying this framework are that "high professionally oriented teachers in high bureaucratic schools-measured by Punch's Organizational Inventory(OI)[68] -will conflict more than high bureaucratic oriented teachers-when measured by Gerhardt's Conflict Assessment Questionnaire(CAQ)"[69]-and that high bureaucratically oriented.

---

68) Keith F. Punch. Bureaucratic Structure in Schools and Its Relationship to Leader Behavior: An Empirical Study(Ph. D. Dissertation, The University of Toronto, 1967).
69) Ed Gerhardt, Staff Conflict, Organizational Bureaucracy and Individual Satisfaction in Selected Kansas School Districts (Doctoral Dissertation,

<Table 8> Basic Assumptions

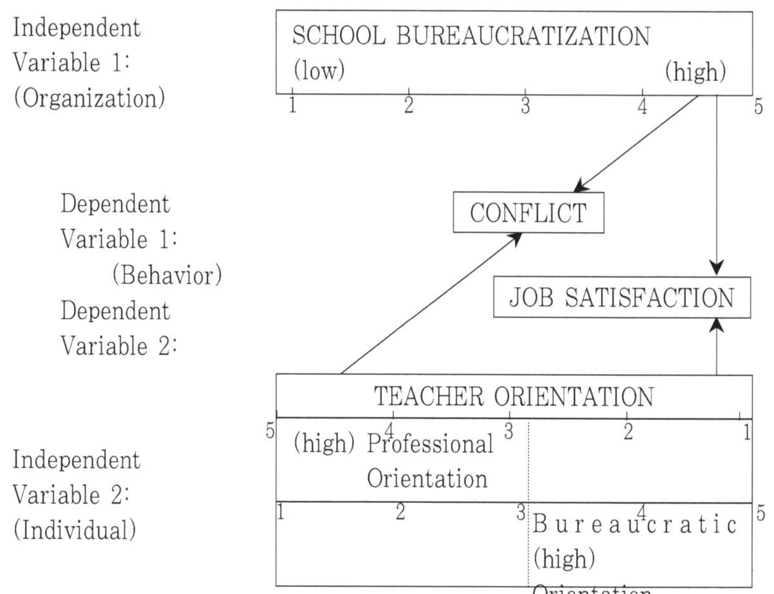

teachers even in high bureaucratic schools will be more satisfied than high professionally oriented teachers-measured by
Minnesota Satisfaction Questionnaire(MSQ).[70] In other words,
conflict will appear as professionally oriented teacher's behavior and satisfaction as bureaucratically oriented teacher's.
The writer identifies four variables; as independent variables,
(1) School Bureaucratization, (2) Teachers' Professional and
Bureaucratic Orientation, and as dependent variables, (3)

The University of Kansas, 1971).

70) D. J. Weiss and others, Manual for the Minnesota Satisfaction
Questionnaire, Minnesota Studies in Vocational Rehabilitation: 22,
Bulletin 46(Industrial Relation Center, University of Minnesota,
Oct., 1967).

Conflict, and (4) Job Satisfaction.

Basic assumptions with four variables are summarized in ⟨Table 8⟩

B. Research Questions and Empirical Studies

Research questions come from four variables identified in above section and from their combinations.

(1) Are there significant differences in (a) teachers' orientations, (b) perception of bureaucratization, (c) conflict, and (d) job satisfaction in terms of (a) teaching experience, (b) level of academic degree, (c) sex?

This is a question for demographic study. As separate questions; who are the more professionally oriented teachers?; who are the more bureaucratically oriented teachers?; who perceives as more bureaucratic in the same school?; who experience more satisfied?

These questions are summarized in the following table.

⟨Table 9⟩ Demographic Study

Demographic Characteristics	Variables	Teacher Orientation		Perception of Bureaucratization	Conflict	Job Satisfaction
		Profess-ional	Bureaucratic			
Teaching experience	High Low	?	?	?	?	?
Level of academic degree	Over MA Under BA	?	?	?	?	?
Sex	Male Female	?	?	?	?	?

Empirical Studies Related to Professional Orientation

According to Colombotos' study,[71] academic males are more profe ssional than nonacademic men in teaching; teachers with advanced training are found to be more professional than those less well educated; liberal arts graduates are more professional than graduates of teachers colleges; secondary teachers are more professionally oriented than elementary teachers; and generally, women tend to be more professionally oriented.

Kuhlman and Hoy's study[72] adds some new and different results. Experience in the school organization for beginning teachers is related to decreased professional orientation, but there is no significant difference between the professional orientations of men and women, and between elementary and secondary teachers.

Korncher's study[73] says that relatively more males than females are classified as professional, but Corwin[74] gets results that professional orientations do not differ between the sexes or different age groups. Fris[75] concluded his study by saying

---

71) John L. Colombotos, Sources of Professionalism: A Study of High School Teachers, Cooperative Research Project of the U. S. Office of Education Project No.330(Ann Arbor: Department of Sociology, University of Michigan, 1962)
72) Edward L. Kuhlman and Wayne K. Hoy, The Socialization of Professionals into Bureaucracies: The Beginning Teacher in the School, The Journal of Educational Administration, 7: 2(Oct., 1974), pp.28~27
73) Mildred Kornacher, How Urban High School Teachers View Their Job, U. S. Office of Education Cooperative Research Project, No.5-8144(1966).
74) Ronald G. Corwin, Militant Professionalism: A Study of Organizational Conflict in High Schools, op. Cit., p.184.
75) Joe Fris, Professionalization and Militancy Among Ontario Secondary School Teachers(Ph. D. Dissertation, University of Toronto, Canada, 1976)

that differences in professional aspiration are related in sex and teaching experiences.

Robinson[76] has research results which indicate that teachers with a university degree collectively more professionalism than those without degrees. From a study of officers, social workers and teachers, Peabody[77] points out that younger and career oriented police officers with college training, and small-town cops attach importance to authority of competence, and that elementary school teachers attach importance to authority of professional competence and that is related to amount of graduate education.

As we see from the above empirical researches, the results are inconsistent. Wells[78] recommens that further study is needed in order to know the effect such variables as age, sex, race, educational training and teaching experience have upon militancy and professional orientation. The researchers also interested in further determination of who are the more professionally oriented teachers. Because age is closely related to teaching experiences, it is not included as a characteristic

---

76) N. Robinson, A Study of the Professional Role Orientation of Teachers and Principals and Their Relationship to Bureaucratic Characteristics of School Organizations(Ph. D. Dissertation, The University of Alberta, 1966).

77) Robert L. Peabody, Perceptions of Organizational Authority: A Comparative Analysis, Administrative Science Quarterly, 6(March 1962), pp.463~82.

78) John Carroll Wells, Teacher Militancy and Professional Orientation Among Black Teachers in New York State(Ed. D. Dissertation, New York University, 1976).

variable.

Empirical Studies Related to Bureaucratic Orientation

Similar confusion exists concerning Bureaucratic Orientation as does the research on Professional Orientation. Berger[79] indicates that the older, western-exposed civil servants are more highly predisposed to emphasize rationality, efficiency, and universality and less predisposed to emphasize the power of position, the authority of the superior official, and the propriety of obedience by the subordinate, and that age, civil-service grade, social mobility and job satisfaction related to bureaucratic scale. Previously, Peabody's study gives some suggestions about age, experience and level of education for the demographic study of bureaucratic orientation.

Wermuth[80] also indicates that age, sex, marital status, level of education and tenure status are related to loyalty and acceptance of rules.

Corwin's above cited study points out that men and younger teachers have statistically lower bureaucratic orientation than their opposites. Previously Kuhlman and Hoy's study results in no significat difference between the bureaucratic orientations of men and women, but that experience for beginning teachers is related to increased bureaucratic orientation. These kinds of confusion stimulatce the writer to study demographic charateristics.

---

79) Morroe Berger, Bureaucracy East and West, Administrative Science Quarterly, 1(Sep. 1956), pp.518~29.
80) Melvin Allen Wermuth, Relationship of Professional of Orientation and Organizational Involvement to Organizational Commitment(Ed. D. Dissertation, Columbia University, Teachers College, 1977).

Empirical Studies Related to Perception of Bureaucratization

Sorensen[81] points out from his research that less experienced persons in the lower positions fell that there is too much bureaucracy, while the more experienced people in higher positions feel that there is too little. This phenomenon can be explained by Corwin's[82] and Kuhlman and Hoy's socialization studies. Beginners of teaching tend to perceive the same school structure more bureaucratically. As they gain experience they begin to bureaucracy.

The writers are interested in the fact that teachers differently perceive same degree of school bureaucratization.

Empirical Studies Related to Conflict

Only one demographic study in this area is appropriate. Miskel and Gerhardt's study concludes that younger, males and secondary teachers experience higher conflict than their female and elementary counter-parts.

Empirical Studies Related to Job Satisfaction

Miskel and Gerhardt's study[83] concludes that male and secondary teachers are less satisfied.

---

81) James Elliot Sorensen, Professional and Bureaucratic Organizations in Large Public Accounting Firms(Doctoral Dissertation, The Ohio State University, 1965).

82) Ronald G. Corwin, The Professional Employee : A Study of Coflict in Nursing Roles, American Journal of Sociology, 66(May, 1961), pp.604~15.

83) Cecil Miskel and Ed Gerhardt, Perceived Bureaucracy, Teacher Conflict, Central Life Interests, Voluntarism, and Job Satisfaction, The Journal of Educational Administration, 12: 1(May, 1674), pp.84-97.

(2) Is there a relationship of teachers' professional and bureaucratic orientation?

Because professional and bureaucratic concepts are not only
different from each other, but also complementary to each
other, a negative relationship is theoretically expected. However empirical studies indicate that there is no significant relationship between teachers' bureaucratic and professional
orientation. This phenomenon can explained by teachers' socialization to bureaucracy by means of their increasing experience.
If the teachers' professional and bureaucratic orientations are
a negative relationship, we need not one of two in predicting
dependent variables, conflict and job satisfaction. Many empirical studies (Corwin, 1965; Berger, 1956; Punch, 1967;
Kuhlman, 1974) reported that there was no significant relationship between professional and bureaucratic orientation
and explained that this phenomenon as socialization to school
bureaucratization. Corwin's study concluded that total professional orientation scale score were not significantly correlated with total bureaucratic orientation scale scores. Therefore,
combinations such as High Professional-Low Bureaucratic
Orientation were possible. Berger indirectly suggested there
was no relationship between the two orientations, saying that
those high on professionalism were also high on the bureaucratic scale, and among those low on professionalism, vir-
tually the same proportion, were also higher on the bureaucratic scale. He once more emphasized that bureaucratic and
professional predisposition may not be unitary tendencies.

Kuhlman and Hoy had interest in socialization of professionals to bureaucracy. The results of their study indicated that experience in the school organization for beginning teachers was related to increased bureaucratic orientation and decreased professional orientation. Their conclusion reconfirmed the belief that bureaucratic and professional orientations are not significantly correlated with each other. Punch's factor analysis results support the idea that professionalization and bureaucratization imply not an antagonistic but complementary relationship. Washburne[84] pointed out problem of Professionals in bureaucracy was that the teacher might have a role conception stressing his professional training but bureaucracy didn't do much about rewarding the good teacher.

In view of these controversies, the writers suggest the necessity of doing a test. From this educational administrators would have some implications for staff development and for personnel management.

(3) Are there differences between professionally and bureaucratically oriented teachers in their perception of bureaucratization?

Do professionally oriented teachers perceive the same school structure as higher bureau-Oratization than bureaucratically oriented teachers? It is important whether school organization is a strict bureaucracy or not, but more interest

---

84) Chandler Washburne, The Teacher in the Authority System, *Journal of Educational Sociology*, 39 (May, 1957), pp.390~394.

is how teachers perceive their school organization. If teachers perceive the same school differently and then behave differently toward school administration, then teachers' perception of bureaucracy gives rise to another problem in educational administration. These are comparisons among subgroups such as HP-HB, HP-LB, LP-HB, and LP-LB in perception of school bureaucratization.

Empirical Studies Related to Question #(3)

According to Hall's study[85] because generally professionalization and bureaucratization have negative relationships and the more professionalized groups are found in less bureaucratic settings, there will be a possibility that professionally and bureaucratically oriented teachers perceive their schools differently.

It was very difficult for the writer to find related empirical studies.

(4) Do the independent variables: school bureaucratization and teacher professional and bureaucratic orientation predict the dependent variable, conflict?

This question can be divided into four parts.

(a) Which is the best predictor among school bureaucratization, professiona orientation and bureaucratic orientation?

---

85) Richard H. Hall, Professionalization and Bureaucratization, *American Sociological Review, 33: 1(Fed., 1968), pp.92~104.*

This is a question for comparison of independent variables to predict the dependent variable, conflict. Spence[86] concluded that the School Organizational Inventory to measure the degree of school bureaucratization is not usable in predicting conflict.

There are some studies that indicates that school structure and teachers' professional and bureaucratic orientation are related to the intensity of conflict, but there are few studies that shown which is a better predictor of conflict.

(b) *Do professionally oriented teachers experience more role conflict than bureaucratically oriented teachers in considering* the organizational variable, the degree of school bureaucratization as constant?

Empirical Studies Related to Question #(4)-(b)

Generally professionally oriented teachers experience more conflict in school organization(Scott,[87] Lusthaus,[88] and Corwin[89]. However, the configuration of professional and employee role conceptions seem to be more important than either role considered separately.[90] Corwin[91] found that High Professional-Low

---

86) James A. Spence, Perceived Bureaucracy, Teacher Work Value, Conflict and Organizational Effectiveness(Ed. D. Dissertation, University of Kansas, 1978).

87) Richard W. Scott, Reactions to Supervision in a Heteronomous Professional Organization, Administrative Science Quarterly, 10: 1(June, 1965), pp.65~81.

88) Everyn Weinrub Lusthaus, Role Coflict of Special Education Teachers: Effects of Organizational Strncture of Schools(Ph. D. Dissertation, State University of New York at Buffalo, 1974).

89) Ronald G. Corwin, Professional Persons in Public Organizations, Op. Cit.,

Bureaucratic Orientation teachers conflict more than those with Low Professional-High Bureaucratic Orientation. Freed's research[92] suggested professional's conflict indirectly. His research suggests that there is significant correlation between teachers grievances and the degree of professional latitude.

If professionally oriented teachers conflict more than bureaucratically oriented teachers, to which subscale will there be more conflict; to Desirable physical work conditions, to Material Inducements, to Personal, non-material opportunities, to School priorities and standards, to Decision-sharing, to Student relationships, to Administrative relationship, and to Staff relationship?[93] This is a question of major interests of the writer.

As another question, are there significant difference between professionally and bureaucratically oriented teachers in experiencing conflict?

(c) Are there significant difference in conflict between teachers in High Bureaucratic schools and in Low Bureaucratic schools?

In other question, will teachers in High Bureaucratized schools

---

90) Ronal G. Corwin, Militant Professionalism, Initiative and Compliance in Public Education, Sociology of Education, 38(1965), pp.310~31.
91) Ibid.
92) Alfred Sherwood Freed, A Descriptive Study of the Relationship of Organizational Structure and Teacher Professional Orientation to Teachers' Grievances(Ed. D. Dissertation, New York University, 1979), Dissertation Abstracts International, 40: 3: 1175-76A(Sep., 1979).
93) Gerhardt's Conflict Assessment Questionnaire Subscales, Ed Gerhardt, Op. Cit.

conflict more than teachers in Low Bureaucratized schools? The previously cited Lusthaus study suggested that organizational structure was related to role conflict, and also Miskel and Gerhardt concluded that the relationships were consistent with conflict increasing as the bureaucratic dimensions increased. However, Stahl's study[94] results concluded that bureaucratism might not influence attrition and that indiscriminate utilization of Hall's Organizational Inventory was inappropriate.

In this question the relationship between school bureaucratization and conflict is dealt with.

(d) Are there interaction effect by School Bureaucratization and Professional and Bureaucratic Orientation in predicting conflict?

In other question, will High Professional-Low Bureaucratic Orientation Teachers in High Bureaucratic Schools conflict more than compared with any other combination? Which subgroup teachers will conflict more? Possible subgroups by considerations are (1) HP-LB in HBS(school), (2) HP-LB in LBS, (3) LP-LB in HBS. (4) LP-LB in LBS. (5) LP-HB in HBS, (6) LP-HB in LBS, (7) HP-HB in HBS, and (8) HP-HB in LBS.

McEwen[95] pointed out professional research talent was

---

94) Bruce George Stahl, Community College Bureaucratism As Related to Student And Faculty Attrition(Ph. D. Dissertation. University of Missouri, Columbia, 1974). Dissertation Abstracts *International, 36: 83A(1975)*.

95) William J. McEwen, Position and Professional Orientation in Research Organization, Administrative Science Quarterly, 1(Sep., 1956), pp.208~224.

disregarded in bureaucratic organizations and Hall[96] also suggested problems indirectly that in a highly bureaucratized situation the highly competent person might not be able to exercise the full range of his competence due to specific procedural specifications, limited sphere of activity, and limited authority due to hierarchical demands. These kind of situations lead to conflict.

(5) Do the independent variables; School Bureaucratization and Teacher Professional and Bureaucratic Orientation predict the dependent variable, Job Satisfaction?

This question is similar to that posed regarding the conflict variable.

(a) Which is the best predictor among School Bureaucratization, Professional Orientation and Bureaucratic Orientation?

According to Jannings' study,[97] structure is of greater importance than role orientation in explaining morale. When we infer morale is related to Job Satisfaction, this study emphasizes the fact that the School Bureaucratization is more predictable for Job Satisfaction. Empirical studies were few.

(b) Are Bureaucratically Oriented Teachers satisfied more than

---

96) Richard H. Hall, The Concept of Bureaucracy: An Empirical Assessment, Op. Cit.

97) Paul Donald Jennings, A Study of the Relationship Between the Organizational Structure of Schools: the Role Orientation of Teachers and Teacher Morale(Ed. D. Dissertation, Columbia University, Teachers College, 1978), Dissertation Abstracts International, *39: 3270-71A(1978).*

Professionally Oriented Teachers without considering the organizational variable?

Mawter[98] indicated research results that professionalism and job satisfaction with supervision are an inverse relationship. This study support only a little part of the positive answer for the above question, but did not compare professionally oriented teachers with the bureaucratically oriented teachers. Except for this study it was difficult for the writers to find the related empirical researches.

(c) Are there significant difference in Job Satisfaction between teachers in High Bureaucratized schools and in Low Bureaucratized schools?

Empirical Studies Related to Question #(4)-(C)

Danese[99] suggested that a negative correlation was found between bureaucracy and satisfaction. Blazovsky[100] indirectly suggested a positive answer to the above question by concluding

---

98) Paul Thomas Mawter, Teacher, Professionalism and Decision-Making Modes in Selected Elementary Schools As Determinants of Job Satisfaction(Ph. D. Dissertation, University of Oregon, 1975).

99) Gino Danese, Perceptions of Bureaucracy and Faculty Satisfaction with Participation in Decision-Making at Unionized and Non-Unionized Institutions of Higher Education(Ed. D. Dissertation, State University of New York at Albany, 1977), *Dissertation Abstracts International, 38: 1143-44A(1977).*

100) Richard A. Blazovsky, School Bureaucracy and Teacher Alienation(Ed. D. Dissertation, Rutgers University, The State University of New Jersey, 1977), Dissertational, 38: 3820A(1977).

that highly centralized and formalized schools were characterized by alienation from work.

However, Moeller and Charters[101] pointed out opposite results in that teachers in highly bureaucratic systems had a significantly higher, not lower, sense of power than those in less bureaucratic systems. Enerio's study[102] also was similar to Moeller and Charters'. Jain[103] said intrinsic motivation which the writer thinks, is related to job satisfaction, was affected by bureaucratic level. However Stewart's study[104] showed different result, structural change does not affect to job satisfaction.

(d) Are there interaction effect of School Bureaucratization and Professional and Bureaucratic Orientation in predicting Job Satisfaction?

In other question, which subgroup experiences the most sat-

---

101) Gerald H. Moeller and W. W. Charters, Relation of Bureaucratization to Sense of Power, in Fred D. Carver and Thomas J. Sergsovanni(eds.), Op. Cit., pp.235~248.
102) Joseph M. Enerio, Perceived Bureaucratic Structure in the Universities and Four-Year Colleges of the State University of New York and Its Relation to the Academic Deans' Perceived Sense of Power(Ed. D. Dissertation, State University of New York at Albany, 1976), Dissertation Abstracts International 37: 5480A(1977).
103) Tej Kumar Jain, Bureaucracy and Motivation: An Empirical Assessment of Weber's And Bennis' Theoretical Position(Ph. D. Dissertation, University of Kansas, 1977), Dissertation Abstracts International, 38: 3845A(1978).
104) David Arthur Stewart, Changing Organizational Structure to Affect Perceived Bureaucracy, Organizational Climate, Loyalty, Job Satisfaction, and Effectiveness(Ed. D. Dissertation, University of Kansas, 1976), Dissertation Abstracts International, 38: 587A(1977).

isfaction among (1) HP-LB in HBS, (2) HP-LB in LBS, (3) LP-LB in HBS, (4) LP-LB in LBS, (5) LP-HB in HBS, (6) LP-HB in LBS, (7) HP-HB in HBS, and (8) HP-HB in LBS?

The writers have not as yet found empirical research related to this question.

(6) What Is the relationship of Conflict and Job Satisfaction?

Generally speaking we think conflict is negatively correlated with satisfaction as Miskel and Gerhardt's study cited previously, but this relation is not always the same. Koopman-Boyden and Adams[105] found that the relationship between job satisfaction and consensus which is thought as opposite concept of conflict, was shown to be far from strong.

So a test about the relationship of conflict and job satisfaction is significant for common knowledge.

In summary, the research questions are, first, for the demographic study of four variables, and second, the relationships of the four variables to each other.

Turning to the beginning point, will answers to the above questions be helpful to achieve the goals of the school? Demographic studies will give suggestions to the educational administrator about teacher-administrator relationships. Just as individualized instruction is necessary for students, administrator's individualized relationship with teachers is needed in educational admini-

---

105) Peggy G. Kopman-Boyden and Raymond S. Adams, Role Consensus and Teacher Job Satisfaction, The Journal of Educational Adminstration, 7:1(May, 1974), pp.98~113.

stration. By knowing about teachers' conflict and satisfaction, the administrator can cue in and thus foster their working aspirations. Study of bureaucratization and professionalization imply some change of elementary school organizational patterns. These suggestions and implications will be helpful for the growth and development of students, a major goal of the school.

〈요 약〉

공립학교의 관료화와 전문화의 두 경향과
이에 관련된 연구 질문

사회가 관료화되어가면서 공립학교도 점점 더 관료화되어 가고 있다. 이와 동시에 가르치는 일을 비롯하여 교사의 직무는 점점 전문화되어 가고 있으며 또한 전문화가 절실히 요구되고 있다.

그런데 이 관료주의 원리나 특성은 전문주의 원이와 특성과는 상반되는 점이 많다. 그러므로 이 서로 다른 두 경향 속에서 자연히 갈등이 뒤따르게 된다. 특히 전문 지향성이 높은 교사는 학교 조직이나 행정에 대하여 심한 갈등관계를 갖기 쉽다. 약간의 갈등은 조직행동의 활성화를 위하여 필요하나 과도한 갈등관계는 개인 교사의 정신적, 육체적 건강에 해로울 뿐만 아니라 이것이 곧 아동-학생에 직접적으로 영향을 주고 학교 조직의 목적 달성을 위해서도 유익하지 못하다고 볼 때 미국 공립학교에서의 관료화 경향과 전문화 경향은 중요한 연구문제가 된다.

그러나 학교조직의 관료화 속에서도 관료지향적 교사는 그래도 교직에 대하여 전문지향 교사보다는 더 만족할 것이라는 가정은 또한 다른 쪽에서의 연구문제가 된다. 또한 똑같은 하나의 관료화된 학교조직을 전문지향교사와 관료지향교사는 서로 다르게 볼 가능성이 있다. 즉, 전문지향교사가 더 학교조직이 관료화되었다고 보고 갈등을 많이 할 가능성이 있는 것이다.

이와 같이 조직 변인인 (1) 학교조직의 관료화와 개인변인 (2) 교사의 전문지향성과 관료지향성의 상호작용은 교사의 행동과 태도로 나타날 (3)

갈등과 (4) 만족의 정도에 영향을 줄 것으로 보아 이 네 변인들 간의 관계에 따른 여러 흥미 있는 연구 질문이 제기되어 앞으로 실제 자료에 의한 경험적 연구가 기대된다.

4. 관료적 학교조직에서 전문지향
교사의 갈등

I. 서 론

우리 사회는 하나의 조직사회이다. 조직 속에서 태어나고, 조직을 위하여 일하면서 생의 대부분을 보낸다.106) 한마디로 말하면 현대사회에서 인간은 조직을 떠나서 살 수 없다107)고 할 수 있다. 교사도 학교라는 조직 속에서 하루 24시간의 1/4 이상을 일하면서 보낸다. 교사에게 중요한 학교조직은 어떤 성격을 띠고 있는가?

학교조직이 대형화하고 복잡화 경향을 보임에 따라 관료적 성격을 나타내고 있다.108) 그 이유는 조직이 복잡해지면 내적 조정의 필요성이 커지니

---

* 이 논문은 한국교육학회 1976년도 연차학술 대회에서 발표하고 교육학연구 14권 3호(1976. 10) pp.155~168에 게재되었었음.

106) Amitai Etzioni, Modern Organizations(Englewood Cliffs, N. J.: Prentice-Hall Inc., 1964), p.1.

107) 고영부, 김해동, <u>인간관계론</u>(I)(서울: 서울대출판부, 1972), p.64.

108) Norman J. Boyan, "The Emergent Role of the Teacher in the Authority

까109) 자체의 목적을 효과적으로 지원하고 달성하기 위한 행정체제로 관료제를 택하는 것이다.110) 관료주의가 현재 가장 우수한 조직형태의 대표111)라고는 하나 관료주의의 병리적 측면을 수반하고 있는 경우가 많으며, 획일주의와 형식주의, 비밀주의와 할거주의, 관료독선과 책임전가 등 바람직하지 못한 경향112)을 띠어 오늘날 우리 교육의 문제를 행정의 측면에서 볼 때 한 가지 심각하게 반성해야 할 문제는 교육체제 안에서의 관료화의 촉진이라 할 수 있다.113) 어쨌든 학교조직이 관료적 특성을 가지고 있다고 한 마디로 정리해 놓기로 한다.

관료적 사회를 만들어낸 사회적 압력(social forces)은 또한 다른 형태의 조직을 만들어냈는데 이것이 전문가원리로 고용사회(employee society)114)와 맞서고 있다.115) 교직이 전문직이냐, 아니냐에 대하여는 많은 학자들의 논의의 대상이 되어 왔으나 극단적으로 "이다", "아니다"로 단언하지 않고 정도의 차이, 수준의 차이는 있으나 전문직이라는 사실은 인정하고 있으며, 더구나 전문직이어야 한다는 당위성에는 반론의 여지가 없다.116)

Structure of The School" in Fred D. Carver & Thomas J. Sergiovanni ed., Organization and Human Behavior: *Focus on Schools*(N. Y: *McGraw-Hill Book Co., 1969), p.200.*

109) Ronald G. Corwin, "Professional Persons in Public Organizations", in Ibid., p.217.

110) Robert G. Owens, Organizational Behavior in Schools(Englewood Cliffs, N. J. Prentice-Hall Inc., 1970), p.56.

111) Corwin, op. cit., p.213.

112) 김종철, "우리나라 교육 오늘의 문제" 교육연구 제8권 7호(서울: 교육연구사, 1975) p.111.

113) Ibid.

114) 고용사회란 말은 Petre F. Drucker, "The Employee Society" *American Journal of Sociology, LVIII(Jan, 1952), pp.352~63*에서 쓰고 있다.

115) Ronald G. Corwin, "The Professional Employee: A Study of Conflict of Nursing Roles," American Journal of Sociology, LXVI(may, 1961), pp.604~15.

116) 최근에 대한교련, 새교육 통권 261호 1976. 7. pp.17~48에서 특집으로 "교직 전문성의 재검토를 싣고 있으나 교직이 전문직이어야 한다는 것을 전제로 하고 있다.

오늘날 모든 조직체와 기관기능이 분화되고 전문화되는 경향에 따라 교육 역시 변화 발전하여 전문화117)되고 있으며, 교사들도 교수와 교육과정에 관한 의사결정에 있어서 점점 더 보다 많은 전문적 자율성과 권위, 그리고 관료적 지배로부터의 자유를 요구118)하고 있으며 UNESCO와 ILO도 "교원의 지위에 관한 권고문(Recomendation Concerning The Status Of Teachers)" 6항에서 "교육은 전문직으로 간주되어야 한다고 권고하고 있으며 교직의 전문성은 어느 국가에서나 강화119)되고 있는 것은 사실이다. 여기서 학교조직에는 전문적 특성이 또 있음을 확인해 둔다.

이상에서 우리는 학교조직은 교사에게 있어서 중요하며 관료적 원리(bureaucratic Principle)와 전문적 원리(Professional principle)의 이중원리(dual Professional and bureaucratic principles)120)가 있음을 알았다. 더구나 앞으로도 계속하여 더욱더 관료적 성격을 띨 것이고 집권화의 경향이 강화될 것이며, 이에 반하여 교원의 전문성 역시 점차 확대, 강화되어야 할 추세121)에 있다. 학교라는 한 조직 안에 상반되는 특성을 지닌 관료주의와 전문주의가 공존하며, 더구나 집권화, 다계층화(고층조직화) 및 관리적 권한의 우선시122) 등 관료주의가 강화되는 상황 속에서 전문가로서 기대에 어긋나지 않으려 하는, 또 교직의 전문성을 확립하려 하는 전문지향 교사는 어떤 갈등을 가질 것이라는 것이 이 논문의 기본가정이다. C. E. Bidwell123)과 D. E. Griffiths124)는 전교사가 전문지향이거나 관료지향과 전문지향의

---

117) 진보영, "교육행정의 전문성과 권한배분", 교육행정학연구회 제3회 학술발표회 발표유인물, 1974. p.47.
118) Owens, op. cit., p.103.
119) 이규환, "외국에 있어서의 교직전문성", 새교육 op. cit., p.36.
120) Corwin, "Professional Persons……" op. cit., p.214.
121) 남정걸, "학교조직에서의 교원의 역할수행", 교육학연구 제14권 제1호(서울: 한국교육학회, 1975), p.15.
122) Ibid., p.13.
123) C. E. Bidwell, "Administration and Teacher Satisfaction," Phi Delta Kappan, ⅩⅩⅩⅦ(1956), pp.285~88을 인용한 Boyan, et. al op. cit. p.203.

양면성을 지닐 것이라는 가정을 조심스럽게 받아들이고 있는데 그렇다면 우리나라에서도 많은 교사들이 갈등하고 있을 것이 예상되는바 이에 대한 연구는 의의 있다고 본다. 앞으로 학교조직의 이중성을 좀더 살펴보고 거기서 생기는 갈등을 찾아보고 그 해소방안이 무엇인지를 알아보는 순서로 이론적 고찰을 하고자 한다.

대학에서는 행정가와 교수는 행정과 감독의 관계를 분리[125]하여 존재한다고 봄으로 여기서 학교조직이라 함은 대학을 제외한 각급 학교 특히 초등과 중등의 공립학교에 중점을 둔다.

Ⅱ. 학교조직의 이중성

학교조직을 여러 측면에서 볼 수 있다. Owens는 학교조직을 복합조직(complex organization), 사회체제(social system), 관료제(bureaucracy)로 설명하고 있다.[126] 그는 고전주의 조직이론, 신고전주의 조직이론, 두 이론의 종합(synthesis)으로 개관한 다음 공식조직(formal organization)과 비공식조직(informal organization)의 복합조직(complex organization)과 체제이론(system theory)에 의하여 사회체제(social system)를 개방체제(open system)와 폐쇄체제(closed system)로 나누어 설명하고, 마지막으로 관료제(bureaucracy)로 학교조직을 설명하고 있다. 그러나 여기서는 관료제와 전문조직의 관점에서 학교조직을 보고자 한다.

---

124) D. E. Griffiths et al., Teacher Mobility in New York City(N. Y.: School of Education, N. Y. University, 1963)를 인용한, ibid.
125) Boyan, ibid., p.209.
126) Owens, op. cit., pp.45~65.

A. 관료적 특성

Max Weber는 조직을 카리스마조직(charismatic organization), 전통조직(traditional organization), 관료조직으로 나누고 관료조직은 행정가의 역량을 최대로 발휘할 수 있도록 짜여지고 직위가 기능을 바탕으로 이루어지고, 그에 필요한 기능을 익힌 구성원으로 운영되는 조직127)이라고 하였다. 또 정확성, 신속성, 명확성, 사무지식, 계속성, 분별성, 통일성, 엄격한 복종, 부화의 감소, 물적 인적 절약 등이 엄밀한 의미의 관료행정에서는 최적상태에 이른다128)고 하여 장점을 모두 열거했으며 합리적 합법적 권위(rational-legal authority)를 상징하는 것으로 계층적 조직, 기능적 분업, 직무전속주의, 공사의 분별, 합리적 조직이라고 생각하였던 것이다.129)

1. 관료제의 특징

Max Weber는 관료제의 특징으로 6가지를 들고 있다.

(1) 규정 즉 법이나 행정규제에 의하여 정해진 질서정연한 사무범위

(2) 계층의 원이와 등급으로 정해진 권위수준은 상급자가 하급자를 감독하는 상·하관계의 정연한 체제

(3) 현대 사무관리는 문서에 근거를 두고 있다.

(4) 사무관리, 적어도 전문적 사무관리는 대개 완전하고 숙련된 훈련을 전제로 한다.

(5) 사무가 아주 발전되면 활동은 근무시간이 정해져 있다는 사실과 관계없이 최선의 능력을 요구한다.

(6) 사무관리는 일반법칙을 따른다.130)

---

127) Owens, op. cit., pp.56~57.

128) Max Weber, Essays in Sociology, trans H. H Gerth and C. W. Mills(N. Y: Oxford Uni. Press, 1946), p.214를 인용한 215~16 Peter M. Blau, The Dynamics of Bureaucracy, Revised ed., (Chicago: The Univ. of Chicago Press, 1964). p.1.

129) 김종철, "우리나라 교육 오늘의 문제", 전게서 p.111.

영국의 사회학자 H. J. Laski[131]는 (1) 행정에 있어서 일과에 열중, (2) 규정에 있어서 융통성 금지, (3) 의사결정의 지연, (4) 실험적 착오금지를 특징으로 들고 있다. Laski가 약간 부정적 특징을 들고 있는 반면 Robert Presthus는 비슷한 뜻을 다르게 표현하고 있다.

　(1) 규정, 방침, 규제, 법으로 정해진 고정된 사무범위

　(2) 상급자가 하급자를 감독하는 계층의 원이와 권위수준

　(3) 문서에 바탕을 둔 행정

　(4) 훈련된 관리가 운영하는 행정

　(5) 안정되고 종합적인 일반정책에 의하여 계획된 행정[132]이라 하고 있다.

　D. A. MacKay는 (1) 권한－직위, (2) 분업, (3) 구체적으로 정해진 행위, (4) 제한된 절차, (5) 비정, (6) 능력[133]으로 집약했고, Corwin은 (1) 직무의 전문화, (2) 작업의 표준화, (3) 권한의 집중화로 묶었다.

　Victor A. Thompson은 상하관계에서 상급자는 권리를 갖는 반면, 하급자는 의무를 갖는다고 보아 역할관계에서 논하고 있는데 이것이 학교조직에서 중요한 갈등의 원천이 된다고 보아 옮겨본다.

　a. 상급사의 권리

　(1) 하급자의 제안을 거부하거나 동의할 수 있는 권리

　(2) 하급자로부터 복종과 충성을 기대할 권리

　(3) 의사소통을 독점할 권리

---

130) Max Weber, "The Monocratic Type of Bureaucratic Administration" The Theory of Social and Economic Organization, trans by A. M. Henderson and Talcott Parsons(Oxford Uni. Press Inc., 1947).

131) Encyclopedia of the Social Science, Vol.3, 3, pp.70~73을 인용한 Dwight Waldo, Public Administration(McGraw-Hill Book Co., 1953).

132) Robert Presthus, The Organizational Society(N. Y.: Alfred A. Knopf, Inc., 1962), p.5를 인용한 Owens, op. cit., p.57.

133) D. A, MacKay, "Am Empirical Study of Bureaucratic Dimensions and Their Relation to Other Characteristic of School Organization" Unpublished Ph. D. dissertation. University of Alberta, 1964.

(4) 하급자보다 나은 존경을 받을 권리

(5) 조직의 목표설정

(6) 하급자의 업무할당

(7) 의사결정권

b. 하급자의 의무

(1) 상급자에 대한 복종의 의무

(2) 충성의 의무

(3) 차별대우를 감수할 의무

(4) 상급자의 권리행사를 그대로 받아들일 의무134) 등이다. 이는 관료조직을 계층적 측면에서 개념을 형성한 것으로 설명을 더 들어본다.

(1) 계층의 직위에 있는 사람은 바로 자기 위의 상급자로부터 해야 할 의무를 부여받고 다시 하급자에게 추진업무를 할당한다. 이러한 지시가 업무의 분할, 즉 조직을 이루는 것이다.

(2) 하급자는 이 지시에 따라 다시 감독135)되고 마찬가지로 그 보다 낮은 지위의 하급자를 지시감독하게 된다.

(3) 상급자는 하급자가 업무추진이나 지시에 추종하고 이행하도록 하급자를 규제한다. 따라서 권한은 최상위자로부터 이어져 내려오고 의무는 최하위자로부터 최상위자를 향하여 이어져 올라가는 것이다. 학교조직에서도 이런 계층이 강화되는 현상이다.

이상을 종합해 보면 (1) 권한, (2) 계층, (3) 문서, (4) 비정성, (5) 숙련, (6) 규정 등은 관료제에 있어서 빼놓을 수 없는 특징이라고 본다.

이 관료제가 기능적으로 잘 운영만 되면 다음과 같은 장점이 있다.

(1) 능률적이다.

(2) 예측할 수 있다.

---

134) Victor A. Thompson, "Hierachy, Specialization and organizational Conflict" in Carver, op. cit., pp.19~20.

135) Ibid., p.23.

(3) 공사를 분명히 할 수 있다.

(4) 신속하다.136)

이와 같이 관료제가 행정체제로는 더할 수 없는 조직이라고는 하지만 항상 효과적이고 또 항상 건강상태에 있는 것은 아니고 역기능 내지 병리상태가 있는 것이다.

2. 관료제병리

관료제가 원래 경직하고 비생산적인 것은 아닌데 그 과정에서 규칙과 절차, 문서를 절대적인 것으로 여겨 형식주의로 빠지고, 수단과 목표의 전도(displacement of goals)137)의 역기능(bureaucratic dysfunctions), 병리(bureaupathology) 현상으로 나타나기도 한다. 학교에서도 교수를 잘하여 아동－학생의 성장발달을 돕는 것이 주목적일 텐데 교사의 자율성은 줄어들고 상부의 지시, 명령은 늘어나고, 형식적 행사와 잡무가 강조된다면 이것이 역기능 내지는 병리현상인 것이다.

관료제의 성격도 변해왔다. 현대 관료제는 고전적 위계체제에다 전문화를 결합시킨 것이다.138) 조직의 목표를 수입히는 일은 행정기능에 속하지민 그 목표를 달성하는 데 필요한 프로그램은 실제로 전문가의 손에 의하여 이루어지는 업무이므로 조직 내 문제해결에 필요한 유용한 기술과 의사소통의 적정성에 달려 있는 것이다. Eugene Litwak139)는 관료제의 3모델로 나누어 그 변화를 설명하고 있다. 즉 1) Weber의 형태, 2) 인관관계에 바탕을 둔 형태, 3) 전문가관료제(professional bureaucracy)140)로 나누고

---

136) Owens, op. cit., p.60.

137) Robert K. Merton, "The Nature and Sources of Pathological Bureaucratical Behavior" in Robert Dubin, Human Relations in Administration, 4th. ed. (Englewood Cliffs, N. J.: Prentice-Hall, 1974), pp.197~200.

138) Thompson, op. cit., p.24.

139) Eugene Litwak, "Models of Bureaucracy which Permit Conflict" in Carver, op. cit., p.85.

140) Robert Vinter, "Notes on Profession and Bureaucracy,(Un Published

Weber형에는 정부기관(공공성을 띤 사기업—수도, 전기, 가스), 인간관계형에는 국립정신병원, 대광고회사, 전문가형에는 큰 병원, 대학원, 대연구기관, 대사회사업기관 등을 들고 있다.

관료제를 학교조직에 초점을 맞춰 살펴보고자 한다.

(1) 교육부, 시·도 교육청, 교육구청, 교장, 교감, 부장교사, 교사로 이어져 내려오는 계층이 있고, 이 계층에 따른 권한이 있고, 권리와 의무관계가 있다. 그런데 이 위계질서는 더욱 강화되는 현실에 있었다.

(2) 문서주의의 경향도 짙어지고 있다. 이에 따라 교사들은 사무처리에 많은 시간을 보내며, 장학 시에도 통계숫자와 문서의 근거를 따지는 경향이다.

(3) 교사나 교장의 자율성은 낮아지고 지시나 명령, 규정에 얽매이는 경향이다. 학생의 좌석, 성적, 반장임명 등까지 규제하려 한다.

(4) 상급자의 의사결정권은 많고, 대우를 받고, 권한을 갖고 있으니까 교사들은 상위계층으로 올라가기 위해 관료지향이거나 아니면 교사로서의 전문성을 찾기 위해 갈등하며 투쟁하고 도전하는 전문지향의 두 가지 가능성이 있다.

B. 전문적 특성

교직의 전문성 또는 전문지향 교사를 알려면 먼저 전문직이 무엇인가를 알아야 한다. 김종철은 어떠한 직업이 하나의 전문직으로 간주되려면 다음과 같은 지표에 맞아야 한다고 하였다.

(1) 전문직은 고도의 지성을 요구하는 정신적 활동을 위주로 한다.

(2) 전문직은 그 직업에 들어가려는 자에 대하여 엄격한 자격기준을 세우는 것을 특징으로 한다.

(3) 전문직은 그에 필요한 교육·훈련이 단순한 지식이나 습득이 아니고 심오한 학문의 이론과 그 응용에 기초를 두고 있는 것을 특징으로 한다.

(4) 전문직은 이기적 활동보다도 애타적 동기를 중요시하는 봉사활동임을

Manuscript, Sep, 1960)을 인용한 ibid., p.85.

특징으로 한다.

(5) 전문직은 그에 종사하는 자가 자유를 가지는 반면에 중대한 사회적 책임을 느끼는 것을 특징으로 한다.

(6) 전문직에 종사하는 자들은 스스로 자체의 행동을 규율하는 윤리강령을 가지고 있다.

(7) 전문직에 종사하는 자들은 자율적인 조직체를 통하여 사회적 지위를 향상시키고 그들의 전문성을 제고하도록 노력함을 특징으로 한다.[141] 그리고 최근에 지성, 전문기술성, 자율적 책임성, 윤리성, 유인성[142] 등으로 묶어 제시하고 최저기준[143]에 따라 교직 전문성의 현실을 논하여 교직 전문성 확립에의 길은 아직 요원하다고 하였다.

정범모는 전문직이냐 범속직이냐의 척도로 (1) 이론적 배경, (2) 장기훈련, (3) 엄격한 표준, (4) 표준의 신장, (5) 전문직단체[144]라 하고 이런 척도에 비추어 보아 회의적 표현을 하고 있으나 교사의 직업분석에서 (1) 교수, (2) 교육과정계획, (3) 평가, (4) 집단활동의 지도, (5) 사례연구, (6) 사무, (7) 행정참여, (8) 사회연락[145] 등의 활동으로 보아 전문직이어야 한다는 것은 틀림없다.

백현기는 일반직과 구별되는 전문직의 척도로 (1) 고도의 과학적이고 철

---

141) 김종철, <u>교육행정의 이론과 실제</u>(서울: 교학사, 1965). p.30.

142) 김종철, "전문직으로서의 교직의 현위치", 새교육 전게서, p.24.

143) 김종철은 상게문에서 오늘날 일반적으로 공인되고 있는 전문직의 구체적인 최저기준으로 다음 5가지를 들고 있다.
　　1) 적어도 4년제 대학정도에서의 직전 준비교육을 받는다. 현직에 들어와서도 계속적으로 전문적 성장이 보장된다.
　　2) 전문적 기술성을 보장할 수 있도록 엄격히 규정 자격기준의 적용을 받으며 소정의 기준에 도달한 자에 국한하여 입문할 수 있다.
　　3) 업무에 관련된 정책의 수입이나 근무조건의 결정에 참여하며 자율적 규제를 통하여 사회적 책임의 완수에 노력한다.
　　4) 윤리강령을 자율적으로 실천하며 이탈자에 대하여는 강력한 규제와 필요하면 제재를 가하는 것을 서슴지 않는다.
　　5) 직무에 대하여 보람과 긍지를 가지며 만족감을 느낀다.

144) 정범모, "교직의 전문성", 교육과 교사(서울: 현대교육총서사, 1962). pp.20~22.

145) Ibid., pp.11~12.

학적인 이론과 장기적이고 계속적인 전문교육과 훈련을 요하며,

(2) 초임자에게 엄격한 수준을 요구하는 동시에 대 사회관계에 있어 진정한 지도성을 발휘하며,

(3) 자율적인 조직체를 갖고 성문화된 법률적 지위를 향유하는 것으로 인정된다146)는 점을 들고 있다. Myron Lieberman은 전문직을 다음과 같이 정의하고 있다.

(1) 범위가 명확하고 사회적으로 불가결한 일에 독점적으로 종사한다.

(2) 고도의 지적 기술을 행사한다.

(3) 장기의 전문교육을 필요로 한다.

(4) 개인으로서나 집단으로서나 넓은 범위에 걸쳐서 자율성을 가진다.

(5) 자율의 범위 안에서 한 판단이나 행동에 대하여는 직접 책임을 진다.

(6) 영리가 아닌 사회봉사를 동기로 한다.

(7) 적용방법이 구체화되고 있는 윤리강령을 갖고 있다.147)

Gouldner는 전문직의 특징으로

(1) 학식이 많고 전문적 식견이 풍부하여야 한다.

(2) 통일과 단합을 과시하여야 한다.

(3) 강력한 조직을 가지고 고도의 가치를 행하며 구성원의 근무조건이라든가 근무 중의 행동에 관하여 스스로 통제하고 자율화할 수 있는 능력148)이라고 한다.

D. A. MacKay는 전문직의 특징으로

(1) 장기간의 전문적 교육

(2) 직업에 들어가는 요건에 대한 법적 통제

(3) 강력한 윤리강령을 가진 강력한 조직체에의 가입

---

146) 백현기, <u>교육행정의 기초</u>(서울: 배영사, 1969), p.37.
147) Myron Lieberman, Education as A Profession(Englewood Cliffs, N. J.: Prentice-Hall, Inc., 1956). pp.2~6.
148) Gould를 인용한 유동진, "왜 교직의 전문성이 문제되나" 새교육 p.18.

(4) 헌신적 봉사정신[149]을 들고 전문가에 대한 기대로 9가지를 제시하고 있다.

(1) 고객문제에 관한 특수성 강조

(2) 연구 및 변화의 강조

(3) 여러 대안을 가진 규정

(4) 고객지향의 목적달성 강조

(5) 지식의 독점에 바탕을 둔 기술

(6) 전문적이고 특수한 문제의 결정

(7) 법적으로 보장된 전문성에 의하여 규정된 룰(rule)

(8) 전문가집단체와 고객에 대한 충성

(9) 전문적 능력에서 나온 권한[150]

그는 또 전문가는 (1) 고객지향성, (2) 동료지향성, (3) 의사결정, (4) 기술과 지식을 독점하려는 경향성을 가지고 있다[151]고 했는데 이 9개의 기대에 맞추려 하고, 4개의 경향성을 가진 교사를 전문지향 교사라 본다.

Etzioni는 의사결정과 감독의 측면에서 전문성의 정도를 〈그림 II-1〉과 같이 나타내고 있는데 학교는 반전문식으로 보고 있다.

〈그림 II-1〉 조직의 3종류[152]

의사결정측면

높은 정도의 참여→	중간정도의 참여→	낮은 정도의 참여
전문조직	반전문조직	비전문조직
병원 대학교수회의 봉사연구집단	학교 사회사업기관 전문연구기관	공장 기업체 군대조직
동료적→	약간 간섭적(계층적)→	아주 간섭적(완전히 계층적)
	감독적 측면	

---

149) D. A. Mackay, "Using Professional Talent In A School Organiation" in Carver, op. cit., p.228.

150) Ibid., p.229.

151) Ibid.

<표 Ⅱ-1> 전문직과 권한의 이론모형153)

전문적 \ 권환	양	내 용	영 역	행 위	분 화
전 문 직	많 다	복잡화	가치판단	자율적	수평적
비전문직	적 다	단순화	사실판단	타율적	수직적

진보영도 전문직과 권한, 전문직과 의사결정과의 관계에서 〈표 Ⅱ-2〉, 〈Ⅱ-3〉과 같이 이론모형으로 제시하고 전문직의 가장 중핵적 지표는 자유로운 의사결정권한154)이라고 하였다.

<표 Ⅱ-2> 전문조직과 의사결정의 이론모형155)

조 직 \ 의사결정	참여권	책 임	통제형태	과 정
전 문 직	높은 참여	적극적	개방적	직접적
반전문직	낮은 참여	도의적	계층적	형식적
비전문직	참여	소극적	폐쇄적	지시적

이상을 종합하여 볼 때 우리 교직 전문성의 현 위치는 학력, 자격, 사회적 지위 등 모든 면에서 문제점이 있고,156) 여러 학자들이 제시한 전문직의 지표에는 완전히 충족하지 못하여 반전문직 정도로 양보한다 하여도, 전문직이어야 한다는 데는 이론이 있을 수 없다. 교사들은 전문가로서의 기대에 어긋나지 않으려 하고 전문지향하는 반면, 현대조직은 더욱 관료화하고 있어 교사와 행정가 간에 일관된 갈등이 있고 다른 공적으로 인정받는 직업

---

152) Etzioni, op. cit., p.87.
153) Ibid., p.58.
154) 진보영, op. cit., p.56.
155) ★각주 누락
156) 김종철, "전문직으로서의 교직의 현위치", 전게서 pp.24~28.
　　박성내, "초등교원의 전문성과 사회적 지위에 관한 연구" 미출판의 유인물, 1975.
　　대한교련, "교직유인체제확립에 관한 연구(서울: 대한교련, 1969).

의 전문화 과정은 전문화를 위한 투쟁의 과정157)이었다는 점을 생각할 때 전문지향 교사에게는 갈등이 있을 것이라는 기본가정을 더욱 짙게 한다.

Ⅲ. 갈 등

갈등이란 한 개인 어떤 특정의 상황에서 둘 이상의 행동목표나 행동대상에서 선택하게 될 때 즉 거의 같은 장의 힘이 대입된 상태에서 야기되는 것158)으로 크게 두 종류로 나누어 원인을 설명할 수 있다. 첫째는 개인의 내적 갈등(intraindividual conflict)으로 비수락성(unacceptability), 비비교성(incompatibility), 불확실성(uncertainty)의 장태에서 생기고, 둘째는 다른 사람, 집단, 조직과의 갈등인 개인 간 갈등(coflict among individuals)은 공동결정의 필요(need for joint decisionmaking), 목표상의 차(difference in goals), 현실 지각의 차(difference in perception of reality)159)의 상황에서 생긴다고 한다.

A. 갈등의 원천

Thompson은 조직 내의 갈등은 (1) 권리체제(권한), (2) 존경체제(신분), (3) 전문화체제(능력의 배분)의 기본적 행위체제간의 상호작용으로부터 일어난다160)고 하였는데 이런 갈등은 학교조직 내에서도 생긴다고 본다.

(1) 권리체제(권한)에서 생기는 갈등

관료제에서는 상부에 권한이 집중되어 있고 하부는 주로 의무만이 주어진

---

157) Corwin, "Professional Persons……", op. cit., p.214.
158) 김영철, "교사의 역할갈등 및 역할모호성과 학교조직풍토에 관한 연구", 고대대학원교육학과석사학위논문, 1973, p.15.
159) James G. March & Hebert A. Simon, Organizations, (N. Y.: John Wiley & Sons, Inc., 1958), pp.112~15를 인용한 김영철, op. cit., p.16.
160) Thompson, Op. cit., p.30.

다. 학교조직에서 하부에 해당되는 교사는 갈등을 갖게 되는 것이다. 또한 학교장이나 행정가는 위계에 의한 권한을 행사하려는 데 반하여 교사는 전문적 권한을 요구하는 데서 갈등이 생긴다. Peabody의 연구에 의하면 교사, 경찰간부, 복지기관 근무자의 각 집단이 의지하는 권한을 비교했는데 세 집단 중 초등학교 교사가 가장 심하게 자기들의 권위근거를 전문성에 돌린다161)는 것이다.

(2) 존경체제(신분)에서 생기는 갈등

학교장이 존경을 받고, 사회경제적 지위가 높고 모든 면에서 유리한 반면 교사는 존경을 받지 못하고 불리한 데다 사회가 금전지향적 풍토이기 때문에 전문가인 평교사로서의 매력을 느끼지 못하고 갈등은 심하다. 결국 우리 문화풍토에서 성공했다는 말을 듣기 위해서는 높은 계층의 직위를 차지하고, 공적으로 인정되는 존경을 받기 위해서는 위계적으로 성공해야만 하는데 이러한 장황은 전문교사에게 고통스런 갈등을 일으킨다.

(3) 전문화체제(능력의 배분)에서 생기는 갈등

학교행정가는 행정이나 경영으로서의 전문적 영역이 있고 교사는 교사로서의 전문적 영역이 있어야 하는데 교사의 전문적 영역까지 관료적 능력이 침범하기 때문에 갈등이 생긴다. 교사들은 자기들의 전문적 영역에 한해서는 무감독적 장학을 원하는 반면 Washburne의 연구결과처럼 행정가는 교사의 전문적 행위를 무시하거나 질책162)하는 데 갈등이 생긴다.

(4) 역할기대의 위배로 생기는 갈등

관료적 조직에서는 교사가 하나의 관료적 종업원이 되기를 기대하는데 교사가 전문지향일 때 갈등이 야기된다. 소봉암은 "학교조직에 있어서 사문직 성향 교사와 자아실현과의 관계연구" 결과 초등학교에 있어서는 교사의 고

---

161) Robert L. Peabody, "Perceptions of Organizational Authority" Administrative Science Quarterly, VI(March, 1962), pp.463~83.
162) S. Washburne, "Teacher in the Authority system," Journal of Educational Sociology, XXX(1957), pp.390~94.

용자적 지위가 강요당하고 있다고 추론163)하였다.

다음 〈표 Ⅲ-1〉을 보면 종업원지향이기를 기대하는 관료적 학교조직에서 전문지향인 교사의 갈등원천을 알 수 있다.

〈표Ⅲ-1〉 관료지향과 전문지향의 비교164)

종업원지향	전문지향
① 행정지향	고객지향
② 조직에의 충성	전문지향, 전문가동료지향
③ 경험, 인사, 작업표준화에 바탕을 둔 능력	독점적 지식에 바탕을 둔 능력
④ 규정과 절차	의사결정권한
⑤ 공공지향성	일에 대한 통제

① 학교장은 행정위주이고 행정적이길 기대하는데 교사는 학생중심적인 데서 갈등이 생긴다.

② 학교장이 조직에 충실하려 하고 또 교사가 조직에 충성하길 기대하는데 교사는 전문성과 동료, 전문가단체지향적인 데서 갈등이 생긴다. 약간 다른 각도이지만 Argyris는 개인의 욕구와 조직의 요구에서 "성숙"한 개인으로서의 독립, 변화, 도전의 욕구와 의존적이고 순종하는 종업원이 되길 바라는 조직의 요구 사이에 갈등이 예상된다165)고 하였다.

③ 행정가가 경험에 의하여 일을 처리하고 인사와 표준화된 작업으로 권능을 나타내려 하는 데 비하여 교사는 전문이론을 가지고 따지려는 갈등이 생긴다.

④ 행정가는 규정과 절차에 얽매이기를 기대하는데 교사는 보다 많은 재량권을 요구하는 데 갈등한다.

---

163) 소봉암, "학교조직에 있어서 전문직성향교사와 자아실현과의 관계연구", 서울대대학원교육학과 미출판의 석사학위논문 1975. p.57.

164) Corwin, "Professional Persons……", op. cit., p.227의 Employee Orientations Subscales와 Professional Orientation Subacales를 연구자가 표로 대비시킨 것임.

165) Chris Argyris, Personality and Organization,(N. Y.: Haper and Brothers 1957), pp.50~55.

⑤ 행정가가 공공지향적인데 교사는 일의 본질에 열중하려는 데 갈등이 생긴다.

(5) 관료조직과 전문조직의 조직특성에 따른 기대의 차에서 갈등의 요소를 찾을 수 있다. 이것은 〈표 Ⅲ-2〉로 비교하고 설명은 줄인다.

〈표 Ⅲ-2〉 조직의 관료적 원리와 전문가-종업원 원리의 비교[166]

조직특성	관료적-종업원의 기대	전문적-종업원의 기대
표준화 일상적인 일 과정의 계속성 규정의 구체화 정도	고객문제에 있어서 획일성 강조 기록과 서류철의 강조 일반적으로 기술된 규정: 구체화	고객문제에 있어서 특수성 강조 연구, 변화의 강조 대안으로 진술된 규정: 다양성
전문화 직업분화의 근거 기술의 근거	기술의 능률성 강조: 과업지향 실용 우선의 기술	목적달성 강조: 고객지향 지식의 독점에(기본적으로) 바탕을 둔 기술
권 한 의사 결정의 책임성 권한의 근거	일상문제에 대한 규정을 적용하는 결정 공공연히 인정되는 규정 조직과 상급자에 관한 충성심 사무(직위)에서 오는 권한	전문적 문제와 특수문제의 방침결정 합법적으로 인정된 전문성에서 나온 규정 전문가 단체와 고객에 대한 충성 개인적 능력에서 나오는 권한

MacKay는 전문가와 관료적 조직과의 갈등을 〈표 Ⅲ-3〉과 같이 나타내 준다.

---

166) Corwin, "Professional Persons……", op. cit., p.216.

<표 Ⅲ-3> 전문가-조직의 갈등[167]

조 직	전 문 가
1. 권한-직위	기술-지식
2. 분업	개인학생
3. 구체화된 행위	여러 대안을 가진 행위
4. 제한된 절차	융통성
5. 비정적	인간상호관계
6. 능력*	능력

* 여기서 능력은 위계와 직위에서 나온 권능이고 전문가의 능력을 전문적 지식과 기술에서 나온 능력의 차가 있음(필자)

Turner도 관료주의와 전문직간의 규범적 요구의 근원적 대립[168]으로 갈등은 불가피하다고 한다.

<표 Ⅲ-4> 관료주의와 전문직[169]

1. 표준화된 역할행위	1. 융통성 있는 역할행위
2. 자율성이 낮은 의사결정	2. 자율성이 높은 의사결정
3. 조직지향적 역할행위	3. 고객지향적 역할행위
4. 조직의 관리운영에 순응하는 역할 행위	4. 동료와 전문직단체의 기준에 순응하는 역할행위

(6) 관료적 행정가가 전문교사를 평가하고 감독한다는 데서 갈등의 원인을 찾아볼 수 있다.

Goulder가 연구한 바에 의하면 사무분야에 있어서 행정가보다 더 권위 있는 전문가 하급자를 행정가가 자주 감독하고 평가한다는 사실 때문에 많은 긴장이 생긴다[170]는 것이다. 예를 들면 수업을 비롯하여 교사의 모든

---

167) MacKay, op. cit., p.236.
168) 남정걸, op. cit., p.13에서 P. B J. H. Turner, Patterns of Social Organization (N. Y.: McGraw-Hill, 1972), p.167을 인용한 것을 재인용함.
169) Ibid., 제목은 필자가 붙인 것임.

행위를 비전문인인 행정가가 평가하고 감독한다는 데 갈등이 있다. 전문가의 평가는 전문가의 동료의 의견에 바탕을 두어야 한다는 데 복잡성이 있다. 또 Lipham에 의하면 교사의 감독자로서의 교장이란 전통적인 역할과 교수의 전 과정과 교육과정을 현명하게 감독하기에 충분한 능력이 있다는 생각은 더 이상 계속될 수 없다171)는 것이다. 여기서 생각해 볼 점은 교장이 교사출신이라는 데서 교사평가와 감독에 자신감을 갖고 있는 것이 아닌가 하는 점이다. 그러나 교장은 교사로서의 전문성을 잃고 관료지향이 되고 있다는 것이 문제점이다.

(7) 학교조직목표의 전도에서 갈등의 원인을 찾아볼 수 있다.

학교조직의 주요목표는 교수-학습을 잘하여 아동-학생의 성장발달을 돕는 것일 텐데 과도한 관료화와 행정우위현상으로 행사, 사무 등이 목적처럼 전도되는 데서 갈등이 생긴다. 초등학교 학력을 가진 사람이면 할 수 있는 일을 전문교육을 받았다는 교사가 하면서 많은 시간을 허비한다면 심한 불만과 갈등이 될 것이다. 더구나 전문적 영역보다 관리적 영역에 능숙해야 좋은 평가를 받고, 승진할 수 있는 풍토라면 문제가 된다. 목적문제에서 또 하나는 행정가가 목표를 세우고 다른 사람(교사)의 도움으로 조직목표를 달성하려고 하는 데172) 문제가 있다.

(8) 학교조직에 관료주의의 팽배로 인한 관료적 병리 때문에 전문지향 교사의 갈등은 더욱 심해진다.

우정남173)의 연구에 의하면 관료제병리와 학교집단성취도와는 관계가 있

---

170) Alvin W Goulder, "Organizational Tensions" Sociology Today. ed, Robert Merton, et al.(N. Y.: Basic Book, 1956), pp.400~28.
171) James M. Lipham "The Role of the Principal" The National Elementary Principal, *XLIV, No.5(April 1965), pp.28~33.*
172) Paul F. Lazarsfeld & Daniel E. Griffiths, "The Social Sciences and The Study of Adminstration: A Rationale" The Social Science *and Educational Adminstration, ed. Lawrence W. Downey & Frederick* Enns,(Edmonton: The University of Alberta, 1963), p.e.
173) 우정남, "관료제의 병리와 학교집단의 성취도연구" 미출판의 유인물 1975.

고, 일선 교사들에 지각되는 학교관료제의 병리는 ① 과중한 각종 장부정리
의 형식화, ② 각종 회의의 형식적 의식화, ③ 아동의 학습활동에 오히려 지
장을 주는 지시 전달내용과 절차의 강조, ④ 규정과 규칙의 경직화된 강조로
나타났다. 관료제가 정상적으로 운영되어도 앞에서 살펴본 바와 같이 근원적
인 갈등이 발생할 가능성이 있는데 병적으로 운영될 때는 더욱 심할 것이다.

이외에 학교행정가의 관료적 성향(bureaucratic orientation)이 교사
의 자율성을 견제174)하려는 데서, 의사소통의 단절로, 전문가와 행정가가
실재(reality)를 다르게 지각하는 데서 갈등이 생기며 가치갈등도 있다.

갈등의 분야는 Corwin의 연구에 의하면 ① 권한－48.7%(·교육과정운영과
학급에 대한 권한－17.%, ·학생규율－15.6%, ·학교에 대한 권한－6.8%, 학
교와 지역사회관계－1.8%, ·교사 간의 논쟁－7.1%), ② 재정－25.2%(·교사
의 경제적 지위와 직무－13.1%, ·목과문제－10.4%, 학교재정－1.5%), ③ 가
치갈등－22.1%(·도덕적 이념적, 인간상호관계 문제－8.6%, ·교육철학－4.9%,
·학교방침－8.6%) ④ 기타 3.9%175)로 나타났는데 참고가 된다.

B. 갈등의 결과

그러나 조직적 갈등은 백해무익한 것인가. Lewis Coser176)는 갈등이
전연 없는 집단은 없으며 파괴적인 요인만 되는 것이 아니고 사회에 필수적
인 현상이라고 하여 긍정적인 면에서 보는 데 반하여 조석준177)은 조직의
능률과 개인의 심리적 건강에 유해한 것으로 보고 있다. R. L. Kahn178)은
갈등의 양면성을 들어 성숙하고 유용한 인간을 만들지만 과도한 정신적 긴장

---

174) C. E. Bidwell, "Administration and Teacher Satisfaction" Phi Delta
　　　Kappan, ⅩⅩⅩⅦ, 1956, p.285.
175) Corwin, op. cit., p.220의 표에서 백분율만 따온 것임.
176) Lewis Corser, The Functions of Social Conflict(N. Y.: The Free Press
　　　of Grencoe, 1956), p.31.
177) 조석준, 조직론(서울: 법문사, 1973), p.225.
178) R. L. Kahn, et al, The Social Psychology of Organization(N. Y.: John
　　　Wiley & Sone, 1966), p.65를 인용한 김영철, op. cit., p.19.

으로 유해하다고 하였고, Kenneth Boulding[179]도 약간의 긴장을 수반하는 갈등은 발전적이고 생산에 필요한 반면, 개인적으로 사회적으로 낭비를 가져온다는 입장을 취하고 있다. 필자도 약간의 갈등은 일을 촉진하는 활력소가 되고 일에의 도전의욕을 불러일으키지만 과도한 불만은 교사 개인으로나 사회적으로나 해가 된다고 보고 그 영향을 적어본다.

(1) 직무수행에의 영향

전문직 교사의 주요활동이 정신적 심리적 활동이기 때문에 갈등은 곧 교사의 직무수행에 영향을 미친다. 교사의 주요 직무수행은 학생을 가르치는 것으로 바로 학생지도와 연결되어 피해는 학생들에게 옮겨지고 교수-학습의 능률을 기하기 어렵다고 본다.

(2) 전직(Turnover)

심한 경우는 전직으로 발전하게 되고 당장 행동으로 옮기지 않는다 하더라도 벌써 교직으로부터의 심리적 이탈(psychological deviation)상태에 있게 된다.

(3) 정신적 건강에의 영향

갈등이 쌓이고 쌓이면 긴장감, 정신병, 신경병 등의 원인이 될 수 있다.

(4) 대인관계에의 영향

교사는 학생, 동료, 학부모 등과의 인간관계로 많은 시간을 보내게 되는데 갈등의 영향이 이들에게 직접 옮겨질 수 있고 가족에게까지 영향을 줄 수 있다.

(5) 투쟁(Militancy)

갈등의 돌파구가 행정가와의 논쟁, 공개적 논쟁, 열띤 논쟁, 중대사건으로 발전하여 교사의 전문성을 찾기 위한 투쟁의 형태로 나타날 수 있다. 가장 온순하고 과묵한 교사일지라도 어떤 압력 밑에서 일하게 될 때는 투쟁적이기 쉬운 것이다. 이외에도 결근, 태업, 좌절, 의욕상실 등도 생각할 수 있다.

---

179) Kenneth Boulding, Conflict and Defence(N. Y.: Harper & Pow, 1962) pp.305~307을 인용한 Ibid.

Ⅳ. 요약 및 결론

학교조직이 대형화하고 복잡해짐에 따라 관료화되고, 또 교직의 전문성이 제고됨에 따라 전문화되는 경향이 있다. 이런 두 줄기 흐름이 부딪치는 곳에 어떤 갈등이 있을 것으로 보고 연구를 시작하였다. 먼저 학교조직의 관료적 특성과 전문적 특성을 살펴보고 그 둘을 대비시켜 갈등의 원천을 찾아보았다. 그 결과 갈등의 원천은, (1) 권리체제(권한), (2) 존경체제(신분), (3) 전문화체제(능력의 배분), (4) 역할기대의 위배, (5) 조직특성에 따른 기대의 차, (6) 교사의 평가와 감독, (7) 학교조직목표의 전도, (8) 관료적 병리가 갈등의 원천임을 확인되었다.

이어서 우리는 과도한 갈등으로, (1) 교사의 직무수행, (2) 전직, (3) 정신건강, (4) 대인관계, (5) 투쟁, (6) 결근, 태업, 좌절, 의욕상실 등에 영향을 준다고 보았다. 그래서 더욱더 전문성 확립을 저해하고. 그 결과 다시 관료주의를 강화하게 되고, 다시 갈등하게 되는 순환관계에 있다고 본다. 이제 이 문제의 갈등을 해소하는 방안을 제의함으로 결론을 맺고자 한다.

갈등을 해소하려고 하는 행위는 변화로 유도된다.[180] 교육에 있어서 변화·혁신이라는 것도 하도 복잡하고 관여집단이 얽혀 있기 때문에 어느 한 부분만을 건드렸다가 역기능과 부작용이 나타날 수 있음을 알아야 한다. 그러나 갈등해소방안은 그의 원천제거에 초점을 맞추어야 할 것이다.

(1) 교직의 전문적 분화

학교행정 기능과 교사의 전문적 기능이 서로 분화되고 행정기능은 교사의 전문적 기능의 지원체제가 돼야 한다.

(2) 교육행정전문가 양성을 교사양성처럼 대학원과정에서 따로 해야 한다. 행정가의 기능을 제대로 못하면서 교사의 전문적 영역까지 침범하고 있

---

180) 김영식, "교직의 변화·혁신을 위한 이론적 고찰과 그 정립을 위한 예비적 연구(Ⅰ)", 교육학연구, 제14권 제1호, 한국교육학회, 1976, p.31.

다. 그 주원인이 교사출신으로 경력 연수만 채워 올라갔고 현행 행정가 양성과정으로 부족하기 때문이다. 현재 교무부장 교사 등이 하는 많은 일이 교장이 사무직원의 보조를 받아 할 일이라고 본다.

(3) 존경체제(신분)에 있어서 학교행정가와 교사가 대등하거나 평교사가 우위에 있어야 한다. 그래야 행정이 지원체제가 되고 교사가 상위지향 관료지향이 안 되고 평교사로서의 전문성을 누리는 데 만족하여 사명감과 책임감을 갖고 교육에 전염할 것이다.

(4) 권리체제(권한)에 있어서도 관리적 권한과 전문적 권한이 서로 다른 영역에서 작용하고 침해하지 않도록 해야 한다.

(5) 교사의 평가와 감독을 전문가가 해야 한다.

현재는 학교장이 모두 평가하기 때문에 관리적 기능, 사무, 처리 등 겉에 드러난 것을 많이 평가하는 경향이다. 수업을 잘해서 우대받고 있는 교사가 교장이 되기는 어려운 반면, 잡무를 잘 처리하여 교장 되기는 쉬운 실정인 것이다.

(6) 교사의 의사결정권을 확대해줘야 한다.

교육과정, 교수, 학생지도 등의 전문영역에서는 교사에게 재량권을 주고 학교의 주요의사결정에도 교사가 참여해야 한다. 학교장의 지시, 명령에 의해서 모든 조직이 움직인다면 학교는 공장이나 회사의 수준으로 전락되고 만다.

(7) 학교조직목표를 바로잡아야 한다.

과도한 관료화 경향에 따라 행정우위 현상으로 교수나 학생지도보다 행정을 우선시하는 목표전도를 바로잡아 교사의 갈등을 해소해야 한다.

(8) 관료적 병리현상 제거

위에서 들은 목표전도, 형식주의, 각종잡무 등을 제거하여 교사로 하여금 본업에 전염케 하여 보람을 느끼게 해야 한다. 통계나 사무가 어쩔 수 없이 필요하다면 학급마다 또는 학년마다 싼 임금의 사무직원을 두어 처리해야 할 것이다.

(9) 행정가의 지도성 변경

행정가는 전통적 지도성으로 교사를 법규나 강압, 지배, 외관적 복종으로 묶어 놓으려 하지 말고 능력을 최대한 발휘할 수 있도록 해야 할 것이다. 다시 말하면 교사의 전문적 태도나 행위를 저지하기 보다는 강화해줘야 한다.

(10) 무엇보다 중요한 것은 전문성 신장과 과도한 관료화 방지를 위한 교사들 자신의 노력이다.

교사의 전문성이 약하기 때문에 비전문인이 침범해 오고 교권은 도전받고, 그래서 갈등은 더욱 심하게 되는 것이다. 학력을 높이고, 계속 연수에 노력하여 교육에 관한 한 교사를 믿고 맡길 수 있도록 해야 한다. 고도의 전문성을 누리는 직업도 모두 전문화를 위해 투쟁하고 도전한 결과라는 것을 알아야 한다.

(11) 교사의 전문성 확립에는 교직단체, 사회 및 국가가 같이 협조해야 한다.

교사를 낮은 대우와 보수로 하나의 관료적 종업원으로 전락시켜 세밀히 지시, 명령, 통제하여 부려먹는 것이 유리한가, 아니면 전문가로서의 지위를 확고히 해주이 자율과 책임, 사명감과 신념을 갖고 스스로 일하게 하는 것이 국가이익에 유리한가를 심각하게 검토해 봐야 할 것이다. 세계 여러 나라와의 교육경쟁, 특히 공산주의와의 대결에서 이겨야 하는 우리 교사 위치의 중요성을 알고 학교조직의 과도한 관료화 방지와 교사의 전문화 촉진에 교사, 교육행정가, 교직단체, 사회, 국가가 다같이 노력해야 할 것이다.

참고문헌

고영부, 김해동, <u>인간관계론</u>(Ⅰ), 서울: 서울대출판부, 1972.

김영식, "교직의 변화·혁신을 위한 이론적 고찰과 그 정립을 위한 예비적 연구(Ⅰ)," <u>교육학연구</u>, 제14권 1호, 서울: 한국교육학회, 1976.

김영철, "교사의 역할갈등 및 역할모호성과 학교조직풍토에 관한−연구", 고대대학원 교육학과 석사학위논문, 1973.

김종철, <u>교육행정의 이론과 실제</u>, 서울: 교학사, 1965.

김종철, "우리나라 교육 오늘의 문제", <u>교육연구</u>, 제8권 7호, 서울: 교육연구사, 1975.

김종철, "전문직으로서의 교직의 현 위치", 새교육 통권 261호, 서울: 대한교련, 1976.

김종철 외, "교원직무부담에 관한 분석 및 그 적정 직무량에 관한 연구"서울: 한국교육학회 1973.

남정걸, "학교에서의 교원의 역할수행" <u>교육학연구</u> 제14권 1호, 서울: 한국교육학회, 1975.

대한교련, "교직유인체제확립에 관한 연구", 서울: 대한교련, 1969.

대한교련, <u>새교육</u> 통권 261호, 1976.

박성내, "초등교원의 전문성과 사회적 지위에 관한 연구" 미출판 유인물, 1975.

백현기, <u>교육행정의 기초</u>, 서울: 배영사, 1969.

소봉암, "학교조직에 있어서 전문직성향교사와 자아실현과의 관계연구" 서울대 대학원 교육학과 석사학위논문, 1975.

우정남, "관료제의 병리와 학교집단의 성취도 관계연구" 미출판의 연구유인물, 1975.

류동진, "왜 교직의 전문성이 문제되나" <u>새교육</u> 통권 261호, 서울: 대한교련, 1976.

이규환, "외국에 있어서의 교직전문성" 새교육 통권 261호 서울: 대한교련, 1976.

정범모, "교직의 전문성", 교직과 교사, 서울: 현대교육총서사, 1962.

조석준, 조직론, 서울: 법문사, 1973.

진보영, "교육행정의 전문성과 권한배분" 교육행정학연구회 발표유인물, 1974.

Bidwell, C. E. "Administration and Teacher Satisfaction" *Phi Delta Kappan,* XXXVⅡ, 1956.

Blau, Peter M., *The Dynamics of Bureaucracy,* Revised ed., Chicago: The University of Chicago Press, 1964.

Boyan, Norman J., "The Emergent Role of the Teacher in the Authority Structure of the School" in Carver, Fred P. & Sergiovanni, Thomas J., ed., *Organizations and Human Behavior: Focus on Schools,* N. Y.: McGraw-Hill Book Co., 1969.

Carver, Fred D. & Sergiovanni, Thomas J., *Organization. and Human Behavior: Focus on Schools,* N. Y.: McGraw-Hill Book Co., 1969.

Corwin, Ronald G., "The Professional Employee: A Study of Conflict of Nursing Roles," *American Journal of Sociology,* LXVI, may. 1961.

Corwin, Ronald G., "Professional Persons in Public Organizations", in Carver, Fred D. & Sergiovanni, Thomas J., ed., *Organizations and Human Behavior: Forcus on Schools,* N. Y.: McGraw-Hill Book Co., 1969.

Coser, Lewis, *The Functions of Social Conlict,* N. Y.: The Free Press of Grencoe, 1956.

Downey, Lawrence W. & Enns, Frederick, ed., *The Social Sciences and Educational Administration,* Edmonton: The University of Alberta, 1963.

Drucker, Peter F., "The Employee Society," *American Journal of Sociology,* LVⅡ, January, 1952.

Dubin, Robert, *Human Relations in Administration,* 4th ed., Englewood Cliffs, N. J.: Prentice-Hall, Inc., 1974.

Etzioni, Amitai, *Modern Organizations,* Englewood Cliffs, N. J.: Prentice-Hall, Inc., 1964.

Gouldner, Alvin W., "Organizational Tensions", *Sociology Today,* ed, Merton, Robert, et al, N. Y.: Basic Book, 1959.

Lieberman, Myron, *Education As A Profession,* Englewood Cliffs, N. J.: Prentice-Hall, Inc., 1956.

Lipham, James M., "The Role of the Principal" *The National Elementary Principal,* XLIV, No.5, April, 1965.

Litwak, Eugene, "Models of Bureaucracy Which Permit Conflict", in Carver Fred D. & Sergiovanni Thomas J., ed., *Organizations and Human Behavior: Focus on Schools,* N. Y.: McGraw-Hill Book Co., 1969.

MacKay, D. A., "Using Professional Telent in A School Organization," in Carver, Fred D. & Sergiovanni, Thomas J., *Organizations and Human Behavior: Focus on Schools,* N. Y.: McGraw-Hill Book Co., 1969.

Owens, Robert G., *Organizational Behavior in Schools,* Englewood Cliffs, N. J.: Prentice-Hall Inc., 1970.

Peobody, Robert L., "Perceptions of Organizational Authority" *Administrative Science Quarterly* VI, March, 1962.

Thompson, Victor A., "Hierachy, Specialization and Organizational Conflict," in Carver, Fred D. & Sergiovanni, Thomas J., ed., *Organizations and Human Behavior: Focus on Schools,* N. Y.: McGraw-Hill Book Co., 1969.

Waldo, Dwight, *Public Administration.* N. Y.: McGraw-Hill Book Co., 1953.

Washburne, S., "The Teacher in the Authority System," *Journal of Educational Sociology,* XXX, 1957.

Weber, Max, "The Monocratic Type of Bureaucratic Administration", *The Theory of Social and Economic Organization,* trans, by Henderson, A. M. & Parsons, Talcott, Oxford University Press, Inc., 1947.

ABSTRACT

A Study on Professionally Oriented Teachers' Conflicts in Bureaucratic School Organization

I

In a school organization there are two different subsystems. One of these is best exemplified by the bureaucracy for school management; the other by professionalization for teaching pupils.

Large size and organizational complexity of the modern school tend to generate more bureaucratic tendency, because the more complex the organization, the greater need for internal coordination which enhances the power of administrators whose primary internal function is coordination.

On the other hand, the growth of systematic knowledge in teaching and firm sense of responsibility of teaching pupils support teachers' aspiration to monopolize over certain aspects of teaching, which is the basis of professional image. Teachers are increasingly demanding greater professional autonomy and authority in the making of decision regarding instruction and curriculum and freedom from bureaucratic domination. Namely, there is other tendency of professionalization in school.

Between these two sets of tendencies there will be at least the possibility of conflicts. That was the basic assumption underlying in present paper. The writer assumed that concurrent development of professionalization and bureaucracy in school would fertilize the soil for conflicts between bureaucracy and professionally oriented teachers.

Ⅱ

Under the assumption the writer studied theoretically school organization on both aspects of bureaucracy and professional, and then compared characteristics of those different subsystem of the school. From that comparison the writer extracted the sources of the conflicts. As the results, the sources of the conflicts extracted were as follows;

(1) Conflicts arose from the disparity between bureaucratic administrators and professional teachers in the system of rights (authority),

(2) in the system of deference,

(3) and in the distribution of abilities.

(4) Conflicts were due to the violation of role expectation.

(5) Conflicts existed between different characteristics of bureaucracy and professional organization.

(6) Much tension could be attributed to the fact that non-professional administrators supervise and evaluate professional teachers who were more competent in their work instruction.

(7) Conflicts arose because of displacement of goals of the school

(8) and because of bureaupathology in school.

In short, the sources of the conflicts came from between professional and bureaucratic principles of the school organization. In other words, individual needs of the professionally oriented teachers who demanded for autonomy, responsibility, flexibility, and exclusive monopoly of knowledge and skill, provided the conflicts with normative demands of bureaucratic school organization.

Excessive conflicts of the teachers were considered to affect to

(1) performance, (2) turnover, (3) mental health, (4) interpersonal relations, (5) militancy and challenge, (6) and absenteeism of the teachers.

Ⅲ

And then the writer concluded present paper by suggesting the alternatives of conflict resolutions.

(1) The teaching professional and administrative functions ought to be operated separately, in that case the latter would become supporting system for the former.

(2) Educational administrators ought to be trained through the graduate course for professional education as teachers.

(3) Teachers' socio-economic status and all other status ought to be treated and respected for similarly as school administrators' level.

(4) Bureaucratic authority and professional authority ought to be functioned in different areas and the former ought not to violate the latter.

(5) Professional teachers ought to be evaluated and supervised not by hierachical administrators, but by professional colleagues.

(6) Decision-making in school ought to be shared by teachers as far as instruction and curriculum.

(7) The goals of the school organization ought to be given priority to instruction, not to administrative behavior or non-instructional chores.

(8) Bureaupathology in school ought to be treated immediately.

(9) Traditional leadership of bureaucratic administrators ought to be transformed into pattern reinforcing professional behavior of teachers.

(10) First of all, teachers ought to do their best for teaching professionalization.

(11) Last and in conclusion, teacher, teaching professional association, society and government ought to cooperate to achieve teaching pro-

fessionalization and to reduce the excessive bureaucratization of school. Especially the write thought that the administrators play a key role in resolving the conflicts.

5. 학교조직의 이중성[181]

I

인간은 조직을 이루고 그 조직 속에서 산다. 조직구성원인 인간은 조직의 목적달성을 위해서 일하고 그 대가로 조직은 개인에게 금전적 보상과 만족 삼을 준다.

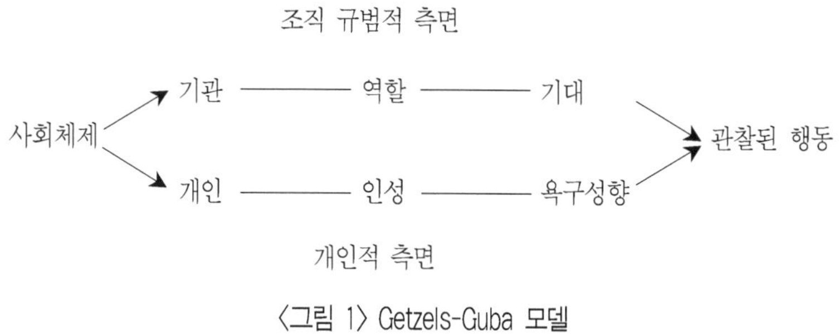

〈그림 1〉 Getzels-Guba 모델

---

* 이 논문은 교육학논총 창간호 1983. 2. 충남대학교 교육학과 pp.64~71에 학생들을 위해 씌어진 것임.

Getzels와 Guba는 인간의 행동을 조직적인 측면과 개인적인 측면의 상호작용으로 다음 〈그림 1〉과 같이 설명하고 있다.

교사라는 개인도 조직규범적 측면인 학교라는 "기관" 속에서 교사라는 "역할"을 각각 맡아 가지고 상급자, 동료, 학생, 학부모 등의 어떤 "기대"를 받으며 생활하고 있다. 그러나 각 교사는 "개인"적 측면의 "인성"과 "욕구성향"이 각각 다르기 때문에 그들의 "행동"은 다르게 나타나게 된다. Getzels와 Guba는 이것을 행동=함수(역할×인성)의 등식으로 나타내고 있다. 어쨌든 교사도 학교라는 조직의 목적달성을 위하여 일하고 조직이 주는 금전 등의 외적 보상과 가르치는 일에서의 보람 같은 내적 보상을 받으면서 동시에 개인의 목적도 달성하면서 생활하고 있다. 여기서 조직의 목적과 개인의 목적이 합치되는 부분(그림 2의 친 부분)이 넓으면 넓을수록 교육의 성과도 높아지고 동시에 교사의 행복감과 만족감도 높아질 것이다. 그러나 조직의 목적과 개인의 목적이 완전 분리된다면 조직에 대한 충성심은 없고 개인은 조직 밖에서 행복을 찾게 되는 것이므로 조직을 위해서도 개인을 위해서도 불행한 상태가 되는 것이다.

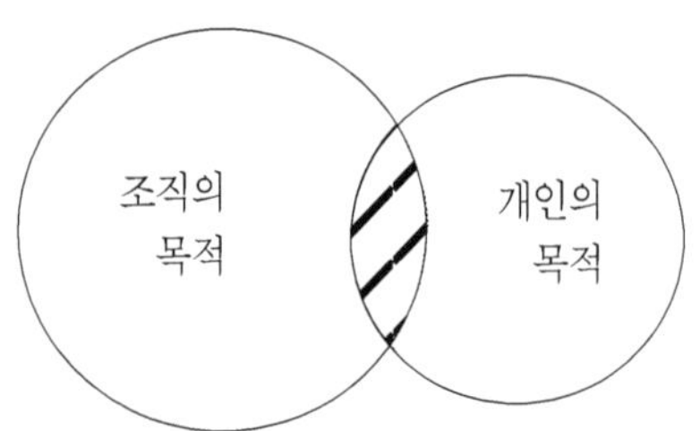

〈그림 2〉 조직의 목적과 개인의 목적의 합치도

Ⅱ

교육행정에 있어서 한때는 조직적 측면과 조직의 목적을 더 강조한 때도 있었고(과학적 관리시대), 어떤 때는 개인적 측면을 더 강조하기도 하였었다(인간관계시대). 그러나 결국 두 측면이 잘 조화를 이루어야 한다는 데 이르렀다(체제적 접근, 행동적 접근).

조직과 개인의 두 측면에 "일"이라는 한 요소를 첨가하여 교사의 학교생활을 "조직" 속에서 "개인"이 "일"을 하면서 생활하는 사회체제로 본다면 "사람(개인)" "일" "조직"의 3자가 학교조직의 목적을 잘 달성할 수 있도록 충분히 조화를 이루어야 한다.(Otto and Sanders, p.393)(그림 3)

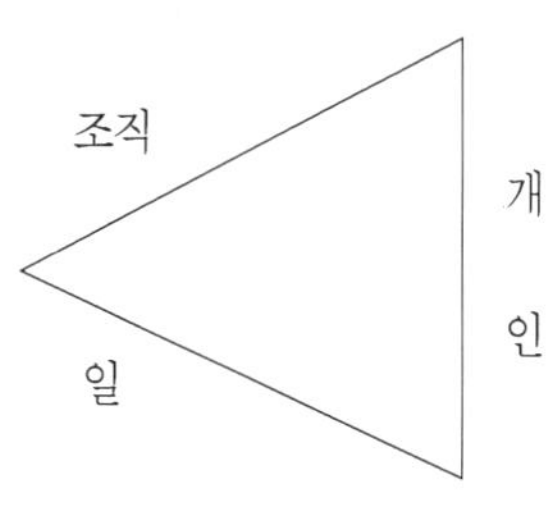

〈그림 3〉 조직, 개인, 일의 조화

그런데 최근 학교소식은 섬섬 더 "관료화"되고 있으며, 그 속에서 일하고 있는 개인인 교사는 점점 "전문화"의 방향으로 나아가고 있으며, 교사들이 하는 "일"인 "교수활동"도 점점 더 "전문화"의 방향으로 나아가고 있다는 데 문제가 있다(그림 3의 조화가 깨지고 있다).

그래서 Getzels-Guba의 모델(그림 1)에 하나의 전문적 차원을 첨가하여 다음 〈그림 3〉과 같이 나타낼 수 있다.

교사는 하나의 관료 조직 구성원으로서의 역할과 기대에 어긋나지 않도록 해야 하는 동시에 교수전문가로서의 역할과 기대에도 맞추어야 한다는 데 어려움이 있다. 더구나 관료주의 역할과 기대는 전문주의 역할과 기대와는 거의 정반대이기 때문에 문제는 더욱 심각하다. 만일 교사의 "인성"이나 "욕구성향"이 관료적 측면과 전문적 측면 어느 쪽으로 더 기우느냐에 따라 교사에게 갈등감 또는 만족감을 주어 교사의 학교생활에 많은 영향을 주게 된다. 관료주의와 전문주의에 대하여 살펴보고자 한다.

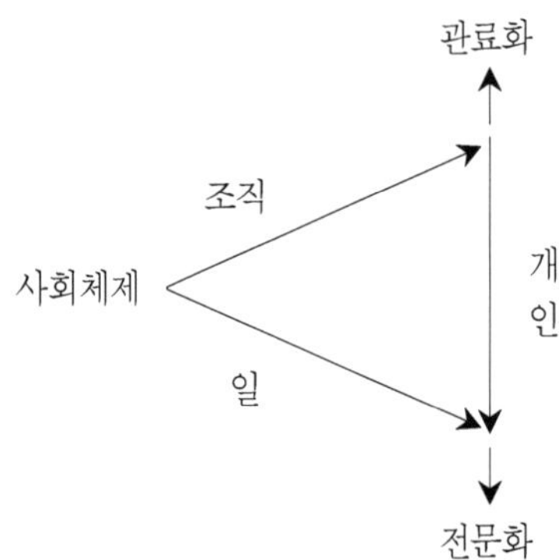

〈그림 4〉 조직의 관료화와 일과 개인의 전문화 경향

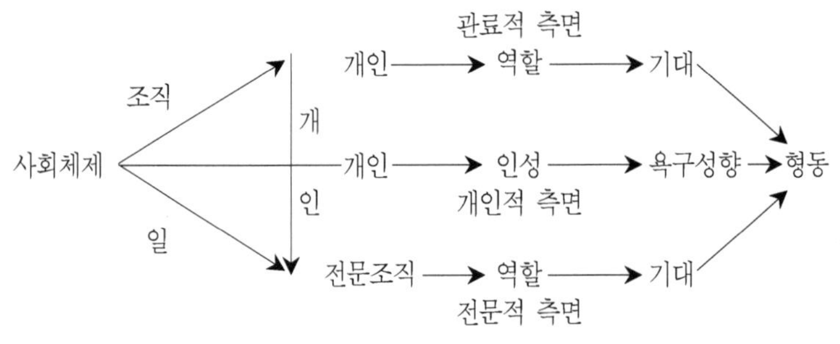

〈그림 5〉 변형된 Getzels-Guba 모델

Ⅲ

관료제를 정의하는 데는 여러 가지 접근이 있으나 관료제의 특성을 들어 정의하는 입장이 많다. 대표적인 것이 Hall(1963)의 6특성이다. 즉 (1) 권위에 있어서 위계가 있다는 점이다. 학교에도 교사-부장교사-교감-교장의 위계가 있다. (2) 일의 전문적 분화가 있다. 학교의 일이 학년별로 과

목별로, 맡은 부서별로 분화되어 있는 것도 사실이다. (3) 규칙과 규정에 의하여 움직인다는 것도 학교에 적용된다. (4) 절차의 명세화도 하나의 특성이다. 학교의 많은 일이 구체적인 절차를 밟아서 처리하도록 되어 있다. (5) 비정성을 특징으로 하고 있다. 관료조직은 인정이나 사적 감정에 쏠려서는 안 되고 또 그렇게 판단되어서도 안 된다. (6) 기술적 능력을 요구한다. 학교조직에서는 어느 조직 못지않게 조직 구성원의 기술적 능력을 요구하고 있다는 것은 뚜렷한 특징이다.

관료제의 창시자인 Max Weber는 관료제야말로 가장 이상적이고, 아직까지 이보다 더 좋은 조직 형태는 없다고 한다. 사실 이 여섯 가지 특성만 잘 갖추고 있다면 이상적일 것이다. 그러나 위의 특성 중 (1), (3), (4), (5)가 너무 지나치게 강조되고 (2)와 (6)은 전문 조직의 특성이기도 한데 이것은 덜 강조되어 현대에는 관료제하면 경직된, 역기능적인, 융통성 없는, 형식주의의 대명사처럼 되어 있다.

그런데 최근 학교조직을 포함하여 모든 조직이 점점 더 관료화되고 있다는 데 의견이 일치되고 있다.

(1) 학교에서도 조직이 점점 너 대형화함에 따라 행정과 통제가 강화되어야 하고 관료화는 어쩔 수 없다.

(2) 또 학교의 기능이 단순히 지식을 가르치면 일로부터 전인을 키워야 하고 사회적 정서적, 심리적, 신체적 발달을 도와야 하며, 영양, 급식, 교통, 불우이웃돕기 등 사회사업 역할도 해야 하며, 범죄를 막아야 하는 경찰적 기능도 때로는 해야 한다. 이렇게 기능이 복잡해지면 조직의 내적 조정이 필요한데 이것이 관료화를 촉진한다.

(3) 또 행정업무가 계속 증가하고 있다. 교생실습에 다녀온 학생들이 이구동성으로 교사들이 가르치는 일 이외의 일이 더 많다는 데 놀라고 있었다. 이것도 관료제 역기능의 산물이다.

(4) 또 학교가 점점 획일화, 규격화되고 있는 현상도 볼 수 있다.

관료적 조직특성은 구성원으로부터 하나의 종업원 또는 관료로서의 행동을 기대한다. Corwin(1965)은 관료적 기대로 다음 7가지를 들고 있다.

(1) 일상적인 일에서 고객에 대하여 획일성을 강조한다.

(2) 과정의 계속성에 있어서 기록과 서류철을 강조한다.

(3) 규정의 구체화 정도에 있어서 구체적으로 규정된 것을 기대한다.

(4) 직업분화에 있어서 능률성과 과업지향을 강조한다.

(5) 기술에 있어서도 일상적인 일에 대한 규정을 기대한다.

(6) 의사결정에 있어서도 일상적인 일에 대한 규정을 적용하는 결정을 한다.

(7) 권한은 조직과 상급자에 대한 충성심과 직위에서 오는 권한을 사용한다.

교사는 이러한 관료적 기대에 얼마나 부응하는 생활을 하느냐에 따라 갈등 또는 만족감이 교차될 수 있다.

학교조직의 관료화 경향과 동시에 전문화의 경향이 점점 뚜렷해지고 있다.

Ⅳ

전문화가 무엇이냐를 정의하는 데도 여러 접근이 있다. 그런데 전형적인 접근은 전문직에 해당되는 특성들을 열거하고 주어진 직업이 이 특성에 어느 정도 맞느냐에 따라 그 전문성의 정도를 따지는 것이다. 그래서 이 특성들을 충족시키는 정도에 따라 Howsam(1980, p.63)은 범속직(occupation)−반전문직(semi-profession)−부상전문직(emerging Profession)−신생전문직(new profession)−기성전문직(established profession)으로 나누고 있다.

Lieberman(1956)의 8개의 전문직 특성의 기준은 다음과 같다.

(1) 특수하고, 명확하고 중요한 일에 대한 사회적 봉사

(2) 봉사하는 데 있어서 지적 기능의 강조

(3) 장기간에 걸친 전문교육

(4) 집단이나 개인에 대한 광범한 자율성

(5) 전문적 자율성의 범위 내에서 행한 판단과 행동에 대한 책임성의 수락

(6) 직업집단에 주어진 사회봉사와 조직에 바탕을 둔 개인의 강조

(7) 완전한 자치조직

(8) 불분명하고 의심스러운 점에 대한 구체적인 사례로 명확히 해석된 윤리강령

이러한 특성에 비추어 볼 때 교사의 위치는 과연 어디인가? 교육에 종사하는 사람은 교직을 전문직이라 주장하고 또 교사를 전문가라고 하지만 아직 판사나 변호사, 의사와 같은 완전한 전문직의 위치에 이르지 못한 것은 누구나 인정한다. 그래서 교사는 반전문직에서 전문직을 향해서 나아가는 것으로 보고 있다. 학교에서 이 전문화 경향이 점점 두드러지게 나타나고 있다.

(1) 우리가 잘 알다시피 교직은 교복으로부터 출발하였고 전산업시대까지도 교직을 전문직으로 생각지 않았다(Parelius and Parelius, 1978, p.187), 그러나 19C말 초기산업시대에 교직은 전문화, 숙연, 전국 교직단체의 구성과 함께 전문직으로 인정되기 시작하였다.

(2) 교사 교육 연한이 점점 높아지면서(위의 특성 3) 전문화에 박차를 가하고 있디.

(3) 컴퓨터 보조 학습, 능력 기준교육, 교수공학 등으로 교사준비 과정이 보다 전문화되고 있다.

(4) 교사의 참조집단이 바뀌고 있다. 옛날에는 교사가 가르치는 데 문제가 있을 때 수석교사인 교장을 찾아갔으나 이제는 전문가 동료나 연구소, 대학을 찾아가고 있다.(Faber and Shearron, 1970. p.378)

(5) 학교에 전문가 자리가 생기고 있다. 생활지도 카운슬러, 교육자료 전문가, 교육 과정 전문가, 과목 전담교사 등은 전문화 경향의 한 증거가 된다. 우리나라의 여러 특수 주임 교사의 출현도 이런 경향으로 볼 수 있다.

관료조직에서 관료적 기대가 따르듯이 전문조직에서도 구성원에게 전문가로서의 기대가 따르게 된다. 역시 Corwin이 제시한 전문가에 대한 기대는 다음과 같다.

(1) 고객의 문제에 대하여 특이성을 강조한다.

(2) 연구, 변화의 강조가 기대된다.

(3) 대안적 규칙의 적용이 기대된다.

(4) 목표 달성, 고객 중심의 강조가 기대된다.

(5) 독점 지식에 기반을 둔 기술이 기대된다.

(6) 전문직 문제나 독특한 문제에 대하여 결정권을 갖는 것이 기대된다.

(7) 전문성에 의하여 규정된 규칙을 적용할 것이 기대된다.

(8) 전문가 단체에 대한 충성과 개인적 능력에서 나온 권위를 내세울 것이 기대된다.

여기서는 전문직의 특성과 학교에서의 전문화의 경향성, 전문가에 대한 기대에 대하여 간단히 살펴보았다.

V

교사는 개인의 목적과 행복을 추구하면서 동시에 조직의 목적을 달성하기 위해서 학교라는 조직 속에서 일한다고 하였다. 학교에서 조직적 측면과 개인적 측면은 중요한 양 차원이다.

조직과 개인, 거기서 하는 일이 잘 조화를 이루면 조직 목적과 개인목적 모두를 위해서 더할 수 없이 좋겠으나 학교 조직은 점점 관료화되고, 그 속에서 일하는 개인과 하는 일 자체는 점점 전문화의 길을 향해서 나아가고 있다. 그런데 관료주의의 특성과 기대는 전문주의의 특성과 기대와는 서로 상반되고 있다. 이 두 틈바구니, 즉 학교조직의 이중성 속에서 교사는 갈등하고, 딜레마에 빠지기 쉽다. 학교 조직 이론가들은 이 두 조직 이론을 포함하고 조화를 이루는 관료적-전문주의조직을 만들어 내려고 하지만 앞으로 안정성 있는 학교조직으로 정착될 때까지는 교사 스스로 각각 다른 이 두 조직 특성과 기대를 조화시키려는 노력이 필요하다. 대개 신임교사는 전술한 전문주의의 기대와 이상으로 기울어지는 경향이 많은데 우리는 이것을 전문지향성이라 한다. 마치 전문의사가 병원에서 환자만 치료하고 연구만 하면 되듯이 교사도 수업만 하고 연구하면 모든 것이 끝나는 것으로 알기 쉽다. 그러나 현실은 그렇지 못하다. 교생실습 나갔던 학생들이 돌아와서 교사의 잡무가 많은 데 놀랐다고 하는 것은 대개 학교의 관료적 측면을 보고 한 소리일 것이다. 대개 경험이 많은 교사는 학교의 관료적 특성과 기대에도 잘 적응하고, 때로는 너무 밀착하여 교수활동에서의 전문성을 잃고 한 사람의 관리와 가깝게 행동하는 경우도 있다. 대개 관료주의에 잘 적응하는 사람이 수업 잘하는 사람보다 교장, 교감, 장학사로 빨리 진출하는 경우가 많다. 물론 전문지향성과 관료지향성, 둘 다 높은 적극적이면서도 능력 있는 교사라면 더할 수 없이 좋을 것이다. 우리는 이런 사람을 양수잡이(ambivalent)라고 할 수 있다.

결론적으로 (1) 우리는 조직의 목적과 개인의 목적을 잘 조화시켜야 할 것이고, (2) 학교조직을 관료적-전문조직으로 발전시켜야 할 텐데 이는 조직 이론가들이 할 일이고 (3) 교사는 현재의 학교조직의 이중성을 잘 이해하고, (4) 전문지향성과 관료지향성 둘 다 높이도록 노력하든가 아니면 이 둘을 잘 조화시키도록 노력하여야 성공적인 교사가 될 것이다.

참고문헌

Corwin, R. G. "Professional Persons in Public Organizations." *Educational Administration Quarterly,* 1: 1-22. Autumn, 1965.

Faber, C. F. and G. F. Shearron. *Elementary School Administration,* N. Y.: Holt, Rinehart and Winston, Inc., 1970.

Getzels, J. W. and E. G. Guba, "Social Behavior and the Administrative Process", *School Review,* 65: 424-41, Winter, 1957.

Hall, R. H. "The Concept of Bureaucracy: An Empirical Assessment." *American Journal of Sociology,* 64: 32-40. Jul., 1963.

Howsam, R. B. "The Workplace: Does It Hamper Professionalization of Peadagogy?" *Phi Delta Kappan,* 93-96, Oct., 1980.

Lieberman, M. *Education As A Profession,* Englewood Cliffs, N. J.: Prentice-Hall, Inc., 1956.

Otto, H. J. and D. C. Sanders, *Elementary School Organization and Administration.* (4th ed.). N. Y.: Appleton-Century-Crofts, 1964.

Parelius, A. P. and R. J. Parelius. *The Sociology of Education,* Englewood Cliffs, N. J.: Prentice-Hall, 1978.

제2부
동기이론

6. Herzberg의 동기 – 위생이론의 검증

Ⅰ. 서 론

A. 문제의 제기

우리 인간은 깨어 있는 시간의 대부분을 일하면서 보내며1) 쉬고 있는 동안의 화제도 자기가 하고 있는 일이나 직업에 관한 것들이 많다. 역사적으로는 원시인에서 현대인에 이르기까지, 한 개인으로 보면 어린아이 때부터 늙어 활동할 수 없을 때까지 일을 하면서 살아간다. 어떤 행운아에게는 이 일이 행복의 근원이 되기도 하지만 다른 많은 사람에게는 슬픔의 근원이 되기도 한다. 일이란 괴로운 것 일이 끝나면 즐거운 것이라는 통상 감정이 있지만 그림에 열중하는 화가나 음악에 도취하는 음악가와 비해 보면 도리어 이상한 감정, 왜곡된 감정이라 할 수도 있다.2)

똑같은 상황에서 똑같은 일을 놓고 어떤 사람은 행복감을 느끼고 어떤 사

---

* 이 논문은 저자의 서울대교육대학원, 1974, 석사학위논문임.
1) Frederick Herzberg et al., The Motivation to Work(N. Y: John Wiley & Sons, Inc., 1959), p.3.
2) 정범모, <u>교육과 교육학</u>(서울: 배영사, 1970), p.161.

람은 불만 속에서 살기도 한다. 인생의 목적은 행복의 추구에 있다[3]고 하는데 어떻게 하면 인간이 자기가 하고 있는 일에서 행복을 구할 수 있느냐는 것이 문제이다.

자기가 하는 일에서 행복감을 느끼기 위해서는 자기, 직무에 만족해야 한다. 자기 직무에 만족하여 행복감을 느끼느냐, 불만족하여 불행감을 가지느냐 하는 직무태도는 "일하는 사람이 자기의 직무로부터 무엇을 원하느냐?" 하는 욕구에 의하여 결정된다고 본다. 자기가 바라는 욕구가 충족되었을 때는 만족하는 태도를 갖고, 직무에서 바라는 욕구가 충족되지 않았을 때는 불만족하는 태도를 갖게 된다. 이렇게 되면 결국 인간이 일을 하는 데 행복감을 갖게 하려면 인간이 자기 직무에서 원하는 욕구를 찾아내서 그 욕구를 충족시켜 주면 된다고 미루어 생각할 수 있다. 또한 과업을 성취하는 데 있어서 그 일에 대한 개인의 태도는 효과성과 밀접한 관계가 있기[4] 때문에 교사의 직무태도에 영향을 주는 요인을 찾아내야겠다는 문제가 제기된다.

이 영역에 있어서 이론적인 기본 가정은 직무에 대하여 만족을 설명하는 요인과 불만족을 설명하는 요인은 개념적인 연속선(conceptual continuum) 상에 있다[5]는 것이었다.

이 연속선 가정은 직무요인이 일하는 사람을 만족으로 이끌 수도 있고 불만족으로 이끌 수도 있는 가능성을 가지고 있다는 것이다.

그래서 불만족요인으로 작용하던 요인을 만족요인으로 전환시킬 수 있고 불만족요인을 제거하면 저절로 만족하게 될 것이라는 가정이다.

---

3) 최정훈, 지각심리학(서울: 을유문화사, 1973), p.131.
4) 김영식과 김옥환, 교원 보수제도 개선을 위한 일 연구, 1973. (미출판) p.8.
5) Thomas J. Sergiovanni, "Factors Which Affect Satisfaction and Dissatisfaction of teachers," in Fred D. Carver & Thomas J. Sergiovanni, ed., Organizations and Human Behavior: Focus on Schools(N. Y: McGraw-Hill Book Company, 1969), p.249.

직 무

부정적 …… 요인 …… 긍정적

불만족 ◀――――――――――――――――――▶ 만족

〈그림 Ⅰ-1〉 연속선 가정

Thomas J. Sergiovanni, "Factors which Affect Satisfaction and Dissatisfaction of Teachers," in Fred D. Carver & Thomas J. Sergiovanni, ed., *Organizations and Human Behavior: Focus on Schools (N. Y.: McGraw-Hill Book Co., 1969), p.250*

그러나 Herzberg와 그의 동료는 1920~1954년 사이에 미국에서 보고된 직무태도 영역의 155편의 논문을 분석하[6]던 중 조사자가 직무만족에 대하여 질문한 논문의 결과에 차가 있다는 데 암시를 받아 1959년 미 피츠버그지역의 11개 업체에서 200여명의 기사와 회계사를 면접연구하여 동기 ―위생이론[7]을 발표하여 종래의 연속선 가정을 뒤엎게 하였다.

그의 동기―위생이론에 의하면 만족요인과 불만족요인은 따로 있어 독립적이고 상호배타적이라는 것이다. 즉 만족요인은 직무만족으로만 이끌고, 불만족요인은 직무불만족으로만 이끌며, 만족요인은 일에 적극적인 동기를 주는 것으로 일 자체와 관련되어 있고, 불만족요인은 일을 둘러싼 환경과 관련된 요인들이라는 것이다.

만족요인을 일에 적극적인 동기를 준다고 하여 동기요인이라 부르고, 불만족요인은 근무환경과 관련되었는데 이 환경이 예방적이고 위생과 같다고 하여 의학용어를 빌어 위생요인이라 부르고 둘을 합쳐 동기―위생이란 말이 나오게 되었다. 이 이론이 미 산업계의 각광을 받고 있으나 아직도 연속선 개념이 우세하고 학계에서 부정적인 반응도 많이 있는바 과연 긍정적으로

---

6) Frederick Herzberg et al., Job Attitudes: Review of Research and Oqinion(Pittsbergh: Psychological Service of Pittsburgh, 1957).
7) Herzberg, The Motivation to Work op. cit.

검증될 수 있느냐 하는 문제가 제기된다.

다음으로는 미국에 바탕을 둔 이론이 상황이 다른 한국에서 그대로 적용되며,8) 일반산업계 종업원을 상대로 하여 세운 이론이 교사집단에까지 일반화할 수 있으며, 교사하위집단간에 차가 없이 긍정되며, 지금까지는 검증 자료수집방법에 따라 약간의 차가 있는 것으로 나타났는데9) 연구방법상에도 차가 있느냐 하는 문제가 제기된다.

요약하면 이 논문의 밑바닥에 깔려 있는 문제는 교사들이 "그들의 직무나 직장에서 무엇을 원하느냐?"10)이며, Herzberg의 동기-위생이론을 한국 교육계에 적용 가능한가 하는 점이 문제이다.

B. 연구의 필요성과 목적

왜 교사의 직무태도에 관하여 연구하는가? 교사, 내용, 학생, 학교환경, 사회환경의 다섯 교육상황 변인11)중에서 교사변인은 다른 어떤 변인 못지않게 중요하다. 그래서 만일 좋은 교사에 빈약한 시설과, 빈약한 교사에 좋은 시설 중 택일하라면 전자를 택할 수밖에 없다.12) 훌륭한 교사를 가진다는 것은 곧 훌륭한 교육을 할 수 있다는 보장이 되며, 교육의 성재가 교육을 담당하고 있는 교원에 달려있다13)고 할 정도로 중요하다. 그러나 실력 면에서 기술 면에서 훌륭한 교사라 할지라도 교직에 만족하지 못하면 그가 가지고 있는 잠재능력을 최대한으로 활용하지 못할 것이다. Davis도 현대 생산성의

---

8) 윤정일, 「게젤스의 사회과정 유형에 관한 가설 검증」(미출판의 석사학위논문, 서울 대학교 교육대학원, 서울, 1970), 머리말.
9) Robert G. Owens, Organizational Behavior in Schools(N. J.: Prentice-Hall Inc., 1970), p.39. Herzberg가 개발, 발전시킨 면접법에 의한 검증은 대체로 지지되는 경향이지만 객관적 방법에 의한 연구는 지지되지 않는 경향이라고 보고하고 있다.
10) 김영식, "조직행위의 기초: 인간욕구와 인간행위", 강길수, 김종철, 김영식, 학교행정(서울: 서울대학교출판부, 1973), p.71.
11) 정범모, 전게서, pp.83~100.
12) 이영덕, 교육의 과정(서울: 배영사, 1971), p.87.
13) 김종철, 세계 안의 한국교육(서울: 배영사, 1970), p.60.

문제에서 종업원의 과업에 대한 태도는 그들의 기초적 기술(fundamental skill)과 직무에 대한 지식(job knowledge)보다도 더욱 생산성과 깊은 관계가 있다14)고 하여 지식, 기술도 중요하지만 직업에 대한 만족, 불만족의 태도가 더 중요하다는 것이다. 그렇다면 직무태도에 미치는 요인을 밝혀서 그중에 불만족의 요인을 제거하고 만족요인을 충족시켜 주어 교사로 하여금 교직에 만족할 수 있게 하여 많든 적든, 우수하든 우수하지 못하든 그들이 가지고 있는 잠재능력만이라도 최대한으로 발휘하도록 하여 교육의 생산성15)을 올려 보자는 데 교사의 교직에 대한 태도에 관한 연구는 필요하고 또한 중요하다.

기계, 산업시설의 100%에 가까운 이용률은 있다고 한다. 그러나 인력의 이용률이 100%가 있는지는 의문이지만 오늘날 유력한 행동과학자들은 일반 정상인은 그의 잠재능력의 10%밖에는 발휘하지 못하고 있다는 견해를 취하고 있다. 이와 같은 사실은 중대한 사실이다.16) 만일 우리 교사의 잠재능력 10%선에서 발휘되고 있다면 현재의 교육내용, 학생, 학교환경, 사회환경조건 하에서도 교육의 성과는 얼마든지 더 올릴 수 있는 여지를 갖고 있는 셈이니 교사의 일에 대한 동기나 교직태도에 관한 연구가 필요하다.

이것은 인간을 조작하여 그 능력을 최대한 부려먹자는 의미로만 해석할 수 없다. 국가적 측면에서 보면 교직태도를 연구함으로써 교사를 불만으로 이끄는 요인을 알아내어 심리적 손상을 줄이고, 현 교육시설의 생산능력을 높이며, 인간자원의 적정이용을 도모할 수 있다는 의의가 있다. 교육계면으로 보면 교사의 사기는 물론 근무의욕17)을 높여 교육의 생산성을 높이고

---

14) Keith Davis, Human Relations in Business(N. Y.: McGraw-Hill, 1957), p.227.
15) 김종철, "교육경영 현대화의 기본문제", <u>교육연구</u> 제6권 제4호(서울: 교육연구사, 1973), p.15.
16) Herbert A. Otto Guide to Developing Your Potential, 소연역, <u>잠재능력을 살려라</u>(서울: 한국생산성본부, 1974), p.23.
17) 대한교련, <u>교직유인체제 확립에 관한 연구</u>(서울: 대한교련, 1969), p.15.

직업전환을 줄이며, 결근태업을 줄이고, 원활한 근무관계를 유지할 수 있기 때문에 교사의 동기를 강력히 요구하고,18) 태도에 관한 연구가 필요하다. 교사 개인적 측면에서 보면 사기 증가방법을 이해함으로 더 큰 행복과 자아실현에 이르게 되고 하루 종일 계약상의 의무 즉 지워진 일을 하고 그 일을 하고 그 일이 끝나면 저녁녘이나 주말만을 즐기는 것이19) 아니고 학교생활에 더 많은 즐거움을 안겨 줘서 하루하루의 의미를 다르게 해 줄 수 있다. 이런 세 측면에서도 교직태도에 관한 연구가 필요하다.

더구나 우리나라의 경우 이 영역의 연구가 잘 정리되지 않아 교사들의 사기를 높이는 요인이 어떠한 것인지를 알아보는 문제는 하나의 중요한 과제라고 박용헌20) 지적하고 있다. 오철진도 석사학위논문에서21) 교직태도에 영향을 주는 요인이 무엇이며 무슨 요인이 강한 영향을 주는지 이 방면에 관한 많은 연구가 필요하다는 결론을 제시하고 있다. Robinson22)은 산업과 교육관계 논문을 조사, 분석해 보고 그중 40% 이상의 논문이 직무만족이나 사기에 관한 것이라는 데 주목하였다. 이렇게 많은 연구가 있었지만 개념적인 정이가 부족하였다.

Herzberg는 1959년 이 영역에서 동기-위생이론으로 정이 발표하여 산업계의 각광을 받아 왔고 그동안 많은 검증이 있었지만 미국과 상황이 다른 한국에서, 더구나 교육계에서는 없었다.

이런 이론이 교육행정 분야에 단순히 소개만 될 때 일선 행정관들에게는 신뢰를 못 받고 오히려 그들에게는 이론이란 현실하고는 거리가 동떨어진 공론에 지나지 않는다고까지 불신을23) 받게 된다.

---

18) 강길수, <u>교육의 과학화</u>(서울: 교학도서, 1964), p.100.
19) 김재만, <u>교사와 교육의 본질</u>(서울: 형설출판사, 1974), p.15.
20) 박용헌, <u>학교사회</u>(서울: 배영사, 1969), p.117.
21) 오철진, 성취동기와 교직태도와의 관계에 관한 연구(미출판의 석사학위논문, 서울대학교 교육대학원, 서울, 1972), p.47.
22) Alan Robinson et al., "Job Satisfaction Researches of 1963." *Personnel and Guidance Journal. XLⅢ, 1964, p.361.*
23) 김영식, "교육행정에 있어서 Getzels류형과 그 영향" 교육학연구 Vol.6. No.2

그래서 이 이론이 우리나라 교육경영에 적용 가능한지 검증할 필요가 있다.

이러한 필요성에 의하여 교사의 직무태도에 영향을 주는 요인을 찾아내서 이 요인들이 Herzberg의 이론대로 상호배타적인 두 부류로 나누어지며, 그 한 부유인 만족요인은 직무자체와 관련되고, 다른 부류인 불만족요인은 일을 둘러싼 근무환경과 관련된 것들인지 밝히고, 이들 요인은 교사의 하위집단 간에 차가 있는지 알아내며, 과연 교사가 교직에 만족하면 직무에 충실한지 확인하고, 마지막으로 연구방법상에 차가 있는지 알아내어 교육경영, 장학행정, 인사행정에 기여하려는 데 좀더 구체적인 목적이 있다.

(1) 교사의 교직태도에 영향을 주는 요인을 알아낸다.

(2) 만족요인과 불만족요인은 상호배타적인가 검증한다.

(3) 이들 요인은 교사의 하위집단 간(남:녀, 초등:중등, 경력연수의 다소)에 차이가 있는지 밝힌다.

(4) 교직에 만족하면 직무에 충실한지 만족요인과 동기요인의 비교로 확인한다.

(5) 면접법과 질문지법에 의한 연구결과에 차가 있는지 밝힌다.

C. 연구의 제한점

이 연구는 많은 부족한 점과 미비한 점 등 제한점이 있다.

(1) 연구표집에 있어서 유층표집이나 무선표집만으로는 면접이란 어려운 협조를 얻을 수 없어 표집 수에 있어서 많은 제한점이 있다.

(2) 면접과 면접분석을 연구자 한 사람이 처리하였기 때문에, 일관성은 있을 수 있으나 객관성을 보장하기 어렵다.

(3) 피면접자의 자기보고로[24] 자료의 근원을 삼았기 때문에 피면접자가 자기 자신에 대해서 아는 것도 있지만 모르는 것도 있을 것이라는 제한과, 대가성(desirability) 또는 요인의 사회적 수용[25]이 크게 작용했을 것이

(서울: 배영사, 1968), p.18.

24) 장상호, "동기와 교육", 정원식 편 정의의 교육(서울: 배영사, 1970), p.90.

다. 즉 돈에 높은 가치를 매기는 것이 좋지 않다고 생각하는 교사는 보수를 만족이나 불만족의 근원이 되는 요인으로 보고하지 않았을 것이다.

(4) 이 연구는 Herzberg의 동기-위생이론의 대체적인 경향은 검증할 수 있지만 요인 하나하나에 대한 확증을 얻기에는 보다 더 정확한 측정방법이 연구되어야 한다.

(5) 직무태도요인-직무태도-직무태도의 영향(Factors-Attitudes-Effects)을 한 틀로 하여 연구하여야 좀더 포괄적인 연구가 되겠으나 연구능력에 벅차기 때문에 Herzberg연구의 핵심적인 일부분만 검증하게 된다.

D. 결과의 요약

Herzberg의 동기-위생이론을 검증하기 위하여 서울 시내 초등교사 50명, 중등교사 50명 계 100명을 면접 분석하고, 연구방법상의 차를 비교하기 위하여 초등교사 115명, 중등교사 65명 계 180명을 질문지로 조사 분석한 결과를 요약하면 다음과 같다.

(1) 가설1 "교사의 만족요인과 불만족요인은 상호배타적이다"는 긍정되는 경향이다. 피면접자가 만족의 근원으로 보고한 만족요인으로는 a. 성취감(만족 50%, 불만족 2%, 그 차의 의의도 .001), b. 인정감(만족 11%, 불만족 3%, 그 차의 의의도 .05), c. 과업자체(만족 14%, 불만족 0%, 그 차의 의의도 .001), d. 책임감(만족 6%, 불만족 0%, 그 차의 의의도 .05)의 4요인이 의의 있게 나타났는데 교사는 일을 성취시키고, 성취에 대한 인정, 일하는 자체, 확대된 책임으로 만족하게 되고 직무자체에 관련되어 있음이 확인되었다. 불만족의 근원으로 보고된 불만족 요인은 a. 근무조건(만족 2%, 불만족 21%, 그 차의 의의도 .001), b. 학교방침과 행정(만족 0%, 불만족 14%, 그 차의 의의도 .001), c. 보수(만족 1%, 불만

---

25) Herzberg, The Motivation to Work, op. cit., p.15.

족 11%, 그 차의 의의도 .01), d. 장학(만족 0%, 불만족 10%, 그 차의 의의도 .001), e. 상사와의 인간관계(만족 0%, 불만족 9%, 그 차의 의의도 .001)의 5요인으로 나타났는데 일을 둘러싼 근무환경과 관련되어 있음을 알 수 있다.

(2) 가설2 "교사의 만족요인과 불만족요인은 하위집단간에 의의 있는 차가 없다"는 대체로 긍정되었다. 즉 하위집단 간에 차가 없이 Herzberg 이론은 지지되었다.

2-a "남교사와 여교사간에 만족요인과 불만족요인에 차가 없다."는 긍정되었다. 단, 32의 가능성 중에 3의 예외가 있다. 여교사가 성취감(남 36%, 여 64%, 그 차의 의의도 .01)에 더 만족하고, 남교사가 과업자체(남 26%, 여 2%, 그 차의 의의도 .001)에 더 만족하고, 발전성(남 16%, 여 0%, 그 차의 의의도 .001)에 더 불만족인 것으로 나타났다.

2-b "초등교사와 중등교사 간에 만족요인과 불만족요인에 차가 없다"는 긍정되었다. 단, 3/32의 예외가 있다. 즉 초등교사가 인정감(초등 16%, 중등 2%, 그 차의 의의도 .02)에 너 만족하고, 학교방침과 행정(초등 12%, 중등 2%, 그 차의 의의도 .001)에 더 불만족하며, 중등교사가 발전성(초등 2%, 중등 14%, 그 차의 의의도 .05)에 더 불만족인 것으로 나타났다.

2-c "교육경력이 적은 교사와 교육경력이 많은 교사 간에 차가 없다"는 완전히 긍정되었다. 즉 교육경력에 차가 없이 Herzberg의 이론은 긍정되었다.

(3) 교사를 직무에 만족하게 하는 만족요인과 직무에 충실하게 하는 동기요인은 일치한다. 만족요인도 동기요인도 공히 성취감, 인정감, 과업자체, 책임감으로 나타났다.

(4) 가설4 "가설1은 면접법과 질문지법에 차가 없다"는 긍정되는 경향이

다. 면접법과 질문지법에 의한 자료 간의 상관관계 $r_{xy} = .88$로 상관리 높고, 면접법과 질문지법 똑같이 만족요인으로 성취감, 인정감, 과업자체, 책임감의 다섯으로, 일치하고, 불만족요인은 보수, 상사와의 인간관계, 장학, 학교방침과 행정, 근무조건으로 일치하고, 질문지법에서 발전성이 첨가되었다.

전체적으로 Herzberg의 동기-위생이론은 긍정되는 경향이다.

II. 이론적 배경

이론적 배경에서는 용어에 대한 설명, 직무태도요인-직무태도-직무태도의 영향의 관계를 살펴보고, Herzberg의 동기-위생이론에 영향을 준 제이론, Herzberg의 동기-위생이론, 선행검증의 순서로 고찰하고자 한다.

A. 용어에 대한 설명

본 논문에서 자주 사용되는 용어를 명확히 정의하기보다는 용어에 대한 안내 정도로 그치고자 한다. 주로 직무태도요인인데 이들은 면접 내용을 분석할 때 어느 요인에 해당됐는지 이해를 돕기 위함이다.

1. 동기요인(Motivators or Motivation Factors)

심리학에서 처음으로 동기현상에 관심을 가진 학자는 McDougall로 "모든 유기체로 하여금 어떤 특정한 목적을 향해서 움직이게 하는 선천적인 성향"[26]에 주목하여 "본능(instinct)"이란 개념을 적용했고 충동이론(drive theory),[27] 목적지향적인 측면에 동기의 초점을 두는 학파도 있다. 이들은

---

26) W. McDougal, An Introduction to Social Psychology, 5th ed. (London: Methuen, 1908)

27) 충동이론가에는 O. H. Mowrer, C. L. Hull, N. E. Miller, J. Dollard, K. W. Spence 등이 있다.

행동의 "지향성"(directness)"[28]에서 찾으려 했고 동기심리학(motivational psychology)을 "행동을 유발하고, 규제하고 방향 짓는 조건을 연구하는 것"[29]이라고 하였다. McClelland는 "동기란 감정상태의 변화가 어떤 단서에 의하여 재생되는 것"[30]이라고 정의하고 있다.

여기서 Herzberg가 말하는 동기요인은 직무만족의 근원이 되는 요인 즉 만족요인이 보다 적극적으로 직무를 충실하게 하는 동기가 된다고 하여 만족요인을 동기요인이라 하였다. 본 논문에서도 같은 요인을 만족요인과 동기요인 두 가지로 강조 의미에 따라 쓴다. 그리고 가설 4에서 직무만족으로 이끄는 만족요인과 직무충실로 이끄는 동기요인과 일치하는지를 검증하게 된다.

2. 위생요인(Hygiene factors)

동기요인과 대조가 되는 것으로 직무에 대하여 불행감을 느끼게 하고, 사기를 저하시키고, 직무에 대하여 나쁘다고 느끼게 하고, 불만족감을 갖게 하는 불만족요인을 위생요인이라 하였는데 이는 의학의 위생과 비슷한 원리로 작용하기 때문이다. 위생은 인간의 환경으로부터 건강의 위험을 제거하지만 치료적 기능을 하지 못하고 예방석이기 때문이다. 불만족요인의 제거는 직무에 대하여 불만족감을 갖게 하는 것을 예방하지만 그렇다고 적극적으로 직무에 만족하게 해주지 못한다는 데서 의학의 위생과 비유가 된 것이다. 구체적으로 본 연구에서는 "교직에 대하여 나쁘다고 가장 강하게 느꼈을 때"를 설명하는 요인으로 나타난 요인을 위생요인이라 한다.

3. 성취감(Achievement)

성공적인 직무수행, 문제해결의 성공감, 자기변호하는 이야기, 일한 결과

---

28) E. C. Tolman, Purposive Behavior in Animals and Men(N. Y.: Cetury, 1932).
29) P. T. Young, Motivation of Behavior(N. Y.: Wiley, 1936).
30) D. C. McClelland, et. al., The Achievement Motive(N. Y.: Appleton-Century crofts, 1953). p.28.

의 목격, 또는 그 반대, 실패에 관한 이야기를 성취감으로 분유한다.

4. 인정감(Recognition)

학교장, 교감, 장학사, 간부, 동료, 학부모, 학생, 전문가, 일반인으로부터의 일의 성취에 대한 인정이 모두 포함한다. 주목, 칭찬, 비난, 비평도 인정감에 속한다. 인정감과 인간상호관계와의 구분은 인정에 강조를 두느냐 인간 상호작용에 강조를 두느냐에 따라 분유한다.

5. 과업자체(Work itself)

직무수행, 또는 과업에 관한 이야기를 할 때 여기에 분류한다. 일상적인 일, 변경된 일, 창의적인 일, 잘못한 일, 너무 쉬운 일, 너무 어려운 일, 가르치는 일, 가르치기 위해 연구하는 일, 학생과 직결되는 일 등이 과업자체에 포함하고 흔히 말하는 잡무는 근무조건에 관련된다.

6. 책임감(Responsibility)

자기자신이나 다른 사람의 일에 대하여 주어진 책임, 또는 새로이 주어진 책임에서 만족감과 책임의 결핍에서 오는 부정적인 태도가 될 때 책임감으로 본다.

7. 승진(Advancement)

여기서 승진은 전문적 성장의 증거로서의 승진이다. 교수기술, 전문성에 있어서의 발전의 표시로서의 승진이다. 교내에서 부서의 이동은 확대된 책임 또는 책임의 결핍으로 책임감에 분류된다.

8. 보수(Salary)

임무수행에서 오는 보상, 봉급의 증액, 증액의 기대, 봉급의 비교에 관한 이야기가 이에 속한다.

9. 발전성(Possibility of growth)

신분상의 변동이나 장래성 등에 관한 것, 타 직업과의 진취성 비교, 친구의 발전과의 비교에 관한 이야기가 여기에 속한다.

10. 학생과의 인간관계(Interpersonal relations-Subordinates)

직무수행상의 학생과의 관계, 개인적인 학생과의 인간관계의 좋고 나쁨. Herzberg는 하급자와의 관계로 했으나 교사로서는 주로 학생과의 관계가 된다.

11. 상사와의 인간관계(Interpersonal relations-Superiors)

교장, 교감, 감독관청 상사와의 우호적 또는 비우호적 관계, 공정·불공정, 경영으로써의 지원, 신뢰성에서 오는 상사와의 상호작용관계를 말한다.

12. 동료와의 인간관계(Interpersonal relations-Peers)

함께 일하는 데 좋은 사람, 싫은 사람, 동료와의 협조·비협조 집단의 응집력 또는 집단으로부터의 고입에 관계되는 내용이다.

13. 장학(Supervision)

장학활동, 장학의 공정·불공정, 장학의 기술, 지나친 감독, 장학의 효과·비효과 등에 관한 언급

14. 학교방침과 행정(School Policy and Administration)

학교경영의 효율성·비효율성, 학교의 조직목표에 대한 찬·반, 누구를 위한 교육인가 하는 의문, 이로운 인사행정, 불리한 인사행정에 관한 사항

15. 근무조건(Working conditions)

일하는 물리적 환경, 업무량, 직무수행에 편리한 시설, 통풍, 조명, 기구, 공간 같은 환경의 적절·부적절에 대한 것.

16. 개인생활(Personal life)

가정생활, 지역사회의 상황, 가족의 욕구 또는 요망 등의 개인적인 생활에 관한 것이다.

17. 신분(Status)

교사라는 신분의 떳떳함, 창피함. 교사라는 것을 다른 사람이 알아 봄. 교사라는 신분의 약함. 자랑스러움 등에 관한 것.

18. 안전성(Security)

교직의 안전성, 근무처의 안정 등에 관한 것.

B. 직무태도요인－직무태도－직무태도의 영향

우리 인간은 살아 있는 동안 끝없이 무엇인가 움직이며 활동을 한다. 이런 수많은 활동들이 모여서 인간의 행위로 나타난다.

인간의 행위도 또한 수없이 많다. 그 많은 행위 중에서 어떤 특정한 행위를 취하느냐를 이해하고 예측하려면 어떠한 상황하에서 그러한 행위를 일으키게 하는가를 알고 인간의 욕구 또는 동기를 이해하여야 할 것이다. 인간 행동이란 근본적으로 목적지향적이라고 할 수 있기 때문에 일반적으로 어떤 목적을 달성하려는 욕구에 의하여 동기화된다. 그래서 김영식은[31] 동기는 곧 행동의 이유이며 인간행위의 진원은 바로 동기 또는 욕구라고 하여 인간의 행동을 일으키게 한다는 점에서 동기와 욕구를 동의어로 쓰고, 목적은 동기가 지향되는 것이기 때문에 유인(자)이 되며, 유인(자)은 가시적인 것(보수, 혜택, 사택, 자녀학비면제, 수당, 연금, 퇴직보험, 작업조건 등)과 불가시적인 것(칭찬, 동정, 인정, 성취감, 존경, 소속감)의 둘로 나누어 설명하고 있다. 동기와 인간행위의 관계는 〈그림 Ⅱ-1〉과 같다.

---

31) 김영식, "조직행위의 기초: 인간욕구와 인간행위", 전게서, pp.47-54.

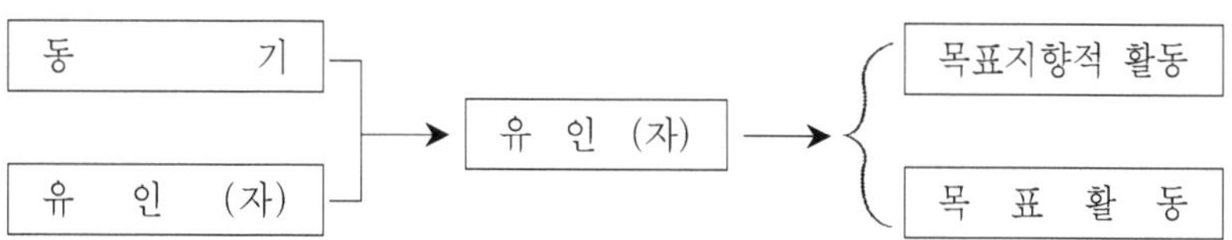

〈그림 II-1〉 동기와 유인(자), 행동의 관계

김영식, "조직행위의 기초: 인간욕구와 인간행위", 전게서, p.51에서

또한 인간은 많은 욕구 또는 동기를 가지며 그 중에서 최강도의 욕구에 의해서 행동으로 표현된다고도 할 수 있다. 〈도 II-2〉에서 욕구 2를 충족시키기 위한 행동으로 나타날 것이다. 교사가 어떤 욕구에 가장 강하게 동기가 되어 행동으로 어떻게 나타나느냐 하는 문제가 중요하다.

즉 "교사가 교직에서 무엇을 원하느냐?"는 본 논문의 밑바닥에 깔려 있는 질문이다.

다시 말하면 동기는 직무태도에 영향을 주는 요인(factors)이 되고 동기에 의한 행동은 곧 태도를 형성하여 직무태도로 나타난다.

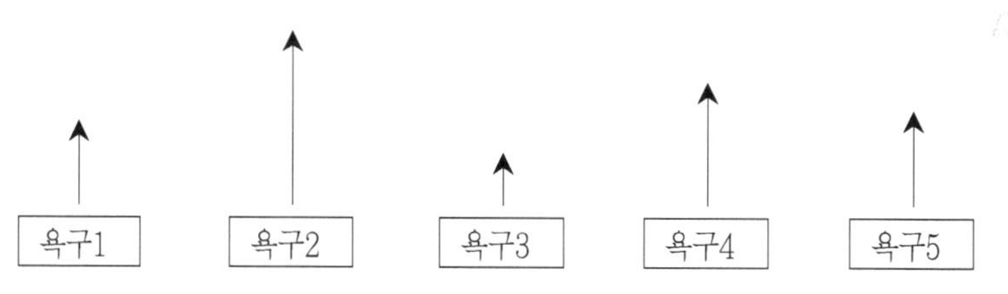

〈그림 II-2〉 가장 강한 욕구의 행동화

김영식, "조직행위의 기초: 인간욕구와 인간행위", 전게서, p.49에서

Newcomb[32]은 생리적 욕구로 구성된 동인에 의하여 목적지향성을 갖는 동기를 형성하고, 다음은 특정의 사물이나 사태에 반응할 준비상태로 태도

---

32) Theodore M. Newcomb, R. H. Turner and philip E. Converse, Social Psychology(N. Y.: Holt Rineuart and Winston, 1965), pp.44-45.

가 형성되며, 이들 태도군의 공통인 가치관을 형성하게 된다는 일반적인 관계를 〈그림 Ⅱ-3〉과 같이 제시하였다.

가치관	: 많은 태도유형이 조직된 공통적인 목표
태 도	: 동기유발된 행동을 위한 일반화된 준비상태
동 기	: 동인에 의해서 자극되어 학습된 목표지향적 심리상태
동 인	: 생리적 욕구

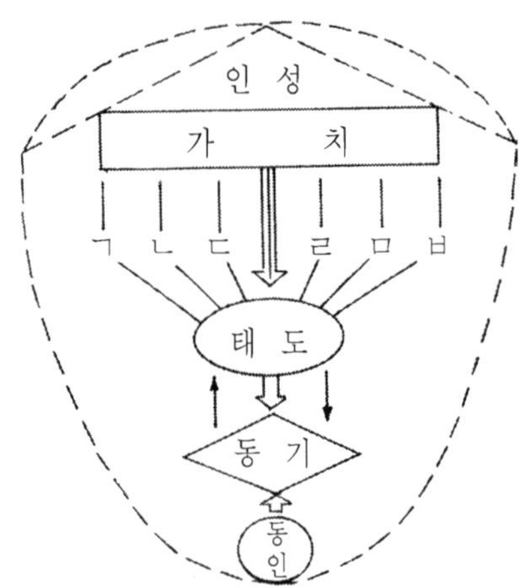

〈그림 Ⅱ-3〉 가치, 태도, 동기, 동인과의 관계

박용헌, "태도와 가치관의 교육", 정원식, 전게서, p.122에서

Newcomb의 부족한 점을 보충하여 박용헌[33]은 이들 개념을 상호작용관계로 설명하여 〈그림 Ⅱ-4〉와 같이 발전시켰다.

〈그림 Ⅱ-4〉 태도와 인성, 가치, 동기, 동인과의 관계

박용헌, "태도와 가치관의 교육", 정원식, 전게서, p.123에서

33) 박용헌, "태도와 가치관의 교육", 정원식편 전게서, pp.122-123.

Herzberg도 욕구, 동기, 행동, 태도의 관계는 김영식, Newcomb, 박용헌의 견해와 다른 것 같지 않다. 그래서 직무태도의 양 극단(만족과 불만족)을 피면접자로 하여금 마음속에서 정한 다음 자기보고로 면접하는 동안 말한 것을 분석하여 태도에 영향을 준 요인을 찾아내고, 직무태도가 직무수행 등에 미치는 영향을 하나의 틀(Set), 요인(Factors) – 태도(Attitudes) – 영향(Effects)(F-A-E)으로 하여 연구하였다. 그는 태도의 영향은 직무수행, 전직, 정신건강, 가족, 친구, 동료와의 상호관계, 사물, 사상에 대한 태도의 변화에 심히 미친다고 보고하고 있다.

본 연구에서는 '연구의 제한점'에서 밝힌 것처럼 교사의 태도의 영향에 대하여는 연구자의 능력의 한계로 다루지 못하고, 또한 동기요인과 위생요인이 상호배타적인가 아닌가가 검증의 핵심이기 때문에 요인 – 태도의 관계만 취급하게 된다. '문제의 제기'와 '연구의 필요성과 목적'에서 제시한 것처럼 교사가 어떤 교육적 태도를 가지고 교육하였느냐가 나타나는 교육효과에 큰 영향을 줄 것34)이라고 믿고 연구를 시작한 것이다.

C. Herzberg의 동기–위생이론에 영향을 준 세 이론

Herzberg의 동기–위생이론은 Maslow의 욕구단계이론과 McGregor의 X, Y 이론을 정리, 확대하고, Argyris의 미숙–성숙 이론의 영향도 받았다.35) Herzberg 이론의 배경이 된 이들 세 이론을 먼저 고찰하고자 한다.

1. Maslow의 욕구단계이론36)

인간은 많은 욕구 또는 동기를 가지며 그 중에서 최강도의 욕구에 의해서

---

34) 이영덕, 전게서, p.26.

35) Paul Hersey and Kenneth H. Blanchard, Management of Organizational Behavior(Englwood Cliffs, N. J.: prentice-Hall, Inc.), 정광복 역 행동과학입문 관리신서 No.16(서울: 한국생산성본부, 1973), p.89.

36) Abraham Maslow, Motivation and Personality(N. Y.: Harper and Brothers, 1954)

행동으로 표현된다고 전절에서 이미 지적하였다.

그런데 Maslow는 최강도의 욕구가 나타나는데 〈그림 Ⅱ-5〉와 같이 다섯 위계가 있다는 것이다. 생리적 욕구는 먹을 것, 마실 것, 주택 등 의식주에 대한 인간의 기본욕구이다. 옛날에는 이 욕구를 직접 채우기 위해 일했지만 현대인은 돈을 벌어서 그 욕구를 간접적으로 채우고 있다. 우리나라 속담에 "금강산도 식후경"이란 말은 바로 이 생리적 욕구를 강조한 것이다.

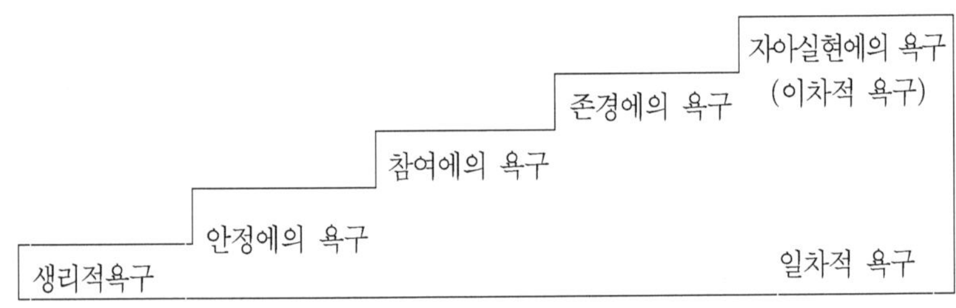

〈그림 Ⅱ-5〉 Maslow의 욕구단계모형

노종회, "학교조직연구를 위한 과업동기의 개념모형분석", 교육학연구 제12권 2호(서울: 한국교육학회, 1974). p.40에서

일차, 생리적인 욕구가 충족되면 다음 단계인 안정에의 욕구가 우세하게 나타난다. 이것은 자기보존의 욕구이다. 현재 뿐만 아니라 미래까지의 의식주를 보장받기 위한 직장과 재산의 유지와 안정에의 욕구이다. 직장에 불안을 느낄 때 다른 욕구는 이보다 덜 중요하다. 두 욕구가 어느 정도 충족되면 참여에의 욕구가 최강도의 욕구로 나타난다. 생각할 여유가 없던 친구를 찾고, 동창회에도 나가고, 취미가 같은 모임에 소속되고, 또 수용되고 싶고, 좋은 인간관계를 맺고자 한다. 어느 정도 인간관계가 맺어지면 같은 모임에서라도 보다 존경을 받고 싶고, 인정을 받으려는 4단계인 존경에의 욕구가 강하게 나타난다. 여기서 존경에의 욕구가 충족되면 그것으로 만족하고 마는 것이 아니고 Maslow의 욕구단계의 최종단계인 자아실현에의 욕구가 우세하게 나타난다. 자아실현에의 욕구는 개인의 잠재능력을 최대한으로 신장

시키는 인간최상의 욕구이다. 음악가는 연주를 통하여, 시인은 시를 통하여, 교육자는 교육을 통하여, 어떤 사람은 이상적인 어머니가 되고자 하는 데서, 행정가는 조직을 통하여, 운동가는 운동을 통하여, 군인은 작전을 통하여 자기능력을 최대한 발휘하고자 한다. 이러한 순서는 대체적인 경향이고 절대적으로 고정된 순서는 아니다.[37]

Herzberg는 인간의 욕구를 "위생욕구"와 "만족욕구(만족에 초점이 된 욕구)"의 두 수준[38]으로 나누었는데 Maslow의 생리적 욕구, 안정에의 욕구, 참여에의 욕구와 존경에의 욕구 일부분까지가 "위생욕구"에 해당되고, 존경에의 욕구 일부와 자아실현의 욕구가 "만족욕구"에 해당되는 내용이다. 인간으로 하여금 일하는 데 고수준의 욕구에 동기가 되도록 해야 한다는 데 Maslow와 Herzberg는 일치한다.

2. McGregor의 이론X와 이론Y[39]

이론X란 대부분의 사람들은 지시받기를 좋아하고, 책임지기를 싫어하며, 안전만을 바라기 때문에 금전과 이익과 처벌로 동기유발시킬 수 있다는 것인데 인간을 부정적으로 보는 인간관리다.

이론Y는 인간은 본래 나태하고 신뢰 없는 것이 아니고 동기유발만 잘 되면 자율적이고 창의적이며 목적달성에 스스로 최선을 다 한다는 긍정적인 인간관리다.

McGregor는 현대사회가 점점 안정되어 가고 풍요해지고, 교육수준도 높아져서 생리적 욕구나 안전에의 욕구 등은 거의 모든 사람에게 충족되기 때문에 참여나 존경, 보다 높은 자아실현에의 욕구에 동기유발되도록 하는

---

37) C. N. Cofer and M. H. Appley, Motivation: Theory and Research *(N. Y.: John Wiley & Sons, Inc., 1964), p.677.*

38) Frederick Herzberg, Work and the Nature of the Man(Clevel and: The World Publishing Company, 1966).

39) Douglas McGregor, The Human Side of Enterprise(N. Y.: McGraw-Hill Book Comany, 1960).

이론Y에 기본을 두어야 한다고 한다.

이런 점에서 Maslow나 Herzberg와 공통점이 있다.

3. Argyris의 미숙 – 성숙이론[40]

McGregor의 이론X에 기초를 두어 인간은 "덜 되고" "못 되었다"고 보아 서로 못 믿고, 인정하려 하지 않으며 구성원을 미숙한 상태로 묶어 놓으려 하며 경영자에게 미숙하다고 해야 구성원에게 유리한 조직이 있으니 미숙에 터한 경영방식이다.

인간을 성숙과 성장으로서의 자아욕구를 충족시켜야 조직의 욕구도 충족시킬 수 있다는 것이 미숙의 반대인 성숙이론이다. 리논Y와 같은 인간관으로 자율성과 책임을 맡겨 주어 자신이 성숙한 인간임을 인정받을 때 조직의 효과도 올라간다.

미숙한 인간으로 보고 Herzberg의 위생요인 같은 물질적 보상보다 성숙한 인간으로 보아 Herzberg의 동기요인인 존경, 자율, 책임, 창의, 자아실현, 성숙 등 정신적 보상을 강조한다는 데 공통점이 있다.

D. Herzberg의 동기 – 위생이론[41]

Herzberg와 그의 동료는 1957년 미국에서 직무태도 영역에 관하여 연구보고된 155편의 논문을 분석 연구하던 중 조사자가 직무만족요인을 찾느냐 불만족요인을 찾느냐에 따라 나온 결과에 차가 있다는 데서 암시를 받아 본격적인 연구를 하게 되었다고 간단히 '문제의 제기'에서 설명한 바 있다.

---

40) Chris Argyris, Personality and Organization(N. Y.: Harper and Row, Publishers, Inc., 1957): Argyris, Integrating the Individual and the Organization(N. Y.: Wiley, 1964)을 인용한 김영식, "조직경영행위", 전게서, p.77.

41) Herzberg, Job Attitudes, op. cit., ; Herzberg, The Motivation to Work op. cit.; Herzberg, Work and the Nature of the Man op. cit.; Herzberg, "One More Time: How Do You Motivate Employee?" Harvard Business Review Jan.-Feb. issue, 1968.

Herzberg의 원연구의 선행연구가 된 이 155편의 분석연구에서는 불만족하는 종업원을 연령, 경역, 성별, 학력, 인성 등에 따른 특징을 연구하고, 책 전체가 직무태도요인 하나하나에 대한 의견을 암시하는 것으로 일관하고 있다. 이 연구에서 만족요인과 불만족요인이 따로 있을 것이라는 가정하에 1959년 미국 피츠버그 지역의 11개 업체에서 기사와 회계사 약 200여 명을 면접하여 무엇이 만족 또는 즐겁게 하고, 무엇이 불만족하게 하고 즐겁지 않게 하느냐를 알아내었다. 여기서 발현한 것이 종업원이 직무에 불만족할 때는 직무자체에 대하여 보다는 근무환경에 관한 것이며, 만족할 때는 직무자체에 관련되었다는 사실이다. 어떤 직무태도요인이 충족되면 직무태도에 긍정적이고, 충족되지 않으면 부정적이라면 Herzberg 연구는 무의미하다. 그러나 연구결과는 어떤 요인은 긍정적으로만 영향을 주고, 어떤 요인은 부정적인 방향으로만 영향을 준다는 것이었다. Herzberg는 종업원을 불만족으로 이끄는 요인은 직무를 둘러싼 주변적인 환경에 관한 것이라 하여 위생요인이라 하였다. 의학에서 주위환경이 병을 예방하는 위생이듯이 근무환경도 불만을 예방한다는 데 비유하여 그렇게 불렀다.

송업원을 만족으로 이끄는 요인을 동기요인이라 하였는데 직무에 만족하게 하여 보다 높은 업무수행을 이룩하는 데 효과적인 동기가 되기 때문이다.

그가 위생요인으로 든 것은 보수, 발전성, 하급자와의 인간관계, 상사와의 인간관계, 감독, 회사방침과 행정, 근무조건, 개인생활, 신분, 안정성의 11개 요인인데 이것들은 업무의 중핵적인 구성요인은 아니고 업무를 수행하는 여건에 관계되었다고 볼 수 있다.

그의 동기요인으로는 성취감, 인정감, 과업자체, 책임감, 승진의 5 요인인데 직무만족에 적극적인 영향을 주고 전체의 생산능력을 향상시키는 데 기여한다는 것이다. 종래의 개념적인 연속선(conceptual continuum)은 만족으로 이끄는 요인과 불만족으로 이끄는 요인은 같은 요인으로 어떤 요인도 양쪽으로 다 작용한다는 것이다. 불만으로 작용하던 요인을 제거하거나 줄이면 저절로 만족으로 작용하여 직무에 만족하게 된다는 것이었다. 그러나 위에서 설명한 것처럼 Herzberg이론은 만족으로 이끄는 만족요인(동기요인)과 불만족으로 이끄는 불만족요인(위생요인)은 상호배타적이고 독립적이어서 불만족요인을 제거한다고 해도 직무에 대한 불만만 사라질 뿐이지 직무만족 현상은 나타나지 않는다는 것이다.

반대로 직무태도에 정적인 쪽으로만 영향을 주는 동기요인을 유지하는 데 실패하였다 해도 이것이 불만족요인으로 바뀌지 않는다는 것이다.

만족요인과 불만족요인이 상호배타적이라는 가설을 그림으로 나타내면 〈그림 II-6〉과 같다. 〈그림 II-6〉에서 만족요인은 중앙 수평선 상단부에 주로 있고, 불만족요인은 하단부에 있으며 굵은 사선을 서로 넘지 않는 경향이기 때문에 불만족요인이었던 것을 사선을 넘겨 만족요인으로 바꿀 수 없다는 가설이다. 두 요인의 구별을 명백히 하기 위하여 김영식[42]이든 예를 요약하여 설명하고자 한다.

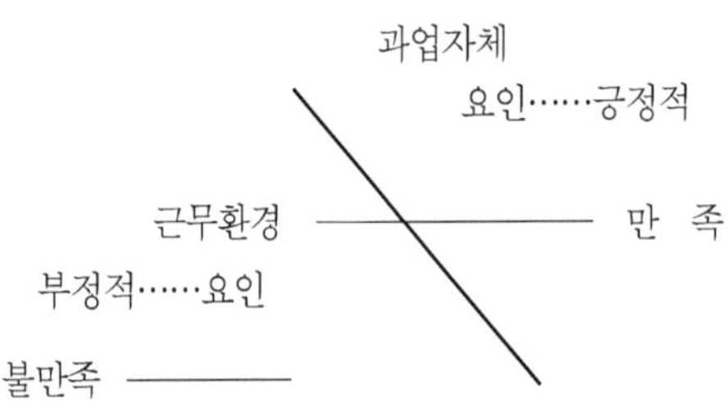

〈그림 II-6〉 만족요인과 불만족요인은 상호배타적이라는 가설

Sergiovanni, op. cit., p.250.

한 교사가 동기화가 높이 되었고 그의 능력의 90% 수준에서 근무하고 있다고 하자. 상사인 교장과의 인간관계도 잘 되었고, 보수, 근무조건, 동료와의 인간관계 등 위생요인이 충족되고 있다. 그러다가 좋은 인간관계를 맺었던 교장이 전출되어 새 교장이 왔는데 사이가 나빠졌다고 하자. 이 교사

---

42) 김영식, "조직경영행위", 전게서, pp.80-82.

는 위생요인이 충족되지 않아서 90% 능력발휘에서 60%로 〈그림 Ⅱ-7〉과 같이 떨어진다.

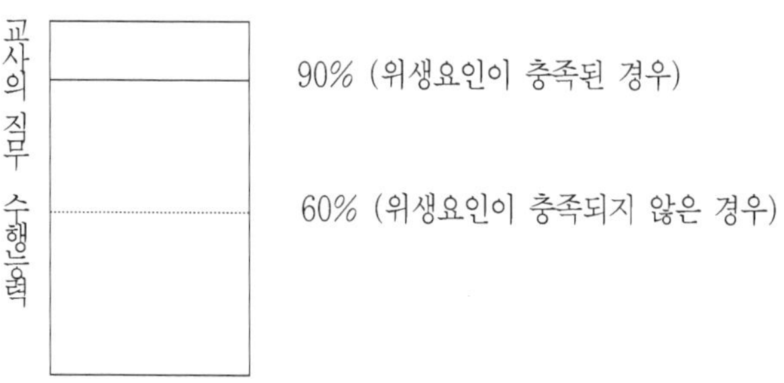

〈그림 Ⅱ-7〉 위생요인이 충족되지 않은 경우의 영향

김영식, "조직경영행위" 전게서, p.80.

그러다 다시 다른 교장을 맞게 되어 처음과 같이 상사와의 좋은 관계와 근무조건이 좋아져 위생요인이 충족되었다 하더라도 그의 능력은 여전히 90% 이상 올라가지 못하고 90% 수준이다.

이제 그에게 성장할 수 있는 기회가 주어지고, 업무 한계가 넓어지고 재량권이 더 주어지고 자기의 실력을 더욱 발휘할 수 있도록 어떤 변화(동기요인충족)가 일어났다면 그는 자기능력의 90% 수준에는 변동이 없을지 모르나 자기의 총 능력 자체가 〈그림 Ⅱ-8〉과 같이 늘어난 능력 중의 90%인 것이다. 점선 부분만큼 교사는 동기요인 충족으로 성장하고 성숙하여 능력까지도 향상된 것이다.

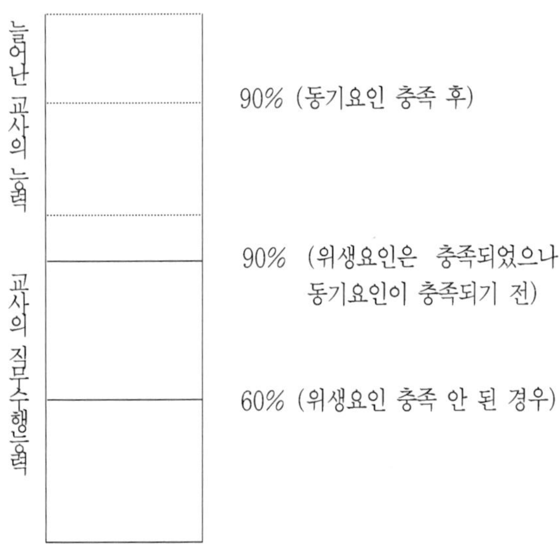

〈그림 Ⅱ-8〉 동기요인 충족의 영향 전게서, p.81.에서

Herzberg 이론과 이에 영향을 준 세 이론을 종합요약하면 〈그림 Ⅱ-9〉
와 같다.

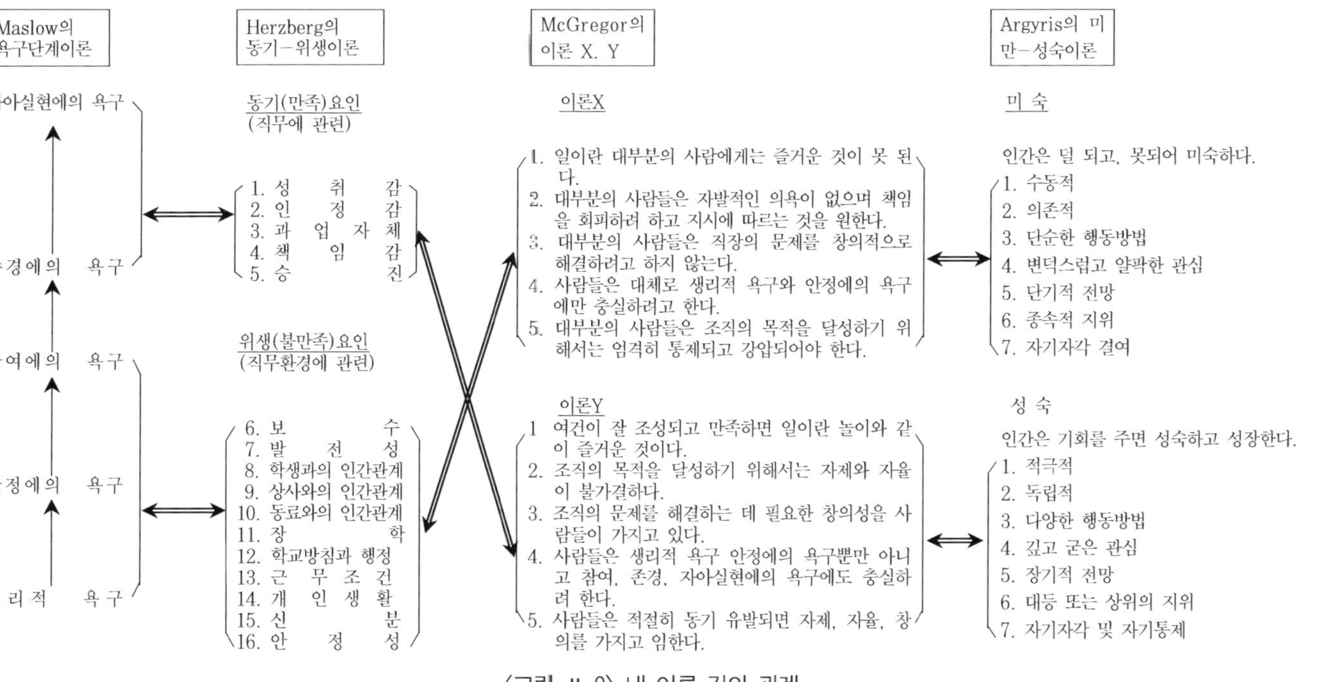

〈그림 Ⅱ-9〉 네 이론 간의 관계

E. 선행 검증

Herzberg의 이론은 흔히 생각해 온 전통적인 연속선 개념을 뒤엎는 새로운 이론이었고 미 산업계의 각광을 받아온 만치 그만큼 검증 수도 많았던 것 같다. 많은 검증들이 대체적으로 긍정적인 경향이나 부정적인 것도 있다. 부정적인 것에는 자료수집으로 Herzberg가 실시한 것과 같은 면접법 이외의 다른 객관적인 방법에 의한 것들이 많다는 데 주목할 점이 있다.

1965연 Halpern[43)의 연구결과는 지지되었는데 동기요인으로 a. 성취할 수 있는 기회, b. 직무 그 자체, c. 직무책임성, d. 승진이 나왔으며 위생요인으로 a. 회사방침, b. 감독의 형태, c. 인간관계, d. 작업조건의 4요인으로 나타나 상호배타적인 것이 확인되었다.

Sergiovanni[44)는 1967년 New York, Monroe 교육청 3,382명의 교사중 121명을 표집하고 그 중에서 면접요청에 응한 71명의 교사를 대상으로 연구한 결과 Herzberg 이론은 긍정되는 경향이고 교사의 동기요인으로 a. 성취감 b. 인정감 c. 책임감으로 의의 있게 나타났고 위생요인으로 a. 학생과의 인간관계 b. 동료와의 인간관계 c. 장학기술 d. 학교방침과 행정으로 나타났다.

이 연구는 Herzberg 이론을 교사에게까지 일반화할 수 있다는 점에서 좋은 삼고가 되었다.

그러나 Ewen[45)은 1964년 1,021명의 보험회사 직원을 대상으로 검증한 결과 만족요인으로 a. 관리자의 관심 b. 훈련정책 c. 보수로 나타나고 불만족요인으로 a. 특권 b. 인정으로 나타나 Herzberg이론대로 만족요인

---

43) G. Halpern, "Relativs Contribution of Motivations & Hygiene Factors to Overall Job Satisfaction" Research Bulletin 65-34, Princeton, N. Y.: ETS, 1965.
44) Sergiovanni, op. cit.
45) R. B. Ewen, "Some Determinants of Job Satisfaction: A Study of the Generality of Herzberg Theory" J. Appl. Psychol., 1964, 48, 161-163.

이 직무자체에 관련된 것이 아니고, 불만족요인으로 인정 등 직무자체에 관련되었다고 한 것이 나타나 부정적이며 Herzberg 이론을 일반화할 수 없다는 결론이다.

한국에서는 정량은[46]이 Herzberg의 이론을 바탕으로 1968년 한국산업인의 직장경험을 실태조사한 결과 산업풍토가 위생요인 지향적이라는 점을 지적하였다. 이 연구는 Herzberg 이론을 소개하는 단계를 넘어 적용연구하였다는 데 의의가 크다. 교육행정도 위생요인 지향적이라는 시사를 얻을 수 있다.

Ⅲ. 연구문제와 방법

이 장에서는 "문제의 제기"와 "이론적 배경"으로부터 형성되는 가설과 그에 따른 연구방법을 제시하고자 한다.

A. 연구문제와 가설

인간은 많은 욕구를 가지고 있으며 가장 우세한 욕구에 의하여 행동으로 나타난다. 어떤 욕구가 교사의 직무태도에 강한 영향을 주며, 어떤 욕구에 동기가 되어 보다 더 직무에 충실할 것인가?

Herzberg 이론대로 피면접 교사들이 대답하는 요인들이 직무만족에 이르게 하는 만족요인(동기요인)과 불만족감을 갖게 하는 불만족요인(위생요인)의 두 부류로 나누어지며, 상호배타적인지 확증을 얻기 위하여 연구가 시작된다. 나아가서 교사의 교직에 대한 만족은 과업자체에서 얻을 수 있으며 불만족은 근무환경에 관련된 것들 때문인가를 확인하려는 것이 주문제이다.

전술한 "이론적 배경"에서 여러 가설이 성립할 수 있겠으나 우선 다음 네

---

46) 정량은, "한국산업인의 직장경험실태조사", 한국심리학회지, 1권 1호(서울: 심리학회, 1968)

가설을 검증하고자 한다.

첫째 Herzberg 이론의 가장 핵심이 되는 것으로 상호배타적 개념이다.

가설1: 교사의 만족요인과 불만족요인은 상호배타적이다.

둘째 Herzberg의 선행연구인 그와 그의 동료에 의한 "Job Attitudes"에서는 연령, 경력, 성별, 학력, 인성, 지위 등의 변인에 따라 사기에 차가 있는 것으로 나타났고, Herzberg의 원래의 연구 "The Motivation to work"에서는 회계사와 기사의 하위집단과 개인에 차가 없이 배타적인 것으로 되었다. Sergiovanni의 검증에서도 교사의 하위집단 간 큰 차가 없이 Herzberg 이론을 지지하는 경향이었다. 만일 하위집단 간에 차가 있다면 교사 전체에 일반화할 수 없고, Herzberg 이론은 교사의 어느 하위집단의 어떤 변인에만 영향 받는 것이 되기 때문에 가설 2가 필요하다.

가설2: 교사의 만족요인과 불만족요인은 다음 하위집단 간에 의의 있는 차가 없다.

2-a: 남교사와 여교사 간에는 의의 있는 차가 없다.

2-b: 초등교사와 중등교사 간에는 의의 있는 차가 없다.

2-c: 교육경력이 짧은 교사와 교육경력이 긴 교사 간에는 의의 있는 차가 없다.

셋째 Herzberg는 종업원이 직무에 만족하면 직무에 충실히 하는 동기가 된다고 하고 다른 학자도 직무만족이 생산성과 직결된다고 하였으나 좀더 확신을 갖기 위하여 교사가 만족할 때의 요인과 교사가 직무에 충실할 때의 요인을 비교 연구하고자 한다.

가설3: 교사를 직무에 만족하게 하는 만족요인과 직무에 충실하게 하는
      동기요인은 일치한다.

넷째 Owens는 "Organizational Behavior in Schools"에서 Herzberg 이론의 검증이 대체로 긍정되는 경향이나 객관적 방법에 의한 연구 중에 부정되는 경향이 많다는 보고에 따라 연구방법에 제한을 받는 이론인가를 밝히기 위하여 가설4가 형성된다.

가설4: 가설1은 면접법과 질문지법에 의한 연구결과에 차가 없다.

B. 연구방법

위의 가설을 검증하기 위하여 다음과 같은 방법과 절차를 밟았다.

1. 예비면접

년섭법의 실현가능성을 타진하기 위하여 계획된 것이다. 피면접교사가 자기의 전 교직경력을 통하여 교직이 좋다고 가장 강하게 느꼈던 때와, 나쁘다고 가장 강하게 느꼈던 때의 양극을 회상하여 말할 수 있을 것인가 알아보려는 것이 하나의 목적이다. 다음은 교사들이 만족과 불만족으로 보고하는 내용을 Herzberg의 직무태도요인에 분류할 수 있는지를 타진하려는 것이다. 만족요인과 불만족요인의 대체적인 경향을 알아보려는 목적도 있다. 이상의 세 목적을 가지고 1974. 6. 5-6. 10. (휴일 제외한 4일간), 서울 시내 초등학교에서 16명(남6명, 여10명)의 교사를 예비면접(1일 평균 4명)하였다.

면접결과 교사에게 자기경험의 양극에 대하여 생각할 수 있는 시간을 주고 마음의 준비를 시키는 것이 좋겠다는 생각이 들어 본 면접에서는 면접내용에 대하여 사전에 언급하기로 하였다.

　다음은 학교에 면접실 같은 장소가 없어 차분하고 안정된 장소와 시간을 정하는 것이 중요하다는 것 이외에는 예비면접의 세 목적을 달성할 수 있었다.

　예비면접 절차는 먼저 면접요청을 하여 승낙하면 면접을 실시하는 데 좀 더 정확한 분석을 하기 위하여 녹음을 하려했으나 대부분의 교사가 녹음을 꺼려하고, 허락한 교사도 녹음을 의식하고 있어 본 면접에서는 쓰지 않기로 하였다. 그래서 면접 중에 또는 면접 바로 후에 분석표에 기록하였다.

면　접　내　용

　선생님의 지금까지의 전체 교직경험 중에서 교직에 대하여 "좋다"고 가장 강하게 느꼈던 때와, 교직이 "나쁘다"고 가장 강하게 느꼈던 때를 회상해 주십시오. 두 경우 중 어느 경우부터 시작할까요?

　1. 그런 느낌이 들었을 때가 지금부터 얼마 전의 일입니까?

　2. 그런 느낌이 얼마 동안이나 계속되었습니까?

　3. 그런 느낌이 들기 시작한 원인은 무엇이었습니까?

　4. 그때 무슨 일로 그런 느낌이 들었는지 그때 상황을 자세히 말씀해 주십시오.

　이제 반대의 경우에 대하여 말씀하기로 하십시다. (위와 같이 반복)

　이제 선생님의 지금까지의 교직경험 중에서 가장 열심히 일하였다고 생각되는 때에 대하여 말씀해 주십시오.

　1. 얼마 전의 일이었습니까?

　2. 어떻게 열심히 일하였나 그때의 장황을 자세히 말씀해 주십시오.

　3 . 그렇게 열심히 일하게 된 근본 동기는 무엇이라고 생각하십니까?

　고맙습니다. 끝으로 저의 연구에 대하여 참고가 될 만한 것이 더 있으면 말씀해 주십시오.

　예비면접의 빈도는 〈표 Ⅲ-1〉과 같았다.

<표 Ⅲ-1> 예비면접의 결과

요 인(Factors)	만 족	불만족	가장 열심히 일한 동기
1. 성취감(Achievement)	13		1
2. 인정감(Recognition)			6
3. 과업자체(Work itself)	2		4
4. 책임감(Responsibility)			4
5. 승진(Advancement)		1	
6. 보수(Salary)	1	2	
7. 발전성(Possibility of growth)		1	
8. 학생과의 인간관계 (Interpersonal relations-subordinates)			
9. 상사와의 인간관계 (Interpersonal relations-superiors)		1	
10. 동료와의 인간관계 (Interpersonal relations-peers)			
11. 장학(Supervision)		2	
12. 학교방침과 행정 (School policy and administrations)		5	1
13. 근무조건(Working conditions)			
14. 개인생활(Personal life)		2	
15. 신분(Status)		2	
16. 안정성(Security)			

초등교사 16명(남6, 녀10) N=16

2. 본면접

이 연구의 주 방법은 면접법이다. 예비면접에서 큰 차질이 없었기 때문에 예비면접과 같이 하였다.

직무태도 연구방법으로는 Hoppock[47]처럼 교사가 직무를 좋아하는지 싫어하

---

47) R. Hoppock, Job Satisfaction.(N. Y.: Harper, 1935)

350 교육조직 연구

는지를 알기 위하여 전면적인 태도조사법, 직무태도의 척도조사법, Hawthorne[48] 연구와 같은 관찰법이 있을 수 있다.

직무태도요인 조사방법에도 이미 정해진 목록을 제시하면 등급을 매기는 방법, 직무에 대하여 좋아하거나 싫어하는 것을 지적하도록 하는 방법이 있을 수 있다. 이들도 편리한 점이 있으나 단점이 있고 면접은 욕구, 동기, 태도 등 경험의 세계를 직접 기술하는 데 좋기[49] 때문에 면접법을 주방법으로 택했다. 다만 하나의 가정은 피면접자가 직무태도의 느낌을 연속선상에 놓고 양 극단의 만족과 불만족을 골라서 보고할 수 있으리라는 것이다. (면접기간 74. 6. 11~74. 7. 18)

a. 면접대상의 표집

면접대상은 서울시내 교사로 실제 수업에 임하지 않는 행정가, 서무, 사서, 양호, 장학사 등은 제외되고 "연구의 제한점에서 밝힌 것처럼 무선표집이나 유층표집만으로는 면접의 협조를 얻을 수가 없어 지역과 교사 수만을 고려하고 면접에 편리한 학교가 참고되어 초등학교 1개교 50명, 중학교 1개교 29명, 고등학교 1개교 21명 계 100명 교사를 면접하였다.

〈표 III-2〉 면접대상표집

N=100

학교급별		성별		교직경력 연수		학력							연령범위 21세-61세 평균연령 33세 9개월 중앙치 32세 2개월	경력 연수범위 4개월-30년 평균경력 9년 10개월 중앙치 9년
초등	중등	남	녀	9년이하	9.1년이상	중졸	고졸	사범	교대	사대	일반대	대학원		
50	50	50	50	50	50	1	6	20	17	35	20	1		

<hr>

48) F. J. Roethlisberg and W. J. Dickson, Management and the Worker (Cambridge, Massachugetts: Harvard University prerr, 1947).
49) 김재은, 교육, 심리, 사회 연구방법(서울: 익문사, 1971) pp.469-470

b. 면접내용

면접내용은 예비면접과 같은데 요약하면 다음과 같다.

(1) 교사가 교직에 대하여 "좋다"고 가장 강하게 느낀 때에 대하여 질문하여 그 대답에서 만족요인을 찾고,

(2) 교사가 교직에 대하여 "나쁘다"고 가장 강하게 느낀 때에 대하여 질문하여 그 대답에서 불만족요인을 찾고,

(3) 교사의 전 교직경험 중에서 가장 열심히 일한 때를 설명하도록 하여 열심히 일하게 하는 동기요인을 찾아냈다.

3. 면접의 분석

요인분석 카테고리를 미리 정해 놓고 면접에서 찾아낸 요인을 찾아내어 빈도로 표시하였다. 요인분석 카테고리는 부록Ⅱ와 같다.

4. 자료처리

가설1을 검증하기 위하여 즉 만족요인과 불만족요인이 따로 있고 상호배타적인가를 검증하기 위하여 피면접자가 만족으로 보고한 각 요인에 대한 빈도와 불만족으로 보고한 빈도를 내어 그 차가 의의 있는가를 검증하였다. 상관표집(같은 표집)의 경우(변화의 검증)이고 극단치가 있기 때문에 Yates의 비연속성 교정공식[50] $X^2 = \frac{(A - D - 1)^2}{A + D}$ 을 써서 .05이하를 의의 있는 차로 보아 만족요인 또는 불만족요인으로 정했다.

가설2. 하위집단 간의 차를 검증하기 위하여 원 빈도로서의 X2계산공식[51] $X^2 = \frac{N(AD - BC)^2}{(A + B)(C + D)(A + C)(B + D)}$ 을 썼다. 가설 3, 4는 가설1과 같은 공식으로 처리하여 비교하였다.

---

50) 정범모, 교육, 심리 통계적 방법(서울: 배영사, 1964) pp.469-470
51) 상게서, p.264

5. 질문지법

　면접법에 의한 검증은 Herzberg 이론을 긍정하는 경향이지만 다른 객관적인 방법에 의한 검증은 지지되지 않는 경향이라는 것은 가설4의 형성에서 설명하였다. 가설4를 검증하기 위하여 질문지법을 채택하였다(기간 74. 7. 19-74. 7. 25).

　a. 표　집

　서울시내 "가" "나" "다"급, 초등학교에서 각각 1개교씩 3개교, "가급" 중학교1, "나급" 고등학교1, 계 5개교에서 초등교사 115명, 중등교사 65명: 남교사 94명, 여교사 86명 계 180명교사가 대상이 되었다. 배부한 질문지 230매 중 202매가 회수되고, 회수된 것 중 180매가 유효하여 성공률 78%이었다.

〈표 Ⅲ-3〉 질문지회수결과표

N=180

학교 급별		성별		교육 경력 년수		학　　　력							연령범위 21세~61세	경력 연수 5월−29년
초등	중등	남	녀	9년 이하	9.1년 이상	중졸	고졸	사범	교대	사대	일반대	대학원	평균연령 32세 6개월 중앙치 32세 2개월	평균경력 10년 중앙치 9년 4개월
115	65	94	86	86	94	0	8	50	40	41	41	0		

　b. 질문지 내용

　질문지 내용은 두 부분으로 되어 있는데 첫 부분은 직무태도요인을 제시해 놓고 면접 내용과 같은 질문에 해당하는 요인을 골라서 쓰도록 되어 있는 선택형이고, 뒷부분은, 면접 내용과 같은 자유기술형으로 되어 두 부분의 답이 일치하는 성의 있는 응답자의 것만 자료로 썼다.

　자료의 처리는 면접법에서와 같다.

Ⅳ. 결과와 해석

자료를 분석처리한 결과를 가설 순서대로 제시하고 해석하고자 한다.

A. 만족요인과 불만족요인

가설1: 교사의 만족요인과 불만족요인은 상호배타적이라는 긍정되는 경향이다.

피면접 교사가 교직에 대하여 가장 만족감을 느낄 때와 가장 불만족감을 느낄 때의 퍼센트와 X2치는 〈표 Ⅳ-1〉과 같다.

교사가 만족으로 표시한 것을 보면 성취감(50%), 인정감(11%) 과업자체(14%), 책임감(6%)의 4요인이 81%를 차지하고, 1위부터 4위까지 차지하고 있다.

이들 4요인은 모두 직무자체와 관련되어 있다. 승진은 0%로 나타났다. 나머지 11요인을 모두 합쳐도 19%에 지나지 않는다.

교사가 가장 불만족감을 갖는 근원으로 표시한 것을 보면 근무조건이 1위로 21%, 학교방침과 행정이 14%로 2위, 신분이 13%로 3위, 보수가 11%로 4위, 장학이 10%로 5위, 상사와의 인간관계 8위의 순서로 나타났다. 이들은 모두 근무환경과 관련되어 있고 교사가 만족으로 표시한 성취감, 인정감, 과업자체, 책임감과 승진에 불만족으로 표시한 것은 모두 합쳐도 6%뿐이다.

만족과 불만족의 근원으로 .05수준(X2치 3.841)에서 의의 있게 차가 있는 것은 다음과 같다. 만족요인으로 성취감*(P<.001), 인정감*(P<.05), 과업자체*(P<.001), 책임감*(P<.05)으로 나타났다.

<표 Ⅳ-1> 교사의 만족과 불만족의 %와 X2치

요 인	만 족	불만족	X2 치	P
	(%)			
1. 성취감	50*	2	46,620	.001
2. 인정감	11*	3	4,082	.05
3. 과업자체	14*	0	12,071	.001
4. 책임감	6*	0	4,166	.05
5. 승진	0	1		
6. 보수	1	11*	6,750	.01
7. 발전성	2	8	2,500	
8. 학생과의 인간관계	5	1	1,500	
9. 상사와의 인간관계	0	9*	7,111	.001
10. 동료와의 인간관계	0	3	1,333	
11. 장학	0	10*	8,100	.001
12. 학교방침과 행정	0	14*	12,071	.001
13. 근무조건	0	21*	19,074	.001
14. 개인생활	5	4		
15. 신분	5	13	2,622	
16. 안정성	1	0		
N=100	100%	100%		

* .05수준(X2=3.841)에서 의의 있는 차가 있다.

불만족요인으로는 보수*(P<.01), 상사와의 인간관계*(P<.001), 장학 *(P<.001), 학교방침과 행정*(P<.001), 근무조건*(P<.001)의 5요인 이 의의 있게 나타났다. 그 외의 발전성, 동료와의 인간관계, 신분은 확실 히 불만족으로 많이 영향은 주고 있으나 만족과 .05수준의 차가 못 된다. 이것은 표집이 크면 차가 커질 가능성도 있다. 학생과의 인간관계, 개인생 활, 안정성은 교직의 특수성에서 오는 영향으로 해석되며 산업계의 종업원 과 비교하여 차를 발현할 수 있다.

만족요인과 불만족요인으로 반응한 것을 도표로 그리면 <그림 Ⅳ-2>와 같다. 〈그림 Ⅳ-2〉는 만족요인과 불만족요인은 상호배타적이라는 가설〈그림 Ⅱ-6〉과 비슷함을 알 수 있다.

요약하면 가설1은 긍정되는 경향이고 만족요인으로 성취감, 인정감, 과업자체, 책임감, 불만족요인으로 보수, 상사와의 인간관계, 장학, 학교방침과 행정, 근무조건으로 나타났다.

B. 하위집단간의 차

가설 2: 교사의 만족요인과 불만족요인은 다음 하위집단 간에 의의 있는 차가 없다는 긍정되는 경향이다. 즉 하위집단 간에 큰 차가 없이 Herzberg 이론을 긍정하는 경향이라고 해석할 수 있다. 그러나 96의 가능성 중에서 6의 예외가 있으니 다음과 같다.

2-a. '남교사와 여교사 간에는 의의 있는 차가 없다'에서 3의 예외가 있다.

여교사가 성취감*에서 만족하고, 남교사가 과업자체*에 더 만족하고 발전성*에 더 불만족하는 것으로 나타났다.

남교사와 여교사의 차는 〈표 Ⅳ-2〉와 같다.

2-b. 초등교사와 중등교사 간에 의의 있는 차가 없다는 긍정되는 경향이다. 즉 초등교사와 중등교사 간에 차가 없이 Herzberg이론을 긍정하는 경향이다. 의의 있는 차가 있는 것은 인정감*, 발전성*, 학교방침과 행정*의 3요인으로 나타났다.

〈표 Ⅳ-3〉을 보면 초등교사가 중등교사보다 인정감*에 더 만족하고 학교방침과 행정*에 더 불만족하며, 중등교사가 초등교사보다 발전성*에 더 불만족하고 있는 것으로 나타났다.

2-c. 교육경력이 적은 교사와 교육경력이 많은 교사 간에는 의의 있는 차가 없다는 긍정되었다.

교육경력 연수를 편의상 평균치와 중앙치에 가까운 9년을 중심으로 두 집단으로 나누어 비교한바 의의 있는 차가 있는 요인은 하나도 없었다.

교사경역에 차가 없이 Herzberg이론을 지지한다고 할 수 있다.

〈그림 Ⅳ-1〉 교사의 만족요인과 불만족요인은 상호배타적이다

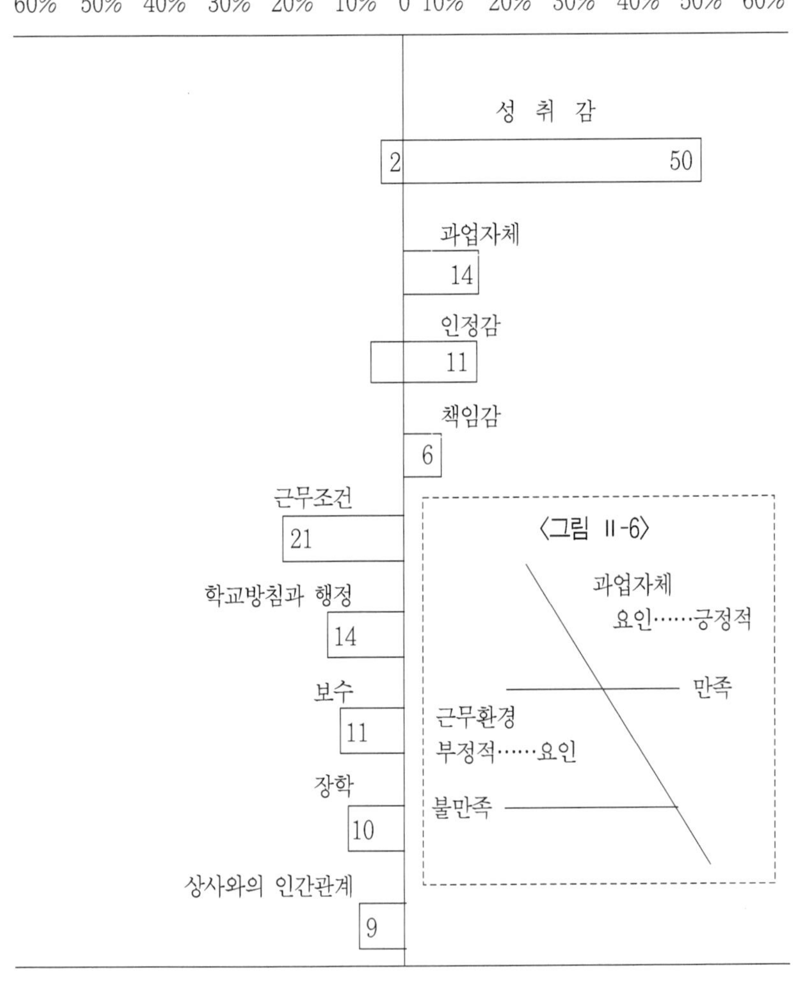

〈표 IV-2〉 하위집단 남교사와 녀교사의 차

요 인	만 족				불만족			
	남	녀	X^2	P	남	녀	X^2	P
	(%)	(%)			(%)	(%)		
1. 성 취 감	36	64*	7,840	.01	4	0		
2. 인 정 감	12	10			4	2		
3. 과 업 자 체	26*	2	11,960	.001	0	0		
4. 책 임 감	6	6			0	0		
5. 승 진	0	0			2	0		
6. 보 수	2	0			16	6	2,500	
7. 발 전 성	0	4			16*	0	8,695	.001
8. 학생과의 인간관계	2	8			0	2		
9. 상사와의 인간관계	0	0			6	12		
10. 동료와의 인간관계	0	0			0	6		
11. 장 학	0	0			12	8		
12. 학교방침과 행정	0	0			12	16		
13. 근 무 조 건	0	0			18	24		
14. 개 인 생 활	8	2			2	6		
15. 신 분	6	4			8	18		
16. 안 정 성	2	0			0	0		
N=100(남50, 여50)	100%	100%			100%	100%		

* .05수준(X^2=3.84)에서 의의 있는 차가 있다.

〈표 IV-3〉 하위집단 초등교사와 중등교사의 차

요 인	만 족				불만족			
	초등	중등	X^2	P	초등	중등	X^2	P
	(%)	(%)			(%)	(%)		
1. 성 취 감	40	60			0	4		
2. 인 정 감	20*	2	8,213	.001	2	4		
3. 과 업 자 체	14	14			0	0		
4. 책 임 감	6	6			0	0		

요 인	만 족				불만족			
	초등	중등	X2	P	초등	중등	X2	P
	(%)	(%)			(%)	(%)		
5. 승 진	0	0			2	0		
6. 보 수	2	0			14	8		
7. 발 전 성	0	4			2	14*	4,891	.05
8. 학생과의 인간관계	8	2			0	2		
9. 상사와의 인간관계	0	0			14	4	3,052	
10. 동료와의 인간관계	0	0			2	4		
11. 장 학	0	0			8	12		
12. 학교방침과 행정	0	0			24*	4	8,301	.001
13. 근 무 조 건	0	0			20	22		
14. 개 인 생 활	4	6			2	6		
15. 신 분	6	4			10	16		
16. 안 정 성	0	2			0	0		
N=100(초50, 중50)	100%	100%			100%	100%		

* .05수준(X2=3.841)에서 의의 있는 차가 있다.

교사경력이 적은 교사와 많은 교사의 만족과 불만족의 차를 표로 나타내면 〈표 Ⅳ-4〉와 같다.

〈표 Ⅳ-4〉 하위집단 교육경력이 적은 교사와 많은 교사의 차

요 인	만 족				불만족			
	9년 이하	9.1년 이상	X2	P	9년 이하	9.1년 이상	X2	P
	(%)	(%)			(%)	(%)		
1. 성 취 감	50	50			2	2		
2. 인 정 감	10	12			2	4		
3. 과 업 자 체	16	12			0	0		
4. 책 임 감	2	10			0	0		
5. 승 진	0	0			0	2		
6. 보 수	0	2			6	16		

요 인	만 족				불만족			
	9년 이하	9.1년 이상	X2	P	9년 이하	9.1년 이상	X2	P
	(%)	(%)			(%)	(%)		
7. 발 전 성	4	0			6	10		
8. 학생과의 인간관계	6	4			0	2		
9. 상사와의 인간관계	0	0			12	6		
10. 동료와의 인간관계	0	0			6	0		
11. 장 학	0	0			12	8		
12. 학교방침과 행정	0	0			18	10		
13. 근 무 조 건	0	0			22	20		
14. 개 인 생 활	6	4			4	4		
15. 신 분	6	4			10	16		
16. 안 정 성	0	2			0	0		
N=100	100%	100%			100%	100%		

C. 만족요인과 동기요인

Herzberg 자신은 직무에 만족하면 직무에 충실하게 하는지 조사하지 않고 만족요인을 동기요인이라 불렀다. 그 점을 밝히기 위하여 가설3이 형성되었다는 것은 이미 설명하였다. 여기서 만족요인은 교사가 교직에 대하여 "좋다"고 가장 강하게 느꼈을 때를 이야기하는 중에 나타난 요인이고, 동기요인은 교사가 가장 열심히 일했다고 보고한 때 나타난 요인으로 하여 그 일치 여부를 알아본 것이다.

〈표 Ⅳ-5〉 만족요인과 동기요인의 관계

요 인	만 족	동 기
1. 성 취 감	50%	19%
2. 인 정 감	11	23
3. 과 업 자 체	14	17
4. 책 임 감	6계81	29계86
5. 승 진	0	0

요 인	만 족	동 기
6. 보 수	1	1
7. 발 전 성	2	1
8. 학생과의 인간관계	5	2
9. 상사와의 인간관계	0	3
10. 동료와의 인간관계	0	2
11. 장 학	0	0
12. 학교방침과 행정	0	1
13. 근 무 조 건	0	0
14. 개 인 생 활	5	2
15. 신 분	5	0
16. 안 정 성	1	0
	100%	100%

$$\Upsilon xy = .65$$

가설3: 교사를 직무에 만족하게 하는 만족요인과 직무에 충실하게 하는 동기요인은 일치한다는 긍정되는 경향이다.

가설1에서 밝혀진 성취감, 인정감, 과업자체, 책임감의 4요인에 만족으로 81%가 반응하고 있는데 교사에게 가장 열심히 일했다고 보고한 동기로는 이들 4요인이 더욱 뚜렷이 나타나 86%가 차지하고, 다른 12요인을 모두 합쳐도 14%밖에 안 되고 있다. 또한 만족과 동기와의 16요인 전체를 어느 정도 상관 있는가를 알아보기 위하여 상관관계를 내었더니 $\Upsilon xy = .65$로 확실히 상관리 있었다. 만족할 때에 나온 요인과 열심히 일하는 동기가 된 요인과의 관계는 〈표 IV-5〉와 같다. 다만 교사의 만족요인으로 성취감이 50%나 되었는데 19%로 줄어든 반면에 교사가 가장 열심히 일하게 된 동기요인으로 책임감이 29%로 수위로 나타났다. 중요한 책임을 믿고 맡겨 줄 때 열심히 일했다고 보고하고 있다. 결과적으로 만족요인을 찾느냐 열심히 일한 동기요인을 찾느냐에 있어 빈도에는 약간의 차이가 있으나 요인자체에는 변동이 없어 만족요인과 동기요인은 일치함을 알 수 있다.

D. 연구방법상의 차

가설4: 가설1은 면접법과 질문지법에 차가 없다는 긍정되었다. 즉 He-rzberg의 동기-위생이론은 면접법과 질문지법의 연구방법상의 차가 없이 긍정되는 경향이다.

〈표 Ⅳ-6〉 면접법과 질문지법에 의한 자료의 비교에서 보면 만족요인으로는 성취감*, 인정감*, 과업자체*, 책임감*의 4요인으로 두 방법 모두 일치하고 질문지법에 의한 자료의 P가 모두 .001수준으로 보다 더 의의 있게 나타났다.

불만족요인으로 보수*, 상사와의 관계*, 장학*, 학교방침과 행정*, 근무조건*의 5요인으로 두 방법으로 똑같이 나타났으나 질문지법에서 발전성*이 하나 더 추가되었다. 질문지법에서 발전성에 불만으로 표시한 기여자는 중등교사, 그 중에서도 교육경력이 9.1년 이상이 되는 경력이 많은 교사이다. 이 한 요인의 차는 표집, 조사대상 수, 질문지 작성 방법, 분석과정 등의 정밀성 부족에서 오는 차로 해석하고 질문지법이기 때문에 온 차로만 해석하기 어렵다. 질문지법에서 한 요인이 불만족요인으로 근무환경에서 첨가되었다는 것은 오히려 Herzberg 이론이 질문지법에 의하여 보다 더 긍정적이지 부정적인 경향은 아니라고 해석된다.

〈표 Ⅳ-6〉 면접법과 질문지법에 의한 자료의 비교

요 인	면접법에 의한 자료				질문지법에 의한 자료			
	만족	불만족	$X2$	P	만족	불만족	$X2$	P
	(%)	(%)			(%)	(%)		
1. 성 취 감	50*	2	46,620	.001	35*	2	59,016	.001
2. 인 정 감	11*	3	4,082	.05	14*	3	15,750	.001
3. 과 업 자 체	14*	0	12,071	.001	28*	0	48,020	.001
4. 책 임 감	6*	0	4,166	.05	5*	0	7,111	.001
5. 승 진	0	1			0	2	2.25	
6. 보 수	1	11*	6,750	.01	1	12*	17,391	.001
7. 발 전 성	2	8	2,500		1	17*	25,757	.001

요 인	면접법에 의한 자료				질문지법에 의한 자료			
	만족	불만족	X^2	P	만족	불만족	X^2	P
	(%)	(%)			(%)	(%)		
8. 학생과의 인간관계	5	1	1,500		2	3		
9. 상사와의 인간관계	0	9*	7,111	.001	0	8*	12,071	.001
10. 동료와의 인간관계	0	3	1,333		2	1		
11. 장 학	0	10*	8,100	.001	0	3*	4,166	.05
12. 학교방침과 행정	0	14*	12,071	.001	0	11*	18,050	.001
13. 근 무 조 건	0	21*	19,072	.001	0	27*	46,020	.001
14. 개 인 생 활	5	4			4	2		
15. 신 분	5	13	2,622		6	8		
16. 안 정 성	1	0			2	1		
	100%	100%			100%	100%		
	N=100 (초등50, 중등50)				N=180(초등115, 중등65)			

결과를 요약하면 교사의 만족요인과 불만족요인은 상호배타적인 결과로 나타났으며 만족요인은 일 자체와 관련된 성취감, 인정감, 과업자체, 책임감으로 나타났으며, 불만족요인은 보수, 상사와의 관계, 장학, 학교방침과 행정, 근무조건의 근무환경과 관련되어 Herzberg의 동기-위생이론은 긍정되는 경향이다.

하위집단 간에 큰 차가 없었으며 만족요인과 동기요인은 일치했으며 연구방법상의 차가 없이 지지된다고 해석된다.

V. 논 의

전술한 결과에 의하여 논의를 전개하고자 한다.

A. 상호배타적인 양극요인

직무태도에 영향을 주는 요인들이 본 연구에서는 상호배타적인 양극요인으로 나누어지는 것이 확인되었다. 한 극인 동기요인은 성취감, 인정감, 과업자체, 책임감의 4요인으로 나타났고 그 반대 극에는 위생요인으로 보수, 상사와의 인간관계, 장학, 학교방침과 행정, 근무조건의 5요인으로 나타났다. 양극으로 나누어진 요인 이외의 요인들은 만족과 불만족간의 .05(X2치 3.841) 수준 이상의 의의 있는 차가 없었기 때문에 잠정적으로 양극으로 갈라질 가능성을 가진 것으로 보고 앞으로 보다 많은 표집으로 연구하여 빈도의 차를 보아야겠다.

B. 동기요인

교사가 보수나 안정만을 위하여 교직에 종사한다고 볼 수 없다는 것이 확인되었다. 학생을 지도하는 과정에서 성장하고 발전하는 모습을 보고 희열을 느끼며, 최소한 수업에 자아몰입하는 순간만은 나쁜 근무환경을 잊는다는 사실을 실제 면접에서 많이 들었다. 일에 동기가 된 교사는 나쁜 근무환경인 위생요인도 잘 감내해 낸다. 보수 같은 외적 보상 때문에만 일하는 교사가 있다면 그 사람은 보다 더 나은 환경을 자꾸 원하게 되고 외적 보상이 끊어질 때는 사기가 심히 저하될 것이다. 그래서 교사의 능력을 최대한 발휘하게 하려면 교육행정이 위생요인에도 노력해야겠지만 동기요인에도 보다 많은 행정력을 경주하여야겠다.

동기요인으로 나타난 각 요인별로 살펴보고자 한다.

1. 성취감

교사의 만족의 근원으로 가장 큰 역할을 하는 요인이 성취감이다. 교사의 성취의 특색은 자기 자신의 성공보다도 학생의 성장, 성공에 관한 것이 많고 교사가 학생을 도달시키고자 하는 목표에 이르게 했을 때 생의 최대의 만족감을 느낀다고 보고하고 있었다. 작게는 한 시간의 수업에 대한 학생의 반응이 정적이었을 때에서, 크게는 돌이킬 수 없는 구렁텅이에 빠진 문제학생을 잘 지도하여 성공시킨 사례에 이르기까지 교사의 반수가 일의 완성에서 오는 성취에 동기가 되고 있다. 성취동기가 높은 사람은 근무환경의 영향을 덜 받고 현 근무환경에도 긍정적이며 과업에 대하여도 도전적인 것이다. 그 예를 우리는 낙도 벽지의 교사가 내부로부터 우러나오는 어쩔 수 없는 정열을 나쁜 근무환경을 잘 참으면서 교육적으로 승화시킨 것에서 찾아볼 수 있다. 보수나 특권이나 지위 같은 사회적 보상이 적은 교사는 정신적 보상으로 학생의 발전, 학급에서의 변화 같은 성취감에서 찾고 있다는 데 교육행정의 눈을 돌려야 한다.

교사로 하여금 자기의 과업을 잘 달성할 수 있도록 행정은 지원해 주어야겠다.

2. 인정감

일을 성취한 데 대한 인정이 만족의 근원으로 크게 작용하며, 특히 교사들이 가장 열심히 일하게 되었던 동기로 23%나 반응하고 있다. 인정해 주는 사람으로는 역시 교장에 관한 이야기가 많이 나왔으며 인정에 대한 동기로는 초등교사(16%)가 중등교사(2%)보다 더 높은 반응을 보이고 있다. 면접과정에서 발현한 사실은 인정을 받기 위해서 열심히 일한 것은 아니라고 일부러 강조하고 있는 교사가 있었으나 그 교사의 마음속에는 인정에 대한 욕구 즉 Maslow의 참여에서 욕구나 존경에의 욕구 같은 인정욕 때문에 일하게 되는 동기가 되었다는 것을 확신할 수 있었다. 그 증거로 새로 전입되어 간 학교에서는 전에 근무하던 학교에서 보다 더 열심히 일했다고 보고하는데 역시 새로 부임해 간 학교에서 인정을 받기 위해서였다.

이 인정감은 일종의 강화현상과 같았다. 일을 한 후 인정을 해주면 보다 더 열심히 일하게 되지만 인정을 해주지 않으면 유능한 교사라 할지라도 교사의 잠재능력을 발휘하지 못하게 된다는 것이다. 이런 교사의 주요 관심은 위생요인이며 여기에서 불만으로 나타난다. 교장 이외에 인정해 주는 사람은 학생, 학부모, 동료교사, 장학사이며 인정의 형태로는 구두, 편지, 전화, 방문 등이었다. 많은 교사가 "스승의 날"에 있었던 이야기를 하고 있었는데 그런 날에 있었던 일이 자극이 되어 보다 더 열심히 일하게 되었다는 것은 작은 일이면서 정신적 보상으로 큰 것이다.

3. 과업자체

과업자체가 불만의 근원이 된 사람은 한 사람도 없었다. 반면 가르치는 일 자체, 수업에 임하고 있는 순간 등 과업자체에 행복감을 느낀다고 한 사람은 14%나 되어서 .001수준 이상에서 그 차에 의의가 있다. 독일어로 "직업"이란 말이 "사명으로 삼고 있는(Berufen sein, 천직인)"뜻에서 왔다고 하는데 교사의 과업자체에서는 천직으로 생각하는 것을 느낄 수 있었다. 인간을 교육시켜야겠다는 불꽃같은 마음은 어쩌면 인간의 본능에 가까운 행동이며, "안 하고는 못 배기는" 정신적 근본충동 같은 것을 면접하는 동안 느낄 수가 있었다. 교사들이 과업자체에서 행복감을 느낄 수 있다는 것은 다행한 일이다. 너무나 나쁜 위생요인을 제거하여 이 과업자체에의 만족감이 밖으로 잘 드러날 수 있도록 해야겠다.

4. 책임감

책임감이 만족의 근원으로 부과 6%라는 것은 교사가 인간교육이란 막중한 사명을 직접 맡고 있다는 점에 비하면 너무나 낮은 빈도이다. 그러나 교사의 책임은 너무나 많은 교육부, 시·도 교육청, 시·군 교육청, 학교의 규제와 규칙, 지시와 명령에 따르다 보면 제한을 받게 되며 자율성이나 창의성은 사라지고 상부에서 하라는 대로만 하면 그만이고, 시키는 대로만 하면 그것은 내 책임이 아니라는 사고방식에서 낮은 빈도로 나타났다고 해석된다. 관료제에서도 이미 정해진 일만 하면 그것으로 끝나기 때문에 자율성이나 창의성, 책임감을 인간 동기로 쓸 수 없는 것은 마찬가지이다. 행정가 자신들이 너무나 많은 지시나 명령을 하여 교직의 전문성을 침해하여 전문성에서 나오는 고도의 자율성과 창의성을 발휘할 기회를 빼앗고, 교사의 책임감, 사명감을 감소시켜 놓고 교사에게서 전문성, 자율성 창의성, 사명감을 요구하는 것이 현 행정의 모순이라고 지적된다.

그러나 일차 믿고 일을 맡겼을 때 열심히 일하는 동기가 되는 동기요인이라는 것은 명백히 밝혀졌다.

책임감은 만족의 근원을 찾는 질문에서는 6%밖에 안 되지만 열심히 일하게 되는 동기를 찾는 질문에서는 29%로 제일 높은 반응이었다.

중요한 책임을 맡기고 책임을 확대시켜 줄 때 교사의 능력은 최대한 발휘된다. 이러한 사실은 행정 방향전환의 중요한 시사점을 줄 것이다. 자유를 주면 교사는 경험을 통해서 자아지향과 책임감을 스스로 배운다는 것을 교육행정가는 알아야 한다.

5. 승 진

교사에게는 승진의 기회가 다른 산업조직보다 적기 때문에 만족요인으로 의의 있게 나타나지 못했다.

전문적으로 성장하기도 힘든 것은 교육행정의 연구과제이다.

C. 위생요인

본 연구에서 동기요인을 강조한다고 해서 위생요인이 동기요인보다 덜 중요하다는 것은 결코 아니다. 또한 위생요인이 전연 일을 하게 하는 동기가 되지 않는다는 것도 아니다. 사기 저하나 근무불만을 막기 위해서는 위생요인의 충족이 절대적으로 필요하다. 다만 보다 높은 차원, 보다 적극적인 동기가 못 된다는 것뿐이다. 위생요인에서 만족을 구하는 교사는 직무자체에서는 만족하지 못하고, 어떻게 하면 보다 잘 직무수행을 할 수 있느냐에는 관심을 보이지 않는다는 점에 주의해야 한다. 동기요인은 좋은 위생환경에서 나타나기가 쉽다. 그러나 동기요인에 동기가 된 사람은 어느 정도 나쁜 위생환경도 잘 극복할 수 있다는 점이 동기와 위생의 중요한 관계이다.

지금까지 산업조직과 교육행정에서도 위생요인 개선에만 중점적인 신경을 써왔다. 그렇지만 교사는 여전히 이 방면에 불만을 가지며 앞으로 개선된다

해도 계속 이 방면에 대한 불만은 남아 있을 것이다. 위생요인 개선에 노력하면서 병행하여 소홀하였던 교사의 동기부여에 연구가 필요하다.

1. 보 수

보수가 교사를 교직에 유인하고 교직에 머무르게 하는 중요한 요인임에는 틀림없다. 교사에게 보다 많은 보수를 준다는 것은 좋은 일이고 어느 수준까지는 열심히 일하게 하는 동기가 된다.

그러나 보수는 외적 동기로 일의 질에 있어서도 차가 있을 뿐만 아니라 어느 수준에서 멈추고 만다. 교직유인체제에서 교사의 초임봉이 타직 공무원보다 높아 금전으로 유인했으나 수십 년 후 다시 타직과 비교하여 금전면의 유인이 사라질 때 즉 위생요인이 충족되지 않을 때 교사는 더욱 사기를 잃게 된다. 면접에서 11%가 보수가 가장 불만족이라고 하며 1%가 자유당 시절의 수입이 좋았던 때 교직이 좋다고 가장 강하게 느꼈다는 것이다. 자유당 시절에 수입이 좋았어도 만족감을 느끼지 못했다는 것은 보수가 만족요인이 되지 못한다는 것을 말해 주고 있다.

2. 상사와의 인간관계

상사의 인정과 상사와의 인간관계를 구분 짓기가 곤란한데 인정에 중점을 두느냐 인간 상호작용에 중점을 두느냐에 따라 분석하게 된다. 인간관계가 사기를 높이는 요인이라고 보고된 것이 종래에 많았다. 대표적이고 고전적인 것이 Hawthorne연구이다. 그러나 이 연구에서는 불만족요인으로 밝혀졌다.

3. 장 학

교사를 도와주고 교수기술을 향상시켜 교직의 전문성을 높이고자 하는 장학이 역효과로 불만의 근원으로 강한 반응을 보인다는 것은 반성과 재고의 여지가 있다. 앞으로 어떻게 해야 인본적 민주장학을 하느냐 하는 많은 연구가 있어야겠다. 그래서 만족의 근원은 되지 못한다 해도 최소한 불만의 요인으로는 나타나지 않도록 해야겠다.

4. 학교방침과 행정

학교방침과 행정이 교사의 많은 불만의 근원이 되고 있다.

특히 인사행정에 심한 불만이 있었다. 인사행정에 불만이 있는 사람이 있으면 반면에는 현 인사행정으로 혜택을 받은 사람도 틀림없이 있어야 할 것이다. 혜택을 받은 사람은 만족으로 표시하여야 할 텐데, 인사행정으로 혜택을 받았더라도 교직에는 만족으로 반응하는 사람은 한 사람도 없었다. 이것을 보면 학교방침과 행정은 불만족으로만 작용하는 불만족요인임에 틀림없다. 따라서 아무리 인사행정의 혜택을 받아도 그것 때문에 교직에 만족하게 되지는 않는다. 다만 그때는 불만족요인으로 나타나지 않을 뿐이다.

5. 근무조건

근무조건에 21%가 불만족으로 반응한 반면 만족으로 반응한 사람은 한 사람도 없어 그 차의 X2치가 19.074이며 불만요인의 수위로 나타났다. 최근 교사의 근무조건에 관한 논의가 자주 일어날 만한 높은 빈도이다. 많은 불이한 근무조건 중에서도 물리적 시설이 나쁘다는 반응은 100명 중 단 1명으로 "학교의 기능이 은행만치 중요하지 못해서 모든 은행이 거의 다 시설한 에어컨 한 대 없어야 할 이유가 무엇이냐?"는 것이었다.

나머지 21%는 학생교육과 직접적인 관계가 없는 잡무와 학생수의 과다, 업무부담의 과다로 질식상태라는 것이다. 초졸, 중졸 정도의 사무직원이 해야 할 잡무를 시켜놓고 교직의 전문성을 찾으라는 것은 모순이다. 미국 산업계에서 아무리 작업환경을 개선해도 생산은 개선된 만치 오르지 않는다는 데 경영자들은 불평을 해왔다. 작업환경이 개선되어 근무조건 요인이 충족되면 불만족요인으로 나타나지 않을 뿐이지 일에 적극적 동기가 되지 못한다. 그러나 나쁜 근무조건 속에 있는 교사에게 교직에 대한 만족감을 갖도록 하기는 어렵기 때문에 현 근무조건 개선에 계속 노력해야겠다.

6. 그 외의 요인

Herzberg가 불만요인으로 그의 연구에서 지적했으나 본 연구에서 의의 있게 나타나지 않은 요인은 발전성, 학생과의 인간관계, 동료와의 인간관계, 개인생활, 안정성은 교사에게 있어서는 어느 정도 충족되어 불만족요인으로 나타나지 않은 것으로 본다. 그리고 발전성 같은 요인은 교직의 특수성 때문에 이미 체념하고 발전이 적은 것으로 인정해 버린 것이기 때문에 불만족요인으로 의의 있게 나타나지 않았다. 면접에서 젊은 초임교사가 많은 것을 배울 수 있고 수양이 된다고 만족으로 표시하며, 어머니 교사들이 자기자녀 교육에 많은 도움이 되고, 많은 사실을 배울 수 있다고 만족으로 반응하는 것을 알 수 있었다. 학력이 초등교사보다 높은 중등교사 그 중에서도 교육경력이 많은 교사는 발전성에 심한 불만을 표시하고 있다. 그래서 이 요인만은 불만족요인으로 나타날 가능성이 크다는 점을 지적해 두고 싶다.

D. 하위집단

교사의 하위집단 간에 동기—위생이론 전반에는 큰 차가 없이 지지하는 경향이다. 바꾸어 말하면 Herzberg의 동기—위생이론은 교사의 어떤 특별한 하위집단만의 영향을 받거나 그 하위집단에게만 적용되는 것이 아니고 교사 전체에 적용 가능하다고 할 수 있다. 그러나 요인의 빈도에 약간의 차가 있으니 다음과 같다.

1. 남교사와 여교사

여교사(64%)가 남교사(36%)보다 더 성취감에 만족감을 느끼고 있다. 여교사가 더 학생의 변화와 조그만 일이라도 완성했을 때 쾌감을 느끼고 있음을 실제 면접에서도 포착할 수 있었다.

과업자체에 남교사(26%)가 여교사(2%)보다 만족으로 높은 반응을 보였다는 것은 특별한 관심을 갖게 한다. 교직이 여성화하고 있고, 여자에게 알맞은 직업이라고 하는데 남교사가 더 과업자체에 만족하다는 점은 특이하다. 실제 면접에서 남교사의 반응은 불만투성이였다가도 수업에 몰두할 때만은 행복감을 느낀다는 내용이 많았다. 교직이 여성에 알맞다는 것은 특히 초등에서 학생의 건강을 살피고 생활을 보살펴 주고, 옷을 입혀주고 코를 씻겨주는 등 섬세한 일을 요하기 때문이나 남교사도 최소한 그런 일이 싫지는 않다는 결론을 내릴 수 있다.

발전성이 없는 것을 남교사(16%)가 여교사(0%)보다 더 불만으로 표시하고 있는 것은 여교사는 교직을 부업 정도로 생각하는 반면 남교사는 생업으로 여기는 차에서 온 것으로 본다.

2. 초등교사와 중등교사

일에 대한 인정감에 초등교사(20%)가 중등교사(2%)보다 더 만족하고 있는데 그 이유는 잘 밝힐 수 없었다. 다만 초등교사가 타인의 인정에 영향을 많이 받는 것으로 해석된다.

발전성에 있어서 중등교사(7%)가 초등교사(1%)보다 .05수준에서 더 불만족으로 차가 있게 반응하였다. 그것은 중등교사의 학력이 높기 때문인 것으로 본다. 중등교사 중에서 자기와 똑같이 대학을 나온 친구의 예를 많이 들고 있었다.

학교방침과 행정에 초등교사(12%)가 중등교사(2%)보다 더 불만을 표시하고 있는데 그 원인은 전술한 학교장의 McGregor의 이론X식 경영에 대한 불만과 인사행정에 대한 불만이었다.

3. 교육경력

교육경력이 적은 교사와 많은 교사 간에는 전연 의의 있는 차가 없다.

E. 만족과 동기

교사가 교직에 만족감을 느끼게 하는 요인과 직무에 충실하게 하는 동기가 된 요인은 빈도의 수치는 차가 있으나 4요인이 높은 빈도로 나타났다.

교사에게 무엇 때문에 열심히 일하게 되었느냐고 묻는 질문에서 4요인이 고르게 더욱 높은 빈도를 보였다. 성취감, 인정감, 과업자체, 책임감은 교사로 하여금 교직에 대하여 만족감을 갖게 하고 열심히 능력껏 일하게 하는 요인으로 밝혀졌음을 다시 한 번 확인하였다.

F. 연구방법상의 차

행동과학의 정밀성, 확실성의 결여와 측정방법의 문제로 Herzberg이론도 검증방법에 따라 상이한 결과가 나온 것으로 알려졌으나 본 연구에서는 면접법과 질문지법 모두 지지하는 경향이라는 결론을 얻었다. 지지되지 않는 경향이라고 알려졌던 질문지법이 오히려 면접법보다 확실히 지지하는 경향이었다. 그리고 면접법에 의한 자료와 질문지법에 의한 자료간의 상관관계 $\gamma_{xy}=0.88$로 높은 상관이었고 두 방법이 모두 Herzberg의 동기-위생이론을 지지하는 경향이어서 본 검증을 한층 더 신뢰감 있게 해준다.

VI. 요약 및 결론

A. 요 약

가설은 검증을 거쳐서 이론이 되고 이 이론에서 다시 많은 가설이 형성되어 검증을 거치는 동안에 완전한 이론으로 굳어져 간다. 일과 동기에 관하여 새로운 이론을 제기하여 미국 산업계의 각광을 받고 있는 Herzberg의 동기-위생이론이 한국에서 경영학, 심리학, 교육행정학 분야에 많이 소개는 되고 있으나 그 이론이 적용가능한 것인지 검증이 없었다. 그래서 본 연구에서는 교사를 대상으로 하여 일반화의 가능성을 타진하여 교육행정에 보탬이 되게 하고자 연구를 시작하였다.

구체적인 목적은 다음과 같았다.

(1) 교사의 교직태도에 영향을 주는 요인을 찾아낸다.

(2) 만족요인과 불만족요인은 상호배타적인가 검증한다.

(3) 이들 요인은 교사의 하위집단 간(남:여, 초등:중등, 경력 연수의 다소)에 차이가 있는지 밝힌다.

(4) 교직에 만족하면 직무에 충실한지 만족요인과 동기요인의 비교로 밝힌다.

(5) 면접법과 질문지법에 의한 연구결과에 차가 있는지 밝힌다.

이런 연구목적과 이론적 고찰을 통하여 다음과 같은 가설을 설정하였다.

가설1: 교사의 만족요인과 불만족요인을 상호배타적이다.

가설2: 교사의 만족요인과 불만족요인은 다음 하위집단 간에 의의 있는 차가 없다.

　　2-a. 남교사와 여교사 간에는 의의 있는 차가 없다.

　　2-b. 초등교사와 중등교사 간에는 의의 있는 차가 없다.

　　2-c. 교육경력이 적은 교사와 교육경력이 많은 교사 간에는 의의 있는 차가 없다.

가설3: 교사를 직무에 만족하게 하는 만족요인과 직무에 충실하게 하는 동기요인은 일치한다.

가설4: 가설1은 면접법과 질문지법에 차가 없다.

위의 가설을 검증하기 위하여 서울시내 초등교사 50명, 중등교사 50명, 계 100명을 면접하고, 초등교사 115명, 중등교사 65명 계 180명을 표집 질문지 조사하였다. 교사가 만족으로 반응한 빈도와 불만족으로 반응한 빈도를 내어 그 차의 의의도를 내기 위하여 X2검증한 결과 네 가설이 모두 긍정되는 경향이었다.

(1) 교사의 만족요인과 불만족요인은 상호배타적이고, 만족요인은 직무자체에, 불만족요인은 직무환경과 관련되어 있음이 확인되다. 직무만족요인으로는 성취감, 인정감, 과업자체, 책임감으로 나타났고, 교사의 불만족요인으로는 근무조건, 학교방침과 행정, 보수, 장학, 상사와의 인간관계로 나타났다.

(2) 교사의 하위집단 간에 직무태도요인은 큰 차가 없고 6/96의 예외가

있었다.

(3) 교직에 만족하게 하는 요인과 직무에 충실하게 하는 동기요인은 일치하여 직무에 만족하면 직무에 충실하다고 할 수 있다.

(4) 면접법과 질문지법의 두 연구방법상에 큰 차가 없이 Herzberg의 동기-위생이론에 관한 가설검증은 긍정되는 경향이다.

B. 결론 및 제안

Herzberg의 동기-위생이론에 관한 4개의 가설이 모두 긍정적으로 검증되었다. 표집과 연구방법상 미일치한 점이 많아 성급한 결정적인 결론을 내리기에는 부족하나 일차 하나의 작은 연구가 끝났으니 나타난 결과대로 결론을 맺고 몇 가지 제안을 하고자 한다.

교사를 만족으로 이끄는 만족요인과 불만족으로 이끄는 불만족요인은 따로 있고 상호배타적인 것이 밝혀졌다. 따라서 행정은 만족요인과 불만족요인을 충족시켜주기 위해서 따로따로 노력해야겠다는 결론에 이른다. 만족요인은 직무자체에 관련되어 있으므로 앞으로 교사로 하여금 직무자체에서 성공감을 느낄 수 있도록 해야겠다는 점이 시사된다. 그렇다고 교사의 근무환경에 대한 욕구는 무시해도 좋다는 결론을 내릴 수 있을 것인가? 어느 정도까지는 감내하기 힘든 근무환경에 처해 있는 교사라 할지라도 직무자체에 동기가 되면 직무만족으로 놀랄 만한 직무수행을 이룩할지도 모른다. 그러나 좋은 근무환경일 수록 직무만족요인이 잘 나타나도록 돕고, 또 나타나는 확률을 높일 수 있다. 또한 불만족요인은 교사의 사기저하를 막을 수 있기 때문에 계속해서 근무환경 개선에 노력해야 한다.

또 교사의 하위집단, 연구방법에 관계없이 Herzberg의 이론을 지지하는 경향이기 때문에 한국 교사에게까지 일반화할 수 있고 교육행정에 적용 가능하다는 결론을 내릴 수 있다. 교육행정 실제에서 지금까지 동기요인을 등한히 하고 위생요인 개선에만 노력을 집중했던 것에서 교사의 동기요인 충족에 노력하여 직무자체에서 자아실현을 돕도록 해야겠다는 행정의 방향을 제시해 준다. 즉 교사의 직무태도에 대한 부정적인 면으로의 접근보다는 긍정적인 면으로의 접근을 강조한다.

마지막으로 몇 가지 제안을 하고 끝맺게 된다.

(1) 교사로 하여금 직무자체에서 즐거움을 느끼고 일의 질도 높일 수 있도록 전문성 신장에 행정적 지원을 강화해야 한다.

(2) 교사로 하여금 일에서 성공감을 맛볼 수 있고, 일에 도전하고, 성취생활을 강화하여 일에 관심을 집중하도록 현직교육이나 장학활동을 통해서 도와주는 체제가 되어야겠다.

(3) 지시나 명령보다 자율성과 자유를 보장하여 스스로 전문지식과 경험을 통해서 직무를 수행하도록 해야겠다.

(4) 교사의 성취나 성공에 대한 인정과 우대가 따르는 제도와 기풍이 요청된다.

(5) 교수프로그램 개발이나 실천에 개인적인 책임을 주고, 교사의 직무에 관계되는 일을 결정할 때는 교사를 참여시켜 책임을 확대해줌으로써 보다 나은 만족감과 직무수행 동기를 줄 수 있을 것이다.

(6) 교사의 동기가 이렇게 단순하지 않고 보다 복잡할 것이라는 추측도 있으므로 앞으로 교사의 동기에 대한 보다 깊은 연구가 기대된다.

(7) 계속적으로 위생요인 개선에 노력하여 동기요인의 출현도 돕고, 사기 저하 예방에도 힘쓰는 것은 당연하다.

(8) 교사가 긍정적인 교직태도를 갖고 있으면서도 현 근무환경이 너무나 나쁘기 때문에 정책적 배려를 요구하려는 의도로 이런 종류의 질문지에 일부러 부정적인 태도로 반응할 가능성이 있음을 이 방면의 연구자는 고려해야 한다.

(9) 발전적인 연구로 교직태도가 직무수행 등에 어떻게 영향을 주는가에 대한 연구가 기대된다.

(10) 마지막으로 본 연구의 윤리성 문제이다. 본 연구결과를 교사를 조작하여 능력을 최대한 이용하려는 의도로 적용되지 않기를 바란다. 예를 들

면 인정감이 교사의 동기요인으로 확인되었다 하여 가식적으로 인정하여 교사의 행위를 조작하려 해서는 안 된다. 보다 중요한 것은 교사 개인으로 하여금 일에서 즐거움과 정신적 만족감을 느끼도록 하고, 심리적 성장과 자아실현을 도우려는 의도에서 적용되길 바란다.

참고문헌

강길수, <u>교육의 과학화</u>, 서울: 교학도서, 1964.

강길수, 김종철, 김영식, <u>학교행정</u>, 서울: 서울대 출판부, 1973.

김영식, "교육행정에 있어서 Getzels 유형과 그 영향", 교육학연구 Vol.6, No.2, 서울: 배영사, 1968.

김영식, 김옥환, 교원 보수제도 개선을 위한 연구, 미출판, 1973.

김재만, <u>교사와 교육의 본질</u>, 서울: 형설출판사, 1974.

김재은, <u>교육 · 심리 · 사회 연구방법</u>, 서울: 익문사, 1971.

김종철, <u>세계 안의 한국교육</u>, 서울: 배영사, 1970.

김종철, "교육경영 현대화의 기본문제", 교육연구 제6권제4호 서울: 교육연구사, 1973.

김종철 외, 교원직무부담에 관한 분석 및 그 적정직무량에 관한 연구, 서울: 한국교육학회, 1973.

노종희, "학교조직연구를 위한 과업동기의 개념 모형분석", 교육학연구 제12권 2호, 서울: 한국교육학회, 1974.

대한교련, 교직유인체제 확립에 관한 연구, 서울: 대한교련, 1969.

박용헌, <u>학교사회</u>, 서울: 배영사, 1969.

소 연역, <u>잠재능력을 살려라</u>, 서울: 한국생산성본부, 1974.

오병수, <u>현대인사관리</u>, 서울: 박영사, 1973.

오철진, "성취동기와 교직태도와의 관계에 관한 연구" 미출판의 석사학 위논문, 서울대 교육대학원, 서울, 1972.

윤정일, "게젤스의 사회과정 유형에 관한 가설 검증" 미출판의 석사학위논문, 서울대 교육대학원, 서울, 1970.

이영덕, <u>교육의 과정</u>, 서울: 배영사, 1969.

정광복 역, <u>행동과학입문</u>, 서울: 한국생산성본부, 1973.

정범모, <u>교육과 교육학</u>, 서울: 배영사, 1969.

정범모, <u>교육·심리 통계적 방법</u>, 서울: 배영사, 1964.

정원식, <u>정의의 교육</u>, 서울: 배영사, 1970.

최정훈, <u>지각심리학</u>, 서울: 을유문화사, 1973.

Argyris, Chris, *Personality and Organization,* N. Y.: Harper and Row, Publishers, Inc., 1957.

Carver, Fred D. and Sergiovanni, T. J., ed., *Organizations and Human Behavior: Focus on School,* N. Y.: McGraw-Hill Book Co., 1969.

Cofer, D. N. and Apploy, M. H., *Motivation: Theory and Research,* N. Y.: John Wiley & Sons, Inc., 1964.

Davis, Keith, *Human Relations in Business,* N. Y.: McGraw-Hill, 1957.

Ewen, R. B., "Some Determinants of Job Satisfaction: A Study of the generality of Herzberg Theory". *J. Appl. Psychol.,* 1964.

Halpern G., "Relative Contribution of Motivation & Hygiene factors to Overall Job Satisfaction" *Research Bulletin 65-34, Princeton,* N. Y.: ETS, 1965.

Herzberg, Frederick, et. al., *The Motivation to Work, 2nd ed.,* N. Y. 3 / 4 John Wiley and Sons, 1959.

Herzberg, Frederick, et. al. *Job Attitudes: Review of Research and Opinion,* Pittsburgh: Psychological Service of Pittsburgh, 1957.

Herzberg, Frederick, *Work and the Nature of the Man,* Cleveland: The World Publishing Co., 1966.

Herzberg, Frederick, "One More Time: How Do You Motivate Employee?" *Harvard Business Review,* Jan.-Feb. issue, 1968.

Hoppock, R., *Job Satisfaction,* N. Y.: Harper, 1935.

Maslow, A. H., *Motivation and Personality,* N. Y.: Harper and Brothers, 1954.

McClelland, D. C., et. al., *The Achievement Motive,* N. Y.: Appleton-Century Crofts, 1953.

McDougal, W., *An Introduction to Social Psychology,* 5th ed. London: Methuen, 1908.

McGregor, Douglas, *The Human Side of Enterprise* N. Y.: McGraw-Hill Book Co., 1960.

Newcomb, T. M., et. al., *Social psychology,* N. Y.: Holt Rineuart and Winston, 1965.

Owens, R. G., *Organizational Behavior in Schools,* N. Y.: Prentice-Hall, Inc., 1970.

Robinson, A. et. al., "Job Satisfaction Researches of 1963" *Personnel and Guidances Journal* XLⅢ, 1964.

Sorgiovanni, T. J., "Factors Which Affect Satisfaction and Dissatisfactions of Teachers" in Fred P. Carver and Others, (ed.) *Organizations and Human Behavior: Focus on School,* N. Y.: McGraw-Hill Book Co., 1969.

Tolman, E. C., *Purposive Behavior in Animals and Men,* N. Y.: Century, 1932.

Young, P. T., *Motivation of Behavior,* N. Y.: Wiley, 1936.

ABSTRACT

I. The Purpose

The purpose of this study is to test Herzberg's hypotheses on his moti-vation-hygione theory at Korean schools.

The study is directed toward more specific problems as described below.

1) To find factors which affect job attitudes of teachers.

2) To identify whether or not the factors distribute themselves into mutually exclusive satisfaction and dissatisfaction categories.

3) To identify variety of the distribution of factors for subpopulation of teachers.

(1) male teachers V. female teachers,

(2) elementary school teachers V. secondary school teachers,

(3) teachers having short length of service V. teachers having long length of service

4) To confirm that if teachers are satisfied to his job they are motivated to their job performance.

5) To find the difference of results between interview method and questionnaire method.

II. Herzberg Theory

Herzberg hypothesized that some factors were satisfiers when present but not dissatisfiers when absent: other factors were dissatisfiers, but when eliminated as dissatisfiers did not result in positive motivation.

Namely, satisfiers and dissatisfiers are mutually exclusive as Figure<2-5>.

Herzberg's research with accountants and engineers tended to confirm the existence of the satisfier and dissatifier phenomenon.

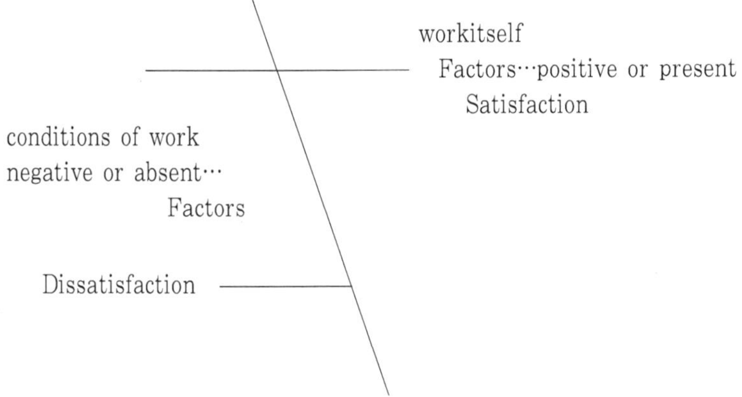

〈Figure 2-5〉. Herzberg hypothesis: satisfaction factors and dissatisfaction factors are mutually exclusive

Satisfiers and dissatisfiers appeared in his research are as follows.
Satisfiers(found in work itself)

(1) Achievement.   (2) Recognition.

(3) Work itself.   (4) Responsibility.

(5) Advancement.

Dissatisfiers(found in the environment of work)

(1) Salary.

(2) Possibility of growth.

(3) Interpersonal relations(subordinates).

(4) Status.

(5) Interpersonal relations(superiors).

(6) Interpersonal relations(peers).

(7) Supervision-technical.

(8) Company policy and administration.

(9) Working conditions.

(10) Personal life.

(11) Job security.

Will the distribution of factors vary for subpopulations of teachers?

And we should confirm that if we motivate teachers by satisfiers, teachers would work hard as found by Herzberg.

Ⅲ. Hypotheses.

The hypotheses to be tested in present study were formulated from the Herzberg Motivation-Hygiene Theory.

1) Hypothesis 1: Satisfiers and dissatisfiers of teachers would be mutually exclusive.

2) Hypothesis 2: There would be no significant difference for teachers subpopulations in satisfaction factors and dissatisfaction factors.(Subpopulations included: (1) male teachers V. female teachers, (2) elementary school teachers V. secondary school teachers, (3) teachers having long duration of teaching experience V. teachers having short

duration of teaching experience.)

3) Hypothesis 3: If teachers satisfy to their job they would be motivated to work hard.

4) Hypothesis 4: There would be no significant difference between the
interview and questionnaire method in the results of
the Hypothesis 1.

Ⅳ. Methodology.

To test the above hypotheses the writer undertook two methods, interview and questionnaire.

Questionnaire were adopted to test Hypothesis 4 and to find difference
of the results between two methods.

A. The Interview

The population for the interview consisted of teachers in Seoul, Korea.

One hundred respondents were selected at random(teachers) and by
stratified sampling(schools).

The sample included 50 male teachers and 50 female teachers for
interviews. Elementary teachers of both sexes were 50, and secondary
teachers of both sexes were 50.

The respondents ranged in age from 21 to 61 years with an average
age being 33 years and 9 months, and median age being 32 years and 2
months.

Years of teaching experience ranged from 4 months to 30 years with
average experience being 9 years and 10 months and median experience
being 9 years.

The writer asked teachers to explain next three sequences during the
interviews.

1) A time when they had felt unusually high or good about their job.
2) A time when they had felt unusually low or bad about their job.
3) A time when they had become enthusiastic to their job performance in their teaching experience history.

The scheme used for content analysis in this study was a direct adoption of 16 categories developed and used by Herzberg.

The writer coded factors appeard during interviews into the Herzberg's categories.

Statistical methods used in this study were percentile and value of Chi squared.

B. Questionnaire

The writer adopted questionnaire method additionally to compare the difference of the results between interview and questionnaire. Because there was a report that "Research which depends on interview for obtaining data tends to support the Herzberg theory, but studies which employ so-called objective techniques tend not to support this theory."[52]

180 respondents were selected among teachers in Seoul, Korea.
    The sample included 94 male teachers and 86 female teachers;

115 elementary school teachers and 65 secondary school teachers.
    The respondents ranged in age from 21 to 61 years with the average age being 32 years and 4 months, and median age being 32 years.

Years of teaching experience ranged from 4 months to 61 years with the average experience 10 years, and median experience being 9 years

---

52) Robert G. Owens, Organizational Behavior in Schools(N. J.: Prentice-Hall Inc. 1970). p.39.

and 4 months. Contents of questionnaire were based on the interview and Herzberg's categories of factors.

Statistical methods were equal to the interview.

〈Table 4-1〉 The percentage and values of Chi-squared for frequency for total groups.

Factors	Satisfaction	Dissatisfaction	X^2	P
1. Achievement	50*(%)	2(%)	46.620	.001
2. Recognition	11*	3	4.082	.05
3. Work itself	14*	6	12.071	.001
4. Responsibility	6*	0	4.166	.05
5. Advancement	0	1		
6. Salary	1	11*	6.750	.01
7. Possibility of growth	2	8	2.500	
8. Interpersonal relations-subordinates	5	1	1.500	
9. Interpersonal relations-superiors	0	9*	7.111	.001
10. Interpersona relations-peers	0	3	1.333	
11. Supervision	0	10*	8.100	.001
12. School policy and administrations	0	14*	12.071	.001
13. Working conditions	0	21*	19.074	.001
14. Personal life	5	4		
15. Status	5	13	2.622	
16. Security	1	0		

* Difference between Satisfaction and Dissatisfaction is significant, Chi-squared value required for significance at the .05 level is 3.841.

V. Results

1) Satisfiers and dissatisfiers tend to be mutually exclusive.

   Table 4-1 includes the per centage and values of Chi-squared for frequency for total groups.

   81 percent of the high attitudes included Achievement(50%), Recognition(11%), Work itself(14%), and Responsibility(6%), Factors which appeared significantly as lows(as contrasted with highs) were Salary (11%), Interpersonal relations-superiors(9%), Supervision(10%), School policy and administrations(14%), and Working conditions(21%).

2) Subgroup of teachers tend not to differ in their responses to sources of high and low job feelings.

   But significant differences were found in 6 of 96 possibilities.

   (1) Achievement appeared as a source of high job feeling for female teachers in 64 percent and this factor was in contrast to 34 percent for male teachers.

   (2) Work itself factor appeared as a source of high job feeling for male teachers in 26 percent but this factor was only 2 percent for female teachers.

   (3) Possibility of growth appeared in 16 percent for male as a source of high job attitudes but did not appeared for female teachers.

   (4) Elementary school teachers responded to Recognition as a source of high job attitude in 20 per cent but secondary school teachers responded it in only 2 per cent as same source.

   (5) Possibility of growth factor as a source of low job attitude appeared for elementary school teachers in 2 per cent but for secondary school teachers in 14 per cent.

   (6) Elementary school teachers responded to as school policy and administrations factor in 24 per cent as a source of low job

feeling but secondary school teachers did to it in 4 per cent as same source.

There was no significant difference by length of service.

3) Satisfaction factors and motivation factors of teachers tended not to differ in their responses.

Satisfaction factors appeared Achievement, Recognition, Work itself, and Responsibility as above description. Factors which motivate teachers to work hard were equal to above four satisfaction factors.

4) The difference between the interview method and questionnaire method tended not to appear in the results of Hypothesis 1.

Only one factor, Possibility of growth, added to factors appeared by interview as a source of low job feeling by questionnaire.

VI. Conclusions

1) This study provides support for the hypothesis that satisfiers and dissatisfiers tend to be mutually exclusive. Further it was confirmed that satisfaction factors of teachers were related to work itself and dissatisfaction factors were related to the conditions or work environment. So, we could conclude that the elimination of dissatisfiers would tend not to lead to job satisfaction. However, we must too know that it is hard for teachers to experience work satisfaction without elimination or temperating of dissatisfiers.

2) We could generalize Herzberg theory in all teachers in Seoul, Korea, without difference of teachers' subgroups.

3) We must help for teachers to drive achivement feeling from work-centered activity.

   To do so, we could help for teachers' self-actualization.

4) The both methods, interview and questionnaire used in this study supported the Hypothesis 1.

부록 Ⅰ. 면접요청

선생님, 오늘도 교육사업에 얼마나 노고가 많으십니까?

이번에 본 연구실에서는 교사가 교직에 대하여 만족감을 갖게 하는 요인과 불만족감을 갖게 하는 요인, 열심히 일하게 하는 요인이 무엇인가에 대하여 연구하고자 하는데 이에 관한 선생님의 실제 경험담을 듣고자 하오니 바쁘시더라도 교육행정연구에 기여하시고 본 연구실을 돕는다는 뜻으로 틈을 내주시면 고맙겠습니다.

일시: 1974년   월   일 오전·후   시
장소:

서울대학교 교육대학원 교육행정연구실

(   ) 선생님 귀하

면접협조에 대한 감사

바쁘신 중에도 면접에 협조하여 주신 점 진심으로 감사드립니다. 본 연구가 교육행정연구와 실제에 조금이라도 도움이 된다면 선생님 은혜에 보답하는 길이 되겠습니다. 선생님 개인의 면접내용은 비밀이며 연구목적 이외에

는 절대로 쓰지 않을 것을 약속드립니다. 가능한 한 연구보고서나 지상을
통하여 연구결과를 보고 드리겠습니다.

1974년   월   일

서울대학교 교육대학원 교육행정 연구실

(   ) 선생님 귀하

부록 Ⅱ. 요인분석

A. 성취감

1. 직무의 성공적인 완성 또는 그 측면

2. 좋은 아이디어, 문제해결

3. 학교에 대한 성공적인 기여

4. 의심을 갖거나 도전해 오는 사람에 대한 정당성 제시

5. 직무상의 실패 또는 그 측면

6. 일의 결과에 대한 목견

7. 일의 결과를 보지 못함

B. 인정감

1. 일에 대한 칭찬, 보답의 있음, 없음.

2. 일의 지적 또는 지적하지 않음.

3. 좋은 아이디어를 받아들이지 않음.

4. 잘못한 일에 대한 비난, 비평.

5. 성공한 일에 대한 비난, 비평.

6. 상사나 다른 사람이 일에 대하여 믿음.

7. 학교 당국이 좋은 아이디어를 받아들임.

C. 과업자체

1. 가르치는 일

2. 일상적인 일

3. 변화된 일

4. 창의적 또는 도전적인 일

5. 너무 쉬운 일

6. 너무 어려운 일

7. 일할 수 있는 기회

D. 책임감

1. 감독 없이 일할 수 있도록 되어 있음

2. 자신의 노력에 대한 책임

3. 다른 사람의 일에 대하여 주어진 책임감

4. 책임이 없음

5. 새로이 주어진 책임

E. 승진

1. 기대하지 않은 승진

2. 승진의 실패

3. 전문적 성장의 증거로서의 승진

F. 보수

1. 보수의 증액

2. 보수 증액 기대의 실패

3. 보수의 양

4. 비슷한 또는 동일 직종에 있는 다른 사람과의 보수의 비교

G. 발전성

1. 예기치 않은 발전

   2. 신분상의 변동

   3. 장래성

   4. 타 직업 친구의 발전과의 비교

H. 학생과의 인간관계

   1. 학교생활에 있어서 학생과의 좋은 인간관계

   2. 학교생활에 있어서 학생과의 나쁜 인간관계

   3. 개인적으로 학생과의 좋은 인간관계

   4. 개인적으로 학생과의 좋은 인간관계

I. 상사와의 인간관계

   1. 상사와의 우호적인 인간관계

   2. 상사와의 비우호적인 인간관계

   3. 상사에 대하여 많이 앎

   4. 상사가 직권으로 누름

   5. 상사가 지지하지 않음

   6. 상사의 정직, 부정직

   7. 상사가 제안에 귀를 기울임 또는 외면함

   8. 일을 하는 데 상사가 믿어줌. 또는 믿지 않음

J. 동료와의 관계

   1. 함께 일하는 데 좋은 사람

   2. 함께 일하는 데 좋아하지 않음

   3. 같이 일하는 사람과의 협조

   4. 같이 일하는 사람의 협조 부족

   5. 집단과 밀착되어 있음

   6. 집단에서 고립되어 있음

K. 장학

1. 장학사의 능력 또는 무능
2. 장학사가 철저하게 비판적이다
3. 장학사가 호의적임
4. 장학활동, 지나친 감독
5. 장학의 효과, 비효과

L. 학교방침과 행정

1. 일의 효과적인 조직
2. 일의 비효과적인 조직
3. 적절한 인사방침
4. 인사방침에 대한 불만
5. 학교목표에 대한 동의 또는 반대
6. 학교행정가에 대한 비판

M. 근무조건

1. 일과의 유리
2. 일하는 사회환경
3. 좋은 또는 나쁜 물리적 환경
4. 좋은 시설 또는 나쁜 시설
5. 일의 적절한 분량
6. 과다한 업무량 과소한 업무량

N. 개인생활

1. 가정생활 문제
2. 사회와 다른 외부 상황
3. 가족의 욕구와 봉급에 대한 열망

O. 신분

1. 신분의 표시
2. 신분의 떳떳함, 창피함.
3. 신분의 약함, 자랑스러움

P. 안정성

1. 직업안정의 객관적 표시
2. 직업안정의 결여

부록 Ⅲ. 교직 태도 요인 조사 질문지

선생님께

 선생님, 오늘도 교육사업에 얼마나 노고가 많으십니까?

 이번에 본 연구실에서는 교사가 교직에 대하여 만족하게 하는 요인과 불만을 가지게 하는 요인, 열심히 일하게 하는 요인에 관계되는 연구를 하고자 하는바 바쁘시더라도 교육행정연구에 기여하시고 본 연구실을 돕는다는 뜻으로 질문지에 답해 주시면 고맙겠습니다.

1974. 7.   .

서울대학교 교육대학원 교육행정 연구실

※ 다음 중 해당란에 ○표, 또는 기입해 주십시오.

1. 성별	2. 학교 급별	3. 연령	4. 교직경력	5. 학 력						
남 · 여	초등 · 중등	만 ( ) 세	총 ( ) 년	중졸	고졸	사범	교육대	사범대	일반대	대학원

설 명

선생님의 전체 교직생활 중에서

첫째: "교직이 좋다"고 느낀 중에서 가장 강하게 느꼈을 때와

둘째: "교직이 나쁘다"고 느낀 중에서 가장 강하게 느꼈을 때,

셋째: "가장 열심히 일했다"고 생각되는 때의 세 경우를 잠시 회상해 주십시오.

〈일단 언제, 무슨 일로 그렇게 느끼게 되었던가 확실히 생각하신 후〉

다음 〈보기〉 1~16까지의 요인을 모두 살펴보신 후 해당되는 요인을 골라 그 번호를 다음 질문의 ( )에 써 주십시오. 그 요인이 중복되어도 좋습니다. 보기에 알맞은 요인이 없으면 질문 아래의 빈칸에 써 주십시오.

질 문

질문 1. "교직이 좋다"고 가장 강하게 느끼게 한 대표적인 요인은?

(   )번

보기에 없을 경우(   )

질문 2. "교직이 나쁘다"고 가장 강하게 느끼게 한 대표적인 요인은?

(   )번

보기에 없을 경우(   )

질문 3. 선생님이 가장 "열심히 일하게 된 동기"는 지금 생각하니 (   )번 같다.

보기에 없을 경우(   )

<보 기>

1. 성취감―직무상의 성공감, 실패감, 학생의 성장·발달, 또는 실패.

2. 인정감―상사, 동료, 학부모 또는 학생으로부터의 내가 한 일이나 나에 대한 인정 또는 불인정.

3. 과업자체―학생의 가르치는 일, 교사 본연의 직무.

4. 책임감―책임을 맡겨 줌 또는 책임을 맡겨주지 않음.

5. 승진―전문적 성장의 증거로써의 승진 또는 좌천에 관계 되는 일.

6. 보수―봉급의 많음, 또는 적음.

7. 발전성―신분상의 발전가능성, 장래성.

8. 학생과의 인간관계―학생과의 인간관계의 좋음 또는 나쁨.

9. 상사와의 인간관계―상사, 학부모와의 인간관계의 좋음 또는 나쁨.

10. 동료와의 인간관계―동료와의 인간관계의 좋음, 나쁨.

11. 장학―장학제도, 장학의 설정, 장학사에 관계되는 일, 장학활동, 장학기술.

12. 학교 방침과 행정―학교방침, 행정, 인사에 관계되는 일.

13. 근무조건―근무시설, 업무량의 많음, 적음.

14. 개인생활―개인생활, 가정생활, 사회적인 사생활.

15. 신분―교사신분에 관계되는 일.

16. 안정성―교직의 안정, 불안정.

질문 4. 무슨 일로 "교직이 좋다"고 가장 강하게 느끼게 되었는가 그 일에 대하여 가능한 한 자세히 적어 주십시오.

질문 5. 무슨 일로 "교직이 나쁘다"고 가장 강하게 느끼게 되었는가 그 일
에 대하여 가능한 한 자세히 적어 주십시오.

질문 6. 선생님께 가장 열심히 일하였던 때의 동기 또는 그 원인을 가능한
한 자세히 적어 주십시오.

「끝」

7. 교육경영에 Herzberg의
동기-위생이론의 적용

I. 서 론

우리나라 교육경영에서 널리 논의되지 않은 Herzberg의 동기-위생이론을 간단히 소개하고 교육경영에의 적용 시 교육행정 방향의 전환을 모색해 본다.

A. 문 제

E초등학교 4학년 12반 담임교사는 저녁 8시인데도 아직 교실에서 무엇인가 열심히 그리고, 쓰고 있다. 전기시설이 안 되어 촛불을 켜고 환경미화와 수업준비에 여념이 없는가 보다. 교장에게 잘 보이기 위한 것도 아니다. 교장은 퇴근한 지 이미 오래다. 이 교사는 교장의 명령이나 지시에 따라 타율적으로 일하는 게 아니다. 이 교사는 원래 명령이나 지시에 의한 타율적 방법은 쓸 줄을 모른다. 이 교사는 무엇 때문에 남들이 개인생활을 즐기고

---

* 이 논문은 새교육(1975. 3) 대한교육연합회 pp.20-25에 게재되었던 것임.

있는 이 시각까지 스스로 일하고 있을까? 다른 교사가 보면 분명 미쳤다고 할 것이다. 정말 이 교사는 미친 것이다. 도깨비가 아닌 일에 미친 것이다. 우리나라 대부분의 교사를 이렇게 일에 미치게 할 수는 없을까?

"시골 학교에 근무할 때였어요. 그 학교에 여교사가 저 혼자뿐이었어요. 물론 그 학교에 오시는 손님 접대는 제가 도맡아야 했어요. 교장 선생님이나 동료 선생님들은 모두 제 솜씨를 칭찬해 주셨어요. 형식적인 것이 아니고 진정한 의미였던 것 같아요. 장학사님들이 오면 모두 싫어하지 않아요? 그런데 저는 오히려 속으로 은근히 기다려지기까지 했어요. 제 솜씨를 칭찬받을 기회가 되거든요. 그리고 군 주최 또는 도 주최 무용대회에 어린이들을 지도해 나가서 나갈 적마다 상을 받아 왔어요. 교장실에 있는 트로피와 상패가 그때 많이 불어났어요. 교장실에 들어서기가 즐겁기만 했어요. 이제 서울로 와서 100여 명 선생님들 속에 파묻혀 생활하다 보니 학교생활에 재미라고는 하나도 없어요."

이 교사를 시골 학교에서처럼 즐겁게 근무하도록 할 수는 없을까?

"교장 선생님께서 나를 인정해 주었어요. 학교의 중요한 일을 모두 맡겼어요. 나는 일이 많다고 불평하기보다 오히려 내 실력을 인정해 주는 데 감사했어요. 토요일, 일요일이 없었어요. 틈만 있으면 기쁜 마음으로 학교에서 일했어요. 뼈가 부서져도 좋으니 그런 때가 다시 왔으면 좋겠어요."

일을 많이 하던 때가 편한 지금보다 좋다니 무슨 이유일까? 인간은 일을 싫어하는 것이 아닌가?

"육상선수를 지도했어요. 오랜 기간을 선수들과 같이 합숙했어요. 그 결과 우승했어요. 우승기를 앞세우고 교가를 부르며 학교에 들어설 때가 내 생애에 제일 기뻤던 때 같아요. 육상에서는 전 도내를 우리 아이들이 휩쓸었어요. 교육감 상도 그때 탔어요. 참 그때는 멋있게 선생 노릇했던 것 같아요."

승전고를 울리며 교문을 들어오는 이 교사의 모습을 그려 봅시다.

> "5·16 혁명 직후 안양에 근무할 때였어요. 조기회를 지도하고 꽃길 가꾸기를 하였지요. 지금의 새마을 운동을 그때 한거죠. 새벽에 일어나 자전거를 타고 몇 동네를 쭉 돌며 지도했지요. 성과가 좋다고 교육감, 장관 표창을 한꺼번에 받았어요. 말없이 일하는 사람도 그때는 알아주더군요. 그때는 참 신 났어요."

우리 선생님들을 이렇게 자기 마음속에서 우러나서 진정으로 아동과 교육을 위해서 열심히, 그리고 즐거움을 가지고 근무하게 할 수는 없을까? 선생님들이 실역이 없더라도 좋다. 기술이 부족한 것도 좋다. 다만 가지고 있는 실역, 있는 기술만이라도 마음속에서 우러나 일할 수 있는 경지에 다다르게 하면 되는 것이다. 그런 경지에 이르는 교사라면 아마도 실력을 기르기 위해서도 노력할 것이다. 위에 든 다섯 예 중 첫 번째는 필자가 직접 본 것이고 그 나머지는 석사학위 논문[53] 자료수집 관계로 100여명 초·중·고 교사를 면접하던 중의 대화에서 나온 것이다. 낙도·벽지의 교사가 근무환경이 나쁜데도 환경이 좋은 교사보다 더 열심히 일한다는 말을 많이 듣는다. 그 이유는 무엇일까?

선생님들의 보수만 올리면 저절로 열심히 일할까? 각 교실에 냉·난방시설을 하면 더 열심히 가르칠 것인가? 직원의 친목을 잘 다지고 인간관계를 잘하면 얼마나 교육의 성과가 올라갈 것인가?

시설물 100퍼센트 활용이면 그 활용도는 높다고 한다. 우리 교사들의 능력의 활용도를 잴 수 있다면 과연 얼마나 될까? 더 이상 활용할 잠재능력은 없을까?

지금까지의 문제에 두자 나름대로 대답해 보고 다음으로 넘어가야겠다.

---

53) 주삼환, Herzberg의 동기-위생이론에 관한 가설검증, 미출판의 석사학위논문, 서울대교육대학원, 1974.

B. 욕구·동기·일

인간은 한없는 욕구에 의해서 행동하고 또 생활하게 된다. 집 없이 남의 집 월세방에 사는 사람은 돈을 모아 전세방을 얻기 위해 저축한다. 전세 사는 사람은 조그만 것이라도 자기 집을 마련하려고 어려움을 무릅쓰고 저녁 늦게까지 일한다. 작은 집을 마련하게 되면 보다 나은 집을 마련하기 위해서 일할 수도 있고, 이제는 자녀 교육을 위해서 노력할 수도 있다. 이것은 흔한 예이지만 하여간 인간은 크건 작건, 높은 수준이건 어떤 욕구, 또는 필요, 희구 등 무엇인가 바라는 것이 있다. 그 바람 속에서 우리 인간은 일을 한다. 일을 해서 얻은 보수로 자기가 가지고 있는 어떤 욕구를 채울 수도 있고, 일하는 자체에서 얻는 어떤 즐거움이나 보람 때문에 일할 수도 있다. 이것은 인간이 가지고 있는 욕구에 의해서 일을 하게 되는 동기가 되었다고 말할 수 있다. 김영식은

> "인간은 행위를 이해하고, 예측을 할 어떠한 상황에서 그러한 행동을 일으키게 하는 인간의 욕구 또는 동기를 이해하여야 할 것이다. 인간행동이란 근본적으로 목적지향적이라고 할 수가 있다. 인간의 행동은 일반적으로 어떤 목적을 달성하기 위한 욕구에 의하여 동기화된다."[54]

고 하여 동기와 욕구를 비슷한 뜻으로 썼고, 동기는 행동의 이유라고 하였다. 욕구·동기·일의 삼자를 한마디로 종합하여 연결시켜 보면 인간은 끝없는 욕구를 가지고 있고, 그 욕구를 채우기 위해서 일을 하게 되는 동기가 된다고 할 수 있다. 한 사람이라도 여러 개의 욕구를 가지고 있겠는데 그중에서 가장 강하게 나타나는 욕구에 의해서 행동하고 일하게 되는 것이다. 이 욕구가 강하게 나타나는 데는 순서가 있다는 이론을 정립하는 사람이 Maslow이며, 욕구단계이론이다.[55] Maslow에 의한 순서는 생리적 욕구,

---

54) 강길수, 김종철, 김영식, <u>학교행정</u>, 한국방송통신대학(서울대출판부, 1973), p.47-48.
55) Abrabam Maslow, Motiuation and Personality(New York: Harper and Brothers, 1954).

안정에의 욕구, 참여에의 욕구, 존경에의 욕구, 자아실현에의 욕구이다. 인간의 가장 기본적인 욕구는 생리적 욕구이다. 생리적 욕구는 배고픔·목마름·추위·더위·비·바람 등을 피하려는 욕구, 자거나 쉬고 싶은 욕구 등 주로 의식주에 관계된다. 이 생리적 욕구가 가장 강하게 나타나는 사람은 이 생리적 욕구에 동기가 되어 일하게 된다. 원시인은 주로 이 생리적 욕구를 채우기 위해서 활동하고 일했다. 일단 이 욕구가 충족되면 다음 단계인 안정에의 욕구가 다른 욕구보다 가장 강하게 나타나고 이 단계의 욕구에 동기가 되어 일하게 된다. 직장의 안정, 생활의 안정 등은 자기보존의 욕구이다. 안정에 위협을 받을 때는 이에 동기가 되어 활동하고 일하게 된다. 지금까지의 두 단계인 생리적 욕구와 안정에의 욕구는 현대인의 대부분에게는 생활이 윤택해지고 살기 좋게 됨에 따라 일단 충족이 되어 동기가 되지 않는다는 것이다. 다음 단계가 참여에의 욕구이다. 의식주와 안정에 어느 정도 걱정이 없게 되면 참여에의 욕구가 강하게 나타난다. 사람들과 어울리고 싶고 어떤 집단에 소속되고 싶고, 좋은 인간관계를 맺고 싶은 것이다. 참여에의 욕구가 어느 정도 충족되면 그 인간관계에서도 존경을 받고 싶은 존경에의 욕구가 강하게 나타난다. 높이 평가받고 싶고, 다른 사람에게 영향력을 미치고 싶은 것이다. 욕구단계의 최종단계는 자아실현에의 욕구이다. 자아실현은 각자가 가지고 있는 잠재능력을 최대한으로 발휘시키도록 하는 것이다. "음악가는 음악을 통하여 시인은 시를 쓰는 데 있어, 장군은 전투에 승리하는 데 있어, 그 잠재능력을 극대화 하려고 하는 욕구이다.56) 지금까지 욕구·동기·일의 관계를 살펴보았는데 이보다 더 흥미 있게 이론을 전개한 사람이 Herzberg인데 그의 동기-위생이론으로 본론에 들어가고자 한다.

---

56) Panl Hersy, Kenneth H Blanchard, *Management of organizational Behavior*(Englewood Cliffs, New Jersey: Prentice-Hall, Inc.)를 번역한 정광복 역, 행동과학입문, 한국생산성본부.

Ⅱ. Herzberg의 동기 - 위생이론

Herzberg의 동기-위생이론은 위에 설명한 Maslow 이 욕구단계 이론과 여기서는 설명하지 않았지만 Argyris의 성숙-미성숙이론57)과 Mcgregor의 X리논 Y이론58)을 확대하고 정교하게 정리한 것이다. 1955년 Herzberg와 그의 동료가 연구한 직무태도에 관한 자료59)를 분석하는 가운데 그때까지에는 없었던 직무태도에 관한 인간행동의 가설을 세웠다. 이 연구는 피츠버그 지방의 11개 부문 산업에서 많은 연구지원을 받고 이 11개 부문에서 200여 명의 기사와 회계사에 대하여 포괄적인 면접을 실시하였다. 면접 내용은 피면접자들이 직무수행에 있어서 어떠한 일로 가장 행복하게 되며 또 만족하고 사기가 높게 되는가에 대하여, 또 어떤 일로 불행을 느끼고 불만족하고 사기가 낮게 되는가, 그리고 그런 태도의 영향은 무엇인가에 대한 질문이 주가 된다. 즉, 요인-태도-영향(Factors-Attitudes-Etfects)을 한 단위로 하여 직무태도에서 요인을 알아내고 그 태도가 직무수행에 미치는 영향에 대하여 연구하여 1959년 "The Motivation To work"란 책으로 보고서를 내놓게 된 것이다. 그때까지 직무태도 영역에서 이론적 기본가정은 종업원의 직무에 대하여 만족하게 하는 요인과 불만족하게 하는 요인은 개념적인 연속선(conceptual continuum)상에 있다는 것이었다. 그림으로 그리면 다음과 같다.

---

57) Chris Argyis, Personality and Organization(New York and Row, pnblishers Inc., 1957)와 Chris Argyris, Integration the Indiv*dual and the Organizations(New York: wiley, 1964)*.

58) Douglas McGreg'or, The Human Side of Enterprise(New York: McGraw-Hill Book Company, 1960).

59) Fredericks Herzberg, Bernard mansner, Richard Peterson and Dora Capewell, Job Attitudes: Review of Research and Opinion *(Pittsbergh: psychological Service of pittsbrngh, 1967)*.

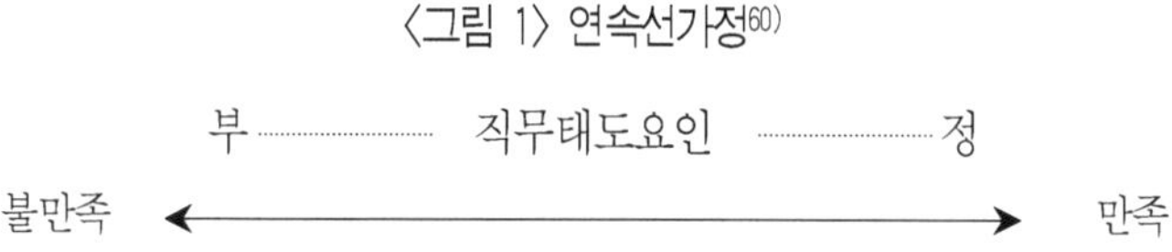

〈그림 1〉 연속선가정[60]

이 연속선 가정의 직무태도에 영향을 주는 요인이 연속선상에 있는 것으로
보아 직무만족으로 영향을 주다가도 충족이 안 되면 직무불만족으로 이끌게도
한다는 것이다.

그러나 Herzberg 이론으로는 직무만족으로 이끄는 요인과 직무불만족으
로 이끄는 요인은 상호 배타적이라는 것이다. 그래서 직무만족요인은 만족
으로만 영향을 주고 그 요인이 충족되지 않을 경우는 직무태도 요인으로 나
타나지 않는다는 것이다. 직무불만족 요인은 영향을 줄 때는 불만족으로 영
향을 주지만 불만족요인에서 사라진다고 해서 만족요인은 되지 않는다는 것
이었다.

〈그림 2〉에서 굵은 사선을 서로 넘지 않기 때문에 불만족요인을 만족요
인으로 바꿀 수 없다는 것이다. 더구나 만족요인은 직무자체에 관련된 요인
들이고 불만요인은 근무환경과 관련된 것들이라는 데 주목하였다. 직무자체
에 만족하는 사람은 더욱 적극적으로 직무수행하는 동기가 된다고 하여 동
기요인이라 부르고, 환경과 관련된 불만족요인은 보다 적극적인 동기가 되
지 못하고 다만, 불만을 예방하는 작용만 한다고 하여 의학용어를 빌려 위
생요인이라 불렀다. 예를 들면 대기오염, 식수오염, 쓰레기, 하수구 등은 환
경적이고 위생적이며 이들을 좋게 고친다 해도 환자를 직접 치료하는 기능
을 하지 못하는 것처럼 종업원의 근무환경 개선이 일을 열심히 하게 하는
직접적인 동기가 되지 못한다는 데 서로 비유가 된 것이다. 이들 두 부류의

---

60) Thomas J. Sergiovanni, "Factors which affect satisfaction and dissatisfaction
   of teachers" in Fred D. Carver, Thomas J. Sergiovanni(ed) Organizations
   and Haman Behavior: Focus on School, (N. Y.: McGraw-Hill Book company,
   1969) p.249.

요인에서 동기−위생이론이란 말이 나왔다. 그가 든 동기요인은 ⓐ 성취감, ⓑ 성취에 대한 인정감, ⓒ 일 자체, ⓓ 확대된 책임, ⓔ 전문적 성장의 증거로써의 승진의 다섯을 들고, 위생요인으로는 ⓐ 회사방침과 행정, ⓑ 감독, ⓒ 직무조건, ⓓ 상사와의 인간관계, ⓔ 하급자와의 인간관계, ⓕ 동료와의 인간관계, ⓖ 보수, ⓗ 직업안정, ⓘ 개인생활, ⓙ 신분, ⓚ 성장가능성을 들고 있는데, 미국산업계가 그동안 아무리 종업원의 근무환경개선을 위해 경영자가 노력해도 생산은 그만큼 올라가지 않는 데 불만을 갖던 중 Herzberg 이론으로는 동기요인 충족을 위해서도 따로 노력하여 종업원으로 하여금 일에 동기가 되도록 하여야 한다는 데 일이가 있다 하여 그의 이론은 각광을 받은 것이다.

Herzberg는 동기요인을 강조했지만 그렇다고 위생요인을 무시한 것은 아니다. 좋은 환경은 만족요인의 출현을 돕고, 나쁜 근무환경에서 직무만족을 기대하는 것은 쓰레기 더미 위에서 보약을 먹는 격으로 볼 수 있다.

〈그림 2〉 Herzberg의 가설: 만족요인과 불만족요인은 상호배타적이다[61]

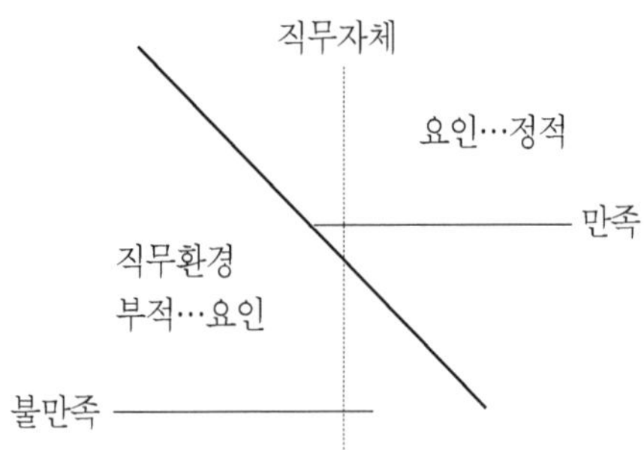

---

61) Ibid.

Ⅲ. 교육경영에 동기 – 위생이론의 적용

Herzberg가 1959년 많은 산업계 재벌들의 후원을 받아 연구보고한 후 산업계에서는 새로운 각도에서 종업원을 대하게 되고, 이 이론이 각광을 받기 시작하였다. 그때까지 기업체에서는 임금제를 어떻게 개선할 것인가, 보너스제, 연금제, 부가급제, Background music, 휴가급제, 인간관계개선, 근무시간 중의 이발 허용, 종업원이 자가용 구입 시 회사에서의 보조, 스포츠와 오락시설 등 주로 직무의 환경개선에 신경을 써 왔는데 이런 것들은 모두 생산에 적극적으로 영향을 주지 못하고 소극적이고 예방적이라는 데 놀라지 않을 수 없었던 것이다. 또한 실제로 기업체들이 이런 좋은 시설과 대우를 해주었어도 생산은 늘지 않고 겨우 하락을 방지하는 정도였으니, 이 이론이 각광을 받게 된 것이다. 그래서 기업체에서는 Herzberg이론대로 근무환경 개선과 병행하여 종업원으로 하여금 일 자체에 동기를 주는 데 대한 연구를 하게 된 것이다. 그러나 학계에서는 긍정적 반응도 있지만 부정적 반응두 있기 직무태두의 다요인설두 나오고 있다. 앞으로 이 이론을 한국의 교육경영에 적용가능한가 타진해 보고 적용 시의 행정방향을 제시해 보고자 한다.

A. 교육경영에의 적용 가능성

아무리 좋은 이론이라도 현장에 적용가능한지 모를 때 그것은 하나의 공론에 지나지 않는다. 더구나 Herzberg이론은 우리와 상황이 다른 미국에 바탕을 두고, 또한 산업계에 적용한 이론을 한국 교육경영에도 적용할 수 있느냐가 문제이다. 이 문제를 해결하기 위해서 서울시내 초·중·고 교사 100명을 표집 면접하고, 180명을 질문지 조사한 결과 대체로 Herzberg 이론은 긍정되는 경향이었다. 질문의 초점은 교사의 교직태도에 영향을 주는 요인으로 교사가 교직에 대하여 행복감을 느끼거나, 만족감을 갖게 하는 요인을 찾는 것과, 불행감이나 불만족감을 갖게 하는 요인을 찾는 데 있었다. 그 결과 만족요인으로 ⓐ 성취감, ⓑ 과업자체, ⓒ 인정감, ⓓ 책임감의 4요인으로 의의 있게 나타났고, 불만족요인으로는 ⓐ 근무조건, ⓑ 학교방침과 행정, ⓒ 보수, ⓓ 장학, ⓔ 상사와의 인간관계의 5요인이 표〈1〉과 같이 의의 있게 나타났다.

<표 1〉 교사의 만족과 불만족의 퍼센트와 X2치

요　인(Factors)	만　족	불만족	X2 치	P(의의도)
1. 성취감(Achievement)	50(%)	2(%)	46,620	.001
2. 인정감(Recognition)	11	3	4,082	.05
3. 과업자체(Work itself)	14	0	12,071	.001
4. 책임감(Responsibility)	6	0	4,166	.05
5. 승진(Advancement)	0	1		
6. 보수(Salary)	1	11	6,750	.01
7. 발전성(Possibility of growth)	2	8	2,500	
8. 학생과의 인간관계(Interpersonal relations-subordinates)	5	1	1,500	
9. 상사와의 인간관계(Interpersonal relations-superiors)	0	9	7,111	.001
10. 동료와의 인간관계(Interpersonal relations-peers)	0	3	1,333	.001
11. 장학 또는 감독(Supervision)	0	10	8,100	.001
12. 학교방침과 행정(School policy and administrations)	0	14	12,071	
13. 근무조건(Working Conditions)	0	21	19,074	
14. 개인생활(Personal life)	5	4	2,622	
15. 신분(Status)	5	13		
16. 안전성(Security)	1	0		
	100%	100%		

* 0.5수준에서 의의 있는 차가 있다.(X2=3.841)

이들 요인을 보면 한쪽 방향으로 강하게 나타났고 만족요인은 일 자체와 관련된 것들이고, 불만족요인은 일을 둘러싼, 일 자체가 아닌 환경적인 요인들인 것을 알 수 있다. 그래서 Herzberg의 동기-위생이론은 지지되는 경향이고 우리나라 교육경영에 적용 가능한 것으로 나타났다.

B. 행정방향의 전환

이제 Ⅰ. 이론의 1. 문제에서 예를 든 열심히 일하는 동기가 된 교사를 이해하고 그 이유를 알 수 있을 것이다. 촛불을 켜고 저녁 늦게까지 일한 교사는 전등도 없는 나쁜 근무환경(위생요인)에서도 직무자체와 일의 성취에 동기가 된 것이다. 다른 교사들이 싫어하는 장학사나 상부의 손님을 은근히 기다리는 여교사, 일요일, 토요일 구별 없이 학교 일을 내 일처럼 즐겁게 일한 교사, 우승기를 앞세우고 교문에 들어서는 성취에 도취된 교사, 새벽에 자전거를 타고 조기회 꽃길 가꾸기를 지도한 교사, 낙도 사치 분교의 농구를 지도한 교사, 산간벽지 낙도의 어려운 여건에서도 묵묵히 최선을 다하는 교사들의 동기를 이해할 수 있는 것이다.

그렇다면 봉급을 올려 주는 것만으로, 냉·난방시설을 하는 것만으로는, 직원친목과 인간관계를 도모하는 것만으로는 아동교육이란 보다 높은 차원의 생산을 하기에는 부족하다고 할 수 있다. 물론 봉급을 올려 주고, 시설을 개선하고, 인간관계를 좋게 하는 것은 모두 일을 열심히 하도록 간접적으로 도와주는 기능은 하지만 직접 일에 동기를 주는 치료적 기능은 하지 못한다. 이런 환경적인 요인에 노력하면서 따로 동기요인인 교사의 내적 욕구, 보다 높은 차원인 일 자체에서의 자아실현의 욕구에 불꽃을 붙여주는 행정이라야 하겠다. 그래서

첫째로 교육행정은 교사의 위생요인과 별도로 동기요인 충족에 노력해야 한다는 점을 제시한다. 우리는 지금까지 너무나 일을 둘러싼 환경적인 것에만 집중해 왔고, 사실 그것마저도 해결하지 못했다. 외부적인 환경에 동기가 된 교사가 있다면 그는 끝없이 더 높은 수준의 좋은 환경을 요구하고, 만일 외적 유인가가 사라질 때 그 교사의 사기는 말할 수 없이 떨어지고 말 것이

다. 불만족요인 제거에 노력하는 행정을 '교사중심행정'이라고 한다면 앞으로의 행정은 '과업중심행정'으로 전환해야겠다. 즉 일을 성취함으로써 만족을 느끼고, 행복감을 갖도록 하고, 일에서 교사가 가지고 있는 잠재능력을 최대한으로 발휘하게 하는 자아실현을 돕는 행정이라야 하겠다. 민주주의 교육의 최대 목적이 개인의 자아실현을 돕는 데 있다면 학생의 자아실현을 돕는 교사의 자아실현부터 먼저 도와주어야 한다는 것은 교육행정의 책임이다.

둘째 교사에게 성취에 동기를 주라. 오철진[62]은 성취동기와 교직태도는 정적인 상관관계가 있다고 하고 필자의 연구에서도 〈표 1〉에서와 같이 성취감 때문에 50퍼센트가 행복감 또는 교직에 만족감을 갖게 된다고 보고하고 있다. 교사가 일의 성취에 동기가 됐을 때는 어려운 근무조건도 어느 정도는 잘 감내해 낼 수 있다. 마치 음악가가 음악에 도취하고 화가가 작품에 열중하는 경지에 이르게 할 수 있다. 일의 성취에 동기가 될 때 근무환경의 영향을 덜 받을 뿐만 아니라 과업에 대해서도 도전적이다. 보수나 특권이나 지위 같은 사회적 보상이 적은 교사는 정신적 보상으로 학생의 발전, 학급에서의 변화 같은 성취감에서 보람을 느낀다는 것을 제시해 둔다. 구체적으로 교장이나 행주가는 어떻게 교사로 하여금 성취감에 발동이 걸리게 하느냐는 좀더 연구해야겠고, 본제를 가지고 밝히기에는 벅차다.

셋째 일의 성취에 대하여 인정해 주라

이 인정감은 강화현상으로 인정을 받으면 더 열심히 일하게 되고 인정을 못 받으면 자신의 잠재능력을 발휘하려 하지 못하고 더구나 능력이 있으면서도 인정을 받지 못한 교사의 주요 관심은 위생요인으로 돌려지게 된다. 순환근무제에서 새로 전입되어 간 학교에서 첫 해에 교사들은 인정을 받기 위해 열심히 일하는 사람이 많다. 그러나 교장이나 학부모로부터 인정을 받지 못할 때 그들의 관심은 다른 데로 돌려진다. 교사를 인정해 줘서 행정가가 손해 볼 것은 하나도 없다.

---

62) 오철진, 성취동기와 교직태도와의 관계에 관한 연구, 미출판의 석사학위논문 서울대교육대학원, 서울, 1972. p.47.

넷째 책임을 확대해 주어야 한다.

Argyris[63]의 연구에서 책임감이 능력을 확대해 준다는 것이 명백해졌다. 그는 라디오류 조립공장에서 12명 한 조로 분업을 하고 있었는데 바꾸어 한 사람이 독자적으로 전 과정을 완성하고 제품에 자기의 성명을 표시하고 책임지도록 했다. 첫 1개월은 생산고가 70%로 떨어지고 6주째는 사기도 형편없이 떨어졌다. 그러나 8주에서부터 오르기 시작하여 15주에는 종전 어느 때보다 최고 수준이었을 뿐만 아니라 불량품이나 반송품이 96%나 줄어들어 생산비를 줄일 수 있었다. 이와 마찬가지로 교사를 성숙한 인간으로 인정하고 책임을 맡길 때 그의 능력을 최대한 발휘할 수 있는 것이다.

어느 회사의 청소원들을 일을 시키는 방법 대신 모든 청결문제를 완전히 일임했을 때 회사는 말할 수 없이 달라지고 자발적이었다는 예가 있다.[64] 교사에게 너무나 많은 지시명령만 하달한다면 그들은 그 지시명령 이행에만 급급하고 더 이상을 기대하기는 어렵다. 믿고 책임을 주고 자율성과 창의성을 기대하는 편이 교육행정으로써 훨씬 바람직하다.

디섯째 교사로 히여금 괴업자체에서 즐거움을 찾도록 해야 한다.

교사가 자기가 하고 있는 일 자체에 동기가 되지 않고 보수나 외적 환경에 동기가 된다면 보다 적극적인 직무수행을 기대하기 힘들다. 우리 인간은 남을 가르치고자 하는 욕망, 자기가 알고 있는 사실을 남에게 전달하고자 하는 마음은 하나의 본능 같은 것이라고 생각한다. 한 원시인이 카누(배)를 만들고 토템 장승에 무엇인가 새기기에 열중하고 있다. 그때 한 소년이 다가온다. 그 원시인은 잠시 작업을 멈추고 그 소년에게 조각에 대하여 무엇인가 가르친다. 이런 남을 가르치고 전달하고자 하는 욕망을 가지지 않은 교사는 없을 것이다. 교사가 맡은 가르치는 일, 보여주는 일(수범)에 몰두하고 동기가 되도록 행정은 신경을 써야 한다. 교사로 하여금 일이 끝난 여

---

63) Chris Argyris, Personality and Organization, (N. Y: Harper and Row, Publishers, Inc., 1957)
64) 정광복 역, 행동과학 입문(서울: 한국생성본부 1973), pp.96-99.

가나 토요일, 일요일을 즐기게 하는 것에서 직장에서 근무하는 동안, 학생과 접촉하는 동안에 즐거움을 갖고 행복감을 갖도록 해야 한다.

의사결정에 교사를 참여시키고 과업을 성취하도록 고도의 창의성과 자율성, 전문성을 신장하고 교수에의 자유, 중요한 일을 믿고 책임을 주는 일, 성공적인 직무수행에 대한 인정 등으로 과업자체에 동기가 되도록 하는 '과업중심행정'으로의 행정 방향 전환으로 집약될 수 있다. 많은 지시와 명령만 받아 행할 때 교사는 직무에서 만족감을 가질 수 없다. 전문의가 원장이나 보건사회부의 지시명령을 받아 처방하지 않듯이 교사에게 그런 전문성과 능력과 자유와 대우를 주어야 그들은 즐겁게 일하고 교육의 성과는 올라갈 것이다.

8. 인간과 일65)

Ⅰ. 일과 행복

우리 인간은 잠자지 않고 깨어 있는 시간의 대부분을 일하면서 보내고 있습니다. 우리 선생님의 경우를 보더라도 하루 24시간의 거의 1/3을 지장에서 보내고 있습니다. 죽어 있는 상태와 거의 다를 바 없는 잠자는 시간을 빼고 나면 최소한 하루의 반 이상은 학교에서 또는 직장을 위해서 보내고 있는 것입니다. 사실 따지고 보면 이 세상에서 가장 가까운 사이라고 하는 부부간에 같이 지내는 시간이나, 가족과 같이 지내는 시간보다 직장에서 동료나 상사 또는 학생들과 보내는 시간이 더 많을 것입니다.

우리가 역사적으로 더듬어 보더라도 원시인에서부터 현대인에 이르기까지, 또 한 사람의 일생을 통해서 보더라도 어린아이로부터 늙어서 활동할 수 없을 때까지 우리는 무엇인가 일을 하면서 살아가고 있습니다.

그런데 어떤 행운아에게는 이 일이 행복의 근원이 되기도 하지만 다른 많은 사람에게는 이 일이라는 것이 괴로운 것, 하기 싫은 것이 되며, 심지어

---

* 이 글은 서울시 남부교육구청 강서제1지구 장학협력회에서 강연하고 <u>수도교육</u> 제69호 82. 3. 53-58에 게재되었던 것임.

는 슬픔과 불행의 근원이 되기도 합니다.

Douglas McGregor의 X이론은 이 슬픔과 불행의 근원이 되는 쪽을 설명해 주고 있습니다. 대부분의 사람들은 지시받기를 좋아하고 책임지기를 싫어하며, 안전만을 추구하고, 될 수만 있으면 일을 회피하려 하기 때문에 돈과 이익 그리고 처벌로써 인간으로 하여금 일을 하게 시킬 수 있다고 하여 인간을 부정적으로 보는 것입니다.

그러나 인간이 반드시 이렇게 부정적인 측면만 가지고 있는 것은 아닙니다. 아침 해가 빨갛게 떠오르는 것을 바라보면서 오늘도 또 즐겁게 일할 수 있는 하루를 가질 수 있다고 생각하며 가슴 뿌듯해하는 사람도 많습니다. 한 폭의 그림에 자기 자신을 실현하려고 자기 자신을 잃고 있는 사람, 피아노 건반 위에 도취된 피아니스트가 있는 것을 우리는 잘 알고 있습니다. 다시 McGregor의 Y이론은 인간의 다음과 같은 면을 말해 주고 있는 것입니다. 만일 인간이 만족한다면 정신적인 일이나 육체적인 일 모두를 놀이나 스포츠처럼 재미있게 느낀다는 것입니다. 인간은 자기가 속한 조직의 목적을 위해서—교사는 학교의 목적을 위해서—스스로 일하고 스스로 자기 자신을 통제해 나간다고 보는 것입니다. 소속감은 최상의 보상이며, 최상의 보상은 바로 인간으로 하여금 자기 자신을 실현할 수 있도록 하는 것이라고 보고 있습니다. X이론과는 달리 대개 사람은 책임지기를 좋아하며 창의성이나 재능은 몇몇 소수인에게만 있는 것이 아니고 대부분의 모든 사람이 다 가지고 있다고 보는 것입니다.

하여간 인간이 근본적으로 일을 좋아하느냐 싫어하느냐 하는 문제는 우리가 살아가는 데 있어서 생각해 봐야 할 중요한 문제입니다. 똑같은 조건 똑같은 상황에서 똑같은 일을 하면서 어떤 사람은 불평과 불만 속에서 하기 싫은 일을 하면서 하루해를 보냅니다. 그리고 근무시간, 직장에 있는 시간은 내 인생의 시간이 아니고 퇴근한 후의 시간이나 주말 휴일만이 내 시간인 것처럼 착각하는 사람도 있습니다. 그런가 하면 어떤 사람은 똑같은 조건에서 일하는데도 자기 자신을 잃고 일에 파묻히는 사람도 있습니다. 근무

시간은 물론이고 근무 외 시간까지, 남들이 가족과 즐기는 주말이라는 시간
까지도 직장의 일에 열중하는 사람도 있습니다.

여러분, 이 두 종류의 사람 중에 어떤 부류의 사람이 더 행복한 삶을 영
위한다고 생각하십니까?

우리 같이 생각해 봅시다. 일을 놓고는 어떠한 태도를 취했었는가? 스스로
행복해하고 즐거워했는가? 아침에 잠자리에서 일어날 때 오늘도 즐겁게 직장
에서 일할 수 있다는 데 행복감에 충만하여 즐거움을 갖고 출근했었는가? 아
니면 억지로 일어나서 억지로 출근했었는가? 후자의 경우라면 우리는 그만큼
불행한 삶을 살고 있는 것이라 생각됩니다. 퇴근 후나 주말만 행복하다면 자
기 인생의 반쪽만큼 행복하게 사는 것이라 생각됩니다. 우리 인간은 모두 행
복을 추구합니다. 그러나 행복이란 그렇게 멀리에만 있는 것은 아닐 것입니
다. 바로 가까이 바로 내 마음속에 있는 것입니다. 공식으로 나타내면 〈행복
=만족(충족) / 욕구〉이라고나 할까요. '욕구'란 분모가 커지고 '충족'이란 분자
가 작아질 때 우리의 행복은 작아지게 마련입니다. 소박한 꿈, 소박한 욕구
를 갖고 더 많이 만족해 할 때 우리의 행복은 커질 것입니다.

Ⅱ. 인간의 욕구단계

Abraham Maslow라는 사람은 인간의 욕구를 몇 개의 계단으로 표시했습
니다. 인간의 기본적인 욕구가 충족이 안 되면 그 욕구를 채우기 위해서 일하
고 행동하게 되며, 다른 보다 높은 차원의 욕구는 나타나지 않는다는 것입니
다. 그는 욕구를 〈생리적 욕구→안정에의 욕구→참여에의 욕구→존경에의
욕구→자아실현의 욕구〉의 단계로 나누었습니다.

먹고, 자고, 배설하는 생리적 욕구가 충족되지 않은 사람에게서 우리는
자아실현을 위해서 한 폭의 그림을 그리고 앉아 있거나 시를 읊조리고 있기
를 기대할 수는 없습니다. 생리적 욕구가 충족된 다음에는 가정의 안정, 직

업의 안정을 추구하는 욕구가 나타나고, 그 욕구를 충족시키기 위해서 인간은 일하고 행동한다는 것입니다. 그런 다음에야 각종 모임에도 나가고 클럽에도 들고 싶고, 어떤 사회적인 모임에도 참여하고 싶은 욕망이 생긴다는 것입니다. 그리고 나서는 참여에 그치지 않고, 좀더 존경을 받는 대상이 되고 싶은 것이 인간이라는 것입니다. 인간 욕구의 마지막 계단이 자아실현의 욕구입니다. 사실 교육의 최종 목표도 개개 학생으로 하여금 자아실현을 할 수 있도록 도와주는 것일 것입니다.

처음에 말씀드린 X이론은 낮은 수준의 욕구단계에 맞는 관점이고 Y이론은 보다 높은 수준의 욕구단계에 있는 사람들에게 맞는 경영이론이요 인간관인 것입니다. 하여간 우리가 어떤 수준의 욕구를 얼마나 강하게 가지고 있느냐는 우리의 일에 대한 태도, 우리의 행복감의 정도에 중요한 영향을 준다고 보겠습니다. 그러나 우리가 어떤 단계의 욕구를 충족시키기 위하여 일을 하든 결국 우리는 일을 하고 있을 때 행복한 것이지 일을 않고 일을 도피할 때 행복한 것은 아닐 것입니다. 일을 열심히 한다는 것은 개인의 행복을 위해서도, 또는 기업가나 경영자 나아가서는 국가발전을 위해서도 바람직한 것입니다. 우리가 일을 할 때는 결국 일에서 무엇인가 얻고자 하는 욕구가 있기 때문에 일을 하게 되는 것이라 생각됩니다. 그래서 경영자나 관리자, 행정가들은 그 인간의 욕구가 무엇인가 찾아내서 그 욕구를 충족시켜 주면서 일을 시키려 했던 것입니다. 인간은 돈이란 욕구 때문에 일을 열심히 할 것이라 믿는 경영자들은 봉급을 올려 주고, 보너스를 주고, 연금도 주고 했습니다.

어떤 회사에서는 근무환경을 개선해서 종업원들로 하여금 열심히 일하게 하려고 했습니다. 벽에 페인트칠을 하고, 전등을 밝게 하고, 책상을 새것으로 바꿔 주고, back ground music을 넣어 주었습니다. 어떤 회사에서는 근무 시간에 이발이나 목욕을 할 수 있게 해주고 자동차 살 때 회사에서 보조금을 대주었습니다. 이런 것들은 모두 일을 둘러 싼 주변적인 환경요인들입니다. 이런 환경요인을 개선해 주니까 예상대로 얼마간은 종업원들이 열심히 일하고 생산도 올라갔습니다. 그러나 얼마간 올라간 다음부터는 먼저 그대로이고 더 이상 계속 생산이 오르거나 종업원이 계속해서 정말 마음에서 우러나 열심히 일하는 것 같지는 않았습니다. 다시 말하면 이런 환경적 주변적인 요인들이 충족되면 불만족감은 막아 주지만 사람으로 하여금 일에서 보람을 느끼고, 가치를 느끼며 행복감을 느끼게 하지는 못한다고 보는 것입니다.

Ⅲ. 일하도록 만드는 동기

그러면 우리는 우리의 일, 또는 직업 어디에서 행복감, 만족감 또는 보람을 느끼는 것인가? 한 설계자가 자기의 설계에 의하여 놓여진 그 다리 위를 지날 때마다 그 설계사는 한없는 보람을 느낀다고 토로합니다.

우리는 이것을 성취감이라 부릅니다. 저는 100명의 초·중·고 선생님들을 인터뷰하고, 200명의 선생님들께 질문지로 조사 연구한 적이 있습니다. '선생님, 교직생활 전체를 통틀어서 가장 보람을 느끼고, 가장 만족감을 느꼈을 때가 언제였는가?'를 회상해서 말해 달라고 했었습니다. 어떤 선생님은 봉급 수준이 낮고, 사회적 지위가 낮고, 잡무가 많아 불만에 싸였다가도 일단 수업에 들어가 아이들 앞에 서기만 하면 나 자신을 잃고, 즉 몰아의 경지에 이른다고 합니다.

어려운 처지에 있던 학생, 그늘에 가려져 있던 제자를 도와서 그 아이가 성공해서 선생님 앞에 나타났을 때 그 선생님은 생애 최고의 훈장을 받은 것 같은 느낌이었다고 하는 선생님도 있었습니다. 이들 선생님들은 모두 이 성취감에 도취된 분들이었습니다. 성취감에 발동이 걸린 선생님들이 조사 대상의 약 50%였습니다.

성취동기가 높은 사람은 근무환경의 영향을 덜 받고, 현재의 근무환경에는 비교적 긍정적 태도를 취하는 것입니다. 낙도 벽지의 선생님들 중에서도 근무환경은 말할 수 없이 나쁜데도 자기 내부로부터 우러나오는 어쩔 수 없는 정열을 교육적 성취로 승화시키는 예를 많이 볼 수 있습니다. 보수도, 특권도, 지위도, 명예도 이런 사회적 보상이 낮은 우리 선생님은 정신적 보상으로 제자를 위해서 수업에 몰두하게 되는 것입니다. 우리는 어쩌면 돈을 먹고 사는 게 아니고 정신적 이슬을 먹고 사는 것일지도 모릅니다.

권위 있는 사람, 상급자, 동료, 학부형 또는 전문가로부터 인정받았을 때 그들이 가지고 있던 잠재능력은 발휘되는 것이며, 그들 자신도 열심히 일하면서 스스로 만족해하고, 행복하게 되는 것입니다.

또 다른 열심히 일하게 하는 동기요인은 '일 자체'인 것입니다. 과업자체라고도 표현되겠습니다. 주위환경을 아무리 간접적으로 좋게 개선해 줘도 일 자체에서 재미를 느끼지 못한다면 그는 행복할 수 없는 것입니다. 선생님의 주 업무는 가르치는 일입니다. 아까 성취감을 말할 때 언급했듯이 많은 선생님들은 수업시간만은 그래도 즐거운 시간으로 생각하고 있는 것입니다. 어떻게 보면 인간은 가르치고자 하는 하나의 본능 같은 것을 가지고 있는 것 같습니다. 한 원시인이 Totem Pole에 무엇인가 새기고 있습니다. 그때 한 소년이 옆에 와서 바라보고 있습니다. 이 원시인은 깎던 칼을 잠시 멈추고 열심히 무엇인가 소년에게 가르칩니다. 이렇게 가르치는 일이 인간 사회에서 계속되었기에 오늘날 우리는 이러한 문화를 누리며 살게 되고 또 앞으로도 더욱더 좋은 문화를 누리며 우리의 후세들은 살 것입니다. 가르친다는 일 자체 그것은 무엇보다도 귀중하고 보람 있는 일일 것입니다. 다행히 우리 선생님들은 이런 남을 가르치고자 하는 욕구를 한껏 즐길 수 있는 기회가 있어서 좋은 것입니다.

마지막으로 열심히 일하도록 만드는 동기의 또 하나는 책임감입니다. 처음에 말씀드린 X이론에서는 인간은 책임지기를 싫어한다고 했으나 대부분의 사람은 자기 책임을 다하려고 열심히 일하는 것입니다. 일을 믿고 맡겼을 때는 그들은 최선을 다하는 것입니다. 중요한 책임을 맡기고 그 일에 재량권을 줄 때 사람의 능력은 최대한 발휘되는 것입니다. 일을 시킬 때 책임을 져야지 사고가 났을 때 잘못되었을 때만 책임지라고 하니까 책임을 회피하는 경향이 나타나는 것입니다. 어느 회사에서 있었던 일입니다. 회사 내 건물 청소에 많은 인원과 경비를 투입해도 청결이 유지가 안 되고 여전히 더러웠습니다. 생각 끝에 경영자는 청소부들에게 지금까지 들던 경비 일체를 넘겨주고 약품, 청소 도구를 구입하는 일로부터 청소부를 쓰는 일까지 모든 청소에 관한 일을 자치적으로 해결하도록 책임 일체를 맡겨 버렸습니다. 그 결과 하루아침 사이에 사내는 눈에 띄게 깨끗해졌다고 합니다. 이것이 바로 책임감의 효과였던 것입니다.

Ⅳ. 맺는 말

Herzberg라는 사람은 먼저 언급했던 돈, 근무조건, 행정, 인간관계 등 일을 둘러싼 환경요인들을 위생' 요인이라 불렀습니다. 이들 환경 요인은 의 하에 있어서의 위생 문제처럼 병이 발생하지 않도록 방지하는 역할을 하는 것이지, 위생약이 병을 직접 치료하지 못하듯이 일에 있어서 불만은 줄여주지만 일에 발동을 붙여 주고 만족감으로 이끌게 하는 역할은 못 한다는 데서 비유된 것입니다. 인간을 만족감이나 행복감으로 이끌게 하는 것은 일의 본질과 직접적으로 관련되는 성취감, 인정감, 일 자체, 책임감 등이라는 것입니다.

결론적으로 우리 선생님들, 우리 인간은 행복을 추구하는데 우리는 어디서 행복을 찾을 것입니까? 우리가 일을 할 때 행복이고 불행이고 있는 것이지 일을 안 하는 데는 행·불행을 논할 수도 없습니다. 일을 도피하는 사람, 회피하는 사람이 행복을 찾을 수 있다고 생각하십니까? 사랑하는 아내나 남편, 가족과 보내는 시간보다도 더 많은 시간을 보내는 일에서나 직장에서는 행복을 포기하고 짧은 시간인 여가시간이나 주말에만 행복을 찾으려 하십니까? 또 우리는 일을 해도 그 일에 심취됐을 때 행복을 논할 수 있는 것이지 성의를 다하지 않은 일에서는 행복을 찾을 수 없다는 것을 느꼈을 것입니다. 불만 속에서 하루하루 타령이나 하다 보면 해놓은 것 별로 없이, 제자 하나 후배 하나 똑똑히 키워 놓지 못하고 우리의 젊음은 사라지고 정년에 가까워지게 되는 것입니다.

우리가 우리의 일에서 행복을 찾을 수 있다면 교장이나 교육감이 부러울 것이 없을 것입니다.

우리가 반드시 교장이나 교육감이 돼야만 행복한 것은 아닐 것일진대 우리는 가까운 우리의 마음에서, 우리의 일에서, 순진한 아이들과의 만남에서 행복을 찾을 수도 있을 것입니다. 인생의 황혼기에 서서 내 인생을 정리해야 할 때, 후회 속에서, 아쉬움 속에서, 젊어서 저지른 죄책감에서, 최선을 다하지 못했다는 부족감에서, 더 많이 채우지 못한 욕망 속에서 눈을 감지 못하는 순간이 오지 않도록 하루하루를 알차게 보람차게 보내야 할 것이고, 또 보람찬 둥근 해가 떠오를 내일을 맞을 준비를 마음속에 하고 있어야 할 것입니다.

●저 자 소 개●

주삼환(朱三煥)

●약력●

서울교육대학 교육학과 졸업

서울대학교 교육대학원 교육행정 전공(교육학 석사)

미국 미네소타 대학교 대학원 교육행정 전공(철학 박사)

전 서울 시내 초등학교 교사 약 15년

한국교육학회 회원, 한국교육행정학회 회장(1999)

미국 오하이오 주립대학교 객원교수(2003~2004)

현 충남대학교 인문대학 교육학과 교수

●저서 및 역서●

『사회과학이론입문』(공역, 한국학술징보(주), 2005)

『한국교육행정강론』(한국학술정보(주), 2005)

『질의 교육과 교육행정』(한국학술정보(주), 2005)

『수업분석과 수업연구』(공저, 한국학술정보(주), 2005)

『교육행정철학』(역, 한국학술정보(주), 2005)

『미국교육행정』(역, 한국학술정보(주), 2005)

『입문 비교교육학』(역, 한국학술정보(주), 2005)

『임상장학』(역, 한국학술정보(주), 2005)

『교육행정사상의 변화』(한국학술정보(주), 2005)

『위기의 한국교육』(한국학술정보(주), 2005)

『교양 인간관계론』(공역, 한국학술정보(주), 2005)

『우리의 교육, 몸으로 가르치지』(한국학술정보(주), 2005)

『전환시대의 전환적 교육』(한국학술정보(주), 2006)

『장학: 장학자와 교사의 상호관계성』(역, 한국학술정보(주), 2006)

『허즈버그의 직무동기이론』(역, 한국학술정보(주), 2006)

『대안적 교육행정학』(공역, 한국학술정보(주), 2006)

『전환적 장학과 학교경영』(한국학술정보(주), 2006)

『교육행정 특강』(한국학술정보(주), 2006)

『올바른 교육행정을 지향하여』(한국학술정보(주), 2006)

『교장의 리더십과 장학』(한국학술정보(주), 2006)

『교장의 질 관리장학』(한국학술정보(주), 2006)

『지방 교육자치와 대학자치』(한국학술정보(주), 2006)

『장학의 이론과 기법』(한국학술정보(주), 2006)

『전환기의 교육행정과 학교경영』(한국학술정보(주), 2006)

『고등교육연구』(한국학술정보(주), 2006)

『장학연구』(한국학술정보(주), 2006)

『교육개혁과 교장의 리더십』(한국학술정보(주), 2006)

『교육조직연구』(한국학술정보(주), 2006)

『선택적 장학』(한국학술정보(주), 2006)
『리더십의 철학』(공역, 한국학술정보(주), 2006)
『미국의 대학평가』(역, 한국학술정보(주), 2006)
『교육정책의 방향』(역, 한국학술정보(주), 2006)
『교육행정 및 교육경영』
　　(공저, 학지사, 2003, 개정판)
『미국의 교장』(학지사, 2005)
『교육이 바로 서야』(원미사, 2002)
『교육행정 및 교육경영』
　　(공저, 삼광출판사, 1995)
『장학론』(공저, 한국교육행정학회, 1995)
『장학론』(공저, 한국방송통신대학, 1991)
『인간자원장학론』(공역, 배영사, 1987)
『장학론』(공역, 학문사, 1984)
『교육정책의 새로운 방향』
　　(역, 교육과학사, 1983)
『교육학개론』(공저, 정민사, 1983)
『장학론』(갑을출판사, 1982)
『신장학론』(역, 교육출판사, 1979)

교육조직 연구

• 초판 인쇄	2006년 5월 1일
• 초판 발행	2006년 5월 1일
• 지 은 이	주삼환
• 펴 낸 이	채종준
• 펴 낸 곳	한국학술정보㈜
	413-756 경기도 파주시 교하읍 문발리 526-2
	파주출판문화정보산업단지
	전화 031) 908-3181(대표) · 팩스 031) 908-3189
	홈페이지 http://www.kstudy.com
	e-mail(출판사업부) publish@kstudy.com
• 등 록	제일산-115호(2000. 6. 19)
• 가 격	31,000원

ISBN   89-534-4836-0 93370 (Paper Book)
           89-534-4837-9 98370 (e-Book)